Legalist Empire

Legalist Empire

*International Law
and American Foreign Relations
in the Early Twentieth Century*

BENJAMIN ALLEN COATES

OXFORD
UNIVERSITY PRESS

OXFORD
UNIVERSITY PRESS

Oxford University Press is a department of the University of Oxford. It furthers
the University's objective of excellence in research, scholarship, and education
by publishing worldwide. Oxford is a registered trade mark of Oxford University
Press in the UK and certain other countries.

Published in the United States of America by Oxford University Press
198 Madison Avenue, New York, NY 10016, United States of America.

© Oxford University Press 2016

First issued as an Oxford University Press paperback, 2019

Library of Congress Cataloging-in-Publication Data
Names: Coates, Benjamin Allen, author.
Title: Legalist empire: international law and American foreign relations in the early
twentieth century / Benjamin Allen Coates.
Description: New York: Oxford University Press, 2016. | Includes bibliographical
references and index.
Identifiers: LCCN 2015046611 (print) | LCCN 2015047777 (ebook) |
ISBN 978–0–19–049595–4 (hardcover : alk. paper) | ISBN 978–0–19–005558–5 (paperback : alk. paper) |
ISBN 978–0–19–049596–1 (Updf) | ISBN 978–0–19–049597–8 (Epub)
Subjects: LCSH: International law—United States—History. | International and
municipal law—United States—History. | United States—Foreign relations—20th century. |
Imperialism—History—20th century.
Classification: LCC KF4581 .C63 2016 (print) | LCC KF4581 (ebook) |
DDC 341.30973/09041—dc23
LC record available at http://lccn.loc.gov/2015046611

For Viv, who makes it possible, and
Emma & Juniper, who give it meaning.

CONTENTS

Acknowledgments   ix

Introduction   1

1. International Law in Europe and America to 1898   15

2. Selling Empire, 1898–1904   39

3. Legalism at Home: Professionalizing International Law, 1900–1913   59

4. Legalism in the World, 1907–1913   86

5. International Law and Empire in Latin America, 1904–1917   107

6. Legalism, Neutrality, and the Great War, 1914–1918   136

7. World War, Collective Security, and International Law, 1914–1941   152

Conclusion   177

Abbreviations Used in Notes   185
Notes   187
Bibliography   241
Index   275

ACKNOWLEDGMENTS

This book is the product of many years and of many minds. It would not have been possible without the intellectual guidance of Anders Stephanson; his ability to cut to the essence of a historical problem and ruthlessly pursue its solution remains an inspiration. At Columbia University this project also benefited from the invaluable comments of Sam Moyn, Alan Brinkley, Jack Snyder, Christina Duffy Ponsa, John Witt, and from collaboration and commiseration with fellow graduate students. Elizabeth Blackmar's expert feedback and confident optimism helped me pass several roadblocks along the way. At the American Academy of Arts & Sciences, I received helpful feedback on chapter 1, as well as general encouragement, from Lisa Siraganian, Matt Rubery, Chin Jou, Mary Maples Dunn, Daniel Geary, Benjamin Fagan, Melissa Milewski, and Patricia Meyer Spacks. At Wake Forest University, my colleagues provided essential comments on chapter 2, and Lisa Blee, Nate Plageman, and Mike Hughes generously read additional parts of the manuscript. In addition, I have benefited from comments and conversation along the way from many colleagues, commenters, and friends, including Arnulf Becker Lorca, Dirk Bönker, Brooke Blower, Sarah Bridger, Chris Capozzola, Alex Cummings, Mary Dudziak, Martti Koskenniemi, Paul Kramer, Dan Margolies, Amy Offner, Chris Nichols, Ben Soskis, and Stephen Wertheim. Audiences at the American Society for Legal History, the Harvard Law School Institute for Global Law & Policy Workshop, the American Society of International Law, the Society for Historians of American Foreign Relations, the American Society for Legal History, the Organization of American Historians, and the American Historical Association also helped me to fine tune my arguments. Daniel Geary and Jim Coates helped me track down some images at the last minute, for which I am very grateful.

A book needs material support as well as an intellectual community. Columbia University generously provided several years of academic and summer research funding. Fellowships from the Doris G. Quinn Foundation and the United States

Institute of Peace were invaluable. Serving as a Visiting Scholar at the American Academy of Arts & Sciences provided the opportunity to focus on writing and revising, in addition to exposure to stimulating discussions. My current home, Wake Forest University, allowed me to take a year of leave to complete revisions to the book. My colleagues and students continue to inspire me.

The tasks of research were eased considerably by the helpful staff at the Library of Congress Manuscripts Room and the National Archives II; Special Collections staff at Columbia University's Butler Library, University of California's Bancroft Library, Georgetown University's Lauinger Library, and Harvard Law School; and library staff at Columbia, Harvard, and the magnificent New York and Boston Public Libraries. The staff at Wake Forest's Z. Smith Reynolds Library has been generous with their time and expertise, especially in tracking down requests from Interlibrary Loan. A special note of thanks to Whitney Bagnall at the Columbia Law Library, who facilitated access to John Bassett Moore's uncatalogued papers; and to the American Society of International Law's Kelly Vinopal, who allowed me to read through the Society's early archives. Portions of chapters 5 and 6, respectively, appeared in "Securing Hegemony Through Law: Venezuela, the U.S. Asphalt Trust, and the Uses of International Law, 1904–1909," *Journal of American History* 102, no. 2 (2015): 380–405; and "'Upon the Neutral Rests the Trusteeship of International Law': Legal Advisers and American Unneutrality," in *Caught in the Middle: Neutrals, Neutrality, and the First World War*, ed. Johan den Hertog and Samuël Kruizinga (Amsterdam: Amsterdam University Press, 2011), 35–51. I thank the *Journal of American History* and Amsterdam University Press for permission to use part of these works.

Two anonymous readers at Oxford University Press gave the manuscript a careful review and prompted many changes for the better. My editor at OUP, Susan Ferber, deserves special recognition for supporting this book, for her patience as work on its completion competed for my attention with family and teaching responsibilities, and for attentive editing that improved my prose. Copyediting assistance from Ginny Faber and Maya Bringe was invaluable. Of course, any remaining errors are my own.

I am lucky to have benefitted from the support and the intellectual and emotional camaraderie of inspirational friends and family. A special thank you to Arthur Allen, Margaret Talbot, and Ike and Lucy Allen for hosting me for extended periods as I completed research in Washington. Kevin Murphy generously gave me a place to stay on research trips to New York. Frequent conversations with Julian Feeley keep me in touch with my California roots, and the occasional ups but mostly downs of Oakland sports franchises. Knowing that Jim Coates is only a phone call away gives me the security to try new things. And Vivian, Emma, and Juniper (who arrived just as I finished revising the book) happily distract me at home while inspiring me to hurry up and finish already at the office. This book is dedicated to them.

Legalist Empire

Introduction

In 1906, Oscar S. Straus chose a striking metaphor to justify the creation of the American Society of International Law (ASIL). "We are a world power," he explained, "and we must put world-power clothes on to meet the situation."[1] Straus was not alone in his use of sartorial language, for contemporaries made frequent reference to the "swaddling clothes" of geopolitical innocence that America had so recently discarded.[2] The imagery suggested a nation that had reached a new life stage, one that required a fresh wardrobe of capacities and ideas in order to venture beyond its borders. The evidence of such a transformation was overwhelming: since the Spanish-American War of 1898, the country had not only solidified its position as an economic colossus but, by annexing Puerto Rico and the Philippines, had for the first time added semipermanent, heavily populated colonies unlikely ever to attain statehood. In short order had followed a formal protectorate over Cuba, the "taking" of Panama to build a canal, and Theodore Roosevelt's new corollary to the Monroe Doctrine, which proclaimed an American duty to "police" the Western hemisphere. Empire had been an American practice since the nation's founding, but these new policies were widely understood as departures from traditional methods of territorial expansion.[3] How to match these accessories with the traditional garb of non-entanglement constituted the central preoccupation of US foreign relations in the early twentieth century.

Nevertheless, Straus's imagination of law as an article of "world-power" clothing jars modern sensibilities. Since September 11, 2001, debates about the conduct of the so-called War on Terror have renewed interest in international law. Did harsh treatment of enemy detainees violate anti-torture conventions? Did the 2003 invasion of Iraq start an illegal war? Should those who ordered these policies be tried for war crimes? These debates tend to assume that international law and state power are antagonists. Weak states invoke international law, the thinking goes, to defend themselves from powerful ones, and strong states must find ways around the law in order to exercise their power. Critics also suggest that the administration of George W. Bush departed from historical precedent: its attempt to expand American power around the world violated "a long, proud and continuing history of US support for international law."[4] But, as Straus's statement suggests, the international lawyers of the early twentieth century saw international law as an essential component of the nation's emergence as a Great Power. *Legalist Empire* explains why they thought so and puts lawyers at the center of the effort to create and administer the American empire.

To be a world power, notes historian Michael Hunt, a nation needs three things: economic wealth, a capable government, and a motivating ideology of national expansion.[5] By the turn of the twentieth century, the United States already possessed the first (its economic output surpassed that of all rivals), thanks in part to the corporate lawyers who midwifed the birth of giant industrial trusts. But its governmental apparatus remained underdeveloped, especially at the federal level. In 1890, its army ranked fourteenth among the great powers (behind Bulgaria), and Europeans ridiculed its decrepit navy.[6] While the nation had conquered a continent under the banner of Manifest Destiny, attempts to apply this logic to overseas territories had repeatedly failed since 1870. When president Ulysses S. Grant proposed annexing the Dominican Republic, for instance, Congress refused, in part on the grounds that incorporating an allegedly inferior population was undesirable.[7] Meanwhile, George Washington's admonition to avoid foreign entanglements still had wide appeal. Many thought that the country could not and should not rule formal colonies.

The story of how lawyers and international law helped the United States topple these bureaucratic and ideological barriers to overseas empire between 1898 and 1919 remains to be told. International law, with its lofty promises of peace, reciprocity, and sovereign equality, seems out of place in an imperial age.[8] Standard accounts emphasize Roosevelt's Rough Riders charging Spanish troops in Cuba or gunboats patrolling the Caribbean. A "high tide of regenerative militarism" crested during these years, notes a 2009 historical synthesis, while a 2013 US history textbook flatly characterizes the era's foreign policy as "aggressive and nationalistic."[9] Moreover, it seems hard to square international law with American exceptionalism. If Americans believed that their nation was uniquely a force for good in the world, how could they recognize any law higher than their own manifest destiny?[10]

This book argues that the US empire of the early twentieth century was in important ways a legalist one.[11] Lawyers served government directly. As officials and as informal sources of legal expertise, they advised presidents and made policy. Every secretary of state during this period was a lawyer, and nearly all were founding members of the ASIL.[12] Lawyer-officials like Elihu Root and William Howard Taft helped to administer and justify the American colonization of the Philippines and Puerto Rico, while lesser-known lawyers, such as John Bassett Moore and James Brown Scott, offered legal rationales for taking Panama and entering World War I. When public opinion soured on formal colonial rule, growing numbers of international lawyers in the State Department developed new practices of informal empire by spreading legal regimes that protected the prerogatives of US capital while assuaging opposition from domestic and foreign opponents. At the same time, international lawyers represented US corporations and overseas investors who encouraged gunboat diplomacy. Contrary to the popular image, international lawyers were not isolated idealists spouting naive bromides from the sidelines. Well-connected, well-respected, and well-compensated, they formed an integral part of the foreign policy establishment that built and policed an expanding empire.[13]

In their roles as university professors, public statesmen, and leaders of professional organizations and foundations, international lawyers also performed an important ideological function. They helped to reconcile imperial power with republican traditions and universal principles. International lawyers created a profession in the early years of the twentieth century. The ASIL and other groups, backed by the impressive wealth of the Carnegie Endowment for International Peace, held annual meetings, published journals, and bolstered their identity as experts on international affairs. In so doing, American international lawyers promoted a legalist project for world order. In general terms, *legalism* refers to "the ethical attitude that holds moral conduct to be a matter of rule following."[14] This book uses the term in a particular way: to describe a commitment to expanding the use of legal techniques and institutions to resolve international problems. "Legalists" were those—mostly but not always lawyers—who held such a view. There was no single school of American international law, and legalists held different views about its sources, content, and future.[15] Some advocated a conservative approach that envisioned law as an extension of diplomacy, useful in structuring world affairs and in coordinating and safeguarding interests but unlikely to end war in any but the longest time horizon. This approach had the greatest influence in the late nineteenth century. By 1910, what I term a "judicialist" sensibility of international law had captured the imagination of the profession.[16] This was international legalism in its purest form: a claim that a proper system of legal procedure not only solved conflicts in the present but also created a proper mindset for preventing them in the future. Adherents believed that international law was self-enforcing as long as the public correctly understood national rights and duties. Judicialists did not embrace world government, but called for the holding of regular conferences to codify the rules of law and for the creation of a permanent international court. If staffed by legal experts, such a court would issue precedents to clarify the rule of law, while providing a trusted source of neutral authority to settle disputes. Importantly, this vision of international law proved compatible with the expansion of American power and influence.

The legalist message scaled new heights of popularity in the first decade and a half of the twentieth century. In that era, engaging with global affairs meant engaging with the law. Accounts of treaties and legal debates filled volumes written by diplomatic historians. Political scientists made legal theory central to their conception of the modern state. Aspiring members of the foreign service were tested on their knowledge of international law. So were officers at the Naval War College. Both the advocates of expanded American power and those later generations would call "isolationists" recognized the importance of international law. Not surprisingly, when World War I broke out and the United States attempted to remain neutral, policymaking took place in a context that was as much legal as it was moral or political.[17]

When Americans in these years imagined plans for world organization, they did so in legal terms. Even Theodore Roosevelt—known more for his military bluster than legal finesse—shared important legalist assumptions about civilization and order. Ironically, the most important exception to this rule was Woodrow Wilson, the president often erroneously portrayed as a champion of international law.[18] At the Paris Peace Conference in 1919, when Wilson adamantly declared that he "did not intend to have lawyers drafting the treaty," he was acknowledging the fact that lawyers and legal norms had shaped the existing order he wanted to supplant.[19]

Legalism found a willing audience among the foreign-policymaking elite, many of whom were lawyers. To an extent unmatched before or since, the US government—the executive branch if not always the US Senate—embraced legalist proposals. Washington called for peace conferences and pushed for the creation of a "true" international court. It proposed legal institutions to preserve order in its hemisphere, and it expanded and formalized the provision of legal expertise to its foreign policy decision-makers. Americans often proclaimed themselves leaders in the promotion of international law in these years, and many foreigners agreed.

How can all this international law talk be squared with the violent expansion of American power? After all, the United States made a habit—one that it maintained across the twentieth century—of promoting the creation of international institutions but refusing to submit to their jurisdiction if doing so threatened perceived national interests. In 1919, for instance, America was more responsible than any other state for the establishment of the League of Nations, only to cripple its creation by refusing to join it. After World War II, Washington created modern global institutions in its own image, such as the United Nations and the International Court of Justice, only to turn its back once it could no longer control them.[20]

It would be tempting to chalk up this behavior to hypocrisy and cynicism. But doing so makes the fundamental error of seeing empire and international law as mutually contradictory. It risks falling into a trap that imagines law mattering only when it constrains states by forcing them to do something that they would not otherwise do. Law does sometimes function in this way, and states do sometimes seek to evade it for this reason. But law just as often enables aggressive behavior, and not just by creating "exceptions" to be exploited by the powerful. International law has often permitted the use of force and supported the rights of capital, for example. Behavior that is deemed "legal" is more likely to be considered legitimate by friends and foes alike. Believing in the legality of one's own actions can displace hesitation or guilt.[21] The exercise of American power abroad in the early twentieth century is thus better conceptualized not as a disregard for law, but as the implementation of a particular form of it.

Moreover, viewing law as an independent variable that exerts an outside force on state behavior overlooks the complex ways that legal discourse—lawyers' vocabularies and practices—helps to define the boundaries of acceptable behavior, both inside and outside the policymaking process. Even when law is invoked to serve immediate interests, its language and norms can linger and have unexpected consequences. Conceptualizing conflicts in particular legal frames can shape how policymakers respond to crises.[22] Nor have all states at all times instinctively rationalized their behavior in legal terms. Why the United States emphasized international law in the first place demands explanation, as does the fact that lawyers and policymakers conceptualized the role of law in the nation's foreign policy in different ways at different times. By examining the period when the United States first became a world power, this book aims to do just that.

Of Empire and International Law

In putting international law into the history of American empire, and the history of empire into international law, *Legalist Empire* helps to unite existing scholarship that is fragmented across several disciplines. Historians of the early twentieth-century American peace movement, which was a mostly upper- and middle-class affair, have explored legalists' proposals for international courts and world peace in detail.[23] But in focusing on plans for new international institutions, this work downplays lawyers' participation in the quotidian activities of empire building. Meanwhile, the few books that focus explicitly on the relationship between legalism and foreign policy tend to treat law as either a transparent tool for justifying atrocities or a misguided idealism that prevented the United States from assuming its proper international responsibilities.[24] It is important to recognize that international lawyers were simultaneously idealists and imperialists, dreamers of world order and participants in imperial politics and administration.

Scholars of US legal history and of the history of American foreign relations are also increasingly interested in the intersections between law and empire.[25] Work on the late nineteenth and early twentieth centuries explores the transformations in domestic and constitutional law that made it possible to govern colonies, claim jurisdiction over fugitives and troublemakers beyond US borders, and turn other nations into protectorates.[26] It has also argued that lawyers served as lobbyists and officials who ensured that US policy had a pro-corporate orientation.[27] *Legalist Empire* adds to this scholarship by showing how *international law*—in addition to constitutional innovation and the extension of national jurisdiction—served as a means of expanding power, in part by exploiting the hegemonic potential of international norms.[28] US financial and military might powered the extension of American control overseas.[29] But ideology and rhetoric mattered, too. In addition to exploring the racial and gendered ideas that underwrote justifications for US domination, it is important to recognize how international law both drew on and reinforced these attitudes.[30] Without international lawyers, legitimizing empire would have been more difficult.

Legalist Empire also has implications for understanding the function of international law in global politics. The vast majority of writing on the topic comes from international lawyers themselves and from scholars in the related fields of political science and international relations. This scholarship is concerned most of all with explaining how and why states comply with international law. International law scholar Louis Henkin famously noted, many years ago, that *"almost all nations observe almost all principles of international law and almost all of their obligations almost all of the time."*[31] Most scholars agree, but they disagree on precisely how much ground "almost" covers. Is disobedience so rare as to be inconsequential, or do states habitually ignore laws that contravene important interests? More importantly, why do states comply and should they continue to do so? In explaining state behavior, scholars have highlighted the role of self-interest, the ways in which repeated transnational interactions can lead to the internalization of international law in domestic institutions, and how common rules can help states coordinate their behavior and solve problems of collective action.[32] This scholarship is not blind to the importance of power. Having built international society in their image, some international relations scholars note, powerful states have incentives to comply with particular rules and norms even when doing so may entail short-term costs.[33] Still, much current scholarship implicitly portrays international law as embodying universal values. When states adopt international norms—be they arms control treaties or human rights regimes—it is assumed to be a victory for universal humanity over the irrational parochialism of national interest.

Legalist Empire does not attempt to advance a model of state legal compliance. But by closely examining a specific period and place, it highlights the particularism of international law. Today's scholars note how "transnational norm entrepreneurs" push states to obey international regimes, such as the outlawing of land mines, by incorporating associated norms into domestic laws and political discourses.[34] In the early twentieth century, empire was itself an international norm that was part of, not external to, the law, and many of the "norm entrepreneurs" of that era worked to convince Americans of the benefits and moral necessity of empire.[35] This is a reminder that international law's claims to universalism are just that—claims—and should be treated with caution.[36] This argument builds on the work of international legal theorists who have emphasized the ways that power is built into international law. Even if particular issues are decided on strictly legal (i.e., neutral and doctrinally correct) principles, powerful states tend to have greater say in determining which issues are internationalized in the first place. Concerns such as security, war, and transnational investment become subjects of international intervention, while others, such as economic inequality, remain domestic issues.[37] Moreover, since international legal legitimacy relies simultaneously on ascending arguments (in which a practice is legal when states have agreed, through treaties, legislation, or practices, that it is so) and on descending arguments (which declare a practice legal when it complies with universal values of justice and humanity), there is a built-in ambiguity that can ultimately be resolved only through power.[38] To take a modern example, consider the conflict between a state's sovereign right to control its domestic affairs and the human rights of individuals.

Historical analysis of international law can help to illuminate how and why particular interests are privileged over others by contextualizing law's development and deployment. Relying on published materials, many traditional histories of the discipline tell the story of international law as a series of firsts: the first scholar to base law on state practice, rather than Church teachings; the first treatise of the law of war; the first formulation of human rights, and so on.[39] This presents the history of international law as the natural evolution of a centuries-long tradition of rational inquiry. To understand how actors made sense of law's meaning, however, it is necessary to interpret it through the cultural and ideological prisms of their time and place. Some international legal arguments had greater power to convince, not necessarily because of their fidelity to legal doctrine, but because of how they amplified assumptions about global and national societies. The international law invoked by presidents and secretaries of state, and their advisers, was in many ways a kind of "folk international law," a "lawlike discourse" that mixed legal rules with civilizational ideology.[40] This is not to say that people were disregarding the "true" law but rather to underline the claim that all international law, to one degree or another, relies on such ideological construction. To understand how states invoke legal argument then, it is necessary to understand the political and ideological context in which those arguments are deployed. Scholars of international law have begun to incorporate a historical focus, but so far this work has not paid much attention to the United States before 1945.[41]

America's ideological commitments and position in the international system in the early twentieth century make it an especially fruitful topic of study. In 1900 it acted as a dominant power in its hemisphere but remained a second-rank military power globally. Meanwhile, two geopolitical identities clashed: the United States simultaneously imagined itself a leader of the "New World," with a traditional animus toward "Old World" Europe (as late as 1895, secretary of state Richard Olney had drawn a sharp ideological line between "monarchical" Europe and the republican Americas), and a member of the club of "civilized" and imperial nations.[42] Thus, the United States was simultaneously a "weak" and a "strong" nation, one that alternately embraced and rejected its connections to Europe. Arguments for and against international law thus played out amid shifting contexts of power and interest.

By examining this period of transition, *Legalist Empire* broadens the horizons of the legal geography of empire. From the sixteenth through the nineteenth centuries, as historian Lauren Benton has shown, the enforcement of imperial law was often delegated to locals (magistrates, proconsuls, travelers), in the process creating a series of "layered sovereignties," where different laws applied in different places and to different populations. By the mid-twentieth century, the world had been reconceptualized as a space of juridically equal nation-states with precisely delineated borders of territorial sovereignty.[43] Indeed, as David Armitage and other scholars have argued, the United States served as an important political and ideological model for this transformation.[44] In the decade after 1900, American policymakers flirted with but ultimately decided not to fully embrace a formal imperial law. Instead, they sought a congenial world order grounded in a nominally equal system of international law, an order that permitted hierarchies of power in practice even if it formally embraced state equality. They sought, in other words, to create an empire of nation-states.[45] Because international law prescribed particular rights and duties of states and allowed military measures to enforce them, it provided a useful tool in this effort.

Legalist Empire moves beyond the writings of international lawyers to examine their actions through a wide variety of historical sources. It simultaneously treats international law as a professionalized discipline that created knowledge and justified its members' claims to truth; a body of rules and precedents that guided and prescribed actions in the international sphere; and a political and ideological project that advocated an expanded recourse to law in foreign policy and the creation of international institutions. It is concerned as much with the culture and politics of international law as with its doctrine, for the boundary between them is blurrier than it might seem. The chapters that follow trace the thoughts and actions of international lawyers as they circulated inside the halls of academia, at annual meetings of professional societies, and in the State Department and corporate boardrooms. Often serving in multiple roles simultaneously, they operated as both statesmen for the expanded role of law and as advocates for particular clients. Their personal correspondence, published writings, and the records of their professional organizations reveal the sources and motivations that shaped their actions. State Department archives provide evidence of just how thoroughly law pervaded the policymaking process. Taken together, these sources portray international lawyers as imperial actors and proponents of expanded legal remedies. Their support for law, then, was not simply rhetorical; they believed that a world of law benefited both the United States and the world. Examining the international situation alongside domestic cultural, social, and intellectual contexts explains why.

Explaining International Law's Appeal

Particular political, cultural, and international contexts created the conditions of possibility for the legalist project. International lawyers derived some of their authority from the fact that law was anchored in America's national consciousness and governing institutions to an extent that was unmatched elsewhere.[46] Since the country's founding, lawyers had constituted a political elite in the United States. Though the rise of massive corporations after the Civil War had challenged lawyers' social preeminence, it had also enriched a new class of corporate attorneys who had proven themselves as pragmatic enablers of concentrated power.[47] It was difficult in this environment to argue against "law" in the abstract.

International lawyers also leveraged newly powerful discourses of professionalism that had emerged in the nineteenth century in response to the vast social and political changes brought about by mass industrialization.[48] Academic disciplines as diverse as history, medicine, and law claimed the scientific authority to interpret the world. They embraced a standard repertoire that included holding annual meetings and publishing journals and conference proceedings. By adopting these practices, legalists cast international law as a science and claimed the authority of expertise. They also spoke from within a gendered context, presenting themselves as defenders of an ethic of self-restrained manhood against supposedly "irrational" pacifists and unhinged warmongers. Legalists were serious, scientific men policymakers could trust, or at least so they argued.

The notion that adjudication might replace war seemed plausible because many people believed in the inevitable progress of mankind. Writers such as Brooks Adams, John Fiske, and Josiah Strong reached a wide American

readership while positing laws of historical development, civilization, and progress.[49] A Darwinist vernacular simultaneously asserted the natural domination of
the strong over the weak and the inevitable progress of global society as a whole.
International law embraced this dual "civilizing mission," supplanting force with
reason to govern relations among civilized states while counseling the imperialism of uplift in Africa and Asia.[50] An appeal to international law was also an
appeal to a particular vision of civilized modernity.

International law connected the United States to Europe at a time when
Europe was busy colonizing the rest of the world. "Civilized" states engaged in
the forcible "civilizing" of others. Ideas about law and empire circulated across
the Atlantic and provided Americans a universal language with which to justify
overseas conquest. The rule of law was understood as the application of civilization to restrain irrational behavior. In relations between the Great Powers, this
meant the triumph of reason over the irrational and counterproductive causes
of war. When applied to "backward" areas, it meant the extension of "civilized"
control through empire. Since international law guaranteed certain basic rights
of capital, upholding the rule of law could also mean intervention on behalf of
foreign investors.

International law provided a sort of behavioral grammar for navigating relations with states, "civilized" and "uncivilized" alike. Global politics would be
impossible without fundamental legal categories like "the state" that identify
and categorize units of interaction. For example, without the legal category of
"war" soldiers' lethal actions would simply be "murder."[51] As a young republic,
the United States had been wary of embracing diplomatic and international legal
norms, rejecting them as too aristocratic.[52] (The United States did not promote
anyone to the European-sounding rank of "ambassador" until 1893.)[53] But by
the turn of the twentieth century, the country had embraced the diplomatic
norms of the European empires.[54] Legal expertise was vital in this transformation. Private corporations and the United States government turned to lawyers
to navigate the rules of the international system. Property rights needed defending; rules of law and neutrality, expounding; and the periodic conferences called
to write new norms into international behavior required legal guidance. In short,
a Great Power needed not only an army and navy but also a legal department.

Finally, international law was especially important in the early twentieth century because it helped the United States come to terms with what it meant to be
a "Great Power." Lawyers helped answer the question that Oscar Straus's metaphor implied, just what sort of "world-power clothes" ought to fill Uncle Sam's
closet? The plain haberdashery of the American isolationist seemed out of date.
But the khaki and pith helmet of the European colonizer seemed un-American.
International lawyers proposed instead that Uncle Sam don the long black robe
of the impartial judge. In so doing, the legalist project mediated between two

contrasting ideological desires. On the one hand, promoting international law emphasized the United States' membership in a community of civilized states. This fit with a broader tendency to view Europe as a fertile provider of solutions to problems both international and domestic. Around the turn of the century, "[t]he old division of spheres was breaking down," as historian Cushing Strout has argued.[55] Social reforms, literature, fashion, political thought—all made their way across the Atlantic with particular ease. Empire, too, formed part of a broader global project.[56] International lawyers existed in a transatlantic milieu, corresponding frequently with their European (and, to a lesser extent, Latin American and Asian) colleagues.

At the same time, legalists portrayed international law as an extension of American principles abroad, not a foreign threat to them. The United States had long maintained a "government of laws and not of men," they argued, so supporting international law implied little sacrifice. They explicitly identified the US Supreme Court as the model for an international court and argued that throughout its history the United States had been an exemplary practitioner of international arbitration. The legalist project thus suggested a way for the United States to engage with an ever-closer world without sacrificing any of its national traditions.

A world governed by international law seemed to serve American national interests. International law recognized the right of states to intervene to protect their nationals overseas—be they stranded travelers or misbehaving corporations. It thus protected the rights of capital and incorporated "backward" regions into the sphere of capitalist modernity.[57] Adjudication would prevent wars between European powers that might ensnare the United States. A world of laws perfectly suited a nation happy to maintain its territorial footprint while keeping an open door for market expansion.[58]

Legalists argued that Americans had little to fear from international law. The legalist project was not radical, nor did it seek to do away with the nation-state. It portrayed war as the result of misunderstandings or temper tantrums. Clarification and dissemination of law would prevent conflict. There was no need for an international sovereign with the power to enforce the law, for properly "civilized" states would obey it on their own. Since legalists portrayed the United States as an inherently lawful nation, it need not fear adversarial court decisions.

The notion of international law as a cost-free benefit to the United States depended on important assumptions—about the place of America in the world system, the utility of law as a means of dispute resolution, and the inevitability and desirability of civilizational progress—that were strongest in the early twentieth century. World War I challenged these assumptions in fundamental ways. Law had failed to prevent war or atrocities. Civilization seemed to have perished alongside countless young men in the trenches. Although new internationalist projects proliferated in the interwar years, they no longer relied on the same kind of faith in international law.

Chapter Outline

Legalist Empire traces the intersections between law and empire from 1898 to 1919 and beyond. Chapter 1 provides a brief history of international law, showing how its rules developed in conjunction with the expansion of European economic and imperial power. From its emergence in the nineteenth century, the international law profession promoted a dual civilizing mission: to bring peace and order among states within the European system while also counseling the use of force to "civilize" outsiders. Yet from America's birth, the nation had embraced international law as a way to maintain political non-entanglement with Europe. By the late nineteenth century, leading US international lawyers were interpreting their discipline in conservative ways that accorded with that limited national mission.

The United States' turn to overseas empire after 1898 brought new challenges. Chapter 2 analyzes the political, legal, and ideological debates that followed. It shows how law and lawyers helped to legitimize the actions of the McKinley and Roosevelt administrations. What mattered most in justifying US empire—and in the Supreme Court's ruling that such empire was constitutional—was a mix of legal doctrine and ideological assertions connected to transatlantic discourses of civilization. To be a "civilized" power meant to undertake a "civilizing" mission. Such arguments were more or less sincere, depending on the individual making them, but they reveal the broader plausibility of this discursive frame in these important years.

Chapter 3 turns to the creation of the international law profession in the United States, focusing in particular on the ASIL (founded in 1906) and the Carnegie Endowment for International Peace (founded in 1910). It argues that the agenda of professional organizations reflected legalists' search for authority in the social, cultural, and ideological context of the early twentieth-century United States. The growth of law schools and the law profession, the nature of legal thought, prevailing racial and gender discourses, and the needs of professionalism all contributed. As a result of this context—and of the important personal influence of James Brown Scott—these organizations came to embrace a judicialist sensibility of international law in the years leading up to World War I. Despite a diversity of personal views, the profession as a whole was congenial to elite interests.

Chapter 4 shows how key US elites embraced the legalist project for world order. The US delegation to the 1907 Hague Peace Conference took the lead in supporting the creation of an international court. Meanwhile, the Carnegie Endowment targeted its vast wealth to promoting the judicialist agenda and convincing legalists on both sides of the Atlantic to support it. Thus, in both public and private efforts, the United States was a leading promoter of the international law project. However, close examination of these plans reveals their limitations, especially their assumptions about advancing civilization and the power of elite publications to shape public opinion. A high-profile debate over treaties in 1911 revealed that though the US foreign-policymaking establishment embraced a legalist vision, this did not always result in "legal" behavior.

If debating international law in the European context took on idealistic overtones, Chapter 5 demonstrates that in Latin America between 1904 and 1917, expanding the reach of international law formed part of a hegemonic project. US policymakers in the Roosevelt and Taft administrations and Latin American international lawyers all aimed to create a hemispheric rule of law. They disagreed, however, on whether disputes between states and foreign capital should be subject to international intervention or remain within domestic jurisdiction. The triumph of the position taken by the Great Powers—one that protected investors—demonstrates how the structure and jurisdiction of international law was itself infused with hegemonic content. International law could be a useful tool for projecting power, but it could best promote stability only if wielded with restraint, political acumen, and careful attention to public opinion. By 1913, important constituencies at home and abroad had begun rejecting legal arguments as being overly pro-corporate. The chapter ends by focusing on Woodrow Wilson's fundamental disagreements with legalists. These stemmed both from Wilson's personal philosophical commitments and from domestic challenges to legal supremacy.

Chapters 6 and 7 trace the trajectory of legalism through World War I and the interwar period. The war created unprecedented demands for legal expertise even as it undercut the assumptions and assertions on which legalist programs rested. Chapter 6 focuses on neutrality and the United States' entry into the war. Lawyers provided policymakers with legal opinions, while the United States remained a neutral. As a result of the structure of international law and legalism's ideological commitments, legal advisers (and secretary of state Robert Lansing) supported positions that led directly to the United States joining the side of the Allies.

Chapter 7 examines the war's implications for legalist proposals for world order. Legalists' ranks split, as some key figures began to call for the use of coercion to enforce international law. Thus, as the war came to an end the legalist community was fragmented and unable to effectively propose an alternative to Wilson's League of Nations, which was actively hostile to legalism. Continuing divisions and the decline of the conditions that supported judicialist legalism meant that the nation remained apart from both the League and the World Court. As World War II arrived, American policymakers decided that law must be formally subordinated to power in any future internationalist endeavor.

A relatively small group of men was present at the creation of the international law profession in the United States. *Legalist Empire* highlights their simultaneous presence at the creation of an overseas American empire. Probing this convergence raises difficult questions about international law's promises of universalism and justice. To understand how Americans in 1900 confronted the connections between power and international law requires exploring the centuries-long emergence of international law itself. For international law has long cast an imperial shadow, and even as Americans sought ways to avoid its chill, they imagined extending it to others.

International Law in Europe
and America to 1898

In 1884 an intriguing offer reached the State Department in Washington. German chancellor Otto von Bismarck had invited the United States to attend a diplomatic gathering in his country. The Berlin West Africa Conference of 1884–85 would symbolically inaugurate a period of European colonization that came to be known as the Scramble for Africa and that carved up the continent among European empires. Bismarck hoped that an international conference might prevent England or France from monopolizing the area, guaranteeing free trade and access to the valuable resources of West Africa's interior. The conference also promised to serve humanitarian goals by prohibiting the slave trade and other vices; yet it reeked of the paranoid self-interest of the imperialist powers.[1]

Frederick Frelinghuysen, the alliteratively named American secretary of state, was not sure how to respond to Bismarck's invitation. The United States was emerging as an economic colossus, but it had so far confined its territorial ambitions to its own hemisphere. Americans spoke often of their country's tradition of international non-entanglement (a tradition that later observers often misdiagnosed as isolationism), which they traced back to the wise counsel of their first president, George Washington.[2] Citing a fear of "entangling alliances," the country had even refused to sign the otherwise unobjectionable 1864 Geneva Convention of the Red Cross for eighteen years.[3] The idea of negotiating with imperial powers in Europe over colonial claims in Africa seemed quite outside the country's traditions. Would participation "harmonize with the policy adopted by the United States Government of non-interference?" Frelinghuysen wondered.[4]

There was one way to "harmonize" US policy and Bismarck's invitation. The same impulses that had produced the American doctrine of non-entanglement—namely, the notion that Old World diplomacy was sinful, pointless, and corrupting—also animated a belief that the United States should lead the world in supplanting power politics with peace and rationality. American citizens could be found at the forefront of the emerging international peace movement, and the nation was a leader in the practices of neutrality and the arbitration of disputes. Perhaps an American presence in Berlin could be understood as contributing to the world's progress. "Opening" Africa to Western rule would benefit the natives, the colonizers, and the world at the same time, the conference organizers promised. If European empire were understood as a project of international cooperation, it might be compatible with American non-entanglement. The way the European tradition of international law had integrated law, civilization, and empire gave some hope to this notion. But, as Frelinghuysen would eventually discover, the nation was not yet ready to embrace such an imperial international law. The history of international law, and Americans' understanding of it, explains why.

From the Law of Nations to International Law

The man often called the "father of international law" was a seventeenth-century Dutch humanist named Hugo Grotius. In 1625, as the Thirty Years' War raged in Central Europe, Grotius wrote his masterpiece, *De Jure Belli ac Pacis* (*On the Law of War and Peace*). He hoped that a comprehensive account of moral and legal principles would reduce the horrible destruction of European warfare. Though Grotius wrote frequently on theological subjects, he was no cloistered academic but an active participant in Continental politics. He wrote *De Jure Belli* while in exile in France, after escaping confinement at the hands of political rivals by concealing himself in a box of books.[5] His second most famous work, *Mare Liberum* (1609), which posited a natural right to free navigation, was written in defense of the Dutch East India Company's seizure of a Portuguese ship.[6] Grotius's life and work suggest the many ways in which modern international law was, from the beginning, inextricably bound up with the politics of empire.

The roots of international law stretch deep into human history. One of the earliest surviving treaties, dating to the third millennium, B.C.E., guarantees peace between the Mesopotamian city-states of Umma and Lagash by invoking the wrath of Sumerian gods on lawbreakers. In the following two thousand years, Egyptians and Hittites, northern Indian principalities, and Greek city-states all developed agreements and codes to regulate their foreign relations. The Roman Empire introduced the influential concept of *jus gentium* (usually translated as "law of the peoples"), which applied the law of nature (that is, of moral reason) to humanity. Medieval scholars, such as Thomas Aquinas, further developed this natural law by mixing rationalist logic with quotations from Christian scriptures. Meanwhile, the small states of the Mediterranean developed the *Consolato del Mare* as early as the thirteenth century to regulate maritime commerce, neutrality, and war.[7]

The modern law of nations began to take shape in the seventeenth century. The 1648 Peace of Westphalia put an end to the Thirty Years' War in part by recognizing the equal sovereignty of states. Because Grotius's *De Jure Belli* emerged from this context, many of his successors associated international law with the preservation of European peace and order. In fact, European encounters with the outside world powerfully shaped modern international law.[8] The earliest plans for European international organization, dating to the late thirteenth century, aimed not for perpetual peace but for Western superiority: the concentration of European strength to crush the Saracen menace and retake the Holy Land.[9] European formulations of consular jurisdiction and the law of the sea developed through interactions with the Ottomans in the Mediterranean and the complex rivalries between European trading empires and the states of the Indian Ocean.[10] The conquest of the Americas prompted further developments in international legal thought. Francisco Vitoria (1480–1546), the Dominican monk considered by some to be even more important than Grotius to the founding of international law, demonstrates the centrality of colonial questions to the creation of the discipline. In 1532, he delivered a pair of lectures on Spain's conquest of the New World. Vitoria courageously rebuked the emperor and the pope, who claimed ownership of Indian lands on the theory that pagans had no rights. On the contrary, Vitoria averred, natural law granted rights to all humanity and ensured Indian "princes" title over their own lands. Yet, Vitoria continued, law also mandated certain duties. Indigenous Americans must allow the Spanish to proselytize, for instance, and must not mistreat converts. They must permit the Spanish to trade with them, to anchor ships in their waters, even to mine and export gold and silver. Any violation of these basic rights would, in effect, extinguish Indian sovereignty. The Indians, in short, had no right to disclaim the equal rights and duties imposed universally by (European-invented) natural law. Should they do so, Spain could "legally" seize Indian lands and conduct a "just war" against them. Such a war permitted the use of virtually any means. As Vitoria wrote of just war with the Turks, "[I]t is indubitably lawful to carry off both the children and women of the Saracens into captivity and slavery." By positing a universal law, Vitoria justified atrocities in the language of equal rights.[11]

If there was no global legislature, court, or sovereign, where did international law find its authority? Generally speaking, lawyers approached this problem in one of two ways (and still do today). Natural law outlooks find law in transcendent rules of reason or morality. Law is what God or Reason says it is. Religious texts or rationalist philosophy (and sometimes both) provide sourcebooks. Natural law presents a supranational prescription for states to follow; to disregard it is to cross divine will and natural order. Positive law, on the other hand, builds global order from the ground up. A lawyer in the positivist tradition studies the actions of states. International law is what states have agreed it to be;

formal concurrence (treaties) or habitual behavior (custom) provide evidence of such agreement. A positive approach draws its legitimacy, therefore, from the society of states itself.[12]

An important reason for Grotius's influence is that his work was among the first to explicate natural law and positive law simultaneously. *De Jure Belli* cites biblical and philosophical treatises, alongside treaties and diplomatic chronicles. This seems contradictory, but the contradiction itself is useful: it links material actions with spiritual justifications. Grotius and his successors influenced philosophers and princes alike. The seventeenth-century Swedish king Gustavus Adolphus reportedly carried a copy of *De Jure Belli* whenever he led his troops into battle.[13] Diplomats in the late eighteenth-century relied heavily on the Swiss philosopher Emmerich de Vattel's *Le Droit des gens* (1758), the most popular international legal text of its time.[14]

International law therefore emerged from Early Modern Europe as a useful bundle of complexities and contradictions: simultaneously European and imperial, secular and sacred, descriptive and normative. These contradictions endure today, particularly the last couplet. The rules of international law are frequently mundane: common definitions and agreed-upon rules that grease the wheels of exchange and provide mutually intelligible guides to conduct.[15] But advocates of international law often harbor grander dreams. Plans for perpetual peace—or at least more peace than exists at present—are rarely far from the mainstream of the field. Scratch the surface of an international lawyer, and one might find a prophet. This was especially true among the nineteenth-century Europeans who founded the international law profession.

The Professionalization of International Law

By 1870, international law had a well-developed if not always coherent tradition of authorities and customs, treaties, and treatises. Textbooks illustrated state practices relating to such standard concerns as sovereignty, jurisdiction, neutrality, treaties, and laws of war. A long list of authorities with fantastic names—Bartolus of Sassoferato, Baldis of Ubaldis, Alberico Gentili, Samuel von Puffendorf, Christian Wolff, and Cornelius van Bynkershoek—created a self-referencing community of scholars that stretched across nations and centuries.

Yet this did not add up to a distinct *profession* of international law. None of these writers would have considered themselves international lawyers (indeed, the very term *international* was not coined until 1789, by Jeremy Bentham). Instead, they dabbled in the law of nations while also writing philosophy, history, theology, or jurisprudence. It was difficult to define precisely where the study of diplomacy or public law ended and the study of "international law" began.

If universities taught the subject at all (and many did not), they usually combined it in chairs of "Laws of Nature and Nations" located within philosophy faculties.[16]

Why did this change? The international context had much to do with it. Developments in the second half of the nineteenth century generated hopes and fears that sparked new legal departures. On the positive side, a half-century of peace had comforted Europe after the end of the Napoleonic Wars in 1815. New technologies knit the world ever closer. Expanded economic ties raised hopes for peaceful cooperation, and easier travel and communication boosted transnational interactions. With the advances of the steamship, railroad, and telegraph, scholars and practitioners of the law of nations could come together to create a truly "international" international law—one that gained legitimacy by reflecting the viewpoints of all nations. Instead of lonely scholastics writing treatises, collaboration would enable the codification of international law. (A few scholars, led by Johann Caspar Bluntschli (1868) and David Dudley Field (1872), wrote their own codes of international law, hoping to inspire nations to adopt them.) And when Britain and the United States resolved an especially contentious dispute in the *Alabama* arbitrations of 1871–72, it suggested that law could solve even the weightiest matters of national honor.[17]

The return of violence, meanwhile, spurred international lawyers to action. The Franco-Prussian War of 1870–71, which killed thousands in the heart of Europe, offered a gruesome reminder of the carnage of war. Struggles for national consolidation in Italy and Germany, along with renewed colonial expansion in Africa and Asia, called for newly strengthened legal agreements to regulate them and ensure smooth operations.

In this environment, a transatlantic group of men created the international law profession. Prompted by Swiss publicist Gustave Moynier and Francis Lieber, a German emigré who taught at Columbia University, in 1873 Belgian lawyer Gustave Rolin-Jaequemyns invited twenty-two experts to Ghent. There they founded a new international law organization, the Institut de droit international. The Institut consisted solely of experts, limited to an elected membership of one hundred twenty. Small committees would meet during the year to codify issues of public and private international law, and the entire Institut would assemble annually or biannually to ratify their deliberations. Through "*l'action scientifique collective*," the Institut would develop "scientific" codes of law. Along with a new journal, the *Revue de Droit International et de Législation Comparée*, which Rolin-Jaequemyns had founded in 1869 with the help of British jurist John Westlake and the Dutchman Tobias Asser, international lawyers had demarcated a transnational intellectual space devoted to specialized study.[18]

Noting the frequent references to legal "science," many scholars have termed the late-nineteenth century the "great era of positivism" in international law.

Indeed, the rise of Darwinian science and Comtean positivism made purely natural law arguments difficult to sustain (although a few lawyers tried, such as James Lorimer). Yet it is misleading to consider the Institut solely a positivist effort. Its predecessors might fit the label. Positivist approaches had gained the upper hand in the early nineteenth century. The 1815 Treaty of Vienna, which ended the Napoleonic Wars, gave rise to a notion of European stability and European Public Law. In this environment, law came from states, acting in concert, not from above. War became a political act, an inevitable friction of the system. No longer focused on deeming war just or unjust, law instead provided rules to bracket war's incidence and limit its damages. In the hands of German lawyers like Johann Klüber (1762–1837) and Georg Friedrich von Martens (1756–1821) international law became a catalogue of procedure.[19] The members of the Institut found this insufficient. To determine the real state of the law, one had to go beyond the law as it was currently defined through diplomatic practice. In short, law must accord with the values of advanced civilization. The Institut's first bylaw made this clear. It pledged the organization to become the "organ of the legal consciousness of the civilized world."[20]

What really animated the project of the Institut was not the gradual refining of laws through scientific investigations but, rather, the unspoken attempt to shape legal norms and institutions according to the dictates of an evolving civilization.[21] The Institut maintained a "late-Victorian reformist sensibility," in the words of legal scholar Martti Koskenniemi.[22] It was a bourgeois ideology, advanced by middle-class reformers who also favored free trade, clean government, and public education. Westlake taught math in his spare time at Working Men's Colleges; Ernest Nys "professed to the great principles of the [French] Revolution"; Rolin-Jaequemyns belonged to the liberal party. Léon Bourgeois, one of France's leading legalist voices, led the social-democratic Solidarité party. These men were liberals, not radicals, who opposed socialism and anarchism. They endorsed a gradual amelioration of social tensions and foresaw an inexorable increase in human capacities and well-being.[23]

Most post-1873 international lawyers shared a belief that the progress of law followed from the natural growth of the international community. British lawyer T. J. Lawrence, for instance, described by one historian as "more bluntly positivistic than has ever been the case elsewhere," nonetheless argued that international law followed an evolutionary path that mirrored the domestic: just as private duels had disappeared, so too would war.[24] The "evolutionary idea," as historian Casper Sylvest terms it, effectively stood in for natural law in justifying the internationalist project; it became "the strongest extra-legal foundation for international law."[25] The belief in evolution arose directly from a conviction of common culture: a European (or at least Western) community whose advances evidenced progress and through whose actions humanity would rise as a whole.

The flipside of grounding law in this culturally particularist way was that it seemed to deny law's protection to those outside the anointed community. Thus international law intersected with the colonizing project.

Civilization and Empire

By the nineteenth century, international legal authorities no longer wrote in the immediate shadow of the Crusades. Yet how one defined membership in the "society of nations" continued to be as important as how one defined the rights and duties of those nations. Seventeenth- and eighteenth-century writers, including Grotius, Christian Wolff, and Vattel, echoed Vitoria in arguing for a universal international law grounded in natural law principles that extended to all humanity. But in the nineteenth century, publicists began to argue that international law applied only to Europeans and their descendants.[26] A "standard of civilization" defined the society of nations, and became part of the definition of international law itself. "The Law of Nations, or International Law, is a body of rules *recognized as binding* on civilized independent States in their dealings with one another and with one another's subjects," went a characteristic formulation.[27]

But of what, precisely, did this standard of civilization consist? Sometimes it took explicitly religious form. Henry Wheaton, an American diplomat, stated in his influential *Elements of International Law* (1836) that international law applied only to "the civilized and Christian people of Europe or to those of European origin." References to Christianity and Christian states in international legal texts continued into the early twentieth century.[28]

For the generation of the Institut, a desacralized notion of "civilization" provided the dominant criteria for inclusion or exclusion in the society of nations.[29] Importantly, "civilization" was singular. Early nineteenth-century philosophers had considered the possibility of multiple civilizations: the empires of Asia might be civilized in their own way, for instance. But international lawyers of the late nineteenth century rejected this pluralism.[30] Instead, they arranged humanity hierarchically, drawing on contemporary scientific arguments such as those established in anthropologist Lewis Henry Morgan's *Ancient Society* (1877). Scottish writer James Lorimer repeated Morgan's standard categorization in his *Institutes of the Law of Nations* (1883): "[H]umanity in its present condition," he explained, "divides itself into three concentric zones or spheres—that of civilised humanity, that of barbarous humanity, and that of savage humanity."[31]

What distinguished the savage from the civilized? Sociopolitical organization, most importantly. Civilized states were those that had replaced the capricious rule of man with the rational rule of law. They could be trusted to make and uphold agreements. As John Stuart Mill explained in 1836, "[I]in savage life there is little or no law, or administration of justice; no systematic employment of the collective strength of society, to protect individuals against injury from one another."[32] Civilized states had governments ready and willing to protect the life and property of foreigners. Their representatives dressed and behaved according to Western tastes. By the early twentieth century, most international lawyers recognized Japan as "civilized," a designation Japanese officials had pursued by proclaiming adherence to the laws of war and by trading kimonos for business suits at international meetings.[33]

Yet, in practice, the notion of civilization rested on vaguer assumptions of development. At times, racial considerations appeared explicitly; Lorimer praised "ethnology, or the science of races" for its contributions to "international politics and jurisprudence," and Francis Lieber declared, "Internationalism is part of a white man's religion." John Westlake argued that natives lacked sovereignty because they were "unable to supply a government suited to white men."[34] More often, racial bigotry figured implicitly. Because international law required a common consciousness, as we saw earlier, it could not apply to those who had not yet developed that consciousness. Civilized consciousness was in turn a result of social development and intellectual capacity, which, by assumption or assertion, were products of the West. As T. E. Holland explained, "[T]he family of nations" were those sharing "a common civilization" and "a similar level of moral and political opinion" derived from "their historical antecedents." In practice, he continued, "[T]his may be said to include the Christian nations of Europe and their offshoots in America."[35]

Still, *civilization* remained a term of art. International lawyers believed that they knew a civilized country when they saw one, even one outside Europe. Of Japan, Westlake wrote, "There are differences of detail, but no one who has had a liberal education feels himself a stranger in the houses, schools, law courts, theatres, scarcely even in the churches, of another ['civilized'] country."[36]

Economic and military might also made civilized right. In Japan, Europeans renounced extraterritoriality—the practice whereby foreigners were exempt from the jurisdiction of local courts—only after the Japanese made clear their imperial ambitions and capacities. States that remained "uncivilized" faced serious consequences. Lorimer's tripartite division of humanity mandated distinct treatments. Within Europe, international law promoted peace through toleration. "Civilized" humanity had full sovereignty, which guaranteed the right to determine one's own social order and state policy. "Barbarous" states, including Turkey, Persia, and parts of Asia, merited "partial recognition," which entailed territorial sovereignty but not jurisdiction over foreign visitors. Europeans who committed crimes in Turkey and China, for instance, were tried in consular courts by their own countrymen. And "savage humanity" merited only "mere human recognition." In the words of John Stuart Mill, "To characterize any conduct whatever toward a barbarous people as a violation of the law of nations, only shows that he who so speaks has never considered the subject."[37]

Marshaling these and similar arguments, international lawyers proved to be useful adjuncts to imperial foreign ministries. Not surprisingly, their views often overlapped neatly with national policy. Belgian publicist Ernest Nys offered a full-throated defense of King Leopold's bloody work in the Congo. John Westlake defended British actions in the Boer war. Frenchman Alexandre Merignhac determined that French treaties with African chiefs accorded with international law, while doubting the validity of those signed by the British. "[I]n fact," notes Koskenniemi, "everyone's *conscience juridique* supported the controversial colonial policy of his homeland."[38]

Though in practice "civilization" continued to rely on racial and cultural assumptions, presenting it as a legal category made it potentially universal.[39] The potentiality of universal civilization in turn enabled colonialists to describe the great race for empire in terms of a "civilizing mission." If in principle any people could be made civilized, imperialism could be recast as tutelage—though of course equal rights always remained just beyond an ever-receding horizon. Liberal arguments in this vein did not necessarily or inherently lead to colonialism, as the anticolonial arguments of some prominent British liberals like Richard Cobden and William Gladstone indicate. In fact, some international lawyers considered the "civilizing mission" a mere charade. "Ideas of humanity and of social progress too often hide a spirit of scandalous plunder," complained French lawyer Gaston Jèze. He worried that legal abuses of power in the colonies might surface at home, or even worse, that powerful European states might claim the mantle of civilization to attack their weaker neighbors. Yet Jèze's was a minority position. The international law profession on the whole remained a valuable ally of European imperialism until well into the twentieth century.[40]

To implicate international lawyers in imperial expansion is not to attribute sole or even major responsibility to their writings. European states sought overseas territory for economic and strategic reasons, and also for domestic political advantage and international prestige. Most international lawyers accepted imperialism as a given, and hoped that legal regulation might mitigate its worst abuses. Their writings likely comforted imperial statesmen, though it is unlikely that their criticisms would have dissuaded expansion altogether.[41]

But it is worth highlighting the ease with which a liberal sensibility of international law supported imperialism, because this formed the language with which Europeans—and eventually Americans—understood both the colonial project *and* the internationalist one. Participants in The Hague Peace Conferences of 1899 and 1907 described their actions as the advancement of civilization. So did the countries that collaborated to crush the Boxer Rebellion and cement Western (and Japanese and Russian) domination of China in 1900.[42] Imperial civilizing mission and international law were intertwined. The potential for progress through tutelage justified the civilizing mission in the colonies, just as the potential for progress through evolution made it possible to predict the advance of international law within the society of nations. Both depended on the concept of an advanced, superior European society.[43]

The fact that international law accompanied the violence of colonialism forced those states on the fringes of the "society of nations" to make legal concepts of civilization part of their response to European aggression. Approaches differed. Japan not only hired European international law experts but fundamentally transformed its political system in order to be recognized as an equal. Japanese leaders quite explicitly promised that becoming civilized along Western lines would mean an end to "unequal treaties" that granted extraterritorial jurisdiction to foreigners. China on the other hand incorporated extraterritoriality into preexisting domestic legal conceptions of legal pluralism, in a vain attempt to limit European (and American) incursions. The imperial elites of the Qing Empire refused to acknowledge European definitions of what constituted superior civilization.[44] Meanwhile, international lawyers in Latin America—technically within the sphere of civilization though often marginalized and abused by European empires—appealed to their status as civilized states in attempts to limit Great Power threats to their sovereignty.[45] Even Russia—hardly a rule-of-law state at home—promoted international law abroad in a claim to lead civilization towards peace.[46]

The United States faced this dynamic as well. By 1900 the nation had been embraced as one of the Great Powers. Yet, born as a republic through an anticolonial revolution, it had often defined its identity in opposition to Europe. How would the United States respond to the linking of law and empire?

International Law and the American Foreign Policy Tradition

"[T]he circumstances of a rising State make it necessary frequently to consult the law of nations," noted Benjamin Franklin in 1775. As a weak republic and a fragile confederation, the new United States desperately sought recognition from the international community. This required adherence to standard international behavior. Thus committees of the Continental Congress consulted Vattel's *Droit de gens* (1758) and collections of European treaties. Though the Declaration of Independence is best known today for its second paragraph, headlined by natural law appeals to the "self-evident" truths that "all men are created equal," its first paragraph signals the search for recognition by offering "a decent respect to the opinions of mankind" and appealing to "the powers of the earth." Only by joining the existing international order, the Founders reasoned, could the new nation gain "full Power to levy War, conclude Peace, contract Alliances, establish Commerce, and to do all other Acts and Things which Independent States may of right do."[47]

The Constitution also recognized the importance of international law. Article I, section 8 gives Congress the power to punish "Offences against the Law of Nations," while Article VI declares treaties, alongside the Constitution and congressional laws, to be "the supreme Law of the Land." By signaling the new nation's commitment to existing international law, as David Golove and Daniel Hulsebosch note, the founders "designed the Constitution to facilitate American integration into the wider community of civilized states and ensure that the nation would comply with its international obligations."[48]

The fact that international law served the interests of a fledgling state offered no guarantee that it would continue to appeal to American policymakers in the nineteenth century, however. In the hundred years after the signing of the Constitution, the United States conquered a continent and became a global power. In the process of doing so, its actions came to define what late nineteenth-century Americans could readily define as a "tradition" of foreign policy practice, based on three sometimes contradictory values.[49]

The first, expressed in George Washington's Farewell Address of 1796, privileged commerce over politics and cautioned against entanglement in European affairs. By the early nineteenth century, Washington's warning to "steer clear of permanent alliances" with Europe came to be understood in the words of Thomas Jefferson's broader formulation: "peace, commerce, and honest friendship with all nations, entangling alliances with none." In calling for simultaneous political withdrawal and commercial engagement, the message set the stage for Jefferson's own confused policy: pursuing the latter often made the former impossible. Indeed, the efforts by Jefferson and his White House successor James Madison to ensure trade rights led ultimately to the most entangling of policies: war with Great Britain in 1812.[50]

The Monroe Doctrine provided the second set of traditional values. It originated as a short passage in president James Monroe's 1823 message to Congress: "[T]he American continents, by the free and independent condition which they have assumed and maintain, are henceforth not to be considered as subjects for colonization by any European powers." Though subject to a multitude of interpretations over the years, the doctrine implied two basic assertions about American identity. First, it underlined the idea of two spheres: a fresh, republican, progressive New World compared to a fallen, corrupt Old World. Second, it presented the United States as an anticolonial nation and a friend of self-determination.[51]

Manifest Destiny, a sense of national mission, forms the third component. In 1845, in an effort to legitimate American territorial expansion, journalist

John O'Sullivan's *Democratic Review* declared "the right of our *manifest destiny* to overspread and to possess the whole continent which providence has given us for the development of the great experiment of liberty and federated self government." But the notion of the United States as a providential nation destined to redeem the world predated O'Sullivan. It traces back, in one form or another, to the founding of the nation, and further, to New England's first Puritan settlers. In ascribing divine purpose to American expansion, the concept of manifest destiny converts non-entanglement into exceptionalist unilateralism: why should a "chosen" nation ally with the non-elect? Manifest Destiny also carried with it decidedly secular connotations of racial superiority.[52]

At first glance, the values of unilateralism, commercial expansion, anti-colonialism, and manifest destiny—in addition to being mutually contradictory—seem difficult to reconcile with international law. But in fact, embracing international law offered two ways to promote these values. Promoting arbitration and the law of neutrality, for instance, served the interests of a commercial power desirous of avoiding wars with European powers. Legal infrastructure, in other words, could preserve non-entanglement. Second, standing as a champion of international law could, under the proper circumstances, be conceived of as an American mission to redeem the world. Thus international law figures more prominently in the history of American foreign relations than we might assume given the country's reputation as a "gunfighter nation."[53]

International Law's Champion? Neutrality, the Peace Movement, and Arbitration

Looking backward from the late nineteenth century, some Americans could construe a pattern of special support for international law. For example, in 1886, a congressional joint committee voted to fund the publication of a digest of international law: a multivolume collection of American policies and statements related to the law of nations. The committee's reasoning reveals a nationalistic pride in this international discipline:

> Congress has ... wisely voted large sums to monuments in stone and bronze of our great military chieftains. This vote would erect a monument at least as enduring to those eminent statesmen who established in this country an imperial peace, and have given to the world, as the greatest European jurists now admit, its present system of international law.[54]

While exaggerating American parentage of international law, proponents of such a position could and did point to three things in their favor: the American role in developing the international law of neutrality; the strength of the peace movement in the United States; and a history of resorting to international arbitration to resolve disputes.

Neutrality

The United States played a leading role in transforming neutrality from a questionable and contingent practice into a legally defined regime. During wartime, belligerents naturally distrusted neutrals. Why allow a third party to grow rich supplying the enemy with vital provisions and armaments? Neutral shippers faced threats of seizure and condemnation. As a weak, commercial nation, the new United States had a clear interest in maximizing neutral rights in order to keep itself from being dragged into war, and to gain the greatest ability to trade with both sides.

In 1794, America enacted domestic legislation commanding its own citizens to remain neutral in the wars of others—the first such law in the world. This reassured belligerents that neutral countries could remain rigorously impartial during wartime. It inspired similar legislation in other countries and led, ultimately, to international treaties respecting neutrals. The United States also advocated expansive neutral rights. In 1812, when the young country went to war with England, it did so in protest of Britain's repeated violations of its "rights" as a neutral. In the following years, America updated its neutrality laws at home and pushed for greater neutral privileges abroad, including the notion that private property should be immune from seizure by belligerents at sea and on land.[55]

Neutrality and peace have a natural association: to be neutral means to refuse to take part in war. Yet in the American case, neutrality grew as much from self-interest as from humanitarian sentiment. A commercial power naturally sought the broadest rights to export its goods. The American insistence on the neutrality of property on land also reflected its overwhelming concern with slaves as private property.[56] When self-interest and neutrality failed to align, Americans abandoned the latter: during the Civil War, the American navy intercepted European merchant shipping while its courts justified the seizure of neutral cargoes, even those en route from one neutral port to another.[57] Europeans complained loudly of hypocrisy.[58] Even when not at war, American officials weighed their support for neutrality against a preference for freedom of action. The United States refused to sign the 1856 Declaration of Paris, which granted extensive rights to neutrals, because doing so would have meant abandoning the option to utilize privateers in a future war.[59]

Nevertheless, later observers trumpeted American support for neutrality as evidence of peaceful intentions and the promotion of international law. They pointed, too, to American innovations in the law of extradition and of expatriation (the right of an immigrant to foreswear obligations to his or her previous homeland). That these laws also reflected the special interests of a nation seeking control over a rapidly growing immigrant population did little to restrain advocates' laudatory encomia.[60]

The Peace Movement

Americans could rightly claim a leading role in the international peace movement during the nineteenth century, even if that movement boasted few concrete accomplishments. American pacifists founded the world's first official peace organizations, the New York Peace Society and Massachusetts Peace Society, in 1815. A national body, the American Peace Society, emerged in 1828. Both developed in a broad American reform context, drawing from an emerging middle class that was heavily influenced by Christian evangelism. The peace movement attracted prominent antislavery advocates, such as William Lloyd Garrison, and echoed the abolitionist language of redemption and sin. David Low Dodge, founder of the New York Peace Society, titled an 1815 pamphlet *War Inconsistent with the Religion of Jesus Christ.* Dodge and Garrison represented a powerful nonresistor wing of the early movement. Rejecting defensive and offensive wars alike, their followers even questioned the use of police force within domestic society.[61]

If Christianity infused these early peace activities, advocates did not limit their appeals to scripture. William Ladd, leader of the American Peace Society, was a Harvard-educated former sea captain from Maine whose personal religious conversion experience animated his advocacy. Yet his *An Essay on a Congress of Nations* (1840) featured but a single biblical quotation. It relied instead mostly on international legal texts and Anglo-American philosophy. Ladd compared works by Grotius, Burlamaqui, Puffendorf, and Vattel to illuminate discrepancies and lacunae in the law. He proposed a "Congress of Nations" to redress them by creating an international code. A "Court of Nations" could then draw on this code to settle any future disputes. Ladd saw no need for an enforcement mechanism: "I believe that, even now, *public opinion* is amply sufficient to enforce all the decisions of a Court of Nations," he wrote. Ladd's proposal anticipated much of the legalist project of the early twentieth century. It also closely resembled one floated fifteen years earlier by Bentham disciple James Mill, demonstrating the extent of Anglo-American cooperation in the early peace movement.[62]

Ladd's whiggish plan attracted prominent Whig Party support. In 1833, the American Peace Society enlisted John Quincy Adams and Daniel Webster to judge a competition that awarded $1,000 to the best essay outlining a plan for peace. Whig senator Charles Sumner of Massachusetts became the peace movement's most powerful supporter in Washington. The society itself remained small, but in stressing public opinion and the rule of law, it reflected broader traditions in America. Lawyers held prominent positions in society, and respect for the law helped to maintain order without the need for the centralized state bureaucracies of Europe. For Alexis de Tocqueville, who visited America around the same time, the impressive power of public opinion had a more frightening cast: in democracies, he noted, "tyranny leaves the body alone and goes straight for the soul." In any case, appeals to public opinion had wide resonance: even the Democrat John O'Sullivan endorsed Ladd's plan and introduced resolutions to the New York Assembly calling for congressional action on its behalf.[63]

American peace activism was transatlantic in scope. Twenty-six Americans attended the first international conference of peace advocates, held in London in 1843. A few years later, Elihu Burritt, the "learned blacksmith," who, legend has it, could speak four dozen languages, founded the League of Universal Brotherhood. Its British branch attracted some ten thousand followers. Burritt organized international conferences in Brussels in 1848, Paris in 1849, and London in 1851. In Paris, fifteen hundred attendees witnessed Victor Hugo predict a future "when we shall see those two immense communities, the United States of America and the United States of Europe, holding hands across the sea." Continental Europeans occasionally found American piousness off-putting, but they could not fail to be impressed by the young nation's energy and conviction.[64]

American legal scholars also made an international mark in the early nineteenth century. Chancellor James Kent of New York devoted the first two hundred pages of his highly influential *Commentaries on American Law* to international law. Meanwhile, Henry Wheaton's 1836 *Elements of International Law* was translated into French, Italian, Spanish, Chinese, and Japanese. Americans took special pride in the primacy of Wheaton's text in East Asia. The American minister to China regarded its translation into Chinese (it was the first international legal treatise so translated) with special "patriotic pride."[65]

The Civil War nearly destroyed the American peace movement, however. Faced with a conflict between avoiding war and ending slavery, most peace advocates sided with the latter, responding to Angelina Grimké Weld's call to "baptize liberty in blood." But the war also contained the seeds of a reborn, more influential peace movement. For one, it gave rise to the first modern statement of the laws of war. In 1863, at Abraham Lincoln's request, Francis Lieber (Columbia professor and future cofounder of the Institut de droit international) produced a code of laws that were issued to the Union army as General Orders No. 100. Although, in practice, the Lieber Code, as it came to be called, justified violence as much as it limited it, it inspired similar undertakings by European governments and served as the basis of many future efforts at codification, including elements of The Hague Conventions of 1899 and 1907.[66]

The Civil War also gave rise to the *Alabama* claims, whose successful resolution inspired the peace movement. During the war, British authorities had failed to prevent the fitting out of several Confederate ships in English ports. Led by the *Alabama*, these ships wreaked havoc on Union shipping; the *Alabama* alone burned or captured for ransom over sixty merchant vessels before it was caught and sunk by the Union navy in 1864. Charging England with violating the laws of neutrality, Americans demanded reparation for direct losses and—more controversially—up to $2 billion in "indirect costs" stemming from the prolongation of the war the *Alabama's* predations had allegedly caused. Discussions grew heated; this seemed to be just the sort of issue of "national honor" unsolvable by legal means. So when the two sides created an arbitral tribunal that settled the matter in 1872 (Britain agreed to pay the United States $15.5 million), observers took it as evidence of the power of arbitration.[67]

Arbitration

For later observers, the successful resolution of the *Alabama* claims proved that the United States was a champion of international arbitration. It is true that the country had frequently promoted the practice. The 1794 Jay Treaty with Great Britain established three arbitral tribunals to settle a disputed boundary, the payment of debts to British interests, and the claims of US merchants against Britain; the 1814 Treaty of Ghent provided for three more. Although Britain proved to be America's most frequent arbitral partner, the United States also conducted arbitrations with France, Mexico, Haiti, Chile, and many others. All told, by 1896, the country had submitted to arbitration fifty-one times. By the end of the century, under the influence of the transatlantic peace movement, it began to support calls for general treaties to make arbitration the standard method of resolving disputes. At the first Pan American Conference in 1889–90, the US delegation supported a hemispheric general arbitration treaty, and in 1897, the country signed (though did not ratify) the Olney-Pauncefote Treaty, in which the United States and Great Britain promised to submit, with few exceptions, "all questions in difference between them" that could not be solved through negotiation.[68]

Americans also shaped the practice of arbitration in important ways. Beginning in 1869, when secretary of state Hamilton Fish (himself an accomplished attorney) appointed Francis Lieber to serve as umpire on the US-Mexican Mixed Claims Commission, Americans promoted a professionalized arbitral method. Rather than rely on European monarchs or statesmen—the prevailing approach—US negotiators put forward skilled lawyers to staff arbitral tribunals.

They aimed to substitute legal technique for the quasi-diplomatic negotiations that had often marked the undertakings. (The tribunal in the *Alabama* claims, for instance, based its rulings on an interpretation of law agreed upon by the treaty that created the tribunal in the first place. Before the tribunal even met, then, major legal issues had already been decided, and so the whole affair served a more diplomatic than legal purpose.) By choosing lawyers like Lieber who ruled according to laws created in the image of the European great powers, American officials ensured that the outcomes would favor the interests of a nation seeking to protect its businessmen and investors abroad. Under Lieber's watch, the 1869 Mexican-American claims tribunal awarded over $4.1 million to US claimants, and less than $151,000 to Mexican ones.[69]

Sometimes the United States simply refused to arbitrate. Though the 1848 Treaty of Guadelupe Hidalgo that ended the Mexican-American War contained a clause pledging arbitration of future disputes, the war itself had been one of choice for the United States. In 1891, after two American sailors died in a bar brawl in Santiago, Chile, President Benjamin Harrison forgot his administration's earlier championing of arbitration at the Pan American Conference in his rush to threaten war. Harrison backed down only when Chile paid a $75,000 indemnity. And in 1898, when the *Maine* sank in Havana harbor, President William McKinley rejected Spain's offer of arbitration in favor of war. As the Cuban writer José Marti put it in 1889, "Arbitrage would be an excellent thing, if . . . this still adolescent republic . . . would yield its own appetites to arbitrage." Nevertheless, despite arbitration's mixed record in practice, by the turn of the century, Americans saw themselves as major innovators and supporters of the practice. As a 1908 *American Journal of International Law* editorial quipped, "The United States has been and is a partisan—we might almost say a violent partisan—of international arbitration."[70]

Innocents Abroad in the Congo

Frederick Frelinghuysen ultimately decided that the Berlin West Africa Conference offered the possibility of reconciling this international law of messianic pacifism and unilateralist neutrality with the emerging European international law of civilizational imperialism. True, the United States had no direct colonial interests in Africa, unlike many of the European powers. But the prospect of expanded trade appealed, and the United States did have a special interest in the region by virtue of its connection to nearby Liberia, and the fact that Henry M. Stanley, the explorer who had "discovered" much of the continent's interior, was an American (or so he appeared; in fact, Stanley's strenuous claims of American nationality covered up his humble upbringing in a Welsh workhouse). Thus, while pointedly reserving the right not to sign any final declaration, Frelinghuysen accepted Bismarck's invitation.[71]

John Kasson, US minister to Germany, became the American delegate to the conference. He proposed that the entire Congo River valley be neutralized. Traditional colonialism was counterproductive, he argued. It created exclusive zones of commerce and led to war. "Neither our commerce nor our colonies can prosper, nor the lives of our people be secure, if we allow the standards of foreign war to be transferred to a land full of barbarians," he contended. Kasson supported a ban on the sale of liquor to native Africans, called for strict obligations for native welfare by occupying powers, and proposed obligatory arbitration between the colonizing nations so as to prevent war. The other powers regarded these proposals as utopian and of little consequence; German, British, and French power politics determined the shape and outcome of the conference. But Kasson did embody an American attitude that rejected colonialism as a selfish, violent, counterproductive enterprise even as it supported a collective, civilizing project of internationalist empire. His arguments for neutrality and arbitration pleased American peace advocates, such as the Universal Peace Union.[72]

Americans were not alone in infusing the conference with humanitarian narratives. European international lawyers saw in it the potential to regulate colonialism through law for the benefit of the natives and world peace. In 1883, the Institut de droit international had endorsed a plan calling for freedom of trade and navigation along the Congo River, along with a commission to manage it, so as to avoid conflicts between "*nations civilisées*." Internationalizing the African interior, publicists promised, would arrest the potential for colonial violence while opening the continent to commerce and civilization. The conference did in fact approve such an international commission; it also directed colonial powers to "bind themselves to watch over the preservation of the native tribes," to allow freedom of worship (while simultaneously promoting missionary activities), and to abolish slavery and the slave trade so as to promote the "moral and material well-being" of the natives. As historian Eric Weitz notes, the General Act of the Berlin conference "enshrined the language of civilizing mission" at the international level.[73]

That language was mostly hot air, however. The attempt to regulate new colonial occupation under international law amounted to little. The conference granted the international commission charged with overseeing such guarantees no money and almost no power. Humanitarian provisions made little impact over the following decades as the scramble for Africa accelerated. In fact, the most important outcome of the conference was its decision to officially recognize the International Association of the Congo, an organization directed by King Leopold II of Belgium. Though Leopold promised a neutral, humanitarian venture, the association soon transmogrified into the Congo Free State, a de facto Belgian colony that between 1890 and 1910 engaged in a campaign of gross exploitation, slavery, and murder so extreme that even other colonial powers blanched.[74]

Ironically, the nominally anticolonial United States had much to do with Leopold's unfortunate triumph. America was the first country to officially recognize the International Association of the Congo, pledging on April 22, 1884, to treat its flag "as the flag of a friendly Government." This, combined with France's endorsement the following day, conferred legitimacy on Leopold's supposedly philanthropic organization. Leopold's astute distribution of bribes and blandishments no doubt had much to do with America's endorsement of his project. The entire American delegation at the conference—Kasson, assisted by Stanley and Colonel Henry Sanford—was or had been on Leopold's payroll and consequently promoted Belgian interests equally with American ones. Sanford had bent the ear of Chester A. Arthur after hosting the president at his Florida mansion. But it is unlikely that Leopold could have succeeded had his project not so perfectly appealed to American sensibilities about international affairs. The International Association of the Congo promised a depoliticized imperialism, a civilizing mission open to all, neutral in approach, without commercial monopoly or territorial aims: in short, the very sort of project a "non-entangled" United States could get behind.[75]

Ultimately, however, even this pitch-perfect project scored only a partial victory. Alone among the powers in Berlin, the United States refused to sign the conference's final General Act. The American press was split. Proponents appealed to economic and humanitarian motives. Opponents portrayed the conference as a manifestation of Europe's voracious imperialism. The *Nation* castigated American participation in "the game of treaties, war, and mock philanthropy as a cover for treachery, stratagems, and systematic spoiling of the easily deceived natives," while the *New York Herald* warned that the Berlin precedent might soon cross the Atlantic. How long until the United States awoke to a conference of powers "settling the internal affairs and local administration of Mexico, Panama, or Nicaragua"?[76]

A more general disillusionment followed as the profane realities of Leopold's Congo supplanted its sacred promises. Joseph Conrad's *Heart of Darkness* (1898) expressed its author's discontented realization that the romantic adventures portrayed in Stanley's dispatches had led not to civilization but to savagery. But Conrad's critique of European imperialism did not encompass a cultural pluralism: his narrator pities Africans but evinces no respect for native society. So long as Europeans (and Americans) continued to view nonwhites as uncivilized, the potential for a *truly* civilizing mission remained a powerful rhetorical option.[77] Americans had applied such a rationale to their treatment of Native Americans. But before 1898, they had been reluctant to apply it to overseas colonialism. This skeptical sensibility animated the approach of the nation's most important international legal authorities at the time.

International Law against Empire?

Compared to its status in Europe, international law remained underprofessionalized in the United States in the 1880s and 1890s. Of course, one could find lawyers to litigate matters of international concern, such as prize cases, international investment and claims, and matters of private law—marriages, inheritance—involving litigants in more than one country.[78] By 1879, Coudert Brothers, a pioneering international law firm, maintained offices in New York and Paris.[79] And American scholars continued to write on the topic, although late nineteenth-century production was limited to a handful of treatises.[80]

International lawyers had no institutional presence yet in the United States. Almost no Americans attended the meetings of the Institut de droit international during these decades. Without an official organization, it fell to individuals to represent expert opinion on international law during public disputes. Two of the most prominent were John Bassett Moore and Theodore Salisbury Woolsey. Tellingly, their pre-1898 approaches to international law and politics ran counter to the sorts of arguments that would promote the sort of American empire that emerged in the new century.

Born in Smyrna, Delaware, on December 3, 1860, John Bassett Moore boasted prominent local ancestry and received a nineteenth-century gentleman's upbringing.[81] His secondary education, at the Felton Seminary and Classical Institute (which Moore's father and uncle had helped to found), emphasized the classics, exposition and rhetoric, mathematics, and the arts, as well as "the gentlemanly virtues of 'truthfulness, integrity, modesty, and love for one's fellow man.' "[82] Moore also developed a prodigious work ethic, and matriculated at the University of Virginia, where he studied classics, history, and law.[83] Owing to repeated illnesses, Moore left Virginia in 1880 without a degree.[84]

Like most of his contemporaries, Moore learned the law through practice, apprenticing with a Wilmington lawyer and joining the Delaware bar in 1883.[85] To advance his career, Moore planned to study Roman law in Germany. He contacted the State Department, hoping to finance his studies by working part-time in a diplomatic office in Berlin. However, Thomas Bayard, the new secretary of state, was also a Delaware man, and after learning of the young Moore's talents through a family friend, convinced John to forego European studies and work instead at the State Department in Washington, beginning in 1885.[86] "Thus," reported Julius Goebel Jr., "it was almost by accident that Moore became a specialist in international law."[87]

When Moore arrived in Washington, the entire department, exclusive of the foreign service and support staff, consisted of just thirteen people.[88] Moore soon rose to become third assistant secretary of state and became personally involved in all manner of diplomatic negotiations. Among other duties, he helped draw up the agenda for the first Pan American Conference in 1889–90, prepared for arbitrations with Great Britain, investigated boundary disputes in South America, and, as he later boasted, "personally conducted the correspondence as to the annexation of Hawaii."[89] These experiences impressed upon Moore the importance of international law to the daily conduct of foreign relations. They also established his expert credentials. In 1891, Moore published his first major work, *A Treatise on Extradition and Interstate Rendition*, after "[e]xperience in dealing with cases of extradition soon led me to feel the need of a more thorough and comprehensive work."[90] This earned Moore membership in the prestigious Institut de droit international, although he did not attend its meetings.[91]

In 1891, Moore left government service for a newly created chair in international law and diplomacy at Columbia University, the first full professorship of international law in the country.[92] He remained in New York for the next thirty-three years, aside from two brief returns to the State Department from 1898–99 and 1913–14, and a nearly three-year period of convalescence in 1908–10, after he experienced a degeneration of the muscles in his eyes due to overwork.[93] While teaching, Moore retained close ties to the State Department, often serving as an informal adviser on legal and diplomatic matters.[94] He also represented a series of private clients, allowing Moore "to make some provision for my family"—he married Helen Frances Toland in 1890, and had three daughters—"while wearing myself out on legal and historical writing."[95] Moore's sterling reputation as a scholar and attorney attracted many suitors. Woodrow Wilson traveled to New York to personally offer him a chair in international law and political science at Princeton; Presidents McKinley and Taft offered him a position on the Philippine Commission and the attorney-generalship of the Philippines, and rumors swirled after Wilson's election to the presidency that Moore would be named secretary of state (he settled instead for the department's second-ranking position).[96] Politicians (William Howard Taft), military men (Alfred T. Mahan), and even labor leaders (Samuel Gompers) turned to Moore with inquiries about international law.[97] He was frequently identified as "the greatest living authority in America on international law."[98]

Moore's lone biographer describes him as a "realist" because he counseled pragmatism and opposed sentimentality.[99] Moore embraced positivism. He believed that international law rested on state consensus. In the absence of global legislation, the task of the legal scientist was to establish the actual behavior of nations so as to reveal shared customs.[100] "Principles will be regarded as correct or incorrect in proportion as they reflect existing conditions," he argued in

1912.[101] The value of international legal work depended in large part on how faithfully it reported the historical facts.[102]

Moore's most important publications emphasized the connections between law and policy. He cemented his academic reputation with two multivolume compilations. The first, *History and Digest of the International Arbitrations to Which the United States Has Been a Party* (1898), not only examined the procedural details of every arbitration in American history but emphasized the centrality of diplomacy in convincing nations to arbitrate.[103] The second, *A Digest of International Law* (1906), likewise set international law in a diplomatic context. In eight volumes it summarized every American policy on which international law touched in even the slightest capacity. Moore thus provided what amounted to a diplomatic history of the United States. In the process he revealed how closely law intertwined with policy.[104] Both works aimed at a policymaking as well as a scholarly audience. The digest portion of *History and Digest of International Arbitrations* grouped decisions and diplomatic initiatives under topic headings, everything from "Nationality" to "Intervention" and "War Claims," so that policymakers and attorneys could easily examine international precedents. *A Digest of International Law* was also divided by topic in such a way that a reader could with little effort determine what position the government had taken on neutrality or expatriation, for instance. Recognizing the value of these collections both as handbooks for diplomatic practice and as ready references for American diplomatic history, the US government commissioned and printed them.[105] And Moore's frequent stints in the State Department show him as a willing and useful servant to the wielders of American power.

The point of international law, Moore believed, was not world peace but rational management of global politics and the minimization of war. The United States had throughout most of its history followed this lesson commendably, he believed. "Traditional" policy, he argued, rested on the principle of "non-intervention." This meant first of all "non-interference in the internal affairs of other nations," a notion correlated strongly with the practice of automatic recognition of foreign governments.[106] Secondly, it meant the maintenance of separate geopolitical spheres, as represented by the Monroe Doctrine. Moore was no isolationist, but he was a conservative. The best foreign policy was to continue what had worked for the past century. American statesmen, he argued, had defended the "principle of legality" but had also been "practical"; support for the rights of neutrals protected American trade while limiting the effects of European war. Willing to support the expansion of American power, yet wary of overextending it in pursuit of ill-defined civilizing missions, Moore's attitude on empire is best described as a kind of ironic detachment.[107]

Moore's contemporary, Theodore Salisbury Woolsey, also saw international law as a means to preserve America's traditional foreign policy of political non-entanglement and commercial expansion. Born in 1852 to Theodore Dwight Woolsey, president of Yale College and author of a celebrated 1860 treatise on international law, the younger Woolsey became Professor of International Law at Yale in 1878, and served in that position until 1911. Along with Moore, Woolsey stood out as an expert and a pioneer in international law before the rise of the profession in the United States. He published a new edition of his father's textbook in 1891 and wrote frequently for the *Yale Law Journal*, in addition to teaching law and diplomatic history. Considered an authority on foreign affairs more generally, he often contributed to the public discussion on that topic.[108]

Woolsey had high praise for America's past but, in a typically conservative way, fretted about its present and future. A penchant for jeremiad ran in his family: preacher Jonathan Edwards—famous for his "Sinners in the Hands of an Angry God" sermon—was Woolsey's great-great-grandfather. Through good fortune and wise leadership, Woolsey believed, America had become a free and prosperous society. But since the Civil War the country had become "decadent." Its economic growth had outstripped its "political and social and moral development," and greedy businessmen and corrupt politicians threatened the republic. Woolsey bemoaned the decline of culture, especially "the degeneration of the stage" which had replaced "elevating thoughts" with "the sensational, the spectacular, the sensuous, the idiotic, very often the lascivious."[109]

The same fear of decline characterized Woolsey's estimation of foreign relations and international law. America's policy of non-entanglement had served it well, Woolsey believed. The country had no need of a standing army and carried on a healthy trade with the world. International law—the resolution of disputes via arbitration, where possible, and the promotion of "the neutral program"— helped maintain this blessed state of affairs.[110] Yet, as early as 1892, Woolsey sensed "a departure from the old and safe policy of the fathers." "Jingoism" menaced the "wise counsel" of Washington's Farewell Address. Foreign entanglements produced costly wars and corrupted domestic politics. "A presidential campaign might be decided, not by the belief of a party as to questions of currency or the tariff or the civil service, but by its spirited foreign policy," warned an indignant Woolsey. "Would this be likely to give us better government?"[111] Surely not.

Woolsey studied world affairs closely. The experiences of other nations provided valuable lessons. He envisioned the treaty that neutralized the Suez Canal as a model for ongoing negotiations over the building of a passage across the Central American isthmus.[112] Nevertheless, he approached international law in the context of national interest not international civilization. Force could be employed abroad in order to "[p]rotect the lives and property of American citizens everywhere," but not to right wrongs of no immediate concern. The nation should "observe the law international" because it kept the country safe, and because a reputation for "honorable behavior and fair dealing" led to expanded trade. Woolsey thought war wasteful and hoped arbitration would lessen its incidence, but had few hopes of its eradication in the near future. Fighting a war for civilization was anathema.[113] Thus Woolsey, like Moore, remained skeptical of the fusion of law, civilization, and empire emerging from Europe. Until the United States itself reached for overseas colonies in 1898, this conservative approach to international law seemed adequate to the nation's needs.

By the turn of the twentieth century, the United States had developed a tradition of promoting international law in order to maintain political non-entanglement. Yet even as Americans led transnational pacifist organizations, the profession of international law in the United States, to the extent it could be called a profession, remained attuned to technical detail and historical practice and had not yet joined with its European brethren in the promotion of overseas empire. Yet, because of how international law interacted with the politics of civilization, such a move remained a latent possibility. In 1898 the needs of the new world power would compel the appearance of an imperial international law in the United States.

2

Selling Empire, 1898–1904

Sixteen years after the fact, Elihu Root recalled the surprising circumstances of his appointment as secretary of war. In front of an audience of New York lawyers, Root explained how he, a corporate lawyer who had never held public office (save a short stint as a US district attorney), became the man in charge of occupying, pacifying, and governing the largest overseas colony in America's history. In July 1899, Root narrated, he had just retired for the summer to his country home in Southampton, New York, when he was called to the telephone and offered the job "by one speaking for President McKinley." Root, taken aback, dismissed the notion as "quite absurd, I know nothing about war. I know nothing about the army." McKinley's emissary directed him to hold the line, Root remembered, and a moment later replied, "President McKinley directs me to say that he is not looking for any one who knows anything about war or for any one who knows anything about the army; he has got to have a lawyer to direct the government of these Spanish islands, and you are the lawyer he wants."[1]

Why would a president want a lawyer to direct the Department of War? In 1899, McKinley faced a series of challenges stemming from America's recent military victory over Spain. The Spanish-American War had been justified as a crusade to free Cuba from Spanish colonial misrule. Since 1895 the American public had followed, with increasing dismay, Spain's bloody attempts to put down a pro-independence revolution there. Newspapers featuring images of Spanish villains menacing innocent Cuban maidens proliferated, and *Cuba Libre!* became a popular slogan. In February 1898, 266 American sailors died when the USS *Maine* exploded and sank in Havana harbor, allegedly (though in reality most likely not) with the connivance of Spanish officials. On top of this, Americans had long coveted the island's strategic location (guarding the approach to a future canal through Panama) and economic potential (vast sugar plantations). From McKinley's standpoint, the combination of opportunities that would be created for American capital, political gains as a wartime president, and fear of what might happen should the mixed-race revolutionary movement actually take power ultimately made his decision to go to war obvious.[2]

The outbreak of the Spanish-American war was thus overdetermined. So was its outcome. The "splendid little war," as the secretary of state, John Hay, termed the conflict, lasted only a few months. By late July, with its navy seized or sunk and its army beleaguered, Spain sent out peace feelers to Washington. On August 12, the two sides agreed to an armistice, and in October their representatives began negotiating in Paris. More than Cuba was at stake in these negotiations, for during the war, the United States had seized control of several other Spanish colonies, most importantly, the Philippine islands, whose distance (some 7,000 miles from San Francisco) and population (7 million inhabitants) posed new problems for imperial rule. Under the terms of the Treaty of Paris, signed December 10, 1898, Spain relinquished sovereignty over Cuba and ceded Puerto Rico, Guam, and the Philippines to the United States, in exchange for $20 million.[3]

What was so easily won in war was not so easily kept in peace, however. As anti-imperialists warned that colonizing the Philippines would threaten America's republican traditions and domestic racial order, the Senate nearly defeated the peace treaty. For the United States, imperialism of this sort was "a much more unsettling and problematical undertaking than it had been for the Old World powers."[4] The treaty ultimately passed with but one vote to spare. Across the Pacific, Filipinos had already raised weapons against their new imperial masters. As reports of war and atrocities filtered back to the American press, imperial politics pervaded domestic ones, and a series of scandals threatened McKinley's re-election campaign. Meanwhile, it remained unclear whether the American Constitution permitted colonies to be held indefinitely without the promise of statehood.

When the president chose "a lawyer to direct the government of those Spanish islands," he likely hoped for an attorney adept at the legal alchemy by which damning facts mysteriously become exonerating narratives. Drawing on his experience as a New York City lawyer defending unpopular corporations in the courts of law and public opinion alike, Root would take on the interests "of the greatest of all our clients, the Government of our country" (as he put it) and alternately camouflage or justify them in the language of law to assuage domestic criticism.[5]

International discourses penetrated the domestic politics of imperialism. Policymakers contended that a now clearly "entangled" America must pay its respects to world opinion and international law. Seeking legal expertise, the State Department had hired John Bassett Moore to serve as assistant secretary of state during the war. The nation had also promised to obey the 1856 Declaration of Paris—a convention governing the law of war at sea that it had theretofore refused to sign—and offered generous terms to neutral nations. Soon after the war ended, the Supreme Court resoundingly affirmed that "international law is part of our law."[6]

If empire needed international law, the question was, just what sort of international law? As we have seen, in the nineteenth century, law—especially arbitration and neutrality—served as a vehicle for maintaining American separation and exceptionalism. But with a new imperial client, lawyers would need a new discourse of international law, one conceived of in *international* terms. To defend imperial policies, international lawyers would turn, not to narrow technical obfuscations, but to the broader, morality-infused discourse of civilization.

Among the Civilized Powers

Today's historians tend to see the expansions of 1898 as being continuous with a longer tradition of imperial growth, rather than as a singular "aberration."[7] But contemporaries experienced the period as a rupture ushering in an unexplored era of perils and possibilities. Henry Adams found the country "so full of swagger and self-satisfaction, that I hardly know it." The debate over empire that flared most brightly in 1899 and 1900 turned to a large degree on questions of American exceptionality. Simply put: should the United States follow in Europe's footsteps on the road to overseas expansion?[8]

Anti-imperialists depicted the seizure of the Philippines as an abandonment of American values. When the United States fought to liberate Cuba from Spanish tyranny, wrote Mark Twain, the most famous member of the Anti-Imperialist League, it had been "playing the usual and regular *American* game." But in crushing the liberty-seeking Filipinos, America had adopted European rules for no reason "further than to get ourselves admired by the Great Family of Nations, in which august company our Master of the Game has bought a place for us in the back row." Or, as the New York *Evening Post* put it, "Anti-Imperialism is only another name for old-fashioned Americanism."[9]

Empire threatened American society and government by introducing "foreign" peoples to the body politic, anti-imperialists argued. Giving millions of Cubans and Filipinos the right to vote would produce the heretofore unimaginable spectacle of "Asiatic" senators addressing Congress in "pidgin English." Labor leader Samuel Gompers feared "an inundation of Mongolians" who would steal American jobs. Senator Benjamin R. Tillman of South Carolina warned of the influx of nonwhites, noting that his fellow Southerners had already had bitter experience with "this white man's burden of a colored race." Major General John Dickman made the issue crystal clear: "Uncle Samuel has too many niggers already." Yet, to rule these peoples as colonial wards, argued Yale sociologist William Graham Sumner, would make a joke of the Constitution and discard Americanism for "the European military and monarchical tradition."[10]

Proponents of expansion countered that empire was nothing new. The conquest of the Native Americans was a case in point. To pretend that the nation had no experience in the dispossession and ruling of "savages" was to overlook virtually all of American history. If the anti-imperialists were right, Senator Henry Cabot Lodge observed, "then our whole past record of expansion is a crime."[11] Empire served American self-interest, imperialists claimed. It promised a vast outlet for America's "teeming industries," whose products overswelled domestic markets. The Philippines, along with Hawaii—annexed in 1898—would serve as steppingstones to the fabled China market, "a base at the door of all the East," as Indiana senator Albert Beveridge put it. Military strategists eyed Philippine harbors as potential sites for the naval bases and coaling stations necessary for projecting power across the Pacific.[12]

The imperialist case did not rest solely on national interest. A sense of belonging to a larger transatlantic Western world, rather than parochial exceptionalism, structured pro-imperial arguments. America embraced what Frank Ninkovich calls the "internationalist rhetoric of empire."[13] It did not take much to conclude in 1899 that the course of history led inevitably to imperial expansion in an era often called the "age of empire." Between 1876 and 1915, imperial powers carved up roughly one-quarter of the earth's territory into colonies. As British statesman Joseph Chamberlain observed in 1897, "It seems to me that the tendency of the time is to throw all power into the hands of the greater empires, and the minor kingdoms—those which are non-progressive—seem to be destined to fall into a secondary and subordinate place."[14]

Where did the United States fit in this imperial era? Expansion across the continent during the previous century had been explained in terms of geographic or religious destiny, accompanied by the comfortable assumption that any new territory would come to look much like the old: Mexicans on the West Coast, for instance, would be crowded out by Anglo-Americans until California became a US state like any other. Taking the Philippines forced Americans to confront head-on their similarity with European colonial enterprises. Many imperialists embraced the resemblance with pleasure. The only question concerned precisely how much exceptionalism would remain.[15]

Some proponents conceived of empire in Anglo-Saxon terms. *Imperialism* in the abstract might be bad, but Great Britain provided a model for a benevolent, "progressive" imperialism. The Philippines' tropical climate and the perceived racial characteristics of its inhabitants created a situation analogous to what the English faced in India. One thus finds in much of the writing on the Philippines the call to do "as the English have done."[16]

American Anglophiles—who had for years identified Americans and Britons as two branches of the same Anglo-Saxon tree—encouraged such comparisons. So, too, did the British. Rudyard Kipling famously urged Americans to "[t]ake up the White Man's burden" of empire. The *Spectator* promised that within fifty years of American control, "the Filipinos, who now retain so many savage instincts, will be orderly, law-abiding persons like our own hindoos."[17]

Other imperialists chafed at the idea of equivalence. America would lead, not follow. Senator Beveridge saw "God's hand" at work in the rise of American preeminence. Empire had moved ever westward: from China to Rome to Britain to the United States. He imagined America at the head of nations and hailed "the progress of civilization, which under God, the American people are henceforth to lead until our day is done."[18] The *Outlook* summed up the feeling in 1901, when it explained, "It will be our duty, not to govern the Philippines as Russia governs Siberia, or even as England governs Egypt, but to develop in the Philippines a self-governing community." The "American genius" could discover "a new form of colonial relationship unlike any that has ever been established by Holland, Germany, France, or England."[19]

Yet even those who stressed America's special mission to redeem the world imagined it existing inside a larger international project. If they admitted that what America was doing was "imperial" they argued that the United States would do imperialism better than it had been done before.[20] Behind these arguments lay the idea that history was developing in a singular direction, toward progress, and that imperialism was a way to encourage that development. Empire was a quintessentially modern phenomenon, embraced by many (though not all) progressives as a means of advancing society at home and abroad.[21] Empire spread civilization, whether conceived of in terms of Christianity, natural or social science, governance, or commerce. Indeed, the appeal of the entire civilizing project lay in its ability to combine all these things under the guise of common sense. "[H]e serves his country best who serves the world best," argued preacher and best-selling author Josiah Strong, "because the well-being of the member is found to depend on the health or well-being of the life of which it is a part." What did this mean for the Philippines? "As a part of the great world life, these people cannot be permitted a lawless independence."[22]

While it is tempting to dismiss imperialist arguments as weightless words, most imperialists seem to have convinced themselves, at least in the moment, that their project truly served a common good. "Although I am thoroughly anti-imperialist myself," wrote philosopher and social reformer Felix Adler in a letter declining membership in the Anti-Imperialist League, "at the same time I am persuaded that the civilized races have certain duties toward the backward races."[23] For imperialists, the taking of the Philippines could be understood as a morally virtuous endeavor.

The extent to which foreign policy elites began to imagine the United States linked with Western Europe in a shared imperial mission is evident in the increasing challenges to the Monroe Doctrine. That 1823 statement had been understood throughout the late-nineteenth century as justifying a policy of keeping European influence out of the Americas. When, in 1895, the United States intervened in a boundary dispute between Venezuela and British Guyana, it invoked the doctrine in its traditional sense. In a celebrated communiqué, secretary of state Richard Olney declared that British meddling in South America constituted European interference in American affairs, and demanded that England submit to arbitration. Washington had a direct interest in the matter, Olney declared, because "[t]o-day the United States is practically sovereign on this continent, and its fiat is law upon the subjects to which it confines its interposition."[24]

Olney—a railroad lawyer by training and previously the US attorney general—invoked international law in order to support what he described as America's "traditional policy" of non-entanglement. Washington's farewell address still applied, and Monroe's advice still pertained, because the New World differed fundamentally from the Old. In Olney's dubious description, Europe remained a "monarchical" continent dominated by standing armies. Preventing that influence from crossing the Atlantic was necessary to "the cause of popular self-government" in the Americas. International law, via the process of arbitration, provided the best way to resolve the boundary dispute, neutralize the politics at hand, remove British influence, and keep the Americas "pure" and separate. This was far from a call to unite transatlantic civilization through the bonds of law. Indeed, Olney refused a British proposal to hold an international conference to give a legal definition to the Monroe Doctrine.[25]

Yet by 1898, even Olney had changed his tune. Writing shortly after the outbreak of the war with Spain, he called on his fellow citizens to "shake off the spell of the Washington legend" and embrace both the advantages and responsibilities of great power. "A nation is as much a member of a society as an individual," he explained, and the United States ought to "forego no fitting opportunity to further the progress of civilization." Significantly, he emphasized the goal of ending the "scourge of war" through the expansion of arbitration, turning international law from a means of non-entanglement into a part of civilizing mission. Though Olney later opposed the taking of all of the Philippines (a naval base, or perhaps Manila alone, would have sufficed, he believed), he continued to urge the United States to "act for the relief of suffering humanity and for the advancement of civilization wherever and whenever such action would be timely and effective."[26]

Indeed, by 1901 some observers had declared the Monroe Doctrine obsolete. Writing in the *North American Review*, Walter Wellman complained that under its aegis the United States was preventing Europe from civilizing Latin America. An anonymous "American Business Man" titled a later piece "Is the Monroe Doctrine a Bar to Civilization?" Yes, came the answer.[27] The world's progress depended on empire, and if America wouldn't rise to the challenge, it must allow others to do so.

Making the Constitution Safe for Empire

US imperial elites thus imagined their mission as fitting into a larger Western (or at least Anglo-Saxon) project. Taking Puerto Rico and the Philippines proved American membership in the transatlantic club of empire. Yet many wondered if America's legal institutions would permit the indefinite ruling of dependent colonies made up of noncitizens. "An Englishman, a Frenchman, a Russian, or a German would not presume to discuss the right of his government to seize land anywhere, hold it by any tenure, and rule it at will," attorney Carman Randolph explained in the *Harvard Law Review*. But Washington's powers—even overseas—were bound by "a written constitution interpreted by an independent judiciary."[28] Naval officer Alfred Thayer Mahan put it more colloquially: the American march to empire "is met by the constitutional lion in the path."[29]

Mahan chose an apt metaphor, for constitutional rules on territorial governance were as fuzzy as a lion's mane. The text of the Constitution offered little guidance. Article IV gives Congress the power "to dispose of and make all needful Rules and Regulations respecting the Territory or other Property belonging to the United States." But which territory, and which rules? These remained disputed. In *Dred Scott v. Sanford* (1857), Chief Justice Roger Taney had ruled that the Constitution applied in full to the territories. Congress therefore had no right to ban slavery there. The Civil War and the Thirteenth Amendment settled the slavery issue but left territoriality undefined. Generally speaking, jurists recognized that Congress had extensive power over the territories (it could dictate when they became states, and it could add or take away land) but balanced this with the assumption that territories would eventually be admitted to statehood. They also guaranteed many basic rights to (white) territorial inhabitants.[30]

Meanwhile, as US power expanded overseas, the Supreme Court rationalized the use of state power outside national boundaries. *Fleming v. Page* (1850) held that import duties did not apply in Mexican ports occupied by US soldiers during wartime. Although these ports were under American control, they did not count as American "territory" for legal purposes. In *Ker v. Illinois* (1886), the Court gave its blessing to the extraterritorial kidnapping of an American in Peru by agents of the Pinkerton detective agency. Five years later, in *In re Ross* (1891), the Court further extended extraterritorial powers when it rejected an appeal by a seaman, John Ross. An American consular court had convicted Ross of a murder committed on a US navy ship in Japanese waters. Ross protested the violation of his constitutional guarantee of a trial by jury, but the Supreme Court responded, "The Constitution can have no operation in another country." Consular courts were therefore perfectly legitimate, a judgment enhanced by the fact that such courts were "the uniform practice of civilized governments" in "other than Christian countries."[31]

Unlike the situation in *Ross,* however, neither Puerto Rico nor the Philippines was "another country" but under US control. Was Congress bound by the Constitution, or "[f]ree to establish whatever colonial system it sees fit?" asked the *Harvard Law Review.* The law remained "wholly unsettled."[32] Many scholars asserted that constitutional protections, such as the right to a jury trial, did apply. Inhabitants of Puerto Rico and the Philippines (at the very least, those born after annexation) would become US citizens.[33] The Constitution, Judge Simeon Baldwin argued, did not allow for the category of "subjects."[34] Surveying dozens of precedents, legal scholar Henry W. Bikle declared, in 1901, "The colonial system of European nations cannot be established under our present Constitution."[35] Other experts disagreed. Harvard Law School professor C. C. Langdell asserted that for purposes of constitutional protections, "the United States" included only the states themselves and not the territories. His colleague James Bradler Thayer agreed that constitutional provisions provided no barrier to colonial governance.[36]

A great deal was at stake in this legal debate.[37] All sides assumed that the islands could not be governed successfully if their inhabitants were granted constitutional liberties. "To give the half-civilized Moros of the Philippines, or the ignorant and lawless brigands that infest Puerto Rico, or even the ordinary Filipino of Manila, the benefit of such immunities . . . would, of course, be a serious obstacle to the maintenance there of an efficient government," Baldwin argued.[38] Yet it was also problematic to assert, as Langdell did, that the Constitution did not apply outside the states. Did this mean that a resident of the District of Columbia could be tried without a jury? And if the United States could rule colonies without constitutional supervision, what, then, of the nation's claim to be a republic and a beacon of liberty?

The requirements of power demanded a different interpretation. At an 1899 gathering of the American Academy of Political and Social Science, University of Pennsylvania professor Leo Rowe predicted that the courts would do what they always did—namely, leave politics to the politicians. Asserting that the core American principle "throughout our history" was not liberty but "the maintenance of order and security," Rowe assured his listeners that the courts would not "force upon the political organs of the government a construction of the constitution which would make good government in the Philippines impossible." Newspaper editor Talcott Williams backed Rowe's judgment, appealing to an international sensibility to back an argument-from-necessity. The Constitution "created a nation with the usual international powers needed and demanded by an independent nation, recognized and acting as such under the law of nations," he argued. Though the government's powers might be limited at home, "[w]hen as a national sovereignty, it acts within the international field, it has whatever powers are needed for its work as such." International precedents guaranteed the right to be an empire.[39]

When the US Supreme Court finally ruled on the issue, in 1901, it proved Rowe's prediction right by adopting Williams's reasoning. In *Downes v. Bidwell* (1901), the most important of a series of decisions that came to be known collectively as the Insular Cases, the Court considered the petition of Samuel Downes, who had been forced to pay import duties on oranges shipped from Puerto Rico to New York. Narrowly, the case concerned whether or not the new US colony was a "foreign country" for tariff purposes. But implicitly, the Court addressed the more consequential question of whether or not Puerto Rico (and, by extension, the Philippines) lay within the nation's constitutional order. In short, did the Constitution follow the flag? The Court's answer, Elihu Root famously quipped, was that "the Constitution follows the flag—but doesn't quite catch up with it." *Downes* granted Congress nearly unlimited power over the islands. Certain basic rights—to life, liberty, and property—still applied, but otherwise Congress had a free hand to rule Puerto Ricans and Filipinos as it saw fit.[40]

Critics charged the Court with making a political rather than a legal judgment. As Mr. Dooley, the fictional creation of humorist Finley Peter Dunne, explained, "No matther whether th' Constitution follows th' flag or not, th' Supreme Court follows th' iliction returns."[41] Some argued that by re-electing McKinley in 1900, the nation had ratified America's imperial departure.[42] The Court's majority acted to remove constitutional barriers to this achievement. If the Constitution *did* apply automatically to the new territories, argued Justice Henry Billings Brown, then, by law, even "savages" would become citizens. This would be "extremely serious" because "it is doubtful if Congress would ever assent to the annexation of territory" under such circumstances. The "annexation of outlying and distant possessions" involved "differences of race, habits, laws, and customs of the people, and from differences of soil, climate, and production" that required greater governmental freedom of action. If the Constitution followed the flag, the flag would not go far. "A false step at this time," Brown concluded, "might be fatal to the development of what Chief Justice Marshall called the American empire."[43]

The constitutional argument for empire ultimately flowed from a sense that the United States was now a Great Power among Great Powers, and that it therefore must have the same freedom to act as the others. "To concede . . . the right to acquire, and to strip it of all power to protect the birthright of its own citizens . . . is, in effect, to say that the United States is helpless in the family of nations," contended Justice Edward D. White, citing treatises by Vattel, Wheaton, Halleck, Phillimore, and Calvo. Sovereign states had the right to acquire territory and to rule it as they saw fit. America was a sovereign state. Therefore, international law and norms gave it the right to be an empire. Without these rights, a reporter noted, the country would be "a misshapen, bungling nation."[44]

The dissenting justices attacked the majority's appeal to international law to justify empire. Congress "does not derive its powers from international law," but from the Constitution, argued Justice Melville W. Fuller. Justice John Marshall Harlan underlined the point: America could not simply follow what other nations did. "To say otherwise is to concede that Congress may . . . engraft upon our republican institutions a colonial system such as it exists under monarchical governments." European-style colonialism was, in this view, un-American.[45]

The Court's majority shrugged off these criticisms and eventually settled on a legal mechanism that would make empire compatible with the Constitution. Justice White relied on a concept of "territorial incorporation" that had been proposed by the Harvard professor of government Abbot Lawrence Lowell. Lowell suggested a "third view" between the idea that the Constitution applied fully or not at all. He admitted that constitutional protections extended to American territories. But he argued that it was possible for the United States to acquire possessions "without making them a part of the United States." Since the 1898 Treaty of Paris—unlike the treaties through which America had acquired the Louisiana Purchase or lands from Mexico—made no provision for the status of the inhabitants of Puerto Rico and the Philippines, those islands were part of the United States insofar as other nations were concerned, but constitutional protections did not apply until Congress positively "incorporated" the territories through legislation.[46] These legal gymnastics drew fire from the dissenters—territorial incorporation was an "occult" doctrine, Fuller alleged—and led to tortuously worded justifications, as in Justice White's famous conclusion that Puerto Rico was "not a foreign country" but "was foreign to the United States in a domestic sense." Nevertheless, in 1904 the Court affirmed the concept of territorial incorporation, and its reasoning underlined the continuing importance of international law. The United States "has the powers of other sovereign nations," the majority in *Dorr v. United States* ruled, and these included flexible treatment of colonial possessions. Although the Court had grounded the argument in the Territory Clause of the Constitution, it ultimately relied, as legal scholar Sarah Cleveland has noted, on "theories of inherent sovereign powers and authority under international law."[47]

This internationalist reading of the Constitution suggested that the purpose of embracing international law was to make the United States more like other world powers. This departed from basic tenets of the conservative sensibility of international law. Leading experts in the 1890s had promoted international law as a means of keeping the United States separate from Europe, not of emulating it. Indeed, both John Bassett Moore and Theodore S. Woolsey, scholars who held this view, initially opposed territorial expansion in 1898. Moore favored a protectorate over the Philippines, not a full-fledged colonial occupation. Behind this wariness lay a conservative's lament about the changes in American society. Moore remained skeptical about claims of doing things in the name of civilization, and derided assumptions of American innocence. "Of all human traits,"

Moore was fond of saying, "nothing is more pronounced or more incorrigible than the propensity to indulge illusions." Although, as we will soon see, Moore would play a central role in the expansion of American power during the early twentieth century, he never managed more than an ambivalent attitude about it. Surveying two decades of change in 1918, he described American principles in the past tense, ruefully concluding that "[d]own to a comparatively recent time they were regarded as practically immutable."[48]

Likewise, Woolsey opposed the expansion of US territory across the Pacific. Colonizing the Philippines was unprecedented American behavior, he argued. Previous expansions, he contended (unconvincingly), had involved "territory barely inhabited at all." If the United States kept the Philippines, it "would place itself within the European vortex, to be buffeted and cajoled, thwarted and urged on, forced out from its safe and comfortable isolation into the treacherous sea of enmities and alliances."[49]

To support empire, not just any invocation of international law would do. It was necessary to connect international law to international society—specifically, international civilization.

Law and Empire in the Philippines

The Insular Cases removed constitutional impediments to overseas colonialism. But Filipinos continued to fight for their independence. By 1900, their commander, Emilio Aguinaldo, had abandoned conventional military tactics for guerrilla warfare.[50] Confronted by rebels who set ambushes and feigned friendliness before attacking at close quarters with bolo knives, US troops employed increasingly harsh methods of reprisal. These included the notorious "water cure," in which captors poured several gallons of water down a prisoner's throat and then forced it back out by pressing on his stomach, repeating the process until the prisoner confessed. In the countryside, meanwhile, soldiers herded civilians into "reconcentration camps" that bore an uncomfortable resemblance to those created by Spain's infamous General Valeriano Weyler in Cuba in the 1890s—a practice that Americans had vigorously denounced at the time. In 1901, in response to a particularly sanguinary attack by insurgents on the island of Samar, General Jacob H. Smith urged his subordinates to turn Samar into a "howling wilderness." Take no prisoners, he allegedly ordered, "I wish you to kill and burn, the more you kill and burn the better it will please me."[51]

Accounts of torture and slaughter reached Americans at home via newspaper correspondents and soldiers' letters. This reinvigorated the anti-imperialist movement, which had flagged following McKinley's re-election. Opponents argued that fighting an imperial war in the tropics corrupted American soldiers, turning hale young men into bloodthirsty torturers or dissolute alcoholics and diseased johns. As usual, Mark Twain's sardonic wit captured the essence of the critique. American occupiers needed a new flag, he wrote, one "with the white stripes painted black and the stars replaced by the skull and cross-bones."[52]

Amid these challenges, the McKinley and Roosevelt administrations sought new ways to justify their imperial policies to the public and to themselves. They turned to lawyers for help. The secretary of war Elihu Root used two legal strategies to counter criticism of how the war was being conducted. First, he cited General Orders No. 100, the code written by Francis Lieber for the Union Army in 1863. This code authorized the use of punitive reprisals against guerrillas. Second, Secretary Root put General Smith on public trial for his actions in Samar. Yet Smith faced only the charge of "conduct to the prejudice of good order and military discipline," and, though convicted, he was ultimately punished only by being "retired from the active list." This approach—sometimes combined with an after-the-fact presidential pardon—became a frequent tactic that put the blame for colonial violence on a few bad apples, while pinning a bow of legal legitimacy on the counterinsurgency as a whole.[53]

Peter Maguire calls this practice "strategic legalism"—that is, "the use of laws or legal arguments to further larger policy objectives, irrespective of facts or moral considerations."[54] Yet lawyers' exculpatory narratives did not simply drown the opposition in a flood of legal technicalities. Lawyers also infused their arguments with the moralizing rhetoric of progress and uplift—rhetoric drawn from and set in a context of a transatlantic civilizing project. Lawyers were ideological actors as much as technical advisers.

Consider a speech Root delivered in October 1900, in Canton, Ohio. The text was later titled "The United States and the Philippines" and presented, in a published collection of his speeches, as an exemplar of statesmanship. But Root had a more partisan goal in mind: to rebut criticism from McKinley's challenger, William Jennings Bryan (Root suggested to the editor of the collection that a more accurate title would have been "To Hell with Bryan," though he allowed that "this might restrict the sale of the book for Sunday school libraries").[55] "The charge is that President McKinley has been guilty of something called imperialism. . . . Something so foreign to the character of our institutions and so dangerous to our liberties . . ."[56] To counter the charge, Root began with legal arguments. McKinley was simply fulfilling his constitutional responsibilities. By confirming the peace treaty with Spain, Congress had given McKinley the duty of administering the islands. What others called "imperialism," Root said, was merely the responsibility "to defend and assert the sovereignty of the United States." But this legal justification was clearly not enough. So Root proceeded to delegitimize the Filipino resistance through racial and civilizational discourses. It was merely a "Tagalog" insurgency on behalf of a "tribe" led by Emilio

Aguinaldo, "a Chinese half-breed."[57] There was no "Filipino people," Root said, for the islands were divided among numerous ethnicities.[58] Only the United States, as an advanced, civilized power, could bring order to the archipelago, whose people were "incapable of self-government." Should America abandon its responsibility for tutelage, the "government of the Philippines would speedily lapse into anarchy."[59]

In a broader sense, law could not be divorced from civilization. For legalists, law was what created and sustained civilization in the first place. As Supreme Court justice David J. Brewer argued to the Colorado Bar Association in 1898, if you pick at the thread of justice, all the glories of modern civilization "will crumble into dust and be forgotten as the civilization of Babylon." Imperialists argued that Filipinos currently lacked the capacity for law, and thus required tutelage until they developed a due appreciation for it.[60]

William Howard Taft took a leading role in making this argument. Although his girth and later failed presidency have created the impression of him as a genial ditherer, before Taft took the White House in 1908, he was widely regarded as a capable fixer, "one of the most valuable assets of the United States," in Elihu Root's words. He served as civil governor of the Philippines from 1901 to 1904, and after Theodore Roosevelt appointed him secretary of war, Taft became TR's "proconsul," charged with performing "stubborn tasks at far corners of the earth" and bringing order to "fractious islands," as a glowing 1907 newspaper profile reported.[61]

Taft mixed the legal and moralistic rationales for empire. He seems to have internalized the ideology of uplift and civilizing missions. Law, for Taft, signified disinterestedness and honest administration. As colonial governor of the Philippines, Taft hoped to make the "modern lawyer-politician" the basis of island government and society. Yet he criticized what he saw as corruption among the native elites and insisted on importing American judges. Filipino lawyers, he complained, were "venal" and not "capable and honest enough to administer justice." American judges, on the other hand, would show "what Anglo-Saxon justice means." Lacking law, Filipinos also lacked civilization. "They need the training of fifty or a hundred years before they shall even realize what Anglo-Saxon liberty is."[62]

Even Theodore S. Woolsey employed the discourse of civilization in defense of the war effort. Woolsey never fully embraced the seizure of the Philippines, but once the Senate ratified the Treaty of Paris, he counseled Americans to "make the best of it." Believing the Filipinos incapable of self-government, making "the best of it" meant establishing a government "based upon force" and modeled on the British example in India. When US forces disguised themselves as prisoners in order to capture Emilio Aguinaldo, Woolsey wrote an article in *The Outlook* defending the army's tactics under international law. Woolsey's argument relied in part on technicalities: American forces need not obey the law of war provisions of The Hague Convention because Aguinaldo's forces had not signed it (though how could they have done so, given that they were not considered an eligible state signatory?). But, more broadly, his argument invoked the discourse of civilization. The Filipinos were uncivilized and hence had no rights worth respecting. "When the wider question" of the conflict was considered, wrote Woolsey, the fact that the Filipino insurgents were just that—insurgents—meant that the United States was under no legal obligation to treat them according to the recognized laws of war. "The question is thus one of ethics and policy, not of law." The Filipinos were bound to resort to underhanded methods, Woolsey continued; to expect the United States to observe "the nicest rules of civilized warfare" violated "common sense."[63]

Taking Panama

The arguments of Root, Taft, and even Woolsey eased the sting of anti-imperial opposition. But imperialist enthusiasm ebbed quickly. The Philippine project "seemed, in the opinion of a majority of Americans in 1899, a generous and heroic enterprise," noted the *Atlantic Monthly* in 1902. Yet it had since become all too clear that "we are engaged . . . in subjugating a weaker people who are struggling, however blindly and cruelly, for that independence which we once claimed as an 'inalienable right' for ourselves."[64]

Recognizing the turn in the public mood, Roosevelt declared the war over on the Fourth of July, 1902. The issue of torture quickly receded from public debate. Even though American forces continued to fight against Filipino insurgents, especially in the southern islands, most Americans happily ignored their new colonial possession.[65] Yet the broader debate about America's imperial identity refused to die. As American policymakers turned their focus to the Caribbean, the search for stability and US predominance would lead to a series of interventions that provoked opposition at home.

None loomed larger than Theodore Roosevelt's "taking" of Panama in 1903.[66] The origins of the policy stretched back several decades. The United States had long desired a transisthmian canal for strategic and economic reasons. In 1879, a French company, led by Ferdinand de Lesseps, builder of the Suez Canal, had begun construction on a canal through Panama. The project failed, though not before sparking concern among jealous Americans. US desire for a canal had intensified after the War of 1898. During the war, strategists had fretted when it took the battleship *Oregon* sixty-seven days to travel from its base in San Francisco through the Straits of Magellan to the Caribbean. At first, Congress proposed building a canal through Nicaragua, rather than Panama (which was at the time still part of Colombia). But the New Panama Canal Company—the corporate heir to de Lesseps's ill-fated venture—undertook a massive lobbying campaign to ensure that the United States chose the route through Panama. If Washington did, the company would be able to sell its assets to the US government for millions of dollars. William Nelson Cromwell—the company's general counsel and a partner at the elite Manhattan law firm Sullivan and Cromwell—led the lobbying activities in the United States, while the French engineer Philippe Bunau-Varilla supervised activities in France and Colombia. Their efforts paid off, and in 1902, Congress directed President Roosevelt to purchase the company's assets and begin negotiations with Colombia.[67]

In 1903, the United States signed the Hay-Herrán Treaty with Colombia, gaining the right to build a canal and exercise control over a canal zone in exchange for a payment of $10 million plus an additional $250,000 per year. The Colombian Senate, however, unanimously rejected the treaty. President Roosevelt was at a loss. Determined to go through Panama, he was also absolutely opposed to further negotiations with Colombia's "foolish and homicidal corruptionists."[68]

At this key moment, John Bassett Moore, the international lawyer, appeared with a ready-made solution. Speaking with the assistant secretary of state, Francis B. Loomis, shortly before Colombia's rejection of the treaty, Moore mentioned that he had discovered some relevant precedents that supported an American right to build a canal without further negotiations with Colombia. Intrigued, Loomis shared Moore's thoughts with President Roosevelt, who requested a memorandum on the subject.[69]

Moore's memorandum would prove influential. It provided Roosevelt with a series of arguments that claimed a *right* for the United States to build a canal. It is important to note how "the law" was understood here. International law was not based solely on treaties but also on precedent—specifically, the actions of states. The pronouncements of American statesmen thus figured alongside solemn treaty arrangements in determining what the law was—or what it could be asserted to be.[70]

What did Moore's memo say? Above all, it was a morality-infused narrative of progress and civilization. "The United States, in undertaking to build the canal, does a work not only for itself but for the world," Moore wrote. "May Colombia be permitted to stand in the way?" The answer, of course, was no.

Moore offered two kinds of arguments. The first he identified as "general grounds." These boiled down to a claim that Colombian sovereignty over the isthmus was contingent on its duty to international civilization to allow the construction of a canal. For evidence, Moore cited an 1858 opinion of secretary of state Lewis Cass. Since the language of this opinion would turn up in numerous official statements, it is worth quoting at length:

> The progress of events has rendered the interoceanic routes . . . vastly important to the commercial world, and especially to the United States. . . . While the just rights of sovereignty of the States occupying this region should always be respected, we shall expect that these rights will be exercised in a spirit befitting the occasion and the wants and circumstances that have arisen. Sovereignty has its duties as well as its rights, and none of these local Governments . . . would be permitted in a spirit of Eastern isolation to close these gates of intercourse on the great highways of the world.[71]

This was hardly a "legal" justification at all, except insofar as it represented an official statement of the US government. But, it could be construed as a sort of international "eminent domain."

Second, Moore offered "particular grounds." These stemmed from an 1846 treaty between the United States and Colombia.[72] Article 35 of the treaty related to the isthmus of Panama and offered a mutually beneficial deal: the United States would guarantee the "perfect neutrality" of the area—in short, would protect it from European predators and maintain order—in return for the guarantee of a free right of transit for US officials, citizens, and merchandise. As Moore interpreted it, this right implicitly included an option to build a canal. And since the United States had always fulfilled its side of the bargain, Colombia "is therefore not in a position to obstruct the building of the canal."

In short, whether because of a "general" duty not to obstruct the progress of civilization, or "particular" duties under the treaty of 1846, Colombia was obligated under international law to grant the United States the right to build and operate a canal. Roosevelt took this to mean that the United States had a "color of right to start in and build the canal" by itself.[73]

In mid-September, the president invited Moore to spend the night at his Long Island estate to discuss the matter. Moore claimed later that he had expected the memorandum merely to provide legal ammunition for diplomatic negotiations with Colombia.[74] "I was surprised," Moore remembered, "when the President said that he did not intend to have further negotiations with Colombia and that if Panama should revolt and set up an independent government he would recognize it."[75] But Moore had plenty of experience in Washington. He should have realized the effect his bold language—"May Colombia be permitted to stand in the way?"—would have on a man like Roosevelt. Indeed, historian Richard Collin argues that Moore's memo proved "the decisive influence on Roosevelt's canal policy" because it was a "statement of moral and legal principles, a necessity for the aristocratic and moralistic Roosevelt."[76] In fact, by early October, Roosevelt had decided to act. Relying on Moore's memorandum, he planned to tell Congress that he would proceed to dig the canal without Colombia's permission.[77]

Events soon took a different course. Relying on conversations with Roosevelt, Loomis, and Moore, Philip Bunau-Varilla, agent for the New Panama Canal Company, intuited that the United States would support the Panamanians if they sought independence from Colombia.[78] Encouraged by Bunau-Varilla, Panamanian elites seized control from Colombian officials on November 3. US forces then prevented Colombian reinforcements from suppressing the uprising, and within three days Roosevelt officially recognized the new Republic of Panama.[79] Secretary Hay then signed a new treaty that gave the United States even better terms than the Hay-Herrán agreement had, to the lasting dismay of many Panamanian patriots.[80] Moore's direct role in these events was minimal, and he rejected an offer to serve as counsel to the new government.[81] His real value to the cause was his ability to legitimate Roosevelt's actions.[82]

The president's hasty recognition of the Republic of Panama drew wide criticism. To reformer Oswald Garrison Villard, Roosevelt's actions were "ignoble beyond words." Former secretary of state Richard Olney admitted, "For the first time in my life I have to confess that I am ashamed of my country."[83] He complained to his brother that "we now stand before the world as a bullying, land-grabbing, treaty-breaking power, all the more offensive for the unctuous and pharisaical professions of the public functionaries who represent us."[84] The Daughters of the Confederacy sarcastically endorsed Roosevelt's actions as a defense of the right of secession.[85] True, the opposition never constituted a majority and was heavily concentrated among Roosevelt's partisan opponents.[86] But the attacks were serious enough to warrant a direct response from the president.

On December 7, 1903, Roosevelt included a justification of his Panama policy in his annual message to Congress. Significantly, much of the message seems to have been drawn directly from Moore's memorandum. Roosevelt prominently featured Cass's statement and justified his actions under the 1846 treaty. But Moore's brief was not designed to justify the dismemberment of Colombia, and Roosevelt's address did not satisfy his critics. Instead, the president took a peremptory tone, "The question is simply whether or not we shall have an isthmian canal."[87]

Opponents were outraged. Furious anti-imperialists warned of a new imperial departure. Theodore Woolsey once again assumed a critical stance. Though Woolsey had defended US military actions in the Philippines in 1901, he came to see Roosevelt's "despotic tendencies" as sullying America's "national reputation." "Does any reasoning man believe that the President's construction of the treaty of 1846 can be written into it by any other hand than the mailed fist?" Woolsey asked. The president's message, he concluded was "not a case where law enters, but only politics."[88]

Roosevelt decided that a second message was required and invited Moore to Washington for consultation. After listening to the president's draft, Moore concluded that his new statement "was still vitally defective in containing no discussion of the law or giving any explanation of the hasty recognition [of Panama] that was so much at variance with our policy and practice."[89] Roosevelt had merely referenced the treaty of 1846 and quoted Cass's statement again ("I repeat the quotation here, because the principle it states is fundamental," the president had said).[90] So Moore set out to rewrite the speech, for it was vital that "what had been done be defended on definite legal ground."[91]

Roosevelt evidently valued Moore's advice highly, for he incorporated most of the lawyer's suggestions unchanged.[92] (He later wrote to Moore, "I hope you like 'our' message in its final form. I say 'our' message advisedly, for I feel that you had about as much to do with it as I had."[93]) Moore's most important work came near the end of the speech, where he inserted a full fifteen paragraphs. To justify the recognition of Panama, Moore grouped his reasons into three categories: treaty rights, national interest, and "interests of collective civilization."[94]

Roosevelt's message—eventually delivered on January 4, 1904—has received plenty of attention from historians. Yet its implications have not been fully understood. One historian has called the message "legalistic," while others find it less legal than moral and political.[95] Walter LaFeber, for instance, called the phrase "interests of collective civilization" a quintessentially "Rooseveltian" one, which "better fit the President's prejudices than any international legal or moral standard."[96] But the author of that phrase was Moore, the international lawyer. His personal views of US policy aside, Moore evidently valued a close relationship with the president. And he understood that arguments for empire must now be cast in broad internationalist terms.

Specifically, it is notable that the arguments Moore added to the president's address did little to justify Roosevelt's actions in terms of treaty law.[97] Under "treaty rights," he again cited the 1846 agreement. But there was no plausible way of interpreting that document to give the United States the right to prevent Colombian troops from suppressing a secessionist revolt. And while Moore claimed that the canal was "more than ever essential to our national self-defense," this concern hardly granted a legal right.[98] Even Elihu Root agreed that the letter of the law seemed to favor Colombia: "I suppose Colombia had a good right there, but you must look at the substance."[99]

It seems that Moore's main contribution was to point out the high moral purpose of the endeavor: "If ever a Government could be said to have received a *mandate from civilization* to effect an object the accomplishment of which was demanded in the *interest of mankind*, the United States holds that position with regard to the interoceanic canal," he wrote.[100] America, Moore concluded, had proven its ability to govern in the interests of civilization. As proof, he cited the Platt Amendment, under which the US maintained a de-facto protectorate over Cuba. Instead of exploiting Cuba for its own self-interest, Moore asserted, it had set the island free, thereby acting in the "interest of mankind."

So even as Moore endeavored to defend Roosevelt's policy on "definite legal ground," his argument ultimately relied on a discourse of civilization. Legally speaking, Colombia was not technically "uncivilized": unlike much of Africa and Asia, it was neither colonized nor subject to extraterritorial jurisdiction.[101] As international lawyer William Cullen Dennis explained, although Colombia was "weak, corrupt" and "inefficient" and the United States was "a great nation ready to act as the trustee for civilization," this affected "the ethics of the situation but not the law."[102] On the issue of the treaty of 1846, Roosevelt's critics continued to dispute Moore's tortured interpretation.[103]

Moore's appeals to a "mandate for civilization" nonetheless were persuasive to many. For in a rhetorical sense, the concept of "civilization" connoted, not merely sovereignty, law, and Christianity, but also progress and modernity. A civilized state promoted the advances of engineering and the expansion of trade.[104] By blocking the building of an isthmian canal—sure to be a great engineering feat and a spur to global commerce—Colombia showed itself unfit to control its own territory. Even Richard Olney, a very public critic of Roosevelt's policy, accepted the basic right to exercise a sort of international eminent domain in behalf of "the general welfare of all states."[105] When one considers, too, that writings of the period often portrayed Latin Americans as lazy, backward, and corrupt, it is easy to see why Moore's claims seemed so plausible.[106]

In the final analysis, Roosevelt needed to ask only for forgiveness and not permission. The deed was already done.[107] The Hay-Bunau-Varilla treaty ultimately passed by a vote of sixty-six to fourteen.[108] Roosevelt needed simply to put the matter in a better light, to offer a plausible explanation that assuaged lingering guilt, prevented any further political damage, and protected his legacy. He wanted to convince himself and his supporters that his actions were permissible. Moore provided that reassurance, both for the president and for the country at large. That today we find its reasoning so unsatisfying is not unrelated to the fact that we have a hard time believing in the imminent triumph of international law: stripped of the veneer of civilization, the realities of power loom all too large.

Coda: Legalizing Panama

At the same time as Moore was advising President Roosevelt, he was hard at work on the eight-volume *A Digest of International Law* (1906).[109] Sponsored and printed by the US government, the *Digest* would serve as the premier statement of the US interpretation of international law for the next several decades.

The *Digest* interpreted law through diplomatic records and statements, as well as treaties. Chapter 9, titled "Interoceanic Communication," dealt primarily with American canal diplomacy. It contained all the statements and treaties to which Moore made reference in his memoranda for Roosevelt—including Cass's note. It then included Roosevelt's statements of December 7 and January 4.[110] This had the intended effect of justifying the policy as a legal matter. Admiral Alfred Thayer Mahan had held doubts about the legality of American actions, he told Moore, but became convinced "after reading for this decision the correspondence in your International Law Digest, that our course was just from a legal point of view, as Laws amongst nations go."[111] Moore made no mention in his book of his direct influence in the crafting of Roosevelt's speeches. By acting simultaneously as a student and a shaper of the law, Moore created the illusion of an unbroken tradition, with Roosevelt as modern embodiment of this traditional—and therefore legal—American diplomacy. But of course it was Moore who created this tradition, and placed Roosevelt inside it! Thus did Roosevelt's—and Moore's—appeal to civilization become part of law itself.

Both constitutional and international law played important roles in making American empire possible after 1898. Their enabling effects stemmed only partly from the technical language of statutes and doctrines. More important was how lawyers connected imperial actions to broader ideological claims grounded in discourses of civilization. These arguments did not convince everyone, but they provided enough justification to ensure the establishment of an overseas empire. After 1904, as public opinion on colonialism soured, a new profession of international law would arise. Though it offered a different vision of American policy, it remained amenable to the spread of American power.

3

Legalism at Home

Professionalizing International Law, 1900–1913

In 1899, James Brown Scott had a promising future—and a problem. He had just arrived at the University of Illinois to serve as dean of its newly created College of Law. Only thirty-three years old, Scott had already demonstrated the tireless work ethic and fierce ambition that within a decade would make him the single most important figure in the American international law profession. After having earned undergraduate and master's degrees from Harvard, he studied Roman and international law in Paris, Berlin, and Heidelberg. He then moved to Los Angeles and helped to lay the foundation for the University of Southern California school of law.[1] Glowing letters of recommendation from two Harvard professors and from Nicholas Murray Butler, soon to be named president of Columbia University, had convinced Illinois president Andrew Draper to bring Scott to Illinois.[2] But when Scott proposed teaching international law in the law school, he was met with stiff opposition. The topic had traditionally been offered as part of the liberal arts curriculum, and David Kinley, the dean of the College of Literature and the Arts, had no intention of giving it up. The law school ought to stick to standard subjects like torts, contracts, and property, Kinley argued. Many law professors around the country agreed, and Kinley solicited their opinions and submitted them to President Draper. None carried more weight than the statement from the celebrated legal thinker Oliver Wendell Holmes Jr. "International law, of course, has little to do in any sense, with the practice of the profession," he wrote to Kinley. "I should almost as soon require chemistry."[3]

Thanks to Draper's personal support, Scott prevailed in his confrontation with Kinley in 1899, but only temporarily. He taught international law at Illinois for several years.[4] But Kinley's opposition—and the concurrence of so many legal authorities—signaled a greater challenge. As Scott labored to make international law part of the legal profession (and therefore separate from peace work or diplomacy), he would face continuing skepticism. Indeed, when he tried to establish a journal of international law at Illinois, the administration refused to support him.[5] A frustrated Scott left for Columbia University in 1903. Shortly thereafter, the Illinois law school dropped international law from its curriculum.[6]

There was more at stake here than university politics. As Scott had explained in his first public address, "International Arbitration," which he delivered to the Sunset Club of Los Angeles in 1896, developments in international law were poised to transform the world.[7] Just as men had come to live together peacefully under law, so, too, would states. Legal experts would codify the wisdom of ages; states would sign on to the code; and an international court would adjudicate disputes. The project had seemed achievable in 1896. An ordered and peaceful world had special appeal to a certain segment of the American elite—including the government officials, lawyers, and self-identified capitalists who populated the Sunset Club—who both feared the social disorder being sparked by industrialization and identified themselves as the most qualified men to fix it.[8] The United States and Great Britain were preparing to sign a treaty in which they had pledged to submit their disputes to international adjudication.[9] Arbitration had become a "popular craze" in the Anglo-American world.[10] At the Sunset Club, Scott was so confident that he concluded his talk with a detailed explanation of how to avoid an extended "industrial panic" when nations inevitably disbanded their armies.

But the coming era of peace would have to wait. The Anglo-American arbitration treaty did not pass in the Senate. Its opponents derided peace activists for being unmanly and unpatriotic. And in 1898 the United States sailed off to war, propelled by a mighty tailwind of patriotic fervor. As the new century dawned, international lawyers faced a dilemma. If international law was not law, what was it? If it was merely an advanced form of pacifism, it risked being dismissed as utopian naiveté by the policymaking elites whose attention it required. If it was instead a simple adjunct to diplomacy, a cataloguing of practices that states followed in competing for power, it would have little capacity to make the world a better place.

In the early twentieth century, international lawyers in the United States professionalized their discipline, in part as a response to these challenges of legitimacy and identity. Between 1906 and 1912, they created a series of organizations that sought to develop international law as a science, to spread its knowledge to the public, and to assert their claim as the rightful interpreters—and, at times, makers—of foreign policy. The story of the development of international law has often been told as the natural evolution of a centuries-long tradition of rational inquiry, in which the profession's projects are analyzed as intellectual responses to the perennial problems of world order. But tracing the career of James Brown Scott shows how the ideological, cultural, and social needs of legalists shaped the profession. Responding to the institutional demands of law schools and the jurisprudence of classical legal thought, the international law profession embodied an optimistic reformist sensibility that promoted national and class interests in the guise of universal values. This professional sensibility perfectly fit the interests and assumptions of the period's economic and political elites. Hitching the profession's fortunes to this class of men provided legalists with immediate benefits even as it created hidden weaknesses.

The Need for a Profession

A quick glance at how universities taught international law in the late nineteenth century reveals a split personality. Some professors treated it as a form of moral philosophy that drew heavily from natural law. For instance, when future US president Woodrow Wilson taught the subject at Princeton University in 1894, he combined an overview of European history with philosophical discussions of the great writers on the topic: Grotius, Puffendorf, Vattel, and so forth. According to an undergraduate's notes, Wilson introduced the topic by explaining that international law was "free from technicalities of ordinary Law, yet there is a dash of philosophy in it and it has in it those elements which do much to cultivate and broaden the mind—'It polishes.'"[11] One could be excused for thinking that international law, in Wilson's presentation, was more moral than legal.

Other professors emphasized positive law. In their courses, international law reflected the shared customs of states, based on their explicit agreements and observed behavior. Theodore S. Woolsey taught both international law and diplomatic history at Yale, and his exam questions suggest that he made few distinctions between the two subjects. Woolsey expected his international law students to memorize the rules of international law ("Under what circumstances is it lawful to employ savage troops in civilized warfare?") and to apply them to hypothetical situations ("If New Haven were besieged and bombarded by a land force, what buildings could properly be marked and their destruction by the enemy's cannon thus prevented?").[12] A 1904 final exam for his American Diplomatic History course tested students almost exclusively on topics related to interpretations of boundaries, treaty law, and neutral rights.[13] John Bassett Moore, meanwhile, assembled collections of hypothetical legal situations to use in the training of future officers at the Naval War College.[14]

Moore, whose Columbia University title was Professor of International Law and Diplomacy, had no objection to forging a close connection between law and state practice. The connection revealed how successfully international law had suffused the study of international relations at the turn of the century.[15] But if international law merely catalogued the actions of states, how could it serve as the progressive force for building peace through law that Scott envisioned? A proceduralist international law might not be law at all, but merely the inscription of "international usage."[16]

A venerable strain of legal philosophy made exactly this point. John Austin, a disciple of Jeremy Bentham, had argued a century earlier that international law was not really law, because true law required a central authority to enforce it. Since there was no sovereign above states to sanction lawbreakers, international law was merely "a branch of positive morality."[17] This charge struck a nerve among the perpetually defensive advocates of international law; even today's international lawyers still think it necessary to rebut the "Austinian challenge."[18]

For Scott and his contemporaries, the problem with embracing a moralistic conception of international law was that it left one open to charges of impracticality and naiveté. International lawyers worried about being dismissed as utopian, emasculated dreamers unworthy of inclusion in the councils of state. This fear was especially salient in an era that prized vigorous masculinity. Beginning in the late nineteenth century, scholars assert, Victorian-era definitions of manhood as restrained and upright behavior faced competition from a new vision. Scholars describe the new approach in different ways: as "passionate manhood"; as a period of masculine "performance"; as a shift from mature "manliness" to the more assertive "masculinity."[19] Whatever label one prefers, it is clear that, as historian E. Anthony Rotundo puts it, "Older traits of manliness such as independence and reason were . . . cast in shadow by more physical, 'primitive' qualities."[20] Teddy Roosevelt, the political face of the era, was also the face of the new man, one who practiced a "strenuous life," full of vigorous physical exertion and the indiscriminate slaughter of various and sundry wild animals.[21] These were the years when organized sports first captured the fascinations of middle-class men and when "sissy" and "stuffed shirt" became common insults.[22]

Not surprisingly, the peace movement often encountered opposition phrased in the language of gender politics. In the 1890s, male supporters of international arbitration had been attacked both for their disavowal of martial glory and their alliances with women and women's organizations (women also made up more than half of the audience at the first meeting of the Anti-Imperialist League).[23] According to their jingo antagonists, male peace activists were "effeminate gentlemen" and "deluded by sentimental gabble and persuaded to advocate the theories of gush." The defeat of the arbitration treaty in 1897 and the popularity of the Spanish-American War of 1898 suggested that the country agreed with jingoes that arbitration was an undesirable "exhibition of pusillanimity."[24]

This was but the latest attack on the virility of the mostly middle-class, Northeastern men who dominated official peace and anti-imperialist groups.[25] Many had been mugwump reformers and were derided as "political hermaphrodites" because of their perceived willingness to switch political parties.[26] Since international lawyers belonged to the same class of men, they risked being dismissed in the same way as sentimental or unserious. If international law was not "real" law but simply propaganda for peace, then its practitioners were more akin to ministers than to lawyers. And the ideal minister embodied the feminine virtues of morality, spirituality, and love.[27]

Cultivating a strong identity as legal professionals, rather than moralizing scolds or abstract philosophers, would thus help legalists differentiate themselves from the peace movement. "I share your wish that 'that word "pacifist" did not exist,'" wrote James Brown Scott to the Dutch minister of foreign affairs in February 1914. It would be "fatal" to any legalist institution, he explained, if "it were understood that it was the organ of anything other than enlightened international practice, as based upon principles of international law."[28]

The problem was that law school gatekeepers were reluctant to admit international law into their curriculum. And if one could not teach it in law school, was it really law? The most important figure in defining law school jurisprudence in this era was Christopher Columbus Langdell. In 1870, Harvard president Charles Eliot had appointed Langdell dean of Harvard Law School. To meet the growing social and industrial complexity of post–Civil War America, Eliot wanted to establish a truly scientific university modeled on German higher education.[29] Langdell advanced this program by arguing that law, far from being a mere "species of handicraft," was in fact a science that must be developed by university professors committed to intensive study.[30] Indeed, according to a biographer, Langdell not only transformed law school teaching but also created the model for all modern US professional education.[31]

At the heart of Langdell's legal science lay the so-called case method. Law consisted of principles, or doctrines, which could be inducted from studying judicial decisions. The solution to any particular future legal problem could in turn be deduced from the principles. The work of the legal scholar, then, was to create a taxonomy of law by identifying central principles and presenting a guide to their application.[32] The library was to the legal scholar what the "laboratories of the university are to the chemists and the physicists, all that the museum of natural history is to the zoologists, all that the botanical garden is to the botanists."[33] While equating law to biology seems implausible today, Langdell's conception of science as a historical discipline fit contemporary attitudes.[34]

The case method had important pedagogical implications. Instead of listening passively to lecturers expounding the principles of law, Harvard students worked out those principles on their own by studying cases. Though initially controversial, the Harvard method spread quickly and would become standard in legal education by 1915.[35] This coincided with dramatic growth in law schools. In 1870, when Langdell joined Harvard, there were only 1,600 law students in the entire country. By 1900, there were 12,500.[36]

But the law taught at most law schools pointedly did not include international law. Langdell's legal science was premised on judicial decisions and confined to common law: property, contracts, torts, and so forth. "Statutes, unprincipled distortions of the common law, had no place in scientific legal study," notes a recent history of legal education.[37] Many Langdellians deemed even constitutional law "unscientific" owing to its political character.[38] International law—with its lack of agreed-upon jurisdiction, court, or rules—was anathema. "We are unanimously opposed to the teaching of anything but pure law in our department," argued James Barr Ames, who succeeded Langdell as Harvard Law School dean.[39] In 1898, after Harvard president Charles Eliot forced the appointment of an international lawyer, the law school faculty refused to award degree credit for his courses. International law "has no binding force," complained Professor James B. Thayer, "and we are training young men for a practical profession."[40] As late as 1907, only ten of the nation's eighty-one law schools offered courses in international law.[41]

Professionalization promised to make international law "legal" and thereby avoid the slide into either moralizing pacifism or the ratification of power politics. The late nineteenth and early twentieth century was the golden age of professionalization. Doctors, lawyers, social workers, librarians, and others formed professional associations. So, too, did academic disciplines: the American Economic Association was founded in 1885, the American Historical Association in 1884, and the American Political Science Association in 1903.[42] By developing bureaucratic organizations, emphasizing scientific methods, and issuing codes of conduct, reformers across the disciplines made themselves into credible voices of expertise and authority.[43] Professional organizing offered a means of supporting a program of reform, while it simultaneously presented members as scientific, manly, and respectable experts.[44]

Domestic lawyers offered a blueprint. They faced their own crisis of legitimacy in the late nineteenth century. As corporations grew, elite lawyers increasingly became directly attached to them. No longer primarily acting as trial lawyers, they took part in boardroom and backroom deals to merge industrial behemoths and avoid litigation. The multiplying scandals of the Gilded Age ensnared them alongside their corporate patrons. Some of the founders of the Association of the Bar of the City of New York in 1870 and the American Bar Association (ABA) in 1878 had been implicated in scandals involving the political corruption of Boss Tweed and the improper financial shenanigans of the Erie Railroad. By establishing standards of behavior, corporate lawyers "were trying to address the conditions of their own degradation."[45]

At the same time, the elite bar worried about threats from below. There was an influx of immigrant lawyers (especially Jews) serving poorer clients and victims of industrialization, allegedly functioning as "ambulance-chasers," who were "debasing the noblest of professions into the meanest of avocations."[46] The elites responded by creating professional organizations that would hold their members to high standards and, in the process, exclude undesirables. The ABA advocated raising education and admissions standards and outlawing the solicitation of clients.[47] Though law school professors and practitioners did not always see eye to eye, they each recognized the value of cooperation. Top Harvard graduates could count on high-paying job offers from Wall Street law firms, which trusted the universities to identify promising talent.[48] By restricting membership to educated elites and associating itself with academia's claims that law was a science, the profession as a whole claimed an "exalted social status and cultural authority."[49]

Professional lawyers were clearly *men*. By 1910, for instance, only 1.1 percent of lawyers were women, and the Gilded Age courtroom was an intensely male space, presided over by the stern father figure of the judge.[50] Harvard Law School did not admit a woman until 1950.[51] Langdell reportedly explained that "that the law is entirely unfit for the feminine mind—more so than any other subject."[52] Even the case method could be understood in terms of masculine virility. Instead of passively learning the principles of law from lectures, the Harvard student was metaphorically thrown "into a pit," as the *Centennial History of the Harvard Law School* put it. With "no map," he was forced "to find his way by himself" and to "scramble out of difficulties" until he finally emerged from the wilderness of the cases with a self-made knowledge of the law and faith in his own abilities.[53] The Harvard method created "thoroughly trained men, fit at once to enter upon the practice of a learned and strenuous profession."[54] Professionalization did not fully solve the problems of legitimacy that lawyers faced. Critics continued to paint them as corrupt sycophants of their corporate clients.[55] But professionalization did provide a model for addressing the problem, and James Brown Scott eagerly embraced it.

In a series of articles, Scott attempted to fit international law into a Langdellian frame.[56] English and American judges, he showed, had considered international law to be part of municipal law.[57] "[I]nternational law is part of the English common law," he explained; and "as such it passed with the English colonists to America."[58] Therefore, Scott argued in a 1903 address to the ABA, "if international law is law and is administered in our courts as such, it follows that it should be taught and studied as law."[59] Practical experience trumped Austin's philosophical objections.

In 1902 Scott published *Cases on International Law: Selected from Decisions of English and American Courts* "to show that international law could be taught by the case method of instruction" and "convince even the casual reader, not to say the student, that there was a wealth of adjudged material."[60] It would be difficult to find anyone more enthusiastic about the case method than James Brown

Scott. In 1906 he delivered an address at George Washington University on the scientific and pedagogical virtues of the method, and he used the case method in all his classes.[61] His *Cases on International Law* "held the field in North America for more than twenty-five years."[62] Scott even became director of West's general casebook series.[63]

By recasting international law as municipal legal science, Scott charted a path between moralism and diplomacy. He admitted that international law could be taught as part of a liberal arts education "for purposes of citizenship and general culture." But in such courses "international law becomes a hodgepodge of diplomatic history, political and foreign history, international ethics—a thing of ceremony, courtesy and comity" rather than real law.[64] The "professional man," he argued, "must seek the professional school."[65] International law must be developed by professional international lawyers.

Creating a Profession

In 1905, James Brown Scott attended the eleventh annual Lake Mohonk Conference on International Arbitration, a summer gathering of peace advocates set in a picturesque resort near New York's Catskill Mountains. These yearly conferences attracted the standard variety of reformist elites: ministers, industrialists, educators, professionals, and philanthropists. Participants came every year in increasing numbers—from 35 in the first year to the maximum capacity of 190 in 1905—reflecting the growing popularity of the peace movement.[66] Between 1901 and 1914, some forty-five new peace organizations were founded in the United States, and a National Peace and Arbitration Conference in 1907 attracted 1,500 delegates and an attendance of 40,000, including four Supreme Court justices and eight cabinet members.[67] But in Scott's eyes, this movement was too unfocused and impractical. True progress in international peace required a legal focus, and only lawyers could develop international law.

Together with Columbia Law School dean George Kirchwey and the future secretary of state Robert Lansing, Scott circulated around the Mohonk Mountain House, seeking out others of like mind. Once Scott was assured of a sufficient number of prominent supporters, Kirchwey formally proposed, on June 2, the creation of a "society of international law."[68] In December, Scott and other legalists met at the New York residence of Oscar S. Straus, a prominent businessman soon to be Theodore Roosevelt's secretary of commerce and labor, to advance the plan. On January 12, 1906, at the offices of the Bar Association of New York, the constitution of the American Society of International Law (ASIL) was formally adopted.[69] To distinguish its aims from those of pacifist groups, the society proclaimed itself committed "exclusively to the interests of international law as distinct from international arbitration."[70] As its founders proudly noted, the ASIL became the first international law society in the United States.[71]

The ASIL constitution clearly stated the group's central goal: "to foster the study of international law and promote the establishment of international relations on the basis of law and justice."[72] To advance the science of international law, it published a quarterly journal, the *American Journal of International Law* (*AJIL*), and held annual meetings to which it invited experts on the topic. But it also aimed to educate public opinion so that the electorate would understand the nation's rights and duties under the law and would support the adjudication of international disputes. Thus the ASIL did not confine its membership to legal experts, as the *Institut de droit international* did. Instead, it cultivated "men of affairs" who it hoped would contribute their practical wisdom while also giving the society much-needed legitimacy. The secretary of state, Elihu Root, served as ASIL president, and the organization counted among its vice presidents three Supreme Court justices, three former secretaries of state, and a future US president. Still, despite its promise, the ASIL initially ran on a shoestring budget. It survived its first years mostly on the efforts of one man—its cofounder and secretary, James Brown Scott.[73]

Conditions soon improved dramatically. In 1910, the steel magnate and philanthropist Andrew Carnegie donated $10 million to found the Carnegie Endowment for International Peace. This was a tremendous sum at the time, equivalent to nearly $1.5 billion today (the average worker in 1910 earned just $575 per year).[74] James Brown Scott became the Endowment's secretary and director of its Division of International Law. He ensured that Carnegie's millions would support legalist organizations, such as the ASIL and, after 1912, the American Institute of International Law, which Scott founded with Chilean lawyer Alejandro Álvarez to promote hemispheric solidarity.[75] "I do not want to exaggerate, but in all sincerity I think that a new era is opening for International Law," Scott exulted to his French colleague Louis Renault.[76]

As Carnegie's gift suggested, by 1910 the peace movement had gone mainstream. Political and business leaders embraced the cause with great optimism. What historian Glenda Sluga has called "objective internationalism"—the way new technologies, such as the steamship and telegraph, linked the nations of the world ever closer—made international cooperation seem inevitable.[77] Carnegie was so confident in his new Endowment that he ordered the trustees to direct the money that remained after world peace was achieved to "the next most degrading remaining evil."[78] Increasingly, the movement embraced international law rather than the religious moralizing of the nineteenth-century peace advocates.[79] Codifying international law, educating public opinion, and convincing states to adjudicate their differences seemed the most practical way forward.

Even among international lawyers, the emphasis on the *legal* nature of international law became more pronounced. A growing number of legalists embraced what could be called a "judicialist" sensibility of international law. Judicialists argued that only by creating international judicial machinery could law be advanced and peace be obtained. They made the creation of a permanent international court their obsession. The institutional manifestation of this sensibility was the American Society for Judicial Settlement of International Disputes, founded in 1910 by Baltimore philanthropist Theodore Marburg with Scott's active encouragement.[80] The ASJSID (or "the society of the long name," as one member quipped) was committed to the establishment of a permanent international court that would operate in a "judicial" manner, in distinction to the frequent diplomatic compromises arrived at in "the ordinary arbitration as it has been understood in the past."[81] The society held annual meetings from 1910 through 1916 and published a pamphlet series. Scott served as its first president, and as secretary thereafter. A rotating assortment of other prominent members of the Atlantic establishment—including Marburg, Joseph Hodges Choate, Judge Simeon Baldwin, mining engineer John Hays Hammond, Harvard president Charles W. Eliot, and secretary of state Philander C. Knox—filled the other leadership roles.[82] The profession was making a claim for international law as law.

International Law and Classical Legal Thought

In the eyes of some later critics, James Brown Scott and his allies succeeded too well in marrying international law to domestic jurisprudence. This is because the late-nineteenth century academy embraced "classical legal thought," which, according to critics, was naïvely formalistic. By adopting this jurisprudence, legalists embraced abstractions at the expense of the realities of world politics. Thus the international legalist project was either too idealistic (and therefore unable to address the challenges of global power) or too conservative (and therefore unwilling to abandon the fiction of nation-state sovereignty and accept the necessity of supranational world organization).[83] This criticism demands careful consideration: to what extent did domestic jurisprudence shape the legalist project?

Answering this question requires engaging the complex scholarship on late nineteenth-century legal thought. This scholarship generally focuses on the competition between so-called classical legal thought and its rival and successor, legal realism.[84] Classical jurisprudence dominated the late nineteenth century, but for decades its history was written by its realist critics. They charged that classical thinkers were formalists who interpreted law by rigidly applying fixed principles without due regard for their societal impact. Oliver Wendell Holmes

Jr. famously took aim at Langdell, whom he called "perhaps, the greatest living theologian." Langdell valued logical consistency, Holmes declared, but "[t]he life of the law has not been logic: it has been experience." A true understanding of the law required one to "consider the forces outside of it which have made it what it is."[85] Harvard Law professor Roscoe Pound dismissed classical jurists as "[l]egal monks who pass their lives in an atmosphere of pure law, from which every worldly and human element is excluded."[86] Pound argued instead that law should reflect the real world by incorporating insights from social science. He called this method "sociological jurisprudence," and his successors pushed his critique further by taking aim at the very autonomy of law. If no single "right" answer could be deduced from the law itself, then any answer was by definition political, and the law should be interpreted to maximize social benefit rather than to conform with doctrine or precedent. In its most extreme form, legal realism became a "jurisprudence of legal incertitude" that explained judicial decisionmaking not by the power of reason or the wisdom of precedent, but by the individual will and even psychological profile of judges themselves.[87]

Critics also blame classical jurisprudence for unduly promoting the interests of capital. They point to the rise of conservative judicial activism in the late nineteenth century, when both federal and state courts struck down laws as unconstitutional with increasing frequency.[88] Most infamously, in the 1905 case *Lochner v. New York*, the US Supreme Court invalidated a law that limited working hours for bakers on the grounds that it violated a constitutional right to liberty of contract.[89] Although the courts did allow a good deal of government regulation to stand, scholars refer often to the "Lochner era" to encapsulate this period and to portray the Supreme Court in particular as a defender of corporate privilege against the will of the people.[90]

Recent scholarship paints a more nuanced picture.[91] Some classicists did argue that rights such as due process could be deduced from formal common law principles and that these abstract rights should then be applied without considering their implications.[92] But many others rejected mechanical formalism, and instead practiced a kind of "historical jurisprudence," which argued that the proper interpretation and application of the common law required the careful study of its development in its historical context.[93] For these jurists, the best legal scholarship consisted of the careful study of court reports and judicial decisions, which revealed the development of law across decades and centuries. Historical analysis proved that social custom underwrote and enforced the law, contradicting John Austin's claim that law issued from the commands of a central authority.[94] Moreover, understanding how law had responded to social change in the past (for example, Henry Sumner Maine's famous claim that the basis of social order had evolved from "status to contract") gave the legal scholar privileged insight into the needs of modern society. For this reason, classical scholars argued, judges were better than legislators at shaping the law to fit evolving social custom.[95]

If classical legal scholars were in fact attuned to social reality, this does not mean that they were essentially legal realists *avant la lettre*.[96] What most clearly distinguishes classical jurisprudence from legal realism was its sensibility of history, law, and society. Classical legal thought was rooted in a worldview that believed in the possibility of objective truth, recognizable through scientific study.[97] It held that categories like public and private or law and politics were conceptually separate spheres, and aimed in its scholarship to develop clear concepts to govern the application of law within any particular sphere, as well as to regulate the relationship between them.[98] If it inducted these concepts from the historical study of the law instead of simply deducing them mechanically, as Pound and others charged, it nevertheless tended to do so more confidently than its realist successors.

Classical legal thinkers also relied on a scientific and teleological sense of history. Laws could be evaluated based on how well they fit the level of evolving historical civilization. Classicists invoked history as a justification for law: certain laws existed because they represented the necessary outcome of historical development. Legal realists, on the other hand, sought to historicize law: by revealing its contingent context, one could unmask law as mere politics.[99]

Whatever its methodological underpinnings, classical legal thought frequently contained a kind of "middle-class moralism" based on the belief that individuals were free moral agents who should be left alone to pursue their own interests.[100] Judicial decisions should therefore value the protection of legal rights oer the aim of making society whole. Much of the laissez faire jurisprudence in the Gilded Age stemmed from an older tradition of Jacksonian individualism rather than a pro-corporate bias.[101] For the most part, classical jurists espoused faith in the ability of law and judges to maintain social order by defining the rights and duties of individuals and states.

It was this mindset more than a commitment to jurisprudential formalism that connected international legalism to classical legal thought. Historical jurisprudence figured prominently in legalist literature, which contained numerous references to key historicists, such as Henry Sumner Maine, Rudolph von Jhering, Frederick Maitland, and Frederick Pollock.[102] In many ways, international law was essentially the study of international custom—indeed, one legalist went so far as to argue that his subject simply be referred to as "customary law."[103] But there were limits to this analogy. Lacking a true international judiciary, one could not develop an international common law based on court reports and judicial decisions alone. Although Scott correctly noted that domestic courts in England and the United States recognized international law as part of their municipal law, such decisions were not necessarily legally binding on other states.[104] Thus the "cases" that made international customary law were often the political actions of states—whether or not they obeyed a particular rule in practice—rather than legal decisions per se. The *AJIL* recognized as much, and it regularly included a "Chronicle of International Events," which covered not only court cases but also treaties, diplomatic agreements, wars, and domestic legislation.[105] Moreover, unlike many of their domestic counterparts, international legalists supported codification—that is, they advocated the creation of legal codes.[106] In fact, the *AJIL* devoted a majority of its articles in its first few years to cataloguing the results of the 1907 Hague Peace Conference, which attempted, through a form of international legislation, to spell out rules of war and peace.[107]

Thus classical legal thought's greatest influence on international law was not its methodology, but its sensibility: faith in the power of law to define individuals' rights and duties and thus allow them to coexist in society.[108] Law at its best provided an apolitical expression of reason. This was a basic assumption of the legalist project, as was the conviction that studying the historical evolution of (international) law and society revealed the inevitable path that law would take in the future. Progress in international law, as Yale professor Edwin Borchard put it, was "a natural concomitant of advancing civilization."[109] And like many classicists, most legalists believed that legal professionals were best able to discern and guide this evolution. The legalists' embrace of judicial supremacy fit cleanly within this classical orthodoxy.

Classical jurists' emphasis on the rights of individuals also found an analogue in the international law project. Just as laissez faire constitutionalism questioned the regulatory power of the domestic state, most legalists rejected the notion of world government. "A federal state, seems to me impossible, and inexpedient . . . even if it were possible," Scott wrote.[110] For later advocates of the League of Nations and other supranational institutions, this stance marked prewar legalists as unduly conservative. But international lawyers' "sovereign state-centered consciousness" should not be mistaken for extreme nationalism, for legalists believed that nations were embedded in international society.[111] They wrote of the "interdependent relations of states," embraced the growing "solidarity . . . of the whole body of the peoples and nations of the world," and deemed "international cooperation . . . an ethical duty."[112] The legalist project envisioned an international peace that did not challenge the fundamental form of the nation-state. It reconciled sovereignty and internationalism by assuming that nation-states would learn to act in a more "civilized" manner. No central authority would be required. The key was for each state to understand and obey its rights and duties. International law, like all law, created an obligation, and "public opinion is more compelling in its nature than a sanction."[113] People obeyed the law out of a sense of obligation rather than force.[114] "The true basis of the peace and order in which we live is not fear of the policeman," Elihu Root argued; "it is the self-restraint of the thousands of people who make up the community and their willingness to obey the law and regard the rights of others."[115] The duty of the legalist lay in teaching the public knowledge of and respect for these rights and duties.

Legalists also relied on an optimistic estimation of the power of reason. International lawyers were quick to position themselves as more hardheaded and scientific than pacifists. Pacifists who embraced nonresistance and rejected the authority of the state invited "anarchy," Scott argued.[116] Paul Reinsch complained that the "older pacificism" was "purely negative in character." Moral appeals would not suffice; scientific internationalism was required.[117] But fundamentally optimistic and moralistic convictions often underlay these invocations of science. Take Lassa Oppenheim's 1908 *AJIL* article, "The Science of International Law: Its Task and Method," which has been cited as expounding the "classic 'paradigm' for international legal positivism."[118] Oppenheim, a German-Jewish émigré who eventually held the Whewell Professorship of International Law at Cambridge, pitched the article to Scott as a kind of manifesto and instruction manual.[119] To advance international law, he argued, lawyers must reject the platitudes of "the armchair politician and the moralist" and embrace the "positive method." Law was not what philosophers or even statesmen *wanted* it to be, but what rules states actually followed. "[I]t is a demand of science to stick to the facts," he declared.[120]

If Oppenheim's methodology called for cataloguing the present as it really was, it nevertheless aimed inevitably toward the future. He advocated science not as "an end in itself" but as a means to promote "peace among the nations." What animated this entire project was a belief in the inexorable advance of civilization. Favoring organic metaphors, Oppenheim described international law as "a branch of the history of Western civilization" and compared multilateral conventions to the "grafting-twig on the trunk of the old customary law." To expect progress, one had to assume the continued growth of the trunk. This Oppenheim readily admitted, "Ours is the faith that removes mountains, for our cause is that of humanity. The all-powerful force of the good which pushes mankind forward through the depths of history will in time unite all nations."[121]

Though not universally held, the idea that the goal of law was world peace (rather than the regulation of politics) was powerful. Washington lawyer Jackson Ralston predicted that soon "international law relating to warfare will be as obsolete as is to-day common and statute law relating to the status of slaves."[122] Scott expressed a similar opinion when he revised his casebook in 1912. Instead of dividing the field into rules dealing with "peace" and those governing "war," as traditional treatises had done, he presented it as "a system of substantive law"— analogous "though not identical" to municipal law—that identified the "rights and duties of states."[123] He relegated war from a central fact of international politics to "a minor position," simply an archaic form of "international procedure."

War was, "as you properly see, self-redress, and is nothing but a survival between nations of that form of self-redress which formerly existed within national lines, but which has been discarded by all enlightened communities by the establishment of courts of justice and administrative organs." With the development of international law, "self-redress" would soon disappear internationally as well.[124]

This idealism was not divorced from power. It flattered the very elites at whom the international law project was aimed. Confident talk about the power of public opinion reflected elites' concerns about what that opinion might support. Diplomacy was no longer the exclusive reserve of "a few learned men," but responsible to a mass public, in an age of yellow journalism. The "new system," Root fretted, brought with it "many dangers from which the old system was free."[125] Just as radical voices threatened private property at home, demagogues might take advantage of "the worst impulses of democracy" to foment war abroad.[126] "We are not to be intimidated by the vulgar cry of an excited populace," Root promised.[127]

Managing public opinion thus loomed as a key challenge for legalists. Today "public opinion" suggests the aggregation of individual preferences as revealed through polling or elections. To obey public opinion is to bow to democratic politics. But not only were there no public opinion polls before World War I, the very concept of public opinion was different.[128] When legalists spoke of public opinion what they really had in mind was some sense of national spirit, the expression of a deeper "will of the people." There was a true, proper public opinion that inhered in the national or international community. In practice, this "true" public opinion was nearly inseparable from a Victorian standard of upright, honest behavior. Nicholas Murray Butler, a staunch supporter of the legalist project, conveyed the essence of the idea when he referred to the "international mind." "It is as inconsistent with the international mind to attempt to steal some other nation's territory as it would be inconsistent with the principles of ordinary morality to attempt to steal some other individual's purse," Butler explained.[129]

The legalist project in a sense aimed to serve as the nation's superego, to restrain eruptions of the uncivilized id. As Borchard explained, the best hope of the peace movement lay in the "force of education when aimed at developing self-control, self-restraint and a habit of thought that will compel a submission of disputes to peaceful settlement."[130] In playing this role, legalists resembled the genteel reformers of the Gilded Age.[131] Like legalists, good-government crusaders, such as Carl Shurz and Dorman B. Eaton, emphasized nonpartisanship and the molding of public opinion by elites as the keys to removing corruption from public life.[132] Urban and international reformers shared a concern with elevating reasoned discourse and the belief that ultimately the "best men" should rule.[133] While James Brown Scott and Elihu Root sought to "substitute the rule of law for the rule of man," domestic reformers sought to replace politics with expertise through an elite civil service.[134] By stressing the values of good faith and impartiality, legalism both reflected and appealed to dominant trends in elite reform. This sensibility, more than a commitment to any particular jurisprudence, animated the legalist project of the early twentieth century.

Affirming a Judicial Identity

When international lawyers embraced a judicialist sensibility by trumpeting the benefits of an international court, they projected an identity as much as they designed a practical program. As historian Peter Novick notes, any new discipline needs a narrative that justifies its members' claims to expertise and authority. Often this narrative surrounds a central "myth."[135] Legalist organizations mythologized the figure of the impartial judge who resolved disputes according to scientific rationality. They were not pacifists, they declared, but supporters of law. The Carnegie Endowment "was never meant to be an institution of the kind of a Peace Society," Lassa Oppenheim noted approvingly.[136]

By stressing the *legal* aspect of international law, legalists highlighted their self-control and impartiality and, by extension, their manliness. Legalists made clear that their proposed court would involve "the cold and passionless application of a principle of law to the facts involved in the controversy."[137] A true court required "judges acting under the judicial sense of honorable obligation, with a judicial idea of impartiality."[138] True justice demanded true professionals; and these professionals had to be mature, reserved, impartial, and, by extension, male. In case anyone doubted as much, the ASIL forbade women from becoming members.[139]

Professional insignia also signaled the search for a manly identity. The seal of the ASIL featured a classic allegorical female figure of justice, holding balanced scales. But the ASJSID spurned this figure in favor of a man clad in judicial robes, holding open a book labeled "LEX" and, with a gentle hand, forestalling a workman from loading an artillery shell. Justice here is not a woman who weighs claims according to enlightened reason, but a legal scientist, male, acting according to the received wisdom of the law book. For some supporters, the representation of the stern father figure may have been more than figurative. Simeon Baldwin, for example, favored the revival of flogging criminals for minor offenses, a form of physical coercion at odds with the organization's stated commitment to intellectual and moral suasion.[140]

In any case, by presenting themselves as embodiments of restrained manhood, legalists sought to signal their legitimacy, trustworthiness, and effectuality. Pacifism, according to Scott, was "displeasing to men of affairs, whose support is

Figure 3.1. The seal of the American Society of International Law depicting a traditional female figure of justice. Source: *American Journal of International Law* 1, no.1 (1907).

essential to the triumph of the peace movement."[141] But by avoiding "untried and unworkable nostrums," legalists succeeded in attracting to their movement such "men of affairs" as secretary of state Elihu Root.[142] These supporters in turn allowed legalists to further assert the viability of their project. Scott allowed, for instance, that most reformers "are frequently regarded as dreamers of dreams and as men without experience in the actual conduct of affairs." But even a man who dismissed the resolutions of peace conferences "must be very sure of himself" to dispute the "weighty words" of a "Mr. Root."[143]

The cult of judicial impartiality also goes a long way in explaining the centrality of an international court in the legalist mindset. Adjudication was nothing new, but it had mostly occurred through arbitration. In an arbitration, the disputants would agree in advance on the issues to be settled and the method of procedure to be employed.[144] They would then select a panel of arbiters. Usually, both sides would pick one or two each, and then agree on an umpire from a third country.[145] Sometimes arbiters were recognized authorities in international law, but often they were simply well-regarded politicians or monarchs. Since arbiters rarely ruled against their own nation,

Figure 3.2. An image attached to the official publication of the American Society for the Judicial Settlement of International Disputes, in which a stern judge holding a law book restrains a worker from loading an artillery shell. The image highlights the masculine identity that international lawyers sought to project. Source: American Society for the Judicial Settlement of International Disputes, *Proceedings of International Conference under the Auspices of American Society for Judicial Settlement of International Disputes, December, 15–17, 1910, Washington, DC* (Baltimore: Waverly Press, 1911).

panels often decided cases by 2–1 or 3–2 margins. In 1899 the first Hague Peace Conference had created the Permanent Court of Arbitration (PCA), which promised to be an improvement on this ad hoc procedure. But the PCA was neither permanent nor a court; it consisted simply of a list of eligible arbitrators from which disputants could choose.[146] Over the next decade and a half, judicialists pressed intently for a more durable institution to replace the PCA. Arbitration could only "hope to triumph in the present state of the world, if it be made judicial," Scott argued.[147]

Court procedure would advance international law in ways that arbitration could not. Assembling an arbitral commission could be time-consuming and expensive.[148] More fundamentally, arbitration failed to live up to the values of "true" law. Arbitrations created no enforceable precedents and were not bound by stare decisis, the principle that judges should rule in accordance with past decisions. Worse, according to its critics, arbitration was simply the continuation of diplomacy with new negotiators. No one had much faith in the impartiality of the process.[149] Since arbitrators tended to support the nations that appointed them, it fell to the umpire (jointly selected by both sides) to split the difference. As a result, arbitration was "vitiated by compromise," Scott charged.[150] The PCA faced similar criticism: "more inclined to the pacific function than to the judicial function," it was not a "true international tribunal" but merely "an adjunct to the chancelleries."[151]

A real judicial court, on the other hand, would promote judicial values. It would deliver rulings quickly and cost-effectively, and these rulings would create precedents, allowing judges to develop international law in the same way as the common law.[152] An international court would thus create a "science of law," explained Harvard professor Eugene Wambaugh.[153] "[A]s the result of a long and honorable history," Scott argued, "judges decide the cases before them by judicial standards and by the traditions of the profession."[154] Judges "are bound to follow fixed rules," averred Simeon Baldwin, "adopted long before the controversy arose, for no other reason than that they were believed to be the rules of justice."[155] This argument relied on a formalistic notion of judicial autonomy. Judges would merely apply the rules as they were written. And judges would naturally earn the respect of nations, since they were naturally respectable figures (the fact that some of the ASJSID's biggest backers, such as Baldwin, were judges no doubt made such assertions especially convincing). "Civilized nations" wanted to submit their disputes to adjudication, Root argued. The only thing stopping them from doing so was "doubt . . . as to getting an impartial decision."[156] But a court of "disinterested" judges, Robert Lansing asserted, would attract plenty of willing litigants.[157] An international court, President Taft told the ASJSID, thus represented a "practical suggestion" for peace.[158]

Judicialists maintained an underlying faith in the progress of civilization. A permanent international court would mark the ultimate end of legal evolution. Primitive governments had used the equivalent of arbitration before they had fully functional court systems.[159] Creating an international court "is in such strict accord with the course of judicial development as to appear inevitable," Scott declared.[160] Permanent courts represented "the great step forward in the reign of law and order in the chaos of international affairs," according to professor Charles Gregory.[161] Just as "trial by combat" disappeared inside nations, once "courts of justice were set up," war would vanish in the presence of a true international judiciary.[162]

The fervor for an international court provoked some criticism. Arbitration supporters cited compromise as a great asset: flexibility encouraged peace.[163] Moore noted that even domestic laws—which were far more developed than international ones—were often "exceedingly indeterminate." Had it not taken the courts twenty years to interpret the Sherman Antitrust Act, only to give it a meaning not intended by its authors?[164] Moore doubted that a pure "'judicial settlement' of disputes" would ever be possible.[165] The notion that a court could succeed where generations of peace work had failed was ludicrous, added Maryland lawyer Omer Hershey. International law remained "a mere bundle of contradictory precedents and emasculated fictions," and one that lacked a real enforcement mechanism to boot. "Certainly there is nothing more lawless than unenforceable law," he charged.[166]

Yet, on the whole, legalist organizations supported an agenda that was consistent with judicialists' major goals and self-image: the creation of a profession in the image of science, separate from diplomacy and pacifism and committed to bolstering the authority of international lawyers as neutral scientists laboring to bring peace and order to the world. The *AJIL*, for instance, often praised the proposed permanent international court and reported on its prospects.[167] The ASJSID's publications made the court's realization a direct goal. In 1909 the ASIL created a committee on codification, pointing out that "the establishment of a permanent court of international arbitration" required firm and universally recognized rules.[168]

The profession also encouraged the adoption of international law courses into law school curricula. In 1913, a Carnegie Endowment survey reported that over two hundred colleges (including fifty-one law schools) taught the subject, but fretted that less than one of every five law students, and only 4 percent of undergraduates, actually enrolled in international law courses.[169] The following year, the ASIL sponsored the Conference of American Teachers of International Law and created a standing committee to study the topic. The conference recommended making the subject mandatory for state bar exams—a recommendation echoed by the American Bar Association's Committee on International

Law in 1916—and endorsed the case method because it promoted "a legal way of looking at things."[170] A later meeting of the standing committee resolved that "[i]n the teaching of international law emphasis should be laid on the positive nature of the subject and the definiteness of the rules," while "the widest possible use should be made of cases and concrete facts."[171] Bryn Mawr professor Charles Fenwick questioned the value of the case method, observing that "[a] large part of international law never comes before the courts." But he was overruled.[172]

Paradoxically, the invocations of judicial prestige were also a response to attacks on it. The early twentieth century witnessed a fierce controversy over the political interventionism of conservative courts. Some opponents began to advocate the recall by popular vote of judicial opinions or even judges.[173] Men like Root saw this as an attack not just on judicial independence but on the law itself.[174] As historian C. Roland Marchand has suggested, when international lawyers embraced the "cult of the robe" in their arguments about courts, they implicitly defended the judiciary from its attackers. Indeed, one often finds the same men—most notably, Root and Taft—backing the creation of international courts abroad while steadfastly resisting the introduction of judicial recall at home. Judicial supremacy replaced elites' anxiety over threats from below with a soothing image of social harmony assured by impartial judges.[175]

Legalists offered a reform project containing no serious critique of American society, or even of American foreign relations, and therefore sympathetic to the elite.[176] Among members of the ASIL, those "associated in the public mind with extreme conservatism" far outweighed supporters of progressive reforms.[177] Lawyers' conservatism reflected in part their own privileged class position. Like most professionals, legalists tended to come from upper-middle-class backgrounds.[178] They were clustered along the Eastern seaboard; many were as likely to correspond with an Englishman as an American living west of the Mississippi. The biographer of Joseph Choate, ASIL vice president and conservative lawyer par excellence, claimed that he and his colleagues seemed "to have had little sense of the country west of the Hudson."[179] As late as 1925, when one international lawyer relocated from Washington, DC, to Palo Alto, California, Edwin Borchard lamented his decision to "retire from the active front."[180]

There was another reason for the popularity of judicialism among legalists. Simply put, legalist organizations mostly supported a judicialist agenda because they were mostly controlled by James Brown Scott. Scott expertly exploited power networks. "Without your recommendation I should still have been in Los Angeles," Scott admitted to Nicholas Murray Butler.[181] In Washington, Scott attached himself closely to Root (he later referred to himself as an "understudy"), working for him directly as solicitor of the State Department from 1906 to 1908 and faithfully praising the elder man's views thereafter.[182] Scott also coedited seven editions of Root's speeches and reports, collecting this "masterly exposition" in order to "make known to future generations the literary, artistic, and emotional side of this broad-minded and far-seeing statesman of our time."[183] His position at the Carnegie Endowment he owed, "as I do so much in life, to my good friend, Elihu Root."[184]

Scott made the ASIL a personal project. Working at night and even lending it $1,700 of his personal funds, he solicited articles, planned annual conferences, and wrote most of the *AJIL*'s editorials in its first decade and a half.[185] At the Carnegie Endowment, as director of the Division of International Law, he funneled support to his own projects. At Scott's insistence, the Endowment purchased a thousand copies of the proceedings of the annual conferences of the ASJSID and distributed them abroad.[186] When this was not enough to keep the society in the black—"There have been but few new members," an ASJSID representative admitted—the Endowment kicked in a $5,500 direct subsidy.[187] From this sort of insider dealing emerges, in 1913, the odd spectacle of Scott, at the Carnegie Endowment, addressing a letter to himself, at the ASIL, explaining the terms on which the former organization would subsidize the latter.[188]

Scott also knew how to achieve maximum visibility for his projects. For example, soon after he co-founded the American Institute for International Law, he wrote to a series of European publicists, asking them to bless the new organization. He then persuaded Paul Fauchille, the editor of the *Revue Générale de Droit International Public*, to publish their responses in his journal.[189] A series of admiring letters soon appeared in the *Revue*. But when the Serbian lawyer Milenko Vesnitch submitted a letter that was "not like the panegyrics you have been receiving from our colleagues," Scott and Fauchille did not publish it.[190]

Scott's success—and the suspicion that it reflected his obsequiousness as much as his accomplishments—rankled some of his colleagues. At Yale, Edwin Borchard wrote that he believed Scott had allowed his personal and political concerns to influence the *AJIL*'s book reviews. "The management has not been scientific," Borchard complained.[191] For some, the animus was personal. "At all events his life and action is a lie throughout," steamed Columbia professor Ellery C. Stowell, "and while he possesses the greatest charm of manner and many superficial attractive qualities, he has not one generous or unselfish thought."[192] Others denigrated his scholarship, and the New York lawyer Joseph P. Chamberlain accused Scott of plagiarism.[193] When Scott served as solicitor of the State Department, his underlings formed a faux-secret brotherhood (dubbing it the "Society of the Mockahi") to plot his overthrow.[194]

Of course, Scott had admirers as well. His scholarship often received glowing reviews.[195] What he may have lacked in insight or originality, he made up in ambition, effort, and self-confidence. Sometimes it was hard to tell the difference: "James, I have never been able to make up my mind whether you are a brilliant conversationalist or just an incessant talker," observed Harvard's Samuel

Williston.[196] Above all, Scott promoted a sensibility of international law that flattered those whose support he needed. The international law profession had a similar relationship to American power as a whole.

The International Law Profession and American Power

In the years immediately following the end of the war in 1898, major universities experienced a minor boom in imperialism studies. Historians, legal scholars, and political scientists studied European experiences with new interest, seeking models of colonial governance that might be useful in the Philippines and Puerto Rico. They published books with titles like *Colonial Government* and *The Administration of Dependencies*. And they attended meetings of the American Political Science Association, which, at its 1904 inaugural gathering, devoted one of its five sections, "Government of Colonies and Dependencies," to issues of colonial governance.[197]

It turned out, however, that colonial studies was not the growth industry it had initially seemed to be. Within a few years it became clear that American power would not expand through additional territorial annexation but through subtler means. While issues of race and empire featured prominently in the young discipline of international relations, many scholars increasingly argued that international institutions—in addition to, or at times instead of, colonial projects—provided the best means of "civilizing" the world.[198] For instance, University of Wisconsin professor Paul Reinsch, author of *Colonial Government*, remained a believer in the potential of empire as a means of establishing "law and order . . . throughout the world." But he increasingly turned to the study of global cooperation, and by 1907 had published the first of a series of works on the topic of international unions.[199]

Contemplating an expanded role for international law became a way of imagining a greater international role for the United States, one that promised heightened influence without the political headaches of overt colonialism. Although many international lawyers had supported the war against Spain in 1898, the profession has accurately been described as "ambivalent" on the topic of formal colonialism. John William Griggs, who argued the government's pro-empire case in *Downes v. Bidwell*, and Chief Justice Melville Fuller, who led the dissent, were both ASIL vice presidents in 1907.[200] Nevertheless, the international law profession as a whole proved conducive to the spread of American power.

Legalist publications presented international law from a perspective that was attuned and sympathetic to American interests. While the *AJIL* did make a point of incorporating foreign voices—reviewing foreign-language texts and inviting non-Americans to write articles—the journal tended to focus on topics of special interest to the United States, such as neutrality.[201] And legalist publications generally supported US foreign policy. In part, this reflected the large number of government officials in the ASIL's leadership (those who worked for the State Department included Scott, Moore, Walter Penfield, Root, Lansing, and Chandler P. Anderson, among others). Financial considerations may also have played a role. The State Department took out 450 subscriptions to the *AJIL*, placing copies in every "Embassy, Legation and Consulate of the United States," and in the process improving the society's financial position.[202] Careful not to upset its patron, Scott monitored the *AJIL*'s editorials. "We would not like to do anything which might cause the Department of State to criticize our action or cancel its subscription," he explained to a contributor.[203]

A law-governed world supported the interests of a neutral, trade-oriented power. Convincing European powers to settle their differences through law would prevent an outbreak of war that might ensnare the neutral United States. At the same time, spreading an international rule of law created guarantees for Americans who were beginning to invest overseas in greater numbers.

The story of Jackson Ralston suggests how the structure of the legal profession favored particular interests, even if individual lawyers did not. Unlike most of his fellow legalists, Ralston had little love for corporate capital. An attorney whose private practice in the late nineteenth century focused on land titles, Ralston became an important supporter of Henry George's "single-tax" plan to promote equality by capturing excess wealth from landowners. He had been a personal friend of labor leader Samuel Gompers for decades, and in 1894 even provided legal services to the remnants of Coxey's Army, the troop of unemployed men who marched to Washington to demand government aid.[204] Nor did Ralston have anything nice to say about America's colonial adventures. In 1898, he helped Felipe Agoncillo lobby for recognition of the Philippine Republic and later served as attorney for the Anti-Imperialist League. Ralston criticized America's tendency to "invade the sovereignty" of foreign nations because policymakers "confuse[d] the interests of a few Americans with the interests of the American public."[205]

Ralston embraced the ASIL because he believed that developing international law scientifically would end war. He had come to international law by accident. His experience in land law led to work for the Pious Fund of the Californias, which had brought a case against Mexico. When that case became the first one submitted to the Permanent Court of Arbitration in 1902, Ralston was named agent for the United States. Soon after, he served as umpire in the Italian-Venezuelan claims arbitration of 1903. Struck by the lack of precedent or established procedure, he collected and published records of a number of international mixed commissions.[206] He hoped that this would contribute to the creation of a recognized code of procedure for arbitrations and thus make the process more "judicial," more consistent, and more widely utilized. Law, he believed, should not merely regulate war, but should find ways to prevent it.[207]

Yet if Ralston's political leanings distinguished him from much of the profession, his legal practice put him in the mainstream. Foreign investors often appealed to law to override the decisions of national courts, making arbitration— sometimes backed by a threat of force—a way to compel weaker states to recognize the claims of stronger ones.[208] Despite his criticism of corporations at home, Ralston accepted their overseas business: his clients included the owners of the Candelaria precious metals mine in Mexico, the Mariposa Development Company in Panama, and the Orinoco Company in Venezuela.[209] In a case involving the latter, the threat of US military power ensured the redress of the company's claims.[210] Revealingly, the US envoy charged with negotiating that settlement insisted that national court decisions be disregarded on the grounds that arbitral tribunals were "international and therefore unprejudiced."[211] In a hegemonic context, even ostensibly apolitical expertise could be mobilized for interested ends.

Legalism also provided a narrative of American power that was easier to square with the nation's exceptionalist ideology. As Robert Gordon concluded in his study of New York City lawyers between 1870 and 1910, a lawyer's main function was not to grease the gears of capitalism or even to find new and better ways to make money for their corporate clients. Rather, "the lawyer's job is selling legitimacy." The lawyer mediated "between the universal vision of legal order and the concrete desires of his clients, to show how what the client wants can be accommodated to the utopian scheme."[212] Legalists transferred to the world stage a vision of an ordered society, where calm legal rationality would forestall any threats to the existing order. While explicit defenses of formal colonialism based on the civilizing mission continued to be present (and can be seen in the *AJIL*), on the whole, by 1907 it had become both more politically tactful and internally ideologically coherent to find other ways to justify the spread of US hegemony.[213] Instead of "civilizing savages" through direct occupation, the United States could "civilize" the world as a whole.

Legalism provided language and concepts that helped the United States resolve a tricky ideological problem: how can a nominally anti-imperial republic be an empire? Becoming a Great Power had spurred excitement and pride but also apprehension. Anti-imperialists complained that the quest for "world power" threatened liberty and democracy. As Senator Carl Schurz argued, to be a truly "great" power, the country ought to emphasize being fair to "all other nations great and small."[214] Schurz invoked international comity as an anti-imperialist gesture, but Theodore Marburg argued that America's "noble role" as a traditional proponent of international law gave it the moral authority to control Cuba.[215]

In an ideological context, the judicialist agenda mediated between two seemingly incompatible desires. On the one hand, it emphasized membership in a community of civilized states, something that many Americans embraced in this era. Yet running alongside the desire for integration with Europe was a time-honored belief in American exceptionalism.[216] An ideology of exceptionalism manifested itself in two conflicting visions: America as the city on a hill (in which a "pure" United States serves as a beacon to the world) and as a redeemer nation (America as providential crusader).[217] Each would seem to preclude a role for international law, for law depends—at least in theory—on the equality of states.

Legalists resolved this tension by "domesticating" international law for an American audience. Legalists, in general, and judicialists, in particular, depicted America itself as a "judicial union." They argued that the United States should be thought of as a system of sovereign states, whose disputes were settled not by a world army but by a court. They devoted lengthy discussions to the obvious potential of the US Supreme Court as a prototype of a court of nations.[218] As usual, James Brown Scott pushed the idea to its furthest extent. Noting that the current "Society of Nations" had fifty states, while the "more perfect Union of the United States "had a similar number, he reminded those seeking a path to world peace that "the experience of the framers of the Constitution . . . should be as a lamp to their feet."[219]

This argument ignored the fact that maintaining a peaceful American "union" had required a massive civil war. Nor was the relationship between New York and Virginia in 1783 necessarily analogous to that between Italy and Russia in 1910. But the judicialist goal was less to present a new history of American federalism than to prove the viability of an international court in the present.[220] Along with frequent references to America's special relationship to international law ("From the very beginning of our national existence the people of the United States have been keenly interested in the common law of nations" said the ASIL's founding prospectus), legalists portrayed international law, not as a foreign imposition, but as the emanation of American values.[221] Judicialism suggested an "American" way of being a great power.

Thus legalists reassured Americans that they had little to fear from international law. After all, their proposed system—an international court combined with the codification of legal rules—contained no sanctions against lawbreakers save public opinion. Properly informed public opinion—in short, a genteel, properly "civilized" ethic—would lead states to obey law through their own volition. Since the United States was furthest along this path, it would have little to fear from international tribunals. Moreover, the legalist project would render superfluous more radical plans such as a federation of states, a league of peace, or an international executive power. "We must be careful not to connect ourselves with extremists," Scott explained in 1912, and what could be better calculated to appeal to the restrained sensibilities of "men of affairs" than a court often analogized directly to the highest court in the land?[222]

International lawyers recast the civilizing mission, not as the conversion of savages at gunpoint, but as the leadership of a world movement toward a legalized world order of justice and peace. They reassured Americans that embarking on such a mission would not threaten the country with foreign entanglement but rather promote the expansion of American values. These arguments convinced much of America's foreign policy establishment. Legalists' influence reflected the success they had in framing their project to appeal to dominant values and identities of the era. By the time the legalist project reached the apex of its influence in the five years before 1914, it appeared to those in power to be responsibly manly and eminently practical.

4

Legalism in the World, 1907–1913

In 1899, the six US commissioners to The Hague Peace Conference celebrated America's Independence Day by laying an elaborate wreath on the tomb of Hugo Grotius. Crafted by Berlin's "Court Jeweler," the wreath's gilt silver leaves encircled the Dutch lion and American eagle, nestled above a ribbon inscribed "To the Memory of Hugo Grotius / In Reverence and Gratitude." In front of an audience that included European royalty and "a choir of one hundred voices, carefully selected from among the best singers of the Hague," Andrew Dickson White, US ambassador to Germany, delivered the main address. Grotius deserved special recognition, White said, as a principle founder of "international law and international justice." The Dutchman had planted "the germ of arbitration," which was now producing green shoots of peace. And the United States, with its "widespread study of law," owed him a special debt. "Perhaps in no other country has his thought penetrated more deeply and influenced more strongly the great mass of the people," White asserted.[1] In linking the birth of the United States and the birth of international law, White expressed a growing legalist sentiment at home. As the leading champion of international law, the United States would lead the civilized world to a future of peace.

Transforming these sentiments into policy meant confronting difficult questions about the United States and its place in the world. Would international law serve to ossify the current international distribution of power, enabling the United States and other empires to exploit weaker states? Would submitting to international law subject the United States to corrupting foreign influences? Could the American public be brought along?

These questions had loomed large in August 1898, when America received an invitation from Tsar Nicholas II of Russia to attend the peace conference at The Hague. Hoping to head off an arms race that his country stood no chance of winning, Nicholas had capitalized on pacifist sentiment to call for disarmament.[2] The Tsar's invitation suggested an Old World affair, and Washington hesitated before responding. That same month the United States had acquired sovereignty over the Hawaiian Islands and concluded its war with Spain, resulting in the annexation of Puerto Rico and the Philippines and the occupation of Cuba.[3] Opponents warned that America's geographic expansion threatened its traditional values. Hobnobbing with European aristocrats might further tarnish the nation's republican heritage. However, President William McKinley concluded that sending a delegation would "impress the world" with America's "preference for peaceable means of settling international questions," and accepted the Tsar's invitation.[4]

The Hague Conference made little progress on its stated goal of disarmament, but it did enact resolutions banning the use of dumdum bullets (designed to explode on impact), poison gas, and aircraft (in this case, dirigible balloons) to drop bombs. It also passed a resolution urging nations to seek out third parties to mediate disputes.[5] As White's comments suggest, the US delegates seemed proud of their connection with a movement for international peace. The American commission pushed for a permanent international court but settled for the establishment of the more limited Permanent Court of Arbitration, which, recall, was a list of judges rather than a sitting court.[6] Yet the spread of international law created challenges as well. Third-party mediation might enable European powers to meddle in American affairs, and White feared that the American senate would disavow any potential threat to the Monroe Doctrine. He made a declaration toward the end of the conference that "[n]othing contained in this Convention" would lead the United States "to depart from its traditional policy" of non-entanglement.[7] Split between its desire to reform the world and to insulate itself from global politics, the nation seemed to be simultaneously embracing and avoiding international commitment.

Nevertheless, when a second Hague peace conference convened in 1907, the United States again attended. The second conference offered an auspicious opportunity to enact the judicialist agenda. Unlike previous gatherings, it was a lawyers' conference. Aristocratic diplomats had dominated the Concert of Europe that had maintained order after 1815; the 1864 Geneva conference on the laws of war favored doctors and military men. But in 1907, as the *Chicago Daily Tribune* noted, "the highest places are occupied by men who are distinctly jurists, replacing diplomatists." At the head of the United States delegation sat lawyer Joseph Hodges Choate, "whose ambassadorship to London has not overshadowed his lifelong service to the law." James Brown Scott attended as a technical delegate. Former secretary of state John W. Foster was there as a delegate plenipotentiary for China, having been chosen on account of being "better versed in international law than any Chinese subject likely to be appointed." To serve the delegation as a secretary, Foster brought along his grandson, a nineteen-year-old Princeton student and aspiring lawyer named John Foster Dulles.[8]

Reflecting the influence of legalist ideas on the American foreign policy establishment, the US delegation took the leading role in promoting the creation of

a permanent international court. But here, too, one could not avoid law's political implications. As strong nations clashed with weak ones over the relationship
between sovereign equality and the power of international institutions, US delegates found themselves caught in the middle. Simultaneously viewing themselves as representatives of a new Great Power and as promoters of an expanded
and strengthened international law, they would struggle to reconcile equality,
sovereignty, and international institutions. Legalists imagined that a judicialist
approach could resolve the contradictions, and envisioned the United States
as the agent of historic civilizing change. Sometimes with governmental impri-
matur and sometimes with money from Carnegie's foundations, over the next
seven years, legalists pushed the expansion of international law. But if America's
foreign policy establishment embraced the judicialist project, were these ideas
as popular—abroad and at home—as the lawyers imagined?

Judicialists Promote an International Court at The Hague

In 1907 the United States was poised to make a difference at The Hague.
Proponents of international law had gained increasing power among the foreign
policy establishment. The nation's growing wealth and international influence
were increasingly evident. Industrialist Andrew Carnegie had bankrolled—to
the tune of $1.5 million—the building of the Peace Palace in The Hague to serve
as the eventual seat of a permanent court. President Roosevelt, responding to an
invitation from the Interparliamentary Union, had taken the lead in proposing
the second Hague conference. Unlike in 1899, there was a heavy Latin American
presence at the 1907 conference, made possible in part by US lobbying efforts.
From Brazil's delegation of twelve to Cuba's half-dozen (handpicked by US secretary of state Elihu Root and Cuba's military governor, Charles Magoon) to
pairs of delegates from Ecuador and Nicaragua, all the region's states save Costa
Rica and Honduras were present. This suggested the rising power of the New
World. In view of US imperial influence in the Caribbean, some worried about
a US-dominated voting bloc. "Had there only been time to create a few more
Panamas or Cubas," complained a letter to the *Times* of London, "the United
States would have been assured of an absolute majority in the Conference."[9]

But the primary American consciousness in evidence was not global domination but judicialism. Elihu Root, now secretary of state, made this clear when he
gathered the American delegation together on the eve of the conference. Root,
by then also president of the ASIL, stressed the importance of using the conference to create a permanent international court. He offered a quintessentially
judicialist justification: "[T]he great objection to obligatory arbitration was not

to the principle of the thing," he contended, "but was due to a fear that the arbitration would not really be impartial." Arbitrations too often involved diplomats, resulting in "negotiation, not judicial decision." Nations feared that "politics may well enter into the question, and that political bias rather than the evidence actually submitted will determine the decision," Root continued. What was needed was a truly judicial tribunal that excluded politics and compromise. This would give the nations the confidence to arbitrate. If Root's prescription seems fanciful, it nonetheless reflected his realistic judgment of how nations behaved.[10]

Theodore Roosevelt deemed the court plan "excellent."[11] Roosevelt was an unlikely and uneven supporter of international law. There were many points of difference between the president and legalists. TR did not consider international law to be "real" law because it lacked a "sanction of force."[12] And although Roosevelt had nearly become a lawyer (he attended Columbia Law School from 1880 to 1882), he was "no believer in technicalities."[13] What mattered was "righteousness" and good government. Law was a marker of civilization, but to expand civilization required force. "Barbarous" or "despotic" nations or peoples—and these could include even Japan and Germany depending on the president's mood—demanded armed vigilance.[14]

Here TR echoed the influential Harvard historian John Fiske, who defined civilization as "the gradual substitution of a state of peace for a state of war" but argued that until all barbarous tribes disappeared, "the possibility of peace can be guaranteed only through war."[15] Just as European colonizers brought civilization to the "world's waste spaces," Roosevelt expected the United States to use intervention and occupation to curb "chronic wrongdoing" in its own sphere of interest.[16] Disarmament might come "[i]f China became civilized like Japan; if the Turkish Empire were abolished, and all of uncivilized Asia and Africa held by England or France or Russia or Germany."[17] But until then, disarmament must be avoided, lest there be an "immediate recrudescence of barbarism in one form or another."[18] Meanwhile, "[t]he United States Navy is the surest guarantor of peace which this country possesses."[19] In his annual messages to Congress, Roosevelt invariably followed appeals for peace initiatives with extensive and detailed calls for military preparedness. Under his watch, the Navy doubled its manpower and expanded its fleet of battleships from seventeen to twenty-seven.[20]

But TR believed that, at least among the "advanced" or "civilized" nations, one could expect states to obey the rules.[21] Roosevelt frequently suggested legal remedies for international disputes. In 1903 he convinced England and Germany to submit their dispute with Venezuela to the PCA. In 1905, as he helped Japan and Russia negotiate an end to their war (an act for which he would win the Nobel Peace Prize), he unsuccessfully suggested The Hague court as their best option.[22] To Sir Edward Grey he wrote, "Personally I think that the strengthening of the Hague Court is of more consequence than disarmament."[23] Roosevelt doubted the imminent triumph of law. A truly civilized world could never be attained, for he simultaneously feared "overcivilization." Civilization was thus ultimately a *process*, a constant struggle to sharpen the body and the mind by living the "strenuous life."[24] The fact that it could never end, that mankind must constantly struggle toward civilization without becoming *too* civilized, may help to explain Roosevelt's alternating embrace of and distaste for international adjudication. "No man in public life to-day," John Foster lamented, "has shown such an erratic and inconsistent course in relation to the subject."[25]

Ever the canny politician, Roosevelt certainly understood the political benefits to be gained from supporting peace. He hoped The Hague issue would win him votes. But political concerns could also cut the other direction: he did not want to appear "as a professional peace advocate," he told Root in 1905. "[M]ost of what I have done in connection with foreign affairs . . . " he explained, "has been on an exclusively altruistic basis; and I do not want people to get the idea that I never consider American interests at all."[26]

Considering his well-known embrace of war, this was probably not a likely danger. In any case, Roosevelt had immense admiration for Root (indeed, he hoped his secretary of state would succeed him in the White House) and the president endorsed Root's proposals for The Hague.[27] James Brown Scott—as State Department solicitor and a technical delegate to the conference—drafted a plan for an international court. The US delegates arrived at The Hague ready to promote a judicialist agenda.[28]

A frustrating month of proceedings elapsed before they could officially present their court plans. Those observers who had hoped that the conference might adopt concrete procedures to end the accelerating arms race or agree on a plan for world government were quickly disappointed. Successful agreements to adapt laws of land warfare to the sea and create a provisional international prize court provided only partial mollification.[29]

The US delegates remained optimistic, fixated on an international court. When, on August 1, Choate took the floor to introduce his nation's court proposal, the *New York Times* announced that "the real Peace Conference began to-day." Aged seventy-five, with a career of persuasive court argument behind him, Choate's oratorical eloquence shone less brightly than usual, for he spoke no French and relied on Baron d'Estournelles de Constant to translate a summary of his remarks. But the force of his conviction of the need for a new court was evident to all.[30] The Permanent Court of Arbitration had represented a step in the right direction, he admitted, but, since it was merely a list of potential arbitrators, it was a court "in name only." Its ethereal nature "has been an obvious source of weakness and want of prestige," Choate charged. Only a real, permanent court would do.[31]

James Brown Scott followed Choate. Speaking in French, he called for the "substitution of judicial action for diplomatic action." "A court is not a branch of the foreign office," Scott explained. It must sit "as a judicial, not as a diplomatic or political, tribunal." A permanent court designed along such lines would avoid compromise. It would establish precedents and clarify the law. And it would compel obedience through respect and invite nations to submit their disputes to it. The court would be voluntary and it would deal solely with judicial matters, exempting questions of a "political nature." But its effects would be dramatic nonetheless. The "mere existence of a permanent court" would be a "guarantee of peace," Scott promised. Just as domestic courts had ended "the use of force" to redress interpersonal disagreements, a true international court "will go far to substitute the rule of law for the rule of man, order for disorder, equilibrium for instability, peace and content for disorder and apprehension for the future."[32]

The proposal for a permanent court was seen from the beginning as a particularly American project. "Americans Would Organize Arbitration Court Like Our Supreme Court," read one newspaper headline. A court would represent "another notable contribution of America to the world's peace," said another. Throughout, the delegates and the press referred to the court plan as the "American proposal."[33]

Despite some initial doubts, the conference voted 28–0, with twelve abstentions, to consider the American proposal as a basis for discussion and assigned it to committee.[34] But political differences soon held the court hostage. The nations disagreed, fundamentally, on the goal of international law. Was peace to be achieved by protecting the sovereign equality of all states, weak and strong alike? Or should the club of Great Powers have the authority to determine the contours of world order?[35]

This rivalry fueled a dispute that would cripple the proposed court: how to select its judges. The Permanent Court of Arbitration had preserved sovereign equality. Each nation—no matter how small—named the same number of judges to the list. But a permanent court could not function with forty-four judges (one for each nation represented at The Hague). Choate and Scott suggested that between fifteen and seventeen judges would be ideal. The question was, how to squeeze representatives of forty-four nations into that number of slots? Should tiny Nicaragua have the same presence as the globe-spanning British empire? The Great Powers proposed a system of hierarchical rotation. Judges appointed by nations of the first rank (and the British and Germans insisted that this not include populous yet "undercivilized" states like China and Turkey) would sit for the court's entire twelve-year term, but judges from smaller countries would serve for shorter periods. The smallest countries would be directly represented for only one year out of twelve.[36] The Great Powers seemed poised to control the new court and install a "legalised hegemony," in the words of legal scholar Gerry Simpson.[37]

But Rui Barbosa, the head of the Brazilian delegation, stood in their path. Barbosa criticized the rotation plan for introducing "the principle of inequality" into international law. Giving the Great Powers more effective representation on the court seemed to legalize the notion that might makes right. By undermining sovereignty, it could put weaker states in greater danger of intervention from their more powerful neighbors.[38]

Barbosa quickly became the surprising star of the conference. Nearly fifty-eight years of age, his mental acuity and rhetorical force belied his short stature. Barbosa had been an abolitionist during Brazil's imperial age, and, when the nation became a republic in 1889, served as its first minister of justice and of finance. Trained as a lawyer, he was a man of letters as well as politics who spoke five languages fluently, effortlessly translated Greek and Latin, and kept a library of 40,000 volumes in his home.[39] Ironically, Barbosa shared Scott's admiration of the American political system. He had drafted Brazil's 1889 Constitution and based it explicitly on the US example. The US courts, in particular, served as a model of republican progress for Brazil to emulate: "The security of the United States lies in the divine grandeur of its justice," Barbosa once wrote. Scott could hardly have said it better himself. But Barbosa did not share Scott's belief that the international system could be conceptualized via analogy to US constitutional arrangements. Nations were not the same as individuals or US states. Rather, their survival depended on strict sovereign equality. "Sovereignty is the great fortress of a country," he maintained.[40]

This message struck a chord with representatives from Persia, China, and Central America. For them, being invited to The Hague ratified their status as full members of the community of civilized nations. To accept a subordinate position on the court would be a step backward. Although Brazil was not a small state, Barbosa came to be seen as a defender of the rights of non-Europeans and weak states everywhere. Brazilians acclaimed him as "the Eagle of the Hague" and commissioned a march commemorating his stand for international equality. (The march has since been performed at *Carnaval*—quite a departure from the staid atmosphere of the *Binnenhof*, the gothic castle where the peace conference met.)[41] With the selection of judges trapped between the competing desires of strong and weak, the court plan seemed doomed.

Scott and Choate initially supported granting powerful states greater representation on the court, but they were more concerned with getting a permanent court, per se, than with any particular arrangement of representation on it. In the face of Barbosa's protests, Scott noted apologetically that his proposal was "provisional." The Americans willingly compromised on a number of fronts. In a last ditch effort, Choate suggested that judges be elected by the nations as a unit, voting collectively. He seemed willing to abandon the hierarchical rotation system if it would ensure the court's creation. In fact, the Americans made a plea for considering the court in a context devoid of national interest entirely. "The United States is ready to accept the result of any election whatsoever, even [if] the American candidates were all eliminated," Scott pleaded. Choate offered "to sacrifice all purely American preferences and interests in the interest of justice and humanity."[42] But the divisions remained too deep, and the American delegation was forced to settle for a motion that approved the court plan in principle and urged its adoption in the future once the matter of judges could be settled. Meeting in plenary session, the conference approved this motion 36–0, with six abstentions.[43]

This was a meager accomplishment in a conference of meager accomplishments. But legalists did not despair. "In a good cause a good fight bravely lost is always a victory," Root asserted.[44] Legalists retained their fundamental belief in the inevitable progress of world society. Though limited, the agreement at The Hague would eventually grow into something greater, they believed. The optimistic narrative rested on the claim that the nations had agreed in principle on the judicialist conception of a world court, and that only a technical dispute over the selection of judges blocked a mighty step toward world peace. This is how Scott told the story in his later accounts, and historians generally echo his formulation.[45] In fact, it was not true. When Choate claimed that apart from judicial selection the delegates had "decided with practical unanimity that there shall be such a court," he met immediate opposition from the Roumanian delegate, Alexandre Beldiman, who noted that his country "has not contributed toward this unanimity." Four other delegates voiced similar reservations. As the Swiss representative later argued, his country would reject the American project "even if it were possible to constitute the court in a manner satisfactory to all the States."[46]

Simply put, many nations did not share the American conviction that a "judicial" court was preferable to an "arbitral" or "diplomatic" one. Courts and arbitration were different, Barbosa noted. Arbitration was a process between equals, the essence of which was the right of the disputing nations to choose their own arbitrators. A judicial court, on the other hand, "presupposes a dependence of subjection." While arbitration preserved sovereign equality, "the judicial function has ever been regarded as a delegation of sovereignty." Heinrich Lammasch, an experienced arbitrator and legal expert from Austria-Hungary, echoed this critique. The "court should not set itself up higher than the parties as a power superior to them," which would be implied if nations had to submit their disputes to judges that they had not directed selected themselves. Creating this sort of international power, in Barbosa's eyes, was "utopian," destined to fail, and "incompatible with the notion of sovereignty in international law."[47] Thus it is not clear that the nations were ready to compromise their sovereignty even if they could arrive at the proper mechanisms for doing so. Indeed, since Scott and Choate had agreed to change the name of the proposed institution from the International Court of Justice to the Court of Arbitral Justice, the possibility remained open that the court would continue to exercise an arbitral function.[48]

Contrary to the fears of its opponents, American court advocacy represented an ideological desire to evade politics, not an attempt to undermine sovereignty. In fact, later critics accused Root and Scott of being too sovereigntist; their version of international law was "an international law in the age of nationalism and imperialism," argues one historian.[49] Root frequently noted, in one form or another, that "the fundamental principle of international law is the principle of independent sovereignty." The world was "not ready" for an "international police force" or a "parliament of man," he argued, for these would require "the practical surrender of the independence of nations, which lies at the basis of the present social organization of the civilized world." Such an outcome was impossible. "There is no nation in the world which would seriously consider a proposal" to give control over its policies to "a majority of alien powers."[50]

This should not be read as a valorization of nationalism for its own sake, however. True, national patriotism could be a useful tool to deploy against the perceived perils of working-class unity: better for the masses to consider themselves "Americans" than "workers," or so conservative elites like Root believed.[51] But legalists' conception of the international space is better conceived of as nation-centered rather than nationalistic. They did not envision the weakening of national sovereignty, but they did imagine nations cooperating for international peace, rather than seeking national self-aggrandizement.[52]

Legalists thus argued that states should act according to their rights and duties, and not merely their immediate self-interest. They did not advocate the creation of international institutions with the power to coerce states; rather, they contended that international adjudication and public opinion could prod states to change their behavior. An international court—by clarifying the law, by inducing states to submit their disputes to it, and by modeling the possibility of impartial settlement—could perform this function. The United States need not fear a court's rulings because the United States already acted in the way legalists hoped other states would act. In other words, legalists understood the court primarily as a civilizing institution, and since the United States was already "civilized" in the sense of acting in accordance with international law, it did not need to worry about how judges would be chosen so long as the court was itself created as a judicial institution. Thus the judicialists embraced voluntarism to sidestep the problem of sovereignty.[53]

This was a matter of national identity as much as national interest. The United States was a Great Power but not an advocate of power politics. The country—to itself and to others—stood for the promotion of international law. "The moral ascendency of the American delegation," noted the *New York Times*, "was marked and acknowledged."[54] The actions of the American delegation at The Hague suggested that Washington had committed itself to the legalist project. This effort would continue by private means.

The Court Campaign of Carnegie's Capital

Unbowed by their failure at The Hague, US legalists continued to try to convince governments to establish a court.[55] But government concurrence alone would not be sufficient. In order to function, a true international court would require a true international law on which to base its rulings. But what did that law contain? By 1910, many still disagreed on that question. Treaties provided guidance, but gaps remained. The judicialist project thus required the forging of consensus, the creation of codes, and the identification of precedents, a process known as *codification*. Codification, to be effective, required state approval: one couldn't expect states to obey a law that they didn't recognize as a law in the first place. As Elihu Root pointed out in 1911: "The nations are a law-making power." He could have said *the* law-making power.[56]

But nations were busy. Their foreign offices were occupied with issues of the moment. To build international law, they needed prompting. They needed research. They needed model codes that they could tweak and shape and reshape until they were acceptable to all. They needed, in other words, groups like the Institut de droit international: scholarly experts to clarify the law, to separate the "is" from the "ought to be," and to make a case for the latter. The Hague Conferences of 1899 and 1907 marked an important milestone in this regard. They united "the private persons who had been discussing and formulating and codifying" with "the governments, who alone had power to make law."[57] The 1899 conference had adopted rules of war heavily influenced by the Institut's 1880 *Manuel de lois de la guerre sur terre*.[58] In addition, by 1911 there existed dozens if not hundreds of international groups that aimed to develop codes of conduct that would regulate everything from sports to postal regulations to copyright.[59] American legalists hoped to shape their agendas, where relevant. And when it came to law, no group was more prestigious than the Institut.[60]

So at the same time that official representatives of the US government negotiated with other nations to create an international court, a more diffuse, though no less elite, network of professionals and philanthropists came together to advance the judicialist project through private means. In so doing, they revealed the beginnings of a monumental shift in transatlantic relations. Throughout the nineteenth century, Americans had borrowed from Europe: capital for railroads and factories, ideals of art and culture, models of social and political reform. But now the shoe was on the other foot—or, more accurately, the wallet was in the other pocket. While European legalists barely scraped by, the newly created Carnegie Endowment for International Peace sat on $10 million in US Steel bonds, which generated an income of $500,000 per year. The new endowment "gives me the impression of being the budget of a small State," British international lawyer Lassa Oppenheim marveled.[61] As the governor of this small state's Division of International Law, James Brown Scott disbursed tens of thousands of dollars around the world in an attempt to forge consensus support for his judicialist vision of international law.

Endowment funds followed the lines of preexisting relationships. Both social and professional interactions connected lawyers in Europe and the United States. They read each other's work, contributed to each other's journals, and—in a pre-Internet world—tracked down government documents and rounded up copies of books to send to their colleagues across the ocean. In so doing they created what historian James Kloppenberg calls "a transatlantic community of discourse." "We have so frequently discussed most of these matters and I have read all of your writings . . . that it would be very difficult to find out how many of the ideas are mine and how many yours," Oppenheim wrote to James Brown Scott in what was only a slight exaggeration. While a shared heritage of the common law traditionally linked Americans with British domestic lawyers, US international lawyers did not confine their outreach to the English-speaking world. This was especially true of Scott, who spoke French "*comme langue maternelle*" thanks to his postgraduate education in Europe. "We are as brothers," Scott wrote of the Serbian publicist Milenko Vesnitch; and Scott's correspondence shows particular fondness as well for the Frenchmen Louis Renault and Albert de Lapradelle, the Greek Nicolas Politis, and the Chilean Alejandro Álvarez, in addition to the Germans Walther Schücking and Hans Wehberg. Even John Bassett Moore, who mastered spoken French only after 1908 and otherwise "limped along" in research and correspondence with the help of translators, maintained friendships with the Swiss Max Hüber and the Englishmen John Westlake and Oppenheim. If distance prevented the full flowering of intimate friendships, American and European lawyers carried on at least an amiable collegiality. Some collected each other's portraits, creating in their homes a virtual community of scholars.[62]

Maintaining transatlantic links, in fact, could prove vital to one's professional advancement. American lawyers kept up to date on the happenings and scholarship from Europe. Moore's first academic success (an 1887 monograph on extraterritorial crime), came to the attention of American scholars only after the Belgian publicist Albéric Rolin praised it in the *Revue Générale de Droit International Public*, and the *American Law Review* translated and republished Rolin's review. In 1908, when Cambridge University was looking to fill the Whewell Professorship of International Law, T. J. Lawrence asked Moore to write him a recommendation. "It is most important that the electors should know in what repute my work is held by those competent to judge in the United States," Lawrence explained. The same held true in reverse for Americans. When, in 1910, James Brown Scott applied for the Chichele Professorship of Law and Diplomacy at Oxford University, he appended twenty pages of recommendations from both American and European colleagues.[63]

Carnegie's millions put weight on the western side of the Atlantic. For all its successes, the financial resources of the Institut de droit international were so limited—consisting mostly of the income from its 1904 Nobel Peace Prize and the annual dues it collected of 20 francs (about $4) per member—that it was unable to hold a meeting every year, and many members could not afford to attend the sessions at all. Scott suggested a deal. The Carnegie Endowment would grant the Institut an annual $20,000 subsidy. In return, the Institut would establish a permanent advisory committee to the Endowment. It seemed an ideal combination of European expertise and American capital. And the Institut's stamp of approval would ease the reception of Carnegie's funds overseas. Otherwise, trustee Andrew J. Montague warned, "as soon as the nations of the world found that the Carnegie Institution [*sic*] was trying to make the international law of the world, it would end whatever possibilities of usefulness we might have."[64]

On March 4, 1912, the Institut's leaders accepted Scott's offer of funds, and then put the matter of an advisory committee on the agenda for the upcoming session of the full organization in Christiania (now Oslo), Norway. Scott never made the connection between the donation and the advisory committee an explicit quid pro quo, but he strongly implied one. In June, he warned Rolin that "there was very serious opposition to the subvention" among the Endowment's trustees. "I am very anxious that the appropriation shall be annual, but I cannot do it alone." With Scott's assurance that the Endowment was a truly scientific institution ("*une institution vraiment scientifique*") rather than a vehicle for Carnegie's pacifism, the full Institut voted at the Norway meeting to accept the Endowment's offer, and to create the permanent Comité Consultatif de la Fondation Carnegie.[65]

Scott undoubtedly hoped to benefit from the Institut's expertise. But he also hoped to enlist its help in his campaign for a court. As the disputes at The Hague conference had demonstrated, the court remained controversial. Although some lawyers had decided that strict sovereign equality of the Barbosian variety inhibited the development of international adjudication, many members of the Institut continued to prefer the arbitral model of the Permanent Court of Arbitration. When the Institut voted overwhelmingly to issue an official statement in favor of a permanent international court, some observers wondered whether the Carnegie Endowment's $20,000 subvention had made the difference. John Bassett Moore was sure that the support had been purchased.

"I confess that, since the Institute accepted the bounty offered it . . . I have felt for it a greatly diminished respect," he wrote a few years later.[66]

The Endowment also aimed to further the judicialist vision by creating an entirely new institution: the Academy of International Law at The Hague. The brainchild of Swiss-German Otfried Nippold and a Dutch lawyer, Tobias Asser, the academy would bring together students—diplomats and officials too, its promoters hoped—every summer for a course of lectures by international lawyers. Scott spent $40,000 on its behalf (the greatest single contribution made by the Division of International Law), and insisted that it accord with his vision of international law. Specifically, he directed, it was "to be an Academy in the scientific sense of the word" that could not "ever become an organ of pacifism." Neither should it promote a purely positivistic legal program, one that merely catalogued the actions of states. Rather, it must present law "as a living and growing system of international rights and duties." The academy was officially established in January 1914; a public unveiling was scheduled for October—three months after the shock of the Great War made its operation impossible.[67]

In addition to focusing on organizations and institutions, the Endowment sought to shape the field by subsidizing legal publications around the world. In response to requests, Scott disbursed large sums: $1,500 annually to the *Revue Générale de Droit International Public*, $1,300 to the *Japanese Review of International Law*, funding for publication of Lassa Oppenheim's *Zukunft des Völkerrechts* and Pasquale Fiore's *Il Diritto Internazionale Codificato*.[68] But Scott had a standard: his division refused requests for aid from groups who did not place the scientific development of international law at the center of their vision for public order. Even the esteemed International Law Association—which had over the years focused more and more on private international law—left empty-handed.[69]

Scott's personal projects fared better. In 1913, the ASIL received an extra $8,500—a sum greater than half of the money given to all European journals that year—to publish a Spanish edition of the *AJIL*. Meanwhile, when the Marquis de Olivart, the publisher of the Madrid-based *Revista de Derecho Internatiocional y Politica Exterior*, begged for funding to extend the "precarious" life of his review, Scott declined. Rather than help Olivart expand to Latin America, he preferred to reserve that space for the American journal.[70]

Given the unbalanced financial resources at hand, the Carnegie Endowment's activities might be seen more as the exercise of power than of disinterested scientific rationality. Yet, as long as Americans conceptualized their nation as the agent of civilizing the world through law, this tension could be minimized. US legalists imagined their nation in the vanguard of this civilizing project. But it was not always so easy to convince other Americans to play their assigned roles.

"Are We Pharisees?" Debating International Law in the United States

In 1913 and again the following year, Elihu Root delivered two of the most impassioned speeches of his career on a seemingly mundane topic: shipping tolls. In 1912, in legislation governing the operations of the soon-to-be-completed Panama Canal, Congress had exempted US coastwise ships from paying tolls when transiting the canal.[71] Democrats and Progressives hoped the measure would foster a thriving shipping industry that could compete with the transcontinental railroad monopolies, and President Taft saw the exemption as an effective way to subsidize the American shipping industry—something that Congress had refused to do directly.[72]

Great Britain objected. In the Hay-Pauncefote Treaty of 1901, England had acquiesced in giving America sole control of any transisthmian canal (the two nations had previously pledged to control it jointly), but only on the condition that "[t]he Canal shall be free and open to the vessels of commerce and of war of all nations . . . , on terms of entire equality."[73] Exempting only American ships from paying the toll, the British charged, violated the agreement and would result in higher tolls on foreign ships to make up for lost revenue.[74] But Taft and Knox argued otherwise. They claimed that the phrase "all nations" really referred to all *other* (i.e., non-US) nations. The United States could treat its own ships however it liked.[75]

International lawyers could be found on both sides of the argument, though even in the United States most supported the British position.[76] When nations disagreed on the interpretation of a treaty, arbitration was supposed to settle the dispute. A 1908 treaty between the United States and the United Kingdom obligated each nation to arbitrate. But it contained exemptions for matters that "affect the vital interests, the independence, or the honor" of either party. And it required two-thirds of the US Senate to agree to any particular arbitration. This support was not forthcoming.[77] Washington appeared ready to simply rebuff the British protest. Doing so would "imperil the world's structure of arbitration," warned journalist Henry Herzberg.[78] It would mean "turning its back on a very honorable chapter in its own history," trustees of the Carnegie Endowment asserted.[79] "We cannot ask other nations to arbitrate their differences if we refuse to arbitrate our own," pleaded James Brown Scott.[80]

The American unwillingness to arbitrate challenged the fundamental premises of the legalist account of world order. If the legalist path to peace required nations to accept their rights and responsibilities under international law, how could one expect success if even the United States—allegedly the natural leader—refused a legitimate opportunity to arbitrate? This, Oscar Straus feared, would set the entire peace movement "back for some years to come."[81]

To prevent this disaster, Root—now a senator from New York—introduced legislation in January 1913 to repeal the toll exemption.[82] To attract votes, he delivered two lengthy, impassioned speeches on the Senate floor. The energy he invested in these addresses (which he had prepared with research assistance from Scott, Joseph Choate, and Robert Lansing) reflected the importance he attributed to the issue.[83]

The entire legalist-imperialist complex that Root had constructed from 1900 to 1908 rested on an image of the United States as a trustee for civilization.[84] He repeated this justification in 1913. "We base our title [in Panama] upon the right of mankind in the Isthmus, treaty or no treaty," he said, before citing the message of secretary of state Lewis Cass that John Bassett Moore had so helpfully provided to Theodore Roosevelt in 1903.[85] To claim now that the United States had the right to do what it pleased in Panama made a mockery of this entire justification: "It was only because *civilization had its rights to passage across the Isthmus*, and because we *made ourselves the mandatory of civilization* to assert those rights, that we are entitled to be there at all," he asserted. "[I]t is not our territory, except in trust."[86]

To abrogate these solemn promises was to violate this sacred trust, to "be false" to America's long tradition as a leader in the movement for peace and law. "We think ourselves, and rightly think ourselves, leaders in civilization," he said.[87] "We have been the apostle of arbitration," Root pleaded, ". . . and we have urged it in season and out of season on the rest of mankind."[88] "Oh, arbitration when we want it, yes; but when another country wants it, 'Never, never furl the American flag at the behest of a foreign nation.'"[89] This did not befit an honorable nation. "O Mr. President, are we Pharisees?"[90]

Advocates for repealing the toll exemption liberally sprinkled their legal arguments with appeal to America's honor. "The United States cannot refuse to arbitrate this question, without retiring from its leadership in the advocacy of peace among all nations," exclaimed Chicago lawyer Harold F. White.[91] The trustees of the Carnegie Endowment were similarly concerned. They spent $23,000 to distribute over 700,000 copies of Root's speech and distributed 1.2 million copies of another statement calling for the repeal of the toll exemption or submitting it to arbitration.[92] Colombia's protests in 1904 had not troubled these men nearly to this degree, and the damages to Colombia from losing the entire province of Panama far outweighed America's interest in tolls.[93] Yet only the latter motivated Root to invoke biblical metaphors for American perfidy. Root framed this in terms of civilization: the "opinion of the civilized world is something which we may not lightly disregard," he explained.[94] Certainly, power mattered, but for Root it was just as much a question of identity and sociability. Legalists' transatlantic connections magnified the importance of European and, especially, British viewpoints. It was difficult to ignore the criticism of giants in the field, such as John Westlake,

Ernest Nys, and Lassa Oppenheim.[95] "Those of us who have recently been in Europe or who are in touch with European thought know the criticism to which we justly expose ourselves when we refuse to submit questions arising squarely under a treaty of arbitration," Scott wrote to Butler. "Our prestige has been, I fear, badly shattered, and two or three occurrences of this kind will question the leadership in the peace movement, which was ours until yesterday."[96]

Legalists took it as gospel that the United States had in fact been a "leader" in international law. But how accurate was this claim? The nation had indeed often taken the lead in *advocating* for more international law.[97] But when it came to actually *submitting* to international adjudication, the United States had a mixed record.[98] Washington had been a party (as participant or judge) to sixty-eight arbitrations or similar procedures in the nineteenth century alone, including tricky claims arising from the American Revolution (via the Jay Treaty) and the Civil War (in the famous *Alabama* arbitration).[99] But most of those cases had involved relatively minor issues. Even when they resolved long-running disputes, it would be hard to say that violence might have resulted otherwise.[100] Indeed, at times the United States entered into arbitration mainly to advance the cause of arbitration generally, rather than to solve a pressing political dispute. In 1902, for instance, Theodore Roosevelt had submitted the Pious Fund case to the Permanent Court of Arbitration primarily to give the new court its first case.[101]

Financially speaking, arbitration had been a winner for the United States. A Carnegie Endowment study from 1914 found that the United States had won 78 percent of all the money awarded in the arbitrations in which it had participated. America had done especially well when matched against weaker states. In arbitrations and settlements with Europe, the United States had paid out nearly $20 million while receiving close to $39 million. In arbitrations with Latin America (with the exception of Mexico, to which the United States paid $3 million for the territory it seized following the Mexican-American War) America had received over $13 million, and paid out only $85,000.[102] The figures were so skewed that the clerk in charge of collating them wondered "whether the Summary at the back of the pamphlet should be printed, inasmuch as it is rather an extreme showing in results in favor of one country, namely, the United States."[103]

The nation had frequently evaded arbitrations that threatened its interests. Washington rejected Spanish offers to arbitrate the explosion of the *Maine* and the occupation of the Philippines. It denied Colombia's demands to arbitrate the dispute over Panama. President Roosevelt did agree to submit a dispute with Britain over the Alaska-Canadian boundary to a claims tribunal, but he appointed nationalist politicians—rather than neutral judges—to the panel, and planned to send troops to the region to enforce the American position if the tribunal ruled against the United States.[104] The American people seem willing "to agree to arbitrate anything and be unwilling to arbitrate any specific thing," lamented the *Independent*, a journal sympathetic to peace advocates.[105]

Despite this record of inaction, the country could at least boast that it had signed a number of bilateral treaties in which it pledged to submit future disputes to arbitration. These included the high-profile Olney-Pauncefote Treaty of 1897 with the United Kingdom, and ten treaties signed by Secretary Hay in 1904–5. But despite this executive branch support, the Senate insisted on putting in so many reservations and exceptions that the treaties were never ratified. Finally, in 1908, a frustrated Roosevelt incorporated the Senate's reservations and limitations into a new set of arbitration treaties that were ratified but functionally worthless, as the failure to arbitrate the canal tolls dispute made crystal clear.[106]

Before the Panama controversy broke out, President Taft had called for new treaties that actually "mean something." His secretary of state, Philander Knox, signed two such agreements, with France and Great Britain, on August 3, 1911. Neither contained exemptions for "national honor" or "vital interests," and they created a joint high commission with the power to decide which disputes were eligible for international adjudication.[107] Had they passed, the canal tolls issue likely would have been arbitrated. But winning the Senate's support proved difficult. Although the struggle for new arbitration treaties is forgotten today, it became a centerpiece of the Taft administration. The treaties had given rise to utopian hopes. The *Los Angeles Times* declared them the most praiseworthy presidential action since the Emancipation Proclamation.[108] But the Senate again insisted on crippling reservations. When a twenty-eight-state speaking campaign failed to raise enough public pressure to sway senatorial votes, Taft refused to proceed with ratification, reasoning that compromised treaties were worse than no treaties at all.[109]

The contours of the fight over Taft's arbitration treaties highlight the real nature of the support for international law in early twentieth-century American politics: it was an impressive edifice resting on brittle foundations. Powerful men supported arbitration. Peace philanthropists raised their voices and opened their wallets. It was to support Taft's treaties that Andrew Carnegie had decided to establish his peace foundation in the first place, and the endowment spent nearly $50,000 on a pro-ratification campaign. Other peace groups funded by likeminded elites (publisher Edward Ginn established his own $1 million peace foundation) also advanced the effort.[110]

The treaties had a strong defender in the White House. Though Taft told his aide that he floated the idea of treaties merely to "draw the sting of old Carnegie and other peace cranks" from criticizing naval rearmament, the president too easily belittled his own motivations. Like other members of the growing foreign policy establishment, Taft viewed law as a fundamental institution of political and social order, and supported its extension to global politics. Having been a practicing lawyer and federal judge in the 1890s, he was personally and professionally inclined to this view. Taft famously claimed that he would rather be chief justice of the Supreme Court than president of the United States (he would eventually have the opportunity to do both, as he became chief justice in 1921).[111] In fact, Taft admitted that he had "always believed" in arbitration treaties and would have "got them out of my system sometime later on" even without Carnegie's prodding.[112] Indeed, the president had a long record of support for international law. He had been a vice president of the ASIL, and served as the honorary president of the ASJSID. He argued that "a permanent international court" offered "the solution of the problem of how to escape war, how to induce nations to give up the burden of armaments, and how to broaden and make certain our system of international law."[113] Legalists could count on a White House and State Department sympathetic to their goals, though not unmindful of other political objectives.

For all they claimed to speak for the country (indeed, for humanity) at large, international law promoters represented an interest group of their own. As we have seen, their strong support reflected the inclinations and cultural assumptions of an Atlantic-oriented professional and capitalist class. For them, giving educated experts the power to resolve disputes marked the triumph of civilization, for war itself was "unworthy of civilized men," in Carnegie's words. They trusted that a well-organized process, carried out by learned and rational men, would result in a just outcome. War caused suffering, death, and waste. Taft allowed that the Civil War was necessary to eradicate slavery, but thought that the War of 1812, the Mexican-American War, and the War of 1898 all might have been avoided through arbitration. Sure America might lose a decision or two, but Taft assumed that ultimately the process would redound in the nation's favor.[114]

Others were not convinced. If the country had entered arbitration whenever it was requested, Theodore Roosevelt mused, "it would have meant that we could not have gone to war with Spain, that Cuba would now be Spanish, that we could not have started building the Panama Canal . . . for unquestionably any neutral arbitration court would have decided against real right and justice and for technical legality . . . against us about Cuba and Panama." For Roosevelt, as for some others, vague promises of transatlantic "civilization" balanced uncertainly against the fear that foreigners would judge the United States unfairly, or that a purely "legalistic" decision might be incompatible with true justice.[115]

A different concept of "civilization" also drove the opposition to Taft's treaties. What fundamentally turned Teddy Roosevelt against them was not primarily the fear of an adverse judgment, but the fear that they might succeed in making war impossible. It was not just that matters of national honor *could* not be solved by arbitration (as Root worried), but that they *should* not be. Some issues challenged the manliness of a nation, and to respond in a measured, legalistic fashion would degrade the civilization of a people and a race. Just as "neurasthenia"—a diagnosable deficiency of "nerve force" whose symptoms ranged from headaches to epilepsy and insanity—afflicted sedentary, overstimulated modern men and women, a nation could become "overcivilized" and decline. To litigate a threat to one's honor was degrading: if a man's "wife is assaulted and has her face slapped," Roosevelt posited in a telling choice of metaphor, only a coward would respond with a lawsuit. Taft "is a flabby fool," he complained. The president did not grasp the fundamental fact that the persistence of barbarousness still required a nation "to play the part of the just man armed."[116]

Nonetheless, while the jingoes and peace advocates squabbled, the American public generally supported arbitration. There are no public opinion polls for the period, but editorial opinion overwhelmingly favored Taft's treaties. Large portions of the clergy preached in favor of them. Business groups lobbied for their passage. Knox was so confident in arbitration's political prospects that he even hoped for a high-profile "wrangle" with the Senate over ratification.[117]

But this support was shallow, and could not match the intensity of the institutional and regional interests that felt threatened by arbitration treaties. The Senate balked at a provision giving a joint high commission the power to determine whether or not a particular dispute would be subject to arbitration. This threatened to undermine the chamber's role in foreign affairs—at that time still a robust one. Representatives of some western states feared that arbitral decisions might inhibit their ability to exclude and discriminate against Asian immigrants. Southerners worried that international creditors might force the adjudication of the defaulted debts of several states. Both Irish Americans and German Americans opposed any treaty that promised closer union with the British. Electoral politics took care of the rest. Democrats had taken control of the House in the 1910 midterm elections, and saw no reason to improve Taft's chances for reelection in 1912. Meanwhile, Roosevelt's dissatisfaction with his successor was increasingly obvious, and the emerging split in the party ranks stemming from the prospect of a Rooseveltian presidential challenge in 1912 dimmed any hopes that Senate Republicans would unite behind Taft's standard.[118]

Thus there were good reasons to doubt the legalist image of the United States as a uniquely civilized respecter of international law. But a gap between rhetoric and actions does not always mean that protagonists do not take their own words seriously. Framing policies in terms of the promotion of law and civilization helped to convince not only the public but also policymakers of the rightness of their actions. Once made, such arguments had a tendency to persist. The tolls provision must be repealed, argued Root and his allies, because if the canal was "a trust for mankind" as US policymakers had repeatedly claimed, then it must be available to all on equal terms.[119] Invoking civilization carried ideological weight.

Root's arguments inspired opposition. As US engineers conquered Panama's rough terrain and infectious mosquitoes, lavishly illustrated books praising the technical—even moral—achievement circulated widely. A nationalistic pride took hold. Americans saw the canal as *theirs*.[120] If Root and others clung tightly to the belief that the canal was "a great work for the benefit of the world at large," nationalists instead emphasized its military and commercial value to the United States.[121] What right had England to butt in? Elihu Root and the Carnegie Endowment, then, were suspect. In April 1914, the Committee on Interoceanic Canals, headed by Senator James O'Gorman, called James Brown Scott to testify on behalf of the Carnegie Endowment. O'Gorman accused Scott of holding "a divided allegiance," while other critics condemned his decision "to take sides in a controversy against your own country."[122] International law should never trump national interest, the senator argued. Earlier, O'Gorman had ridiculed Root's claim that "we have been the apostles of the peace movement." This was hardly the case, the senator said. The Senate had often knocked down arbitration treaties, and even those presently in force excluded matters of national honor and vital interests.[123] O'Gorman's America—like the Irish-American community to which he belonged—self-consciously struggled for whatever it could get. "We can never permit a foreign power"—certainly not the hated English—"to intrude upon us its views affecting our domestic policy."[124]

Ultimately, events seemed to confirm Root's faith in his vision of America. Though the 1912 Democratic platform supported the toll exemption, the incoming president, Woodrow Wilson, changed his mind.[125] An *AJIL* article by his friend John Latané convinced Wilson that the toll exemption violated the Hay-Pauncefote Treaty.[126] Wilson's confidante, Edward House, concurred.[127] In late January, the president-elect dined with Root, Butler, and Choate at New York's prestigious Round Table club. He promised them that "[w]hen the time comes for me to act, you can count upon my taking the right stand."[128]

It took over a year, but in early 1914 Wilson took that stand publicly. In what his leading biographer called "one of the most extraordinary displays of leadership of his entire career," he twisted enough arms to convince his Democratic allies to repeal the toll provision.[129] Significantly, his arguments for repeal made few allusions to America's role as a civilizing power. He stressed instead "the interest of the country." American intransigence damaged its reputation with foreign powers, he told a joint session of Congress. He asked for repeal "in support of the foreign policy of the administration."[130] The president did not share the judicialists' reasoning, but he had supported their cause.[131] At the very least, the country would not be a "Pharisee."

Under Roosevelt and Taft, the United States became the leading proponent of the creation of a permanent international court. This reflected the influence of the judicialist sensibility among those in power, and it stemmed from sincere beliefs. It was not necessarily "idealistic," nor was it radical. It imagined an association among law, civilization, and peace, and assumed that promoting those three would advance the interests of the United States and the world. When gaps appeared to open up between US interests and the interests of other "civilized" powers, these assumptions were called into question. In 1912 and 1913, legalists retained enough political and intellectual influence to overcome this challenge in regard to Panama. But that episode suggested that maintaining adherence to a judicialist project would be difficult if others did not share the view of an identity between American interests and those of the world as a whole, or if the assumed progress of civilization did not materialize. In the meantime, however, international law could prove a useful way to promote American interests while seeming to advance universal causes. This, it turned out, was especially relevant as Washington tried to build an empire in its own backyard.

5

International Law and Empire in Latin America, 1904–1917

Late in his presidency, Theodore Roosevelt lamented imperial paths not taken. "In Cuba, Santo Domingo and Panama we have interfered," he observed. "I would have interfered in some similar fashion in Venezuela, in at least one Central American State, and in Haiti already ... if I could have waked up our people so that they would back a reasonable and intelligent foreign policy which should put a stop to crying disorders at our very doors."[1] These "crying disorders," political and economic crises that menaced investments and invited European intervention, seemed increasingly important. The circum-Caribbean (the area that included the islands, Central America, and the northern rim of South America) was vital to America's overseas empire. It controlled the security of the Panama Canal that would link the Atlantic and Pacific. Yet stability was elusive. Foreign investors exacerbated local political crises, fueling revolutions that in turn endangered foreign lives and capital. When local governments repudiated unprofitable or unfair debts and contracts, foreign businessmen turned for help to their home governments: France, Germany, and England most prominently, in addition to the United States.[2] If imperial powers deemed the claims legitimate, they could respond with anything from informal inquiries to diplomatic protests to armed invasion. This further fueled the cycle of instability and threatened to provoke European military maneuvers, perhaps even territorial occupation anathema to Washington's hegemonic pretensions.

To solve these problems, Roosevelt turned to his favorite lawyer. In 1905 he named Elihu Root, the former secretary of war, to the top post in the State Department, and gave him control over Latin American policymaking.[3] Roosevelt admired Root for his tenacity, wisdom, and competence. The president was not alone. Photographs of Root suggest a man of self-confidence and resolve. Where some saw handsomeness—a visiting British novelist described him as "the most attractive of all the Americans"—others described a "frank and murderous smile."[4] Above all, he was a fixer. You turned to Root when you needed something done, and he got it done.

Born in 1845, Root was the son of a Hamilton College math professor. After graduating as Hamilton's valedictorian in 1864 he set off for New York City, the hub of the nation's economic and cultural elite. He graduated from New York University's law school and began practicing in the city. Keen intelligence, an unrivaled work ethic, and a cultural competence and self-confidence

Figure 5.1 An austere Elihu Root faces the camera in this undated photograph. The papers in his hand and on his desk attest to the source of his influence: his deep knowledge of the law and his facility with the written word. The globe behind his left shoulder suggests his connections to world affairs. Courtesy Library of Congress Prints and Photographs Division, Washington, DC. Call number LC-B2- 4471-10 [P&P]. http://hdl.loc.gov/loc.pnp/ggbain.26102.

that insinuated him into the social networks and clubs of New York's upper class led to a rapid rise. By the end of the century, he was one of the foremost attorneys in America.[5] In 1904, the year between his stints at War and State, Root billed his clients the immense sum of $100,000 (over $2.5 million in 2014 dollars).[6]

As a corporate lawyer, Root specialized in problem-solving and crisis management. He would now utilize the same strategies for his new client, the United States government. Some of these solutions relied on narrowly legal skills. Root knew how to manipulate statutes to enable his clients to bypass hindering legislation, as when he used a careful reading of New Jersey corporation law to permit the American sugar trust to enhance its monopoly even after the passage of the Sherman Antitrust Act. But he also had a feel for government bureaucracies. He had helped Manhattan street car operators consolidate their control by "obtaining municipal franchises, blocking by injunction rival endeavors, alleviating tax burdens, and reorganizing mushrooming holdings into efficient and economic operating units."[7] From his time arguing before juries and lobbying municipal government, Root knew how to convince. He also learned the importance of conciliation from being in the middle of internecine capitalist wars over railroads and other industries.

Perhaps most important was Root's worldview: his notions about law, society, power, and reform. He understood the ethical ambivalence of legal service. On the one hand a lawyer earns his fee by doing the bidding of the man who retains him. Root's clients paid him hefty sums because they expected him to make them even more. As one put it, "I have had many lawyers who have told me what I cannot do; Mr. Root is the only lawyer who tells me how to do what I want to do."[8] Yet as a leader of the bar, Root also enunciated lawyers' duty to the law and to justice, as in his often-quoted quip: "[A]bout half the practice of a decent lawyer is telling his clients that they are damned fools and should stop."[9] It was impossible to ever fully reconcile these views, but Root could come close by imagining the legal order in a way that served the larger interests of his clients. Root thus embraced a politics of reformist conservatism. In his eyes, the American industrial and democratic order was essentially sound. Like other elite lawyers, Root supported reforms that would reduce graft and rationalize administration in order to defang protest and preserve the existing class hierarchies of the late-nineteenth century.[10] Setting the rules in an advantageous fashion and then following those rules: this marked the surest path to preserving the status quo. As Root observed, "[A] lawyer's chief business is to keep his clients out of litigation."[11] Root carried this sensibility to Washington. "The main object of diplomacy," he asserted, "is to keep the country out of trouble."[12] To do so he brought legal expertise to bear on the State Department and aimed to create an international rule of law.

America's legalist foreign policy thus applied not only to the search for peace through law at The Hague Conferences, but also to the nitty-gritty of empire building in the circum-Caribbean. Scholars have often been reluctant to group these two aims.[13] Doesn't empire by definition undermine the rule of law? After all, a basic tenet of the rule of law is that it applies to weak and powerful alike and thus constrains power. Some scholars see evidence in the early twentieth century that the growth of international law limited the use of force in this period (certain aspects of The Hague Conventions appeared designed to do so, for example). They attribute this in part to the rise of legal professionalization and the presence of legal professionals in positions of policymaking responsibility.[14]

By regulating what actors *can* do as well as what they can't, law also has an enabling effect. Root and his successors aimed to create what could be called an "empire of nation states." That is, the United States would seek to extend control over other states that were in principle equal and sovereign by insisting that all conform to certain behavioral norms—norms that included protection of foreign capital and submission to particular forms of international oversight. By binding itself to these norms, the United States would legitimate empire itself.[15]

This chapter examines Root's attempt to build an international rule of law as a strategy for promoting US hegemony, and explores its fate in the administrations of William Howard Taft and Woodrow Wilson. It is by necessity a suggestive account. A comprehensive investigation of the intersections of law and policymaking would require a series of local studies that lie beyond the scope of this book (and in any case the lack of a centralized file for legal opinions in the State Department records complicates the matter). International law also had important implications for American policy toward Asia, a subject that has received coverage elsewhere.[16] Outside its formal colonies, it was in the circum-Caribbean that the United States most clearly exerted hegemonic power in the early twentieth century.

Under Root's watch, the State Department developed a reservoir of legal expertise that enabled it to assess corporate claims, reject spurious requests, and develop rationales for intervention. Root also pushed for the creation of new international institutions to manage interstate conflicts through the legal process. He aimed to build what scholars call the "procedural" aspect of the rule of law—the existence of clear laws and systems to adjudicate them. To those on the receiving end of US interventions, however, even if interventions could be justified by existing legal rules, they nonetheless seemed to violate the "substantive" aspects of the rule of law. The letter of the law did not matter if the effect was unjust.[17] US legalists claimed that the linkages between international law and civilization made intervention legitimate morally as well as legally. For Root's plan to succeed, he would need elite audiences, both at home and abroad, to accept the legitimacy of his vision of the rule of law, and of the role of lawyers in

its making. Even if Root could institutionalize international law in foreign policymaking, could he navigate between capital and its detractors in order to build
a pro-United States order founded on consent? By the time Woodrow Wilson
took office in 1913, international law had become vital to American diplomacy
even as its perceived connection to corporations had undermined much of the
legitimacy that Root had attempted to secure.

Globalization and Intervention: Venezuela and the Dominican Republic

"He who comes to Washington should be prepared with one of two things, if he
would do business with the Government," explained General George B. Davis
to the ASIL in 1907. "He must have figures or a brief. Without a brief, without
figures, his words are wasted."[18] The importance of "figures"—that is, economic
considerations—to turn-of-the-century US foreign policy is a staple of American
historiography.[19] But the role of "briefs"—that is, legal argumentation—should
not be overlooked. In the early years of the twentieth century, corporations used
international law in combination with government power to pursue their aims
abroad.

A conflict in Venezuela showed how international law could support corporate interests and undermine stability in the process. Venezuelan president
Cipriano Castro had long antagonized foreign investors, who, he believed,
should contribute more to his government's finances. In 1901, several foreign
businesses—led by the New York & Bermudez Company (NY&B), which mined
asphalt from a huge tar pit in northeastern Venezuela—attempted to overthrow
Castro's government. The asphalt company loaned $145,000 worth of weap-
ons and supplies to a revolutionary movement that plunged the country into
war. Fighting continued until 1903, leaving perhaps 15,000 Venezuelans dead.[20]
Though Castro eventually triumphed, fighting the revolution had worsened his
relationship with foreigners. To prevent smuggling by the rebels from British-
owned Trinidad, for example, Castro had interdicted shipping and briefly occupied an island claimed by London. In December 1902, Britain, Germany, and
Italy captured Venezuelan ships, bombarded the town of Puerto Cabello, and
blockaded the coast, demanding recompense for damage to the interests of their
nationals.[21]

At first, President Theodore Roosevelt acquiesced in these actions. "If any South
American State misbehaves toward any European country," he reassured a German
diplomat, "let the European country spank it."[22] However, the blockade roused
American public sentiment. Some saw in it a serious challenge to the Monroe
Doctrine.[23] After a few tension-filled weeks, all involved agreed to submit the

matter to arbitration.[24] But, in 1903, the Permanent Court of Arbitration ruled that the citizens of countries who used force to compel settlement should be paid back before other creditors and claimants. The law not only permitted the use of force, the court's ruling implied, but rewarded it.[25] The ruling thus incentivized further interventions. British prime minister Arthur Balfour put it clearly: if the United States wanted no more European blockades in its backyard, it must "see that international law is observed" and uphold "the admitted principles of international comity."[26]

This was the context in which Roosevelt issued his famous "Corollary" to the Monroe Doctrine in 1904. The Corollary announced a de facto US protectorate over the hemisphere. In cases of "chronic wrongdoing," some "civilized" state would need to exercise an "international police power," Roosevelt argued. In the Western Hemisphere, Roosevelt volunteered, the United States would be that power.[27] Roosevelt's message suggested a cooperative imperialism: the United States would take responsibility for protecting the rights of foreign property in "its" neighborhood.[28]

A crisis in the Dominican Republic led Roosevelt to put his Corollary into practice.[29] There, too, a US corporation had inspired a political conflict that threatened to incite European intervention. The San Domingo Improvement Company (SDIC), a small-time New York concern, had managed to gain control over much of the Dominican Republic's public debt. Between 1893 and 1897, the SDIC floated a total of $35 million worth of Dominican government bonds in Europe, charging generous fees and being repaid from import taxes collected in Dominican customs houses. Proceeds from these bond sales were supposed to fund the nation's railroads and public works. But mostly they were consumed in SDIC fees, distributed by Dominican president Ulises Heureaux to his allies, or used to pay off previous loans. After Heureaux's assassination in 1899, the country descended into political chaos and civil war, with a new government emerging every few months. Increasingly, all factions blamed the SDIC for conniving in the corruption of the Heureaux years. Denouncing the company's financial power as a foreign imposition, Dominicans attempted to rid the island of its presence.[30]

The SDIC turned to Washington for support and hired John Bassett Moore to represent its interests before the State Department. Moore's value lay in his combination of international legal expertise and the close contacts he had forged in his many years in and out of government.[31] The Dominican government attempted to buy out the SDIC's interests, but the two sides disagreed about the value of the company's assets. To maximize its leverage, the SDIC sought Washington's support. Since individuals and corporations had no standing under international law, the law permitted governments to negotiate with other governments, and even bring legal claims on behalf of their citizens.[32]

The negotiations had legal, diplomatic, and military dimensions. With the US navy providing a constant presence, US diplomats worked out a protocol with the government of Horacio Vásquez in 1903. The Dominican government would purchase SDIC interests for $4.5 million and agree to an international arbitration to establish the terms of the monthly payments and the security in case of default.[33] The arbitration took place in the spring of 1904. In principle, here was an event to make legalists and the peace movement proud: a neutral, international tribunal would resolve a dispute without violence. In practice, the arbitration revealed the corruption of legal process. The protocol signed by Washington and Santo Domingo provided for a panel of three arbitrators. Each nation would select one arbitrator; the Dominicans would select the third from a list of US Supreme Court or Court of Appeals judges.[34] However, the Dominican arbitrator, Manuel de Jesus Galván, had a history of cooperating with foreign interests—indeed, a later Dominican president unsuccessfully tried to recall him for precisely this reason. Moreover, the third arbitrator was the US judge George Gray, a Delawarean and longtime friend of John Bassett Moore.[35] Further undermining the neutrality of the proceedings, the State Department chose Moore—still on the SDIC payroll—to present its case to the tribunal. Moore, in other words, was representing both a public and a private client simultaneously. A potential conflict of interest, no doubt, but as Moore told the SDIC, Washington "extended special consideration to me in that regard, because of their confidence that I would not abuse their trust."[36]

The tribunal issued a far-reaching judgment in favor of the United States and, by extension, the SDIC. Most importantly, it ruled that should the Dominican government miss a payment—which seemed likely—the United States could appoint an agent to take direct control over Dominican customs houses, where the largest portion of government revenues were collected.[37] Through an international legal process, the company had gained a promise of government aid in recovering its investments.

However, the SDIC's victory created political problems. When the Dominican government missed its first payment, Washington appointed an SDIC official to collect revenue directly from the customs house at Puerto Plata, sparking intense local opposition.[38] Meanwhile, since the arbitral award guaranteed payment of debts owed to the SDIC without offering a similar guarantee to European creditors, investors from Italy, France, Germany, and England clamored for redress.[39]

Worried that European governments might intervene, Roosevelt decided to take a more direct role. In early 1905 he reached an agreement with Dominican president Carlos Morales to create a debt receivership. The United States would officially take control of all customs houses in the country. Forty-five percent of the revenue collected would go to the Dominican government and the rest would go to pay off foreign creditors. As part of the deal, the Dominicans agreed to limit government spending and to consult with Washington before changing tariff rates. The agreement amounted to a "de-facto protectorate," in historian David Healy's words.[40]

Although the SDIC lost direct control over Dominican customs receipts, the company fared well financially in the deal. It received payment on 90 percent of its claims, whereas other bondholders had to settle for half, or less.[41] But, as historian Cyrus Veeser argues, the case convinced Roosevelt to end the "earlier policy of unexamined support for private interests" abroad.[42] For instance, when it came time to choose a financial adviser to oversee Dominican finances, Roosevelt looked not to Moore but to Johns Hopkins University economics professor Jacob Hollander—an expert in modern finance.[43] The funds for the deal came from big New York financial firms, such as Kuhn, Loeb, and Company and the Morton Trust Company, not from small-time concerns like the SDIC.[44] In other words, Roosevelt had decided that a combination of government oversight, big capital, and East Coast professionalism represented the best way to maintain US hegemony.

A new flare-up in relations with Venezuela confirmed Roosevelt's intuitions. Here was another case in which corrupt, or at least incompetent, corporate interests seemed to have turned international diplomacy to their own ends. In July 1904, the Venezuelan government seized the property of the NY&B —the firm that had funded the revolution against President Castro a few years earlier.[45] The NY&B reasoned that it could never regain its property by going through the Venezuelan courts, and so it asked Washington to send gunboats to the country on its behalf. Just as the SDIC had done, the asphalt company turned to John Bassett Moore to press its claim.

A mess of contradictory land titles made the company's case opaque.[46] Yet Moore made a mostly convincing legal argument (if not a moral one—the company had tried to overthrow the government, after all) that its property had been expropriated illegally.[47] Central to the dispute was the question of jurisdiction. Venezuela claimed the case was a matter for local courts; Moore and the NY&B asserted the right of a corporation operating overseas to seek protection from its mother country in the event of a dispute. Moore mobilized transatlantic international legal authority to underline the US government's right to intervene. For instance, he quoted Englishman W. E. Hall to support the contention that when "the act of the government has been of a flagrant character, the right naturally arises of immediately exacting reparation."[48] Moore knew that citing European authorities would bolster his case, for it was common practice among State Department legal advisers.[49] He also referenced US precedents—an easy task for him, since he was simultaneously at work on the congressionally funded *A Digest of International Law*.[50] Citing a series of previous US government interventions, Moore concluded that "[t]he Department has had frequent occasion to apply the principles thus laid down by [European publicists] Phillimore, Hall, Bluntschli, and Creasy, to cases arising in Venezuela." In the past thirty years, "there has scarcely been a case" where the United States had insisted upon the exhaustion of judicial remedies and appeals before applying other forms of pressure.[51] As Moore put it, the right of intervention represented "[t]he true rule . . . which is observed by civilized governments on this subject."[52]

Moore also saw arbitration as a tool that would help the NY&B. Remembering his successful experience arbitrating the SDIC's case against the Dominican Republic, Moore confidently told an NY&B treasurer that arbitration would be a "step" on the road toward US intervention: should Venezuela agree to it Moore believed the NY&B would triumph on the narrow legal questions. But if Castro rejected arbitration—as Moore expected—more aggressive measures could follow.[53] Predictably, Castro rejected the invitation to arbitrate, in large part because Washington—at Moore's urging—had insisted that Venezuela return the NY&B's property before arbitration could commence.[54]

Guided by Moore, the case passed through several rounds of legal evaluation in the State Department. (The fact that several prominent Republicans sat on the NY&B board no doubt added momentum.)[55] The structure and precedents of international law made it possible for Moore to construct a winning argument. True, as Venezuela's foreign minister pointed out, there was an established US precedent against intervention for claims that solely involved contract disputes. But if the claimant could show that in the course of breaking a contract, the foreign government had committed gross misconduct, this could constitute a more serious "denial of justice" or "arbitrary tort" that demanded recompense.[56] By focusing on defects in Venezuelan court procedures, Moore made the case that the NY&B's property had been seized unjustly. Thus, even though secretary of state John Hay found the company "shady," he deemed the claims legally valid and forwarded the matter to the US attorney general, who again validated them.[57] The result was an ultimatum sent to Venezuela, in 1905, demanding return of the company's property.[58] The British minister in Caracas declared that US intervention would "eventually become an accomplished fact."[59]

Roosevelt itched to make this prediction come true. He had no respect for Castro, dismissing him as "an unspeakably villainous little monkey."[60] But sending troops was politically risky. The NY&B was unpopular. "Even the Big Stick would not look pretty all dripping with asphalt," a New York newspaper predicted.[61] Complicating matters further, the US minister to Venezuela had accused assistant secretary of state Francis Loomis of taking a $10,000 bribe from the NY&B. Though an official inquiry cleared Loomis, the stink of corruption clung to the company's case.[62] Corporate actions, reinforced with international legal argumentation, had ensnared US foreign policy. Washington would now turn to a professionalized law to resolve the problem.

Legalist Expertise and the Foreign Policy State

Latin American policy had become a headache for Roosevelt. He turned to Elihu Root for relief. "I shall now cheerfully unload Venezuela and Santo Domingo on you," the president explained.[63] Upon taking office, Root complained that being secretary of state was "like a man trying to conduct the business of a large metropolitan law-firm in the office of a village squire."[64] Indeed, the department that Root inherited in 1905 was still a small, tradition-bound, patronage out-fit where political connections frequently trumped expertise.[65] It was the sort of place where an ambitious foreign service officer secured his promotion by sending his beautiful wife to lobby the secretary of state on his behalf.[66] Though faced with a generally uncooperative Congress, Root and his successor, former corporate lawyer and attorney general Philander C. Knox, set out to reform the department. An imperial bureaucracy required access to accurate information and expert officials to interpret it. Personnel more than doubled between 1900 and 1910, and the department's annual expenditures increased in that time from $3.5 million to nearly $5 million.[67] Examinations filtered applicants, and new bureaucratic organization regularized the flow of information.[68]

Law would play an important role in this process of foreign policy state-building. State Department legal expertise worked not as an extension of the aims of the peace movement but as an attempt to grapple with the transnational move-ment of people and capital. Legal advisers ruled on whether or not to grant or request extradition, who qualified as a citizen, and whether European immigrants still owed military duty to their home countries. Questions of cross-border taxa-tion, naturalization, and passports, too, required the solicitor's guidance.[69] The largest single category of tasks involved the evaluation of pecuniary claims.[70]

Since claimants like the SDIC and NY&B often had powerful political con-nections in Washington, Root felt it necessary to formalize the process; after all, he noted, "one of the most remarkable facts . . . was the largeness of the claims presented and the smallness of the awards made when passed upon by a judicial tribunal."[71] He was right: the history of arbitration was riddled with exagger-ated claims reduced by arbitral panels.[72] Bringing competent legal expertise to the department would help insulate it from corporate pressure by allowing it to push back against corporate claimants. When disruptive American sojourners in Asia generated anti-American feelings there, Root created the US Court of China to rein in their behavior, in an attempt to "save imperialism from itself."[73] By reforming the State Department, Root hoped to bring this process to foreign policy as a whole.

In 1906, the department issued instructions to regularize the recording of claims; claimants seeking protection were urged to supplement their applica-tions with legal briefs.[74] Root also chose James Brown Scott to be solicitor, his chief legal officer. As Root later recalled, Scott "came to the State Department without any influence or backing of any kind."[75] But his professional reputation made him seem an ideal candidate to provide a dispassionate evaluation of investors' claims. During Scott's interview for the solicitor position, Root mentioned a single matter that required his immediate attention: Venezuela.[76]

Scott's appointment was part of a broader effort to expand the department's reserves of legal expertise. In 1900, the department's legal staff consisted solely of a solicitor and two clerks. Two assistant solicitors and four more clerks were added by 1906, and four years later there were three assistants and ten clerks.[77] In 1909 department reformers established a new Office of the Counselor.[78] By 1911, fifteen employees worked in the solicitor's office, and three in the counselor's. In a decade the legal staff had expanded sixfold.[79]

Legal officers were among the State Department's highest-paid employees. In 1910, for instance, the solicitor earned as much—$5,000—as the first assistant secretary, who was nominally the department's second-ranking officer. The counselor, meanwhile received $7,500.[80] High salaries were necessary to attract experienced lawyers, though even then they failed to keep up with the private sector. For instance, Standard Oil paid John Bassett Moore $5,000 in 1914 for preparing a single brief for the State Department.[81] Hiring more permanent attorneys also promised to save money, for the department was spending more and more ($49,000 in 1909) on outside legal counsel.[82] Patronage appointees lacked the ability to resolve the greater number and complexity of legal issues referred to the department.

By 1911, the ABA's International Law Committee boasted that "international relations are more and more confided to the administration and control of the legal profession and are more and more withdrawn from military and purely diplomatic control."[83] The *AJIL* was considered essential reading for those who sought to "keep in touch with all that transpires in international and diplomatic affairs."[84] Prospective foreign officers were encouraged to get a law degree, and on a list of recommended readings, a majority of books concerned international law.[85] Even those who doubted that international law might solve the world's problems nonetheless found legal expertise to be a valuable asset. In 1907, a prospective member of the diplomatic service thought it would be useful to send an assistant secretary the notes he had taken in Professor Louis Renault's University of Paris course on the law of neutrality.[86] Foreign service exams customarily covered international law along with history, diplomatic protocol, and language.[87] If it is an exaggeration to claim, as one scholar has, that "the international lawyers held effective control of the State Department," their wide influence is nonetheless worthy of note.[88]

The expansion of legal capacity inside the department went hand in hand with an attempt to use legal tools to solve problems in the hemisphere. Root had first employed such a strategy in Cuba. As secretary of war, he had responsibility for withdrawing US troops who had occupied the island since the defeat of Spain. In 1898 the United States had promised not to annex the island, but Washington was reluctant to cede control to Cuban politicians.[89] Root found a solution in constitutional design. Cuba would gain its independence, but only once it incorporated certain provisions into its new constitution. These provisions were known as the Platt Amendment, after Senator Orville Platt, who introduced them into an appropriations bill at Root's urging. In the key provision, Cuba declared its consent that "the United States may exercise the right to intervene" to preserve Cuba's independence or maintain a government "adequate for the protection of life, property, and individual liberty."[90] Root argued that the clause was simply "the Monroe Doctrine, but with international force."[91] In other words, he believed that putting America's hegemonic relationship with Cuba into legal form would stabilize it and legitimize it in the eyes of the international community. Europe would have to respect such a situation, he believed.[92] Legal scholar Christina Duffy Ponsa has called this strategy "internationalist constitutionalism": the idea that shaping the constitutions of dependent states could provide a legal framework for American empire by codifying hegemony.[93] Washington employed a similar strategy in Panama. Article 136 of that country's 1904 constitution gave the United States "the power to intervene . . . to reestablish public peace and constitutional order."[94] But the constitutional strategy did not bring the stability that Root envisioned. The Platt Amendment incentivized Cuban politicians to appeal to Washington when rivals threatened their power. US troops would return to Cuba from 1906 to 1909 amid political contestation that turned violent.[95] Moreover, only nations under US military occupation or the threat thereof would consent to such a sovereignty-affronting constitutional amendment. The Platt Amendment suggests Root's faith in legalism, but it was not a scalable model for US policy in Latin America.

After 1904 Root traded constitutional law for international law. Rather than codify US dominance in legal instruments, he would attempt to "civilize" the international order to promote stability and protection for foreign investment. Insisting that Latin American states be invited to the Second Hague Peace Conference in 1907 was part of this strategy.[96] Root also supported the creation of the American Institute of International Law (AIIL), a hemispheric network of international lawyers cofounded by Scott to spread the judicialist project to Latin America. Washington's approach to Central America makes even clearer the role that Root expected law to play. When, in 1906, contests for power, especially between Guatemala and Nicaragua, threatened war, Roosevelt sent the US gunboat *Marblehead* to Central American waters. A preliminary peace accord signed aboard the ship paused a growing war.[97] In order to consolidate this peace, Root urged the nations of Central America to create formal international institutions.[98] In November 1907, representatives of Nicaragua, Guatemala, El Salvador, Honduras, and Costa Rica met in Washington, with representatives from Mexico and the United States presiding. The Central American delegates were split. Some wanted to create a federation; others put their faith in a Central American Bureau and a "pedagogical institute" that would development economic ties which would inexorably link the nations. With the conference deadlocked, US representative William I. Buchanan proposed instead the creation of the Central American Court of Justice (CACJ), modeled on the US plans for an international court at The Hague. Mexico backed Buchanan, and the conference adopted his proposal.[99]

Thus from Washington's perspective, legalism provided the key to peace in Central America. The CACJ was the first permanent, obligatory international court of justice—in a small way, the realization of a legalist dream. Its five well-compensated sitting judges could rule on any international dispute among the Central American republics or between them and a foreign nation. It could even take up matters raised by individuals.[100] "It shall not at all be a mere commission of arbitration, but a genuine judicial tribunal," argued Costa Rican foreign minister Luis Anderson. As such, it "will be the practical realization of the ingenious plans formulated and recommended by the American delegates at the Second Peace Conference at The Hague."[101] US Americans viewed the court as a demonstration of their wise benevolence. Andrew Carnegie donated $100,000 to build a "Central American Peace Palace" in Costa Rica.[102]

Establishing a rule of law promised stability and growth. As Mexican ambassador Enrique C. Creel suggested, law, peace, and profits reinforced each other. Peace would bring with it civilization, he said, "and its life-giving elements of wealth."[103] Root put it succinctly: "[I]t will be, from the most selfish point of view, for our interests to have peaceful, prosperous, and progressive republics in Central America."[104] This was not mere rhetoric. When an outbreak of violence threatened in June 1908 and Costa Rica submitted the first case to the CACJ, acting secretary of state Robert Bacon made Washington's commitment clear: if the other Central Americans did not permit the court to function, the United States would intervene.[105]

Whose Rule of Law?

Root embraced legalism as a tool of hegemony, but it is too simple to see international law as a mere imposition on unwilling or naïve neighbors. Though chroniclers of international law have rarely noticed, Latin America had its own rich history of internationalism.[106] In 1826, for instance, Simón Bolívar convened an international congress in Panama to promote regional unification.[107] A few years later, in 1832, the Chilean humanist Andrés Bello published the hemisphere's first international law treatise, *Principios del Derecho de Jentes*, which would serve as a text for university courses throughout Latin America.[108] In the 1850s and 1860s, Colombian diplomat José María Torres Caicedo—whom many historians credit with coining the term "Latin America"—proposed a series of regional leagues and confederacies for self-defense.[109] Washington may have envisioned law walking hand in hand with US hegemony. But Latin Americans imagined a different potential.

Sovereign independence precluded intervention, Latin American jurists argued. Two "doctrines" embodied this principle. The first took the name of Argentine publicist Carlos Calvo. Beginning with his 1868 treatise, *Le droit international théorique et pratique*, Calvo asserted that foreigners had no more rights than nationals. Therefore, their disputes must be confined to domestic courts.[110] Many states in the region embraced his reasoning and forced foreign investors to sign "Calvo Clauses" in which they pledged not to ask their home governments to intervene on their behalf. But neither the United States nor Europe ever accepted the Calvo Doctrine as a principle of international law; they continued to assert that states could intervene to protect the property rights of their citizens abroad.[111]

In 1902 another Argentinian, foreign minister Luis María Drago, added his own doctrine. In response to the Anglo-German blockade of Venezuela, Drago wrote to Washington condemning the use of force to collect sovereign debts. Creditors already took into account the risks of investing in unstable countries, he argued; that is why they could charge high rates of interest. Once states realized the costs of wrecked national credit they would eventually pay up without forcible compulsion. Allowing Europeans to collect debts via gunboats affronted national sovereignty, was counterproductive, and threatened the Monroe Doctrine. International law ought not to permit it. "In a word, the principle which she [Argentina] would like to see recognized is: that the public debt can not occasion armed intervention."[112] Many North American newspapers praised Drago's note; US policymakers were more circumspect.[113] Solicitor Walter Penfield worried, "If the United States Government should definitely abandon all right of forcible intervention, there are some communities . . . in which Americans might . . . be repeatedly . . . despoiled."[114]

At first glance, the divergence between US and Latin American expectations for international law is quite striking. How could two parties with such different goals both commit to a legalist project? Part of the answer can be found in the cultural politics of "civilization." In a time when law and civilization were understood to be mutually constitutive, it was difficult to oppose international law in the abstract. This was especially true for those who were most intent on proving their "civilized" status. Representing areas of questionable "whiteness" in the eyes of Europeans, some Latin American elites highlighted their nations' participation in international legal relations in order to prove their membership in the "civilized world." Carlos Calvo revealed this anxiety when he insisted, "Read the latest editions of [European publicists] Hefter, Sir. R. Phillimore, Bluntschli, Fiore, Sir E. Creasy, Woolsey, Hall, Brentano Sorel, Gessner, Bulmerincq—even Cogordan, Fauchille, Guelle, de Boeck . . . and you will see that since then not one book on international law has been published in which Latin America does not occupy the rank that belongs to her among civilized nations."[115] As Calvo noted, Latin America had long been recognized as civilized, legally speaking. But because the region had been subject to frequent European (and US) military interventions it appeared to hold a place in international society uncomfortably similar to that of the "semi-civilized" areas like China or the Ottoman Empire. This made embracing the politics of civilization all the more important.[116]

A shared discourse of law and civilization offered Root an opportunity to mend relations with Latin American elites, especially those of the wealthy and rapidly growing nations of the Southern Cone. US Americans had long referred to the Argentines (and sometimes the Chileans) as the "Yankees of South America," and even Roosevelt had suggested that Argentina, Brazil, and Chile were "guarantors of the [Monroe] doctrine so far as America south of the Equator is concerned."[117] Root believed that better personal relationships could ameliorate anti-Yankee sentiment. "If you want to make a man your friend, it does not pay to treat him like a yellow dog," he quipped.[118] In 1906 Root became the first US secretary of state to tour Latin America, capping his well-received journey with a magnanimous address to the Pan-American Conference in Rio de Janeiro in which he praised the progress of Latin American civilization, called for the creation of an "all-American public opinion" in support of international law, and assured his listeners that "[w]e wish for no victories but those of peace; for no territory except our own; for no sovereignty except sovereignty over ourselves."[119]

Root sympathized with Drago's opposition to armed debt collection. "[T]he system of forcible collection of debts generated speculators who live on the people of the country," he observed. Such speculators "promote revolutions by advancing money for arms and ammunition, and make at times contracts with distressed governments which are seeking to avert political destruction."[120] Having witnessed the corporate manipulation of international law firsthand, Root supported reform.

This support did not extend to Drago's call for sovereign immunity from outside intervention, however.[121] International law was fundamental to civilization. States must submit to it, for they had duties as well as rights under international law, Root often said.[122] There was a "standard of international conduct" that they must uphold.[123] Mere inability to pay did not violate this standard, Root proclaimed at a dinner with Drago in Buenos Aires, and the United States had "never deemed it suitable" to collect "ordinary contract debts" by force.[124] But lapses in the rule of law did constitute a reason for intervention. This might occur during times of revolution or civil unrest, when a central government lacked control over its territory. It might also apply to countries allegedly lacking in civilization, "countries whose methods of administering justice are very greatly at variance with the methods to which the people of the great body of civilized states are accustomed, such, for example, as China and Turkey."[125] In such cases states must submit to outside authority: a court, if possible, but armed force in the last instance. As Root told the Panamanian government in 1906, "the United States possesses the inherent right to protect its property and enforce its rights wherever located and wherever imperiled."[126] In short, while Drago hoped international law would protect states from intervention, Root insisted that law applied the principles of civilization, and those principles upheld the rights of foreign investors. In making this claim, Root could cite a broad range of legal scholarship defending the right of intervention.[127]

Thus when the Drago doctrine was debated at The Hague Peace Conference in 1907, the US delegation backed an amended version named after US delegate Horace Porter. The Porter Convention—eventually adopted by the conference as a whole—prohibited the "recourse to armed force for the recovery of contract debts."[128] Yet it contained a loophole big enough to admit "a fleet of warships": if a debtor nation refused to submit to international arbitration or failed to submit to an arbitral ruling, creditor nations could legally use force against it.[129] In other words, the convention upheld the superiority of international society over the sovereign rights of states—or so it appeared to Latin American delegates who were disappointed with the outcome. Argentina led ten Latin American nations that entered reservations to the Convention, arguing that resort to arbitration should be allowed only after local courts had ruled, and that "public loans" should never "give rise to military aggression."[130] As Argentine delegate Roque Sáenz Peña put it, the Porter Convention "envisaged international Judges as the adversaries of sovereignty, and as the enemies of national honor."[131] It thus seemed to permit the continuation of gunboat diplomacy.

The triumph of Root's interpretation of international law over Drago's makes clear that international law was not the set of neutral principles that legalists often portrayed it to be. The ideology of the rule of law implies a "rule by no one," as legal scholar Paul Kahn has put it.[132] Yet this is impossible: all laws are created by particular actors with particular agendas. Determining what counts as the law—what constitutes "denial of justice," what defines "civilization"—reflects underlying power. Was the Drago Doctrine a part of international law or not? This was ultimately decided not by rational debate, but power. This makes international law a "hegemonic technique," in the words of legal scholar Martti

Koskenniemi. Invoking law is an attempt to enlist the rules and the prestige of law on behalf of particular political projects.[133]

Yet Drago's challenge also reveals limits to the legitimacy of international law in this period. Latin Americans did not simply accept US (or European) arguments about the right of intervention.[134] Successful enforcement required not only professional legal expertise, but also restraint and an adept politics of suasion. These Root had in abundance, as his resolution of the dispute with Venezuela demonstrates. Root assured the NY&B company's lawyers that intervention was "a sovereign national prerogative."[135] But he resisted their calls to use force, instead making diplomatic arguments that relied on a report he had directed solicitor James Brown Scott to prepare. Scott's report concluded that Venezuela had violated the NY&B's "property rights" through "gross misuse of judicial and executive authority."[136] Though the company's conduct was hardly morally upright, Scott admitted, its claims were good law. Root pressured Venezuela to uphold what he asserted was the law, eventually severing diplomatic relations when Cipriano Castro refused.[137] When Castro was overthrown, new president Juan Vicente Gómez decided that further confrontation with the United States was unwise and agreed to return the NY&B's property.[138] Legalistic arguments, with the reality of US power just barely visible behind them, had resolved the crisis.[139] This success was emblematic of Root's larger ability to pursue hegemonic stability without the use of force (outside of a military occupation of Cuba under the Platt Amendment that began in 1906). Indeed, the extent of praise for Root as a farsighted statesman is as remarkable as its sources: Europeans (he was awarded the Nobel Peace Prize in 1912); elites from both South and Central America; and even from historians who are otherwise quite critical of US foreign policy in this period.[140]

This image owed as much to Root's personal diplomatic qualities as it did to international law. His successor, Philander Knox, and the Taft administration received no such praise. This was not because Knox and Taft abandoned international law. Taft's administration was, if anything, more legalistic than its predecessor. Taft was a former judge and future chief justice of the US Supreme Court. And Knox had served as attorney general under McKinley and Roosevelt after many years at the corporate bar. Taft and Knox supported both arbitration and a permanent international court. Legal concepts infused their foreign policy. For Knox, grumbled British diplomat A. Mitchell Innes, "a treaty is a contract, diplomacy is litigation, and the countries interested parties to a suit."[141]

Knox lacked Root's political acumen and conciliatory nature. He conducted himself more as an advocate for clients than a statesman building the rule of law, resisting compromise in favor of pressing his position when he felt that law supported him.[142] As secretary of state, Knox made it his goal to settle all outstanding claims of American companies.[143] He advocated arbitration, but it was

arbitration "at the point of cannons," as far as most Latin Americans were concerned.[144] This was never clearer than in his handling of the so-called Alsop claim
with Chile.[145] Negotiations between the United States and Chile had, by 1909,
produced a compromise, but upon taking office Knox discarded it. Instead, he
demanded that Chile arbitrate the case and then threatened to sever diplomatic
relations when Santiago balked. Only a last-minute intercession by the Brazilian
ambassador and Root prevented a major diplomatic breakdown. The case went
to arbitration before the king of England, resulting in a generous judgment for
the American claimants.[146] Despite the "successful" arbitration, the whole affair
left Root furious and many Latin Americans dismayed. "When dealing with
weak Latin-American countries, the United States cares as much about international law as about a radish," complained Manuel Foster Recabarren, Chile's
agent in the Alsop claims arbitration.[147] And unlike Root, who had carefully
wooed Latin American elites, Knox "did not conceal the fact that he considered
them inferior."[148]

Meanwhile, James Brown Scott lost his influence in the State Department,
and was ousted at the urging of clerks and assistant solicitors who considered
him too academic.[149] He was replaced by J. Reuben Clark, who had studied
under Scott at Columbia but did not share his former professor's faith in the
power of international legal institutions to transcend man's animal spirit.[150] Legal
contracts ought to be enforced, Clark argued, and American behavior ought to
conform to recognized laws. But the goal was to maximize American interests
in an unfriendly world. In a white paper written in 1912 as an election-year
vindication of Knox's foreign policy, Clark frankly embraced any interventions
this might entail. The paper argued that American finance and enterprise could
reform Latin American states and solve their problems of governance and debt.
Yet it suggested that in the process foreign investors would likely receive injury
at the hands of local governments, and demand intervention. Since the countries
most likely to fall victim to this kind of scenario were those where law was weak
and "force only commands respect," Clark concluded that "[i]t may be necessary at any moment to exercise a compelling physical force."[151] This was a call for
installing the rule of law at the point of a gun. Root had mostly kept his weapons concealed, but Knox and his underlings brandished them more openly. This
reinforced Latin American suspicions that international law, as interpreted by
the United States, did not protect the rights of all nations equally.

Under the Taft administration, the promotion of international law was overshadowed by the policy of "dollar diplomacy." The administration described
this policy as "the substitution of dollars for bullets." Rather than using violence to ensure stability, the thinking went, smart financial management would
bring peace and prosperity to Caribbean nations and foreign investors alike.[152]
Roosevelt had pioneered this policy when he imposed a debt receivership on

the Dominican Republic. In a debt receivership, US-appointed officials would take control of a country's incoming revenue, and then distribute an agreed-upon percentage in payments to the local government; the rest would go to pay off debts. Meanwhile, a financial adviser, usually from a New York bank, would have a say in how the local government spent its portion of the funds.[153] In assuming that neutral, professional expertise would resolve conflicts and promote stability, the policy of dollar diplomacy resembled the legalist project. However, in both Nicaragua and the Dominican Republic, US financial oversight fueled political opposition that ultimately resulted in armed conflicts, at which point Washington would send in the marines.[154] The breakdown of order was less the fault of Knoxian bluster than the inevitable response of Dominicans and Nicaraguans who were unhappy about the continued imposition of foreign financial controls.[155] But the unpopularity of dollar diplomacy redounded upon Knox and Taft.

Criticism of Taft's foreign policy also reflected increasing distrust of East Coast legal and financial elites. In a political atmosphere of increasing resentment of judicial activism at home (Roosevelt's 1912 presidential campaign included proposals for the recall of judicial opinions), the international rule of law became seen less as a way to supplant power with justice, and more as a way to enforce unjust contracts.[156] At the same time, a progressive caucus in Congress attacked what they called the "money trust," alleging that financial interests were manipulating the economy. The strengthening of what historian Emily Rosenberg calls "antibanking discourses" made it difficult for the Taft administration to claim that its foreign policy used dollars (i.e., financial controls) to serve the goals of diplomacy, rather than vice versa. Taft's policy seemed instead to stand for the triumph of private capital over public interests.[157] Knox was "the minister of the steel trust and the Pennsylvania railroad," complained Kansas senator Joseph Bristow.[158] When Taft failed in his bid for reelection, the next administration resolved not to let corporate lawyers control foreign policy.

Wilson the International Law Skeptic

In 1913 Woodrow Wilson became the first Democrat to occupy the White House in sixteen years. Although he shared his predecessors' concerns for maintaining order in the circum-Caribbean, he believed that they had gone about it all wrong. Like other progressives, he criticized Taft and Knox's "dollar diplomacy" as a foreign policy crafted for the benefit of finance capital. True stability required "the consent of the governed," and hemispheric peace required "mutual intercourse, respect, and helpfulness," he stated in his first foreign policy speech.[159] As it turned out, Wilson's Latin American policies would be more similar to Taft's than many expected. But one important difference stood out: Wilson was no fan of the legalist project.

Wilson did not primarily view social reality through a legal lens. The president had a law degree; he had even practiced law for a short time. But he became "most terribly bored" with the details of legal work, which got "as monotonous as that other immortal article of food, *Hash*, when served with such endless frequency."[160] This is not to say that law played no part in his political philosophy. He had an obsession, beginning as a teenager, with writing constitutions and covenants: for a baseball team, a yacht club, even (jokingly) for a "love league" ("for two members only") with his first wife.[161] So, too, the Presbyterian covenanter tradition schooled in him by his minister father identified reciprocal laws of duty and obedience as the basis of all social institutions.[162] From Edmund Burke, one of Wilson's great heroes, Wilson took the lesson that social change must be gradual and legal, never capricious. Yet Wilson's was no static conservatism; change was vital.[163] Society and government formed a symbiotic, organic pair. The latter must change to reflect the burgeoning interdependence of the former. Law was emphatically not the determinant of future action.[164] Law "records life," Wilson said in 1911; "it does not contain it; it does not originate it."[165] By the time he became president, Wilson sided with such critics of classical legal thought as Oliver Wendell Holmes, Jr. Courts should consider political and social realities, not make rules solely according to formal legal precedents. Wilson had faith in the possibility of ordered change to move society closer to ideal principles of liberty and democracy.[166] The true law that would guide these changes was to be found not in "the piecemeal law books, the miscellaneous and disconnected statutes and legal maxims," but in "the life of men." Discerning the latent "common interest" of society required "sympathy" and "vision." "Constitutions are vehicles of life, but not sources of it."[167] Any remaining doubts as to Wilson's antiformalism were dispelled by his 1916 appointment of progressive lawyer Louis Brandeis to the US Supreme Court. William Howard Taft was one of seven former presidents of the ABA who protested Wilson's choice.[168]

Wilson shared many assumptions with legalists: an Enlightenment belief in the rationality of man and the possibilities for progress, a general conviction in the benefits of capitalism, and a strong American exceptionalism.[169] He generally supported arbitration and had joined the ASIL at its founding (though never played an active role in the organization). He had even taught a course on international law at Princeton.[170] Recall, however, that Wilson approached the subject, not as a practical guide to state relations or the basis for building a system of adjudication, but rather as a philosophy of justice. International law was not proper law at all, he had written in his treatise *The State* (1889). It inhabited "a province half-way between the province of morals and the province of positive law" and consisted mostly of "principles of right action."[171] Undue emphasis on particular international rules made little sense; it would be better to substitute broader moral considerations. If peace were to rest in the rule of law, then the substantive aspects of that rule—its promotion of justice—were more important than its procedural institutions. And one could not trust lawyers to defend justice. Lawyers no longer promoted the public good. They had been "sucked into the maelstrom of the new business system of the country."[172]

For secretary of state, Wilson appointed William Jennings Bryan, who had put his broad poitical constituency behind Wilson's bid for the Democratic nomination.[173] Bryan was a lawyer, but a very different kind from Knox or Root. A populist from Nebraska who had thrice won the Democratic nomination for president but lost the general election each time, Bryan was a foreigner in the land of the Atlantic elite. Nothing could have made the point clearer than Bryan's ban on the serving of alcohol at diplomatic functions, a decision that shocked the European diplomatic corps. The press derisively called it "grape juice diplomacy."[174]

Bryan and Wilson embraced international cooperation, but not from a legalist perspective. Bryan promoted "cooling off" peace treaties. These bilateral treaties—which he ultimately signed with thirty countries, and which were eventually ratified with twenty—pledged signatories to submit disputes to an investigatory committee and to postpone hostilities until the committee issued a report.[175] Bryan believed that during this interval public opinion would prevail upon hostile governments to come to a peaceful settlement.[176] Such treaties echoed legalist prescriptions in their faith in rationality and the power of public opinion, but they gave no special place to law per se. Though James Brown Scott supported them publicly, in private he was doubtful: "I do not very well see the part which distinct commissions of inquiry such as Mr. Bryan proposes will play in international development," he complained to the Swiss lawyer Max Hüber.[177] To legalists' dismay, not only did Wilson not seek the creation of an international court, as his predecessors had done, but his administration helped to bring about the dissolution of the CACJ in 1917.[178]

In fact, both Wilson and his secretary of state believed that Knoxian legalism amounted to little more than granting favors to corporations.[179] Wilson promised to change US policy toward Latin America. No longer would outsiders dominate the region; there would be "an emancipation from the subordination ... to foreign enterprise."[180] Change was in the air. Some even expected that a Democrat in office might encourage revolutionaries in Latin America, forcing Wilson to explicitly disavow the rumors.[181] He presented himself as a supporter of equality among states and constitutional democracy within states.[182]

Yet even Wilson recognized that diplomacy was impossible without some measure of legal expertise. The president and his close adviser Edward House feared the diplomatic ramifications of Bryan's folksy manners and lack of

experience.[183] They offered John Bassett Moore the position of counselor, hoping he would keep an eye on the "Secretary of Very Foreign Affairs," as detractors referred to Bryan.[184] Moore accepted the position only with the "greatest
reluctance."[185] Although he was a loyal Democrat who had known Wilson for
years, Moore had little desire to give up his post at Columbia or his remunerative
services for corporate clients.[186] He agreed to take the position on the condition
that it last only a year and that the office be upgraded: Moore would serve officially as acting secretary in Bryan's absence, and he would not "be subject to the
direction of the Assistant Secretaries" nor "be required to wait upon them."[187] To
secure Moore's services, in other words, it was necessary to make him de facto
undersecretary of state.[188]

   In Moore's opinion Wilson was "singularly uninformed" when it came to legal
matters.[189] The secretary of state was even worse. Bryan had "an entire unfamil-
iarity with what is involved" in diplomacy and an "utter inability to grasp ele-
mentary principles" of law.[190] Before Bryan left on a vacation, one story goes,
he called Moore into his office, explained that the counselor would be in charge
during his absence, and gestured toward a set of volumes on the shelf behind
him, saying offhandedly, "I'm told that if there is anything you don't know you
can find it in those volumes over there." The books were Moore's own *A Digest
of International Law*.[191] Moore was primed for confrontation with his superiors,
and it came quickly. The president's response to the Mexican Revolution—
and his subsequent disagreements with Moore—reveal Wilson's skepticism of
international law

Nonrecognition and Intervention in Mexico

The Mexican revolution, which began in 1910, dominated the first year and a
half of Wilson's foreign policy. It had deep roots. Mexico had opened its doors
to foreign capital during the thirty-five-year rule of Porfirio Díaz, and foreigners controlled nearly all the country's railroads, oil wells, and mines. American
capitalists held the largest investment share: over $1 billion in 1911.[192] For many
Mexicans the costs of economic modernization outweighed its benefits. Land
expropriation created thousands of rootless peasants, while plantations relied
on forced labor. Meanwhile, the middle classes resented Díaz's stifling control
over the political system. In 1911 many of them allied themselves with peas-
ant revolutionaries to overthrow the dictator.[193] The new president, Francisco
Madero, came from a wealthy Northern family, and he hoped to maintain the
old economic order while instituting a more open political system. But he was
opposed on the left by revolutionaries seeking land reform and on the right by
reactionary elements of the old regime. He soon lost control.[194] In February

1913, with the active encouragement of US ambassador to Mexico, Henry Lane Wilson (no relation to the president), and much of the US business community, Madero's military commander, Victoriano Huerta, arrested the president and seized power. Madero was shot a few days later, allegedly on Huerta's orders.[195] Ambassador Wilson called on the Taft administration to recognize Huerta immediately, but Taft, by then a lame-duck president, decided to leave the issue to his successor.[196]

President Wilson refused to extend diplomatic recognition to the new government. Huerta faced continuing armed opposition in the South from rebels led by Emiliano Zapata and in the North from a loose alliance calling themselves the "Constitutionalists." Many of Wilson's powerful Democratic supporters had economic connections to the Constitutionalists and pressured the president to side against Huerta.[197] But it was Huerta's personal and political misdeeds that formed the basis of the Wilsonian critique, not the military or economic situation. Wilson and Bryan characterized Huerta as a murderer and a "usurper." At one meeting, Bryan compared him to Judas Iscariot.[198] Huerta had broken the covenant connecting the Mexican people to their government. Since the United States—in the person of Ambassador Wilson—had been complicit in this sin, the country had a duty to make things right.[199] There would be no diplomatic recognition without a constitutional government.

Wilson expanded his critique over time.[200] When European nations extended recognition to Huerta's government, Wilson attributed their actions to the influence of "foreign interests"—specifically the British oil companies. He framed the issue as part of a broader struggle against plutocracy. "We have seen material interests threaten constitutional freedom in the United States," Wilson declared in a speech in Mobile, Alabama, on October 27, and now Mexico and Latin America faced the same menace "not only within their borders but from outside their borders also."[201] The matter was therefore one of anti-imperialism and self-determination.[202]

But Huerta refused to back down. On October 10, 1913, he arrested opposition members of Congress and declared himself dictator. Wilson favored direct aid to the the Constitutionalists, who "represented the same views and aspirations as to government as were entertained by ourselves."[203] He set his opposition to Huerta in the context of a larger Latin American policy that he had first introduced in a March 1913 address.[204] "We hold . . . that just government rests always upon the consent of the governed," Wilson said. The United States ought not to support any political changes that undermined this principle. When Secretary Bryan showed Moore a draft telegram demanding that Mexico hold elections and that Huerta not be a candidate, Moore exasperatedly exclaimed, "What right have we to make such a demand?" As he saw it, "we had no right to dictate who should or should not be candidates for office in a foreign country."[205]

Given Moore's active work on behalf of regime change in the Philippines, Cuba, Panama, and Venezuela, among other places, it seems hard to imagine that his opposition to Wilson's policy reflected a sincere commitment to the sanctity of Mexican politics. (Moore also wrote disparagingly of the "mixed character," "dense ignorance," and "revolutionary habit" of the Mexican population.[206]) In part Moore's opposition was practical—holding little Cuba as a protectorate was one thing, holding giant Mexico was another. [207] More fundamentally, Moore opposed what appeared to be Wilson's disregard of international law. That was the "difficulty" with Wilson and Bryan, Moore complained to his friend, secretary of war Lindley Garrison: "[T]hey did not take a legal view of anything, not even of legal questions," such as recognition.[208]

Moore correctly pointed out that tying recognition to the nature of a state's internal political organization marked a radical departure from US precedent. It seemed to revive the recognition policy of the Holy Alliance, the group of nineteenth-century European monarchies that conditioned membership in the society of nations on having a legitimate dynastic ruler. Since its birth, the United States had held that any state able to maintain order and carry out its international obligations ought to be officially recognized.[209] There was an assumption that any de facto state represented the will of the people in some way, else it could not exist, and it was not up to outsiders to determine whether the will of the people was legitimately expressed.[210] In *A Digest of International Law*, Moore quoted President James Buchanan: "We do not go behind the existing Government to involve ourselves in the question of legitimacy. It is sufficient for us to know that a government exists capable of maintaining itself; and then its recognition on our part inevitably follows."[211] The United States had once recognized five governments in Mexico in a period of five months; surely not all of them were morally unimpeachable. US governments had withheld recognition before—in fact, President Ulysses S. Grant had postponed official relations with Porfirio Díaz for a year—but these actions had always been justified in terms of ensuring that new governments settled outstanding disputes, not of guaranteeing democracy.[212] "We regard governments as existing or as not existing," Moore argued in a lengthy memorandum to Bryan. "We do not require them to be chosen by popular vote. We look simply to the fact of the existence of the government and to its ability and inclination to discharge the national obligations." In Moore's opinion, Huerta's government easily met these criteria.[213] Failing to deal with it only made things worse. As second assistant secretary of state Alvey Adee quipped, "Shall Mexico be recognized or wreckognized?"[214]

When Wilson asked Moore to draft a note to the European powers protesting their support for Huerta, Moore did so but accompanied it with a fierce denunciation of Wilson's position.[215] Neither international law nor the Monroe Doctrine provided any justification for opposing a state's right to protect its nationals and their property abroad, he stated. Foreign capitalists had plentiful rights under the law, and ensuring that local governments upheld them was no sin. It was ridiculous to suggest that European recognition of Huerta constituted intervention in Mexico's affairs. The Europeans, not the United States, were the ones acting "in conformity with practice."[216]

This time, Wilson saw the wisdom of Moore's advice and elected not to send the telegram as written.[217] But the episode highlights the fundamental differences between Wilson's aims and Moore's outlook. The only way to protest economic neocolonialism from within traditional international law was through the reification of sovereignty. Carlos Calvo and Luis Drago based their protests on the rights of sovereign states to govern economic activity inside their borders. But Wilson's claim boiled down to an argument that since Huerta was in thrall to foreign capital, a US intervention to secure his ouster was an *anti*-imperialist move. Such an argument stood little chance of convincing international legal authorities. The only intervention in Mexico that international law would sanction would be one based on American economic rights, reasons of state, or the interests of global civilization.

Confronted with an incompatibility between law and justice, Wilson understandably began to wonder about the value of international law itself. By the end of October, Wilson had decided that Huerta must be removed from office, by force if necessary. He even drew up a message to Congress and a joint resolution authorizing war.[218] Yet he hoped to avoid bloodshed, and so asked Moore to discuss various steps that might be taken short of an actual invasion.[219] The first matter concerned how to isolate the Mexican government and prevent it from receiving money or supplies from Europe. Moore mentioned various types of blockade, and then the conversation turned to neutrality. Moore's notes from the meeting demonstrate Wilson's growing skepticism of international law:

> The President said he supposed that if we declared war, foreign bankers would be prevented from furnishing money to Huerta. I told him not at all; that neutrality did not require neutral governments to prevent the lending of money to belligerents.
>
> He said he thought that was strange, as it was quite as helpful to a belligerent to furnish it with money as it was to furnish it with arms and ammunition. I told him that that might be quite true, but that the law of neutrality like all other human laws was based on human experience . . . and did not proceed from theoretical conceptions having no connection with practical affairs.
>
> He said he supposed the international practice was not very clearly worked out. I told him that it was on the contrary very clearly worked out.

He said he supposed it was an ancient practice. I answered, no; it was
a modern practice worked out almost wholly in the last hundred years
and that the rules were very clear and well defined and rested on reason
and experience.[220]

Even in Moore's straightforward recollection, Wilson's growing annoyance is
palpable. When Wilson then asked about recognizing the Constitutionalists as
official belligerents, Moore again dissented, saying that it would mean "disregarding the precedents which we ourselves had established, particularly in the
case of Cuba."[221] The two men disagreed several more times over the course of
the conversation. It was simply impossible for Wilson to accomplish his goals
within Moore's legal framework. Sensing this fundamental disagreement, in
November Moore drafted a letter of resignation.[222] But Wilson decided not to
ask Congress for a declaration of war, and Moore stayed on.[223]

 Moore's prediction that the policy of nonrecognition would ultimately lead to
intervention came true in April 1914.[224] Seizing on a pretext, Wilson ordered US
troops to invade Veracruz, hoping to drive Huerta from power. Moore's contention that Huerta was not as weak nor the Constitutionalists as united as Wilson's
agents had reported also proved prescient.[225] American marines met serious
opposition and secured the city only after a battle that left nineteen Americans
and perhaps two hundred Mexicans dead.[226] Meanwhile, Venustiano Carranza—
the leader of the Constitutionalists forces—denounced the invasion. Wilson
quickly accepted the mediation of Argentina, Brazil, and Chile to extricate himself from the deteriorating situation.[227] Even after Huerta finally resigned, in July
1914, the violence continued, as the Constituitonalists splintered. Carranza's
forces battled those of Zapata, Francisco "Pancho" Villa, and other rivals. After
Villa raided Columbus, New Mexico, in early 1916 in retaliation for Wilson's
support for Carranza, Wilson again intervened, sending six thousand troops on
a fruitless chase across Northern Mexico. After 1916, however, Wilson resisted
fierce pressure from American economic interests to invade.[228]

Continuities and Departures

By this time, Moore had long since resigned.[229] When he left Washington in 1914,
the press wondered how the administration would survive without his expertise.
"Advices from Washington indicate that there will be no Moore diplomacy there"
quipped the Philadelphia *Public Ledger*, which had been chronicling Moore's
increasing frustrations.[230] "There are not so many eminent authorities on international law connected with the State Department that the administration can afford
to lose the services of the most eminent of them," opined the *New York World*.[231]

Figure 5.2 A cartoon from the Philadelphia *Public Ledger* depicts a frustrated John Bassett Moore leaving behind the Wilson administration's "Mexican muddle." The lawyer grew increasingly frustrated as President Wilson and his secretary of state, William Jennings Bryan, ignored his legal expertise, here depicted as a broken staff of "expert knowledge." Moore preserved the cartoon in his personal files. Box 93, John Bassett Moore Papers, Library of Congress.

Wilson may not have had much appreciation for international law, but he understood the importance of having someone around who did, so he chose Robert Lansing to replace Moore. Lansing belonged to the board of editors of the *AJIL* and had participated in more international arbitrations than any other living American. He even carried Root's endorsement.[232] After William Jennings Bryan resigned as secretary of state in 1915, Wilson promoted Lansing to head the department. The counselor protested that he lacked the political influence common to most of his predecessors. Still, Lansing was the best man at hand and his familiarity with the procedures of diplomacy and the content of international law made him useful to a president who had already decided to act as his own secretary of state.[233] Wilson would rarely consult Lansing while making policy, but he would rely on his secretary to package it in acceptable legal terminology.

Wilsonianism presented a fundamental challenge to legalism. But outside of Mexico, few of the Wilson administration's prewar policies can be accurately characterized as "Wilsonian." John Bassett Moore's fears notwithstanding, the overthrow of Huerta did not inaugurate of a policy of sponsoring revolutions aimed at promoting constitutional democracy. With a few important exceptions, Wilson and Bryan's Caribbean policies were positively Taftian.[234] In Nicaragua, for example, Bryan signed a treaty featuring a Platt-style amendment granting the United States direct oversight of Nicaraguan affairs.[235] "[T]he Democrats have adopted bodily the foreign policy of the Republicans," a surprised British paper exclaimed.[236] Wilson also expanded the essentials of "dollar diplomacy" elsewhere, in the meanwhile beginning occupations in the Dominican Republic and Haiti that would eventually last eight and nineteen years, respectively.[237] As World War I drained European trade and investment from the region, American capital cemented its control.[238] There is rich irony in the fact that the administration that sought to reject the interventionist tendencies of its predecessors in favor of a policy of equality and democracy became the most interventionist of all.[239] This owed in part to Wilson's and Bryan's idealism. They often managed to convince themselves that their policy truly served the interest of the peoples of the hemisphere rather than national self-interest.[240] A healthy dose of ethnocentric racism helped. Geopolitics mattered too. Wilson continued to believe in the strategic importance of the approaches to the Panama Canal and the conviction that US tutelage would bring benefits to "backward" nations.[241] The outbreak of World War I heightened concerns about German influence and limited congressional opposition to Caribbean interventions.[242] Overall the continuities between Wilson and his predecessors suggest how deeply an interventionist mindset suffused the foreign policy state.[243] Stability remained the goal, and US Americans remained convinced that they possessed the power, right, and means to ensure it.

In 1920, a State Department commercial adviser claimed that the transition from Taft to Wilson was "one of the few instances in which no break is shown."[244] Both administrations meddled extensively in the affairs of their neighbors, utilizing financial protectorates and, when those failed, the marines. Thus most of the interventions that Roosevelt had been forced to forego eventually came to pass at the hands of his successors. Elihu Root had believed that the expansion of international law would establish a stable, US-friendly order. He had successfully defended the legal right to intervene if necessary. But he was perhaps too successful in this regard. By pressing legal claims to their full extent, Taft and Knox undermined law's legitimacy. That intervention nevertheless continued under Wilson shows how deeply ingrained interventionist assumptions were.

Yet Wilson did depart from his Republican predecessors in important ways when it came to legalism. He did not share their faith in international law as the ideal ordering method for global civilization. This would have momentous consequences in 1919, when Washington had an unprecedented say in shaping world order. But first the United States would have to decide how to respond to the Great War. And once again, lawyers and international law would find themselves in the middle.

6

Legalism, Neutrality, and the Great War, 1914–1918

"I thought I could not live as I could get no breath and my heart was throbbing day and night." Writing on August 17, 1914, Lassa Oppenheim evoked the apprehensive excitement of the initial weeks of World War I.[1] Frenzy soon gave way to despair. German publicist Walther Schücking pronounced himself "absolutely crushed," as the extent of the "slaughter between the civilized nations" became clear.[2] And James Brown Scott confessed to being "inexpressibly depressed."[3] "I have felt an irresistible desire to write you," he told Elihu Root, "even although I have nothing to say."[4]

Despair seemed natural. The European powers had violated "practically every law which stood in their way."[5] The "acquired habits of civilization" had failed to restrain the "powerful innate tendencies" of man.[6] All that lawyers had worked for—the meticulous Hague Conventions, the compendious legal textbooks, the optimistic peace meetings—seemed to have failed utterly. A sense of work undone, of illusions shattered and verities undermined pervaded legalist writings as 1914 came to a close. "Our disappointment is too cruel," lamented Louis Renault.[7] Sympathetic friends offered condolences to international lawyers, wondering if they planned to "undertake some new form of occupation, in view of the disappearance of international law."[8]

But in fact war only increased the demand for international legal expertise. Congress ordered a thousand copies of John Bassett Moore's *A Digest of International Law* to be printed: 700 for the House and 300 for the Senate.[9] The public, too, hungered for legal knowledge. "[W]e are having difficulty in keeping on hand a sufficient supply of suitable material," complained George Finch, the *AJIL*'s business manager. "[P]ractically the entire periodical and newspaper press" sought out legal expertise, and the *AJIL* could not compete with "the larger audience and in many cases the compensation which the larger magazines offer."[10] Universities prepared for an "enormously increased interest" in the topic, while international lawyers found a paying audience for public lecture courses.[11]

And corporate business boomed as firms navigated the complex legal conditions of wartime. John Bassett Moore kept "exceedingly busy" representing industrial giants Standard Oil and Bethlehem Steel along with smaller concerns like the Savannah Bank Trust.[12] Chandler P. Anderson had so many private clients that he contemplated opening a Washington office of his firm solely to perform international law work.[13] It was a profitable time to be an expert in international law.

The State Department needed more lawyers, too. Complaints, demands, and pleadings filled its mailboxes: from American travelers marooned in Europe in August 1914, shippers whose goods had been intercepted by the Allies, and foreign governments challenging its policies. In all, the department's workload increased 400 percent in the first six weeks of the war.[14] Since William Jennings Bryan knew little about international law, the department added reinforcements.[15] "More Brains to Be Placed Behind Bryan," explained a Boston newspaper headline.[16] By February of 1915, the department was supplementing the work of Solicitor Cone Johnson, Counselor Robert Lansing, and his assistant Lester H. Woolsey with the regular advice of ASIL members James Brown Scott, Chandler P. Anderson, and Eugene Wambaugh.[17] Scott also chaired the Joint State and Navy Neutrality Board, a three-member group created to provide policymakers with official legal opinions.[18]

Legal expertise mattered because the key wartime issues for the United States were defined in legal terms. Neutrality was the most important. When war broke out in Europe, President Wilson declared the country neutral. This stance was logical and seemed likely to endure. The nation had traditionally considered itself a champion of neutrality, and the policy was popular. Moreover, picking a side in the war was fraught with domestic political danger: it was hard to predict how the large number of recent immigrants of diverse ethnicities, who maintained close ties with their homelands, would react in such a situation. Finally, the country had enough power to defend its neutral rights against any belligerent.

Yet maintaining neutrality was difficult. Combatants mobilized entire societies to feed their military machines. Britain and Germany hungered for America's finance capital and raw materials, and schemed to block their enemies from obtaining them. International law gave neutrals and belligerents mutual rights and duties. Neutrals were allowed to continue trading with both sides, under certain conditions. On the other hand, belligerents could inspect and seize neutral cargoes, also under certain conditions. The precise nature of these conditions was disputed and controversial. How participants constructed and defended their interpretations would contribute significantly to the shape of the conflict.

It was under the banner of neutral rights that the United States entered the war in April 1917. But many historians contend that it was effectively "unneutral" before this, by mid-1915. Proponents of this view point to the fact that almost all American exports of munitions and other crucial goods, such as foodstuffs and raw materials, went to the Allies, and very few to the Central Powers. They argue that the Wilson administration did too little to resist the expansive—and illegal—British blockade that enforced this imbalance. Meanwhile, the United States categorically rejected Germany's attempts to use submarines to intercept Allied shipping. And, unlike small European neutrals (such as Belgium or Greece) who abandoned neutrality only under belligerent duress, America entered the war of its own volition.[19] Defenders of Wilson's wartime policy dispute elements of this account. While everyone agrees that American policy disproportionately benefited the Allies, some deny that this policy was illegal or that meaningful alternatives existed.[20] Wilson's motivations remain similarly contested.[21] Nevertheless, it seems clear that American policy failed to uphold "strict neutrality."[22]

Did American unneutrality reflect a disregard for international law? Critics think so. Britain's seizures of American shipping violated clearly defined neutral rights, they argue. By failing to protest adequately, the United States abandoned a viable legal case and allowed British malfeasance to persist. If policymakers had only followed unbiased legal advice, America could and would have remained neutral.[23] A careful examination of the State Department's legal advisers complicates this story. Given the assumptions of prewar legalism and the structure of international law as it had developed over the nineteenth century, actions that seemed to conform to the law of neutrality might also be substantively unneutral. By embracing a legalist orientation, the United States also committed itself to the Allies. In 1917, war was the result.

Changing Conceptions of Neutrality

Americans had always considered themselves leading defenders of neutrality, but the meaning of that concept changed over time. In 1794 the United States enacted national legislation to enforce neutral duties, thereby reassuring belligerents that neutral countries could remain rigorously impartial during war.[24] The United States also advocated expansive neutral rights. In 1812, the young country went to war with England in part to defend the right to trade with any belligerent. In the following years, America updated its neutrality laws at home and pushed for greater neutral rights abroad, including the immunity of private property at sea.[25] These actions helped to transform neutrality from a questionable and contingent practice into a legally defined institution.[26]

Traditional American neutrality reflected the interests of a small, weak nation.[27] Enshrining rights and duties in international law, its promoters reasoned, would prevent US entanglement in European politics and wars while preserving access to profitable trade. In conjunction with the Monroe Doctrine, it might forestall European challenges to American hegemony in the Western Hemisphere. Neutrality, therefore, developed in tandem with a policy of unilateralism and political nonentanglement. A legally defined neutrality supported goals both ideological and pragmatic.[28]

However, during its own Civil War, the United States had claimed extensive *belligerent* rights in order to prevent trade with the Confederacy. The Union navy intercepted European merchant shipping while its courts justified the seizure of neutral cargoes, even those en route from one neutral port to another.[29] Europeans complained that the policy contravened America's previous support for neutral rights.[30] Yet because it remained part of a broader commitment to political non-entanglement, Americans did not admit to any real inconsistency. They continued to consider themselves leading advocates for neutrality, and historians have assumed that the "traditional" approach endured until World War I.[31] But in important ways, changing views of international law and American national identity began to undermine this relationship even before 1914.

Neutrality had different connotations for the legal advisers of 1912 than it had for the policymakers of 1812. In its traditional form, American neutrality meant abstention from entanglement in international conflicts, and therefore made no distinction between belligerents. But, as we have seen, the legalist project that emerged after 1900 had a different set of values. Legalists like James Brown Scott removed international law from the context of diplomacy, privileging the discovery and application of correct principles over the management of competing interests. As a world power, America had a duty, these lawyers believed, to cultivate a global environment in which international law could flourish. To be "neutral" was not to be indifferent to international politics but to actively promote impartial, apolitical judgment.[32] This implied that belligerents could now be *judged*. This echoed the thoughts of some British jurists—such as John Westlake—who had called for a reconsideration of the just war tradition. Law ought not to merely regulate war, but to end it by administering justice.[33] Rather than using international law to protect narrow national interests, the United States would make the protection of law into an interest in itself.

Before 1914, however, international lawyers did not fully appreciate the vast implications of their project for US policy. They promoted international law in the abstract rather than tailoring neutrality laws to suit changing American interests. In 1904, Alfred Thayer Mahan, the famous naval strategist, offered a different approach. He proposed that the United States abandon its customary support for the immunity of private property from capture at sea. "[W]hat was expedient to our weakness of a century ago is not expedient to our strength today," he explained. The United States ought to expand belligerent rights as much as possible so as to "fasten our grip on the sea."[34] While some legal advisers and policymakers sympathized with this argument, they failed to convince

President Roosevelt to change it.[35] National ideology trumped national interests. Immunity of private property, said Joseph Choate, "made for civilization." The question ought not be reduced to "the level of national needs and interests" but should be examined "from the humanitarian and international standpoint."[36]

This logic explains the reaction of American legalists to the failure of the international prize court in 1911. Under existing rules of international law, a neutral ship captured by belligerent forces could be escorted to port, where a prize court operated by the capturing nation would adjudicate the fate of its cargo. Legalists proposed an international prize court to provide neutral owners of seized cargoes with an impartial alternative. But the court plan languished when Britain refused to ratify the Declaration of London (a codified body of maritime law upon which the prize court would have based its rulings).[37] Tellingly, the loss of safeguards for American shippers was not what most upset legalists. As Elihu Root explained, the "real significance" of the British rejection of the Declaration of London was the setback it represented to the movement for a world court: "The Prize Court Convention," he argued, represented "the advance guard of the proposed judicial system, the experiment upon which the success of the whole plainly depends."[38]

In comparison, it is instructive to note John Bassett Moore's reaction. He, too, praised the proposed prize court ("one of the most remarkable advances ever proposed towards the founding of an international jurisdiction") and grudgingly deemed the Declaration "a step in the right direction."[39] But he had grave concerns with the Declaration's implications for neutral trade. He argued in 1912 that the most dangerous threat to neutral shipping, legally speaking, was the right of belligerents to confiscate "contraband" goods. During the nineteenth century, he explained, important neutral rights had been established in international law. The 1856 Declaration of Paris proclaimed that "free ships make free goods" and that neutral goods are always free. In other words, goods owned by citizens of neutral countries could be traded with any belligerent, and neutral ships could carry any goods—even those belonging to the enemy—without fear of confiscation.[40] But these generous conditions pointedly excepted goods defined as contraband—those with military uses. These were still liable to capture. By the time of the 1907 Hague Conference, contraband had been divided into two legal categories: "absolute" contraband consisted of articles used mainly, or solely for war (most obviously arms and munitions, but also items such as military uniforms); "conditional" or "relative" contraband referred to what today we might call "dual-use" items (including certain raw materials and industrial products). If consigned directly to enemy forces, even food could be confiscated as "conditional" contraband.[41] The problem with the Declaration of London, Moore noted, was that it defined conditional contraband so vaguely as to permit nearly unlimited abuse. For example, it allowed confiscation if the items were "destined to a fortified place of the enemy" or sold to a merchant known to supply articles to the enemy government. But, Moore noted, "practically every important port is a 'fortified place'" and any "established" merchant would likely sell to the government.[42] By exploiting such "loose and interested surmises," belligerents could devastate neutral (and in particular, American) trade. That the United States delegation had agreed with these broad terms was especially frustrating, for this was, as Moore saw it, a betrayal of America's traditional behavior, and a threat to its interests.[43]

Scott did not concern himself with these implications. For him, the general advancement of international law outweighed concern for specific rules of neutrality. This is evident from the 1913 publication of *The Neutrality Laws of the United States* by the Carnegie Endowment's Division of International Law.[44] The book's immediate context was the controversy that surrounded the provisioning of weapons to Mexican revolutionaries.[45] On the surface, the publication seemed continuous with past practice: it reviewed American neutrality legislation since 1794 and recommended updates to reflect modern conditions. But for Scott the goal of modernizing neutrality laws was not to make them better conform with current conditions and interests, but to initiate a process of reform that would offer "a model to the nations."[46] As Scott explained:

> When we think of peace, we go on to the presumption that our intentions are honorable as well as pacific, and that the other nations should be, as it were, brought into our camp. It seemed best to us to. . . [put] our house in order, to consider in how far we as a nation conform to the requirements of neutrality.[47]

Unlike in 1794, when neutrality legislation aimed to keep Europe at arm's length, here it was framed as a move to engage the rest of the world and bring it *toward* the United States—"into our camp"—as Scott put it. The commitment to neutrality formed a necessary precondition for American leadership.

Not all of the State Department's legal advisers of 1914 were as legalistic as Scott. But an ideological conception of civilization and law animated even the most skeptical of the bunch, Robert Lansing. Historians have portrayed Lansing as a "realist," who despite being an international lawyer did not really *believe* in international law.[48] According to Daniel Smith, his biographer, Lansing was "not a mere legalist." He believed that because international law could not be enforced, it "therefore represented little more than custom and expedience."[49] Nils Ørvik sees Lansing as a prototypical realist who could see the real interests and power "behind the lofty phrases and the legal spider-webbing."[50]

Yet Lansing was very much involved with American legalists. He became an international lawyer somewhat by chance: he married the daughter of John Foster, a former secretary of state and lawyer. With his father-in-law, Lansing began in private practice. Among other clients, he represented some American corporate antagonists of the New York & Bermudez Co.[51] He was a founding member of the ASIL, and served on the *AJIL*'s editorial board. His legal work also paid him quite handsomely—he complained about the "considerable financial loss" he would incur by joining the State Department in 1913—and he can be considered a member of the proto-foreign policy establishment.[52]

Lansing was a staunch ideologue. His journals reveal a man concerned above all with unrest from below. Woodrow Wilson's often ridiculed imploration to the American people to remain neutral in "thought as well as in action" reflected Lansing's fear of discord among unassimilated immigrants from rival homelands.[53] Worried about encroaching "materialism" among the population, Lansing held a patrician's concern for the decline of national character.[54] The task of the statesman was not merely to preserve the nation's material interests but to sustain its capacity for patriotism and reasoned discourse.

Unlike James Brown Scott, however, Lansing did not express this ideology *through* law, but rather in conjunction with it. In a series of articles in 1907, Lansing took an Austinian view of the law, defining it as the command of a sovereign and declaring that sovereignty was the "*power to do all things without accountability.*"[55] Law should not be confused with morality, he added, but "is simply the application or the menace of *brute force.*"[56] Though he did not directly deny that international law was law, he did not seem to share Scott's obsession with disproving its critics. In a 1912 article he asserted that the "primary purpose of international law" was the "protection of the fundamental rights of states," namely sovereignty.[57] In case of war, international law ceased to exist between belligerents. It did remain in force between belligerents and neutrals, but since the belligerent has its rights, that is, "its sovereignty" at stake, "so far as possible its physical might should be left free and unhampered in the efforts to maintain national existence."[58]

Lansing was a practitioner first and foremost and he seems to have supported the ASIL primarily for professional reasons. Yet like his contemporaries, Lansing did believe in the evolution of civilization toward greater cooperation. As his biographer notes, "Lansing was not a pessimist, for he believed that the inevitable increase in moral sensibilities would eventually transform national societies and thus change profoundly international relations."[59] As we will see, like the other legal advisers, Lansing came to view World War I in ideological as much as strategic terms.

Reacting to Britain and Germany

Legalists' broader ideological project provided a conceptual vocabulary through which the advisers interpreted the law after 1914. A neutrality of abstention no longer seemed respectable. As a leader of neutrals, America's duty consisted not in validating its own rights but in defending the possibility of a law-governed world. James Brown Scott thus complained when the United States did not protest officially the German invasion of Belgium.[60] Neutrals, he explained, had a duty to protest even where their own interests were not directly threatened: "The material injury is . . . the violation of the principle of law, not merely the injury to the life or property of the citizen of the neutral nation."[61] Elihu Root called for the vindication "of the right to every civilized nation to have the law maintained."[62] Scott later lamented that the US government had "only protested when our interests were involved," claiming that this "smacks of materialism."[63] "I was anxious that we should, from the very beginning," he wrote a French correspondent, "stand forth as the advocate of international law."[64] Or as one colleague put it, "[U]pon the neutral rests the trusteeship of international law."[65]

America refused to share the burden of trusteeship. Though some Americans advocated a neutral alliance to diagnose and punish violations of international law, the Wilson administration rebuffed Scandinavian proposals for a conference of neutrals that would defend neutrality collectively.[66] Lansing explained the refusal as a consequence of America's geographical distance from the European neutrals, but it is difficult not to read it as expressing an unwillingness to dilute American leadership.[67]

In any event, in 1914 defending international law meant asserting neutral rights. The State Department declared at the outbreak of the war that American citizens were free to export contraband—including arms and ammunition—to belligerents, subject only to risk of capture.[68] Since the British Navy controlled the high seas, Britain cut off trade to Germany and the Allies reaped the benefits of American industrial production. The United States soon became Britain's arsenal.[69] Though controversial, US policy accorded with law and tradition: American governments had always claimed the right to export, and international law as codified in the Hague Conventions supported them.[70] While other nations had voluntarily banned such exports, legal advisers claimed that changing the law during wartime would be unneutral.[71] Germany groused, but even its ambassador had to admit the legality of the practice.[72] What drew more ire was America's divergent responses to British and German lawbreaking.

At first, Britain posed the greater threat to American neutral rights. In August 1914, the United States requested that all belligerents conform to the rules laid out in the Declaration of London.[73] The Central Powers—recognizing that the declaration's creation of a free list would facilitate the importation of useful goods like copper and rubber—gave their conditional assent.[74] But London signaled that it would accept the declaration only with modifications that permitted tighter control of neutral shipping.[75] Some of these modifications seemed to violate traditional neutral rights.[76]

Over the next month, Lansing, Scott, and Eugene Wambaugh worked in tandem to prepare a response. Their draft note protested vigorously—so vigorously, in fact, that Colonel Edward House (President Wilson's unofficial deputy) together with British ambassador Cecil Spring-Rice prevented its transmission, substituting in its place a more anodyne communiqué.[77] Despite, or perhaps because of, these conciliatory gestures, Britain ignored American entreaties. Over the next several months it added further restrictions, culminating in a March 1915 Order in Council banning virtually all neutral trade with Germany.[78] This stretched accepted rules of international law beyond their breaking points. In effect, the Order claimed the rights of a blockade without assuming its responsibilities under the law.[79] The United States complained but did not press the issue.[80] Since trade with the Allies continued meanwhile, Germany deemed America's position unneutral.[81]

Wilson's legal advisers considered protest essential. Reaffirming neutral rights was vital not solely for the interests of American shippers, but for the sake of international law.[82] A law violated with impunity could hardly be called a law at all. In dozens of memoranda, they rejected British legal arguments and recommended strongly worded protests.[83] Wambaugh complained in September 1914 that British policy was "so injurious to neutral commerce and so inconsistent with general International Law as to bring it wholly within the legal right of a neutral . . . to protect its commerce by war."[84] Lansing warned that to acquiesce to the blockade would place the United States "in a position where its neutrality and impartiality are doubtful or open to question."[85] The Neutrality Board deemed Britain's March 1915 Order in Council "a grave violation of neutral rights" and compared it to the British conduct that had precipitated the War of 1812.[86] Violations must not go unchallenged, for "[t]he maintenance of the public law of the world—international law—is a matter of deepest concern to the whole world, which will lapse into barbarism if respect for international law be lost." So serious were the violations that "a mere protest would be inadequate."[87]

Citing these complaints, some historians have suggested that the United States might have retained its neutrality had policymakers heeded their advisers' warnings. Historian John Coogan calls the Board's response to the March 1915 Order in Council "Scott's policy of confrontation," portraying it as a path not taken.[88] But the confrontation Scott had in mind was only a limited one. To effect a change in British policy, Americans would have needed to accompany their protests with credible threats of reprisal—such as those made to Germany in response to its submarine campaign.[89] While the advisers counseled a sharper tone in American protests, they did not contemplate this type of aggressive action.[90]

In fact, the advisers' greatest fear was that insufficient protest might cause an excitable public to demand war with Britain. Wambaugh fretted that "hot heads" might "insist upon action against Great Britain and the allies," while Lansing worried that bitter reactions might roil the American melting pot, turning American ethnic groups against one other.[91] It was necessary to walk a fine line between protesting enough to assuage public opinion and uphold the law, but not so much as to actually risk conflict with Britain.[92]

British violations of international law could be solved through legal means, the advisers reasoned. Even Wambaugh, who had suggested that violent reprisals might be justified, advocated no more than a formal protest combined with a commitment to pursue post-war arbitration.[93] Arbitration would restore the losses of American shippers and confirm the legitimacy of the international legal system. The Neutrality Board's problem with "mere protest" was not its ineffectuality but its lack of detail. To prove America's legal case irrefutably, the situation demanded not reprisals but scholarship: a lengthy academic explication of "certain broad principles."[94] By 1916, the Neutrality Board deemed the disagreement "irreconcilable by diplomatic methods" but proposed that any further notes close "with a reference to the treaties of arbitration between the two Governments by which the points at issue between them may, and in the opinion of the Board should, be settled."[95] War with Britain was not in the cards.

Legal advisers took a very different stance towards Germany. The Neutrality Board deemed the torpedoing of the British ship *Falaba*—resulting in the death of one American citizen—not only "illegal but revoltingly inhuman."[96] Legal advisers broadly concurred in the Wilson government's strict protest to Germany's initial declaration of a submarine war zone in February of 1915, and Lansing pushed hard for an aggressive response to the sinking of the *Lusitania*, a British ship sunk in May 1915 with the loss of 1198 lives, including 128 Americans.[97] While British violations could be addressed through post-war arbitration, German behavior necessitated ultimatums, armed preparedness, and perhaps war.[98]

Why this difference? The submarine blockade did present unique challenges. Lansing argued that British violations of the law cost only money, while German submarines cost American lives.[99] (British policy also contributed to civilian deaths: some historians have estimated between 300,000 to nearly 763,000 deaths as a result of blockade-induced malnutrition).[100] But ultimately what drove legal advisers was their conviction that a German triumph meant a defeat for civilization. Even before the sinking of the *Lustiania*, Chandler Anderson wrote in his diary that "[i]f Germany wins, it threatens the existence of popular government throughout the world, and it is inconceivable that the greatest republic in the world should lend itself to the destruction of popular government."[101] A few months later, Lansing confided in a personal memorandum that "I have come to the conclusion that the German Government is utterly hostile to all nations with democratic institutions."[102] When the United States finally entered the war in 1917, Scott declared, "I feel that the United States are justified in declaring war against Germany, and I feel that it would have been justified had it done so at a very much earlier date."[103]

Historians have attributed this bias to a combination of propaganda and Anglophilia.[104] To be sure, the legal advisers held England in high regard. Scott venerated British law. In 1913 he coordinated a celebration of the hundred years of peace between the "English-speaking peoples."[105] Meanwhile, lawyers in Allied countries sent letter after letter describing their suffering at the hands of German "barbarians."[106] Lassa Oppenheim told James Brown Scott that Germany's invasion of Belgium was "the greatest international crime" since Napoleon, while another British lawyer called it "an outrage on civilisation."[107] French-speaking correspondents piled on; the Belgian Albéric Rolin, secretary general of the *Institut de droit international*, decried German atrocities while mourning the death of three of his sons in battle.[108] Lawyers from the Central Powers made entreaties of their own. Hans Wehberg assured Scott of Germany's innocence and hoped that its enemies "will be beaten to a frazzle."[109] Karl Strupp and Heinrich Lammasch meanwhile blamed Russia.[110] But as England tightened its control of the seas and telegraph wires, letters from Austria and Germany slowed to a trickle. Privately, the American advisers sympathized with the Allies.[111]

The social and cultural setting in which legal advisers labored shaped how they interpreted the two sides' violations of law. The East Coast establishment to which these lawyers belonged was a hotbed of anti-German and pro-preparedness sentiment. Harvard, Yale, and Princeton men even traveled to Plattsburgh, in upstate New York, to train for military service under the watchful eyes of General Leonard Wood.[112] While some prewar pacifists, such as Andrew Carnegie, opposed preparedness, most of the bankers, lawyers, and businessmen who had supported arbitration before the war now supported a tilt toward the Allies and an arms build up.[113] High-profile legalists including Elihu Root, Henry Stimson, and Joseph Choate served as leaders of the National Security League, an organization that promoted the strengthening of the nation's military forces.[114]

Legalists' mistrust of Germany was not simply a question of ethnic affinities or outraged morality outweighing disinterested scientific appraisal. Rather, legalists' world view made international law inherently susceptible to this sort of ideological deployment. Legalism interpreted international law as a civilizing project. Although Britain violated maritime law, at least the British made an effort to justify their violations in legal rhetoric.[115] The British were willing to play the game, in other words. They acknowledged the validity of law in theory even as they violated it in practice.[116] Combined with the many successful examples of American-British arbitration in the past (arbitrations in which Lansing, Anderson, and Scott had all participated), it was easy to argue that Anglo-American conflicts could be resolved through legal channels after the war.[117]

Germany on the other hand appeared as the antithesis of the legalist project. In the eyes of American legalists, Germany's approach to law had long been suspect. In 1909, Elihu Root called Germany "the great disturber of peace in the world" which had "persistently stood" against "progress" in law.[118] The same year, Indiana University Professor (and frequent *AJIL* contributor) Amos Hershey called Germany "the main obstacle to the world's peace."[119] "It is curious to note," Scott wrote in 1914, that the country alleged to have committed the worst violations of law ... had not, up to a few years ago, a single chair in all its great educational system exclusively devoted to the teaching of international law."[120] German Chancellor Theobald von Bethmann Hollweg's frank admission that Germany's invasion of Belgium was illegal, and his dismissal of treaties as mere "scraps of paper" seemed to confirm Germany as an opponent of law itself.[121] German law professor Joseph Kohler's attempt to defend the claim that "necessity knows no law" only further suggested the gulf between German legal science and progressive legalism.[122]

As most legalists saw it, German values were antithetical to legalism's liberal foundations. Where the future of international law required the triumph of reason, German society valued force. In place of democracy and public opinion, autocracy reigned. Militarism replaced the international mind. The war therefore was "a contest between the two great rival systems of thought—national and international," wrote Ellery Stowell.[123] German "nationalism," if allowed to triumph, would mark the end of any possible future for internationalism.[124] In defining Germany as an anti-legal power, American legalists echoed British accusations.[125] These views of Germany could be exaggerated.[126] But once Germany became discursively identified as hyper-nationalist, its victory became incompatible with a world of law. Rejecting treaties as "scraps of paper" not only threatened international law, it also threatened the rule of law generally, and thus the basis of modern society: debt, money, even marriage licenses were "scraps of paper" as well![127] "Honest difference as to national rights and duties may be settled by arbitration, or judicial decision;" Elihu Root argued, "but, against a deep and persistent purpose by the rulers of a great nation to take away the territory of others, or to reduce others to subjection for their own aggrandizement, all these expedients are of no avail."[128]

Lansing's private diaries reveal a similar outlook. Lansing was always pro-Ally, and by mid-1915 had become convinced that Germany must be defeated. However, as Robert Tucker has noted, Lansing did not dwell on specific threats to the United States or ponder the fate of particular American interests should Germany win.[129] Germany was to be feared not because of what it might mean for American trade, for instance, but because "German absolutism is the great menace to democracy."[130] Even if the war ended in a stalemate, Germany would regroup, and soon ally with Russia and Japan, the other autocratic powers:

> Their success would mean the overthrow of democracy in the world, the suppression of individual liberty, the setting up of evil ambitions, the subordination of the principles of right and justice to physical might directed by arbitrary will, and the turning back of the hands of human progress two centuries.[131]

It was self-evident that "[w]hen we do go into the war, and we might as well make up our minds that we are going in, we must go in on the side of the Allies, for we are a democracy."[132] If Lansing's policy was based on "national interest," he constructed that concept ideologically as well as strategically.[133]

Armed Merchantmen, Submarines, and International Law

Legalists' social and cultural milieu led them to see German violations of law as more threatening than British ones. But their pro-British stance did not result solely from emotion or ideology. It also reflected the fact that prewar international law favored nations with strong navies. As in the dispute over the legal right to intervene in Latin America, the structure of international law itself made true impartiality difficult. If the war was defined as a war to defend law, it mattered what that law was assumed to cover. In short, which "rights" would Americans fight to protect?

The right of Americans to travel on armed British ships—in defiance of German submarine warfare—was the law most directly invoked in the decision to enter the war. A brief look at the legal advisers' opinions on this issue suggests how a commitment to law could just as easily undermine as preserve neutrality. Soon after the war began, the Neutrality Board ruled that armed ships could maintain a peaceful status under law so long as they carried guns solely for "defensive" purposes.[134] This became official US policy.[135] It was a momentous decision, for categorizing all armed vessels as warships—as the Dutch did—might have disrupted British access to American ports.[136] By doing the opposite, the government assured its citizens that they could travel on British ships without fear of attack.[137]

A later critique deemed the ruling "legally unsustainable," contending that any armed ship ought to be treated as a man of war.[138] The Neutrality Board, led by Scott, defended its decision by citing American case law and the opinions of international legal experts.[139] "Visit and search" were the traditional rules governing naval interception of commerce. Enemy or neutral ships would be stopped and boarded to see if they carried contraband. A ship ferrying illegal goods could be sunk in certain circumstances, but only after providing for the safety of passengers and crew (provided the suspected vessel did not resist).[140]

Before the 1850s, merchant ships frequently carried guns to defend themselves from privateers; their weak armament was no match for a naval cruiser, and would not likely be used to interfere with visit and search. But the introduction of the submarine changed the equation. A well-aimed volley from even a small gun could cripple a surfaced submarine.[141] Distinguishing "defensive" from "offensive" armament was therefore difficult. Germany claimed that its submarines could not conduct traditional visit and search if subject to attack. Instead, they would shoot armed belligerent ships—whether civilian or military in character—on sight.[142]

This marked a clear departure from international legal norms. In previous wars states had expanded the definition of contraband and exceeded recognized limits of blockade, but no one had claimed the right to sink merchant or passenger ships without first allowing for the safety of those on board.[143] Thus where pursuing economic warfare was concerned, international law favored those with the naval strength to enforce a blockade with surface ships rather than submarines. This is one reason for Britain's support for international law. German officials complained that this system both reflected and promoted British power. New technology (the submarine) required new laws, they argued. In their analysis, power would determine what those laws were. As Vice Admiral Reinhard Scheer put it, if the Allies won, "England will make sure that legal chains are attached to the submarine for all time, making it harmless to the English position of power."[144] Despite these complaints, it remained the case that practicing unrestricted submarine warfare violated the international law of 1914. If the United States insisted on defending its rights under that legal system, it implicitly aligned itself with England.

The sinking of the *Lusitania* in May 1915 drove home the seriousness of the issue. Presciently, the Board had realized the potential complications of its initial decision. It accompanied its legal opinion with a note counseling against the arming of merchant ships as a matter of policy.[145] "A ship that fights is less safe than one that runs away," it observed.[146] Yet it refused to alter its legal interpretation.[147] And once proclaimed, a *right* to travel in safety upon belligerent merchantmen could not easily be withdrawn. Wilson had invoked "the whole fine fabric of international law" in support of the claim that Americans could travel on belligerent ships.[148] When the House of Representatives introduced a bill to warn Americans from traveling on armed ships in 1916, legal advisers drafted a response arguing that to warn Americans "is to take away from them a right which belongs to them."[149] In speaking against the bill, Wilson echoed this reasoning:

> I cannot consent to any abridgment of the rights of American citizens in any respect. The honor and self-respect of the nation is involved . . . To forbid our people to exercise their rights for fear we might be called upon to vindicate them would be a deep humiliation indeed . . . It would be a deliberate abdication of our hitherto proud position as spokesman, even amid the turmoil of war, for the law and the right.[150]

Wilson used the same language of rights fourteen months later, when he asked Congress to declare war on Germany. Insisting on the legal right for Americans to travel on belligerent ships had made it necessary to cast aside neutrality in order to uphold international law.

A World Safe for Law

After the United States entered the war, three new words appeared on the stationery of the Carnegie Endowment for International Peace. Above the black letters of the Endowment's name now stood the phrase "Peace Through Victory," printed in bright red ink.[151] Crushing Germany had become the "great peace movement."[152] The ideological framing of the war was complete. It was a war for law.

The image of law mattered more than its actual rules in such a contest. What good was academic debate in the midst of a war to save civilization and the very possibility of law? In 1918, the ASIL decided not to hold an annual meeting. "[A]t a time when the existence of International Law is at stake," the executive committee argued, "learned discussions of some of its technical rules would not be commended by the members of the Society nor meet with any sympathetic response from the interested republic."[153] Most members agreed with the decision. To hold scholarly discussions "would be the height of absurdity," argued R. Floyd Clarke.[154] More laconically, Frederic Coudert summarized the reigning attitude: "Useless to talk law while the bandits are in the house."[155]

Most legalists threw themselves wholeheartedly into the war effort. The ASIL and the Carnegie Endowment pledged their resources to the government.[156] Legal scholars volunteered to teach international law to recruits.[157] James Brown Scott joined the US Army's Judge Advocate corps and helped implement the military draft.[158] Lawyers also mobilized public opinion. *AJIL* editors vetted submissions for their effect on the war effort, while the Endowment shared its office space with chief US propagandist George Creel's Committee on Public

Information.[159] In 1918, the Endowment sent purported evidence of German responsibility for the war to "hundreds of thousands" of German sympathizers in order to "beat down the last remaining resistance of German born and German American residents to the righteousness of our national policy."[160]

For an ostensibly scientific group to conduct its work in such an instrumental way might be controversial today. But legalists seemed not to have discerned any incompatibility.[161] For men like James Brown Scott, international law had always been about more than merely defining the rules. It entailed a liberal vision for the future. If "Prussianism" represented a world-historical threat to law, as American legalists came to believe, the future of international law required its destruction. By 1917, legalism meant war.

Legal advisers do not bear ultimate responsibility for America's entry into World War I. President Wilson and his counterparts in Europe made the key decisions. But standard interpretations of international law did not offer a striking alternative. Law's structure favored status quo powers over those seeking to transform world politics. In the hands of its leading adherents, law could not be truly impartial, for it contained its own politics. Legal advisers believed that the triumph of what they viewed as an illiberal power threatened the progress of civilization. Ultimately, the vision of a world governed by law was anything but a "neutral" one. Yet if the fate of America's wartime relationship to Europe became clear by 1917, questions remained about the shape of the postwar order.

World War, Collective Security, and International Law, 1914–1941

In 1898 Americans had debated what it meant for their country to be the new-est member of the Great Power club. In 1919 the rest of the world faced the reality of American preeminence. Much of Europe lay in ruins, its cities shat-tered and fields marred, populations decimated, economies humbled. Across the Atlantic the United States emerged stronger than ever. In fact, its GDP had grown nearly 25 percent during the war.[1] It now boasted the world's largest economy and served as its largest creditor.[2] It also held the international moral high ground, having defeated Prussian militarism while seemingly remaining free of the imperialist taint of its allies France and Great Britain. This was a shift of world-historical proportions: the transfer of global leadership from the Old World to the New. As if to drive home the point, President Wilson traveled to Europe in 1919 to personally attend the Paris Peace Conference. He seemed intent on stamping his own vision on postwar European politics. Great crowds of spectators in England, France, and Italy greeted him as a hero, as British and French leaders looked on warily. Would Wilson and the United States inaugurate a new world order? And if so, would it be a legalist one?

For the generation that followed—and for many historians since—the answer to the latter question appeared to be yes.[3] The Peace Conference culmi-nated in the Treaty of Versailles, which created the League of Nations. Wilson envisioned a world order free of power politics, founded on open democracy, free trade, and self-determination. The League of Nations would ensure peace through rational debate and international cooperation, and its judgments would be made binding by the threat of collective sanctions. For lawyer and historian Mark Janis, Wilsonianism marks the triumph of an American tradi-tion of international law.[4]

Examining the situation through the eyes of American international law-yers, however, tells a different story. By the time the conference opened in

Paris, it had become clear that traditional American legalism had no place in Wilson's new diplomacy. Prominent legalists were nowhere to be found. "So many people here have expressed their surprise at your absence from the US delegation," Edwin Borchard wrote to John Bassett Moore from Paris.[5] China had appointed Moore to represent its interests at the conference, but Wilson discouraged him from attending. "The word has gone around that they do not want 'international lawyers,' as they are likely to be prejudiced in favor of the past, with all its evil associations and practices," Moore wrote to his daughter.[6] Robert Lansing had a similar experience. After the secretary of state asked James Brown Scott—without the president's knowledge—to gather legal precedents and sketch out a draft treaty, Wilson responded "with great candor and emphasis that he did not intend to have lawyers drafting the treaty of peace."[7] The president proceeded to ignore his secretary of state for the remainder of the conference.[8] It is telling that the most influential American lawyer in Paris was David Hunter Miller, a virtual unknown in international law circles before the war.[9] When Moore had inquired about Miller in 1914, a friend reported that "he has a prosperous looking office, and that he seems well-to-do" but "is evidently not well known for I have otherwise been unable to find any one who knows of him."[10]

Wilson not only distrusted lawyers; he also rejected their proposals. When he produced a draft covenant for the League, he pointedly omitted any reference to an international court, even though he had been presented with an earlier draft containing one.[11] The war had undermined the central premise of the judicialist project. It was hard to retain faith in the inevitable progress of civilization after Europe—the center of that civilization—had destroyed itself with mechanized combat characterized by "the butchery of the unknown by the unseen."[12] If a civilized public opinion was not emerging, how would an international court enforce its decisions? For Wilson and his sympathizers, the war proved the need for international institutions with the direct power to enforce their edicts.[13] For others, the war underscored the need to return to a policy of non-entanglement, maintaining a pure United States, unsullied by European wars and empires. Importantly, both sides embraced aspects of international law, though in very different ways. Their antagonism left no place for the self-enforcing law of the judicialist project. Tracing internecine debates within the legalist community highlights the interconnections among law, culture, and politics, and helps to explain two fundamentally important developments. Why, in 1919, did the United States propose a visionary project of world government, only to reject its own creation? And how, in the 1920s, could the nation continue to embrace the language of international law even as it rejected cooperation with international institutions?

Enforced Law

World War I gave rise to important new proposals for world order that paved the way for the League of Nations. In 1915, a group of prominent professionals, philanthropists, and statesmen founded the League to Enforce Peace (LEP).[14] The LEP was committed to the notion that an international court alone was insufficient to end war. To be effective, law needed to be backed by the threat of coercive enforcement. Since its program incorporated many legalist elements and its membership included prominent legalists— including Theodore Marburg, Theodore S. Woolsey, and William Howard Taft—it can be tricky to situate the group in the broader currents of international legal thought. Did it represent a continuation of or a departure from prewar legalism?[15]

The LEP's program consisted of four articles. The first called for all "justiciable questions" to be "submitted to a judicial tribunal," while the fourth proposed that "[c]onferences . . . shall be held from time to time to formulate and codify rules of international law."[16] Both prescriptions echoed the prewar judicialist call for a permanent international court and the codification of law through Hague-style conferences. Article 2 mandated that "all other questions"—those not susceptible to judicial settlement—be submitted to a "council of conciliation." The LEP had adapted this policy from one proposed by a British working group led by Britain's former ambassador to the United States, James Bryce, which had itself been inspired by William Jennings Bryan's "cooling off" treaties.[17] Only in the third article did the league diverge measurably from prewar legalism, by stating that all members "shall jointly use forthwith both their economic and military forces" against any other member that went to war without first submitting its dispute to either of the tribunals specified in the first two articles.[18] Importantly, while the LEP promised to force states to submit to adjudication, it contained no mechanism to enforce the rulings of the court or the council of conciliation. By design, the LEP stopped short of international government.

How important was article 3, the enforcement provision? At first, Taft downplayed it. The former president instead tended to emphasize the LEP's legal aspects.[19] "The League of Peace will furnish a great opportunity for more definitive formulation of the principles of international law," he stated. Neutral judges would generate "a body of judge-made laws of the highest value."[20] An enforcement mechanism was almost an afterthought. But for A. Lawrence Lowell, president of Harvard and chair of the league's executive committee, article 3 was the "kernel of the proposal," the "exact point for which the Conference had assembled."[21] The failure of international law to prevent the war proved the need for a league. Taft soon came around to this view.[22]

Lowell analogized the international arena to the American frontier. The world was a dusty town of heavily armed men quick to shoot to avenge any slight, he suggested. Here, there were no judges and no courts. The law resided instead in the sheriff. The LEP, as Lowell saw it, was the posse comitatus.[23] This image of the league as an international policeman appeared throughout the writings of its supporters.[24] It was not the League for Peace, Lowell reminded his audience, but the League to *Enforce* Peace.[25]

Despite the emphasis on enforcement, a great deal of the prewar legalist sensibility remained. The LEP implicitly relied on an optimistic vision of public opinion. It assumed that the aggressor in any conflict could be easily identified: it would be the state that refused to submit to judicial and mediating mechanisms. The league's vaunted enforcement provision did no more than compel states to put their disputes before a neutral third party. If they still wanted to go to war afterward, they were free to do so—even if a court dismissed their claim as frivolous. League backers argued that the mere act of submitting a claim and awaiting its adjudication would allow reason to triumph over the misunderstandings and irresponsible nationalism that were the real causes of war.[26] The LEP provided "the machinery by which reason can enthrone itself in the world," according to cofounder Hamilton Holt.[27]

The LEP proposals also reassured Americans that belonging to the league would neither entangle the United States in European politics nor subject US immigration policies or the Monroe Doctrine to foreign supervision.[28] As "the leader in the cause of peaceful international settlements," according to Philadelphia lawyer Thomas Raeburn White, the United States need not fear having law "enforced" upon it.[29] Thus, just as James Brown Scott sought to "domesticate" his proposed international court by comparing it to the US Supreme Court, the LEP advocates described their organization as an extension of American principles. "The United States itself is the greatest League of Peace known to history," Holt declared.[30]

As these appeals to American national pride suggest, the LEP's internationalism was narrow. It did not envision a transformation of sovereignty or any real threat to the status quo. Participants at its initial planning meeting argued against admitting any "backward countries," citing the "danger of setting up institutions among people not qualified to practice them."[31] Many LEP promoters assumed that a de facto Anglo-American alliance would predominate in any league, and some thought the league should restrict its membership to the Allies and neutral countries so as to present a unified front against the Central Powers.[32] LEP advocates' assumption that an aggressor could easily be identified stemmed from their certainty that Germany was to blame for the present conflict.[33]

The LEP succeeded in drawing a broad membership, in part by keeping its program vague.[34] Its second public meeting, held in Washington in May 1916, attracted an audience of over 2,000, including President Wilson, high-ranking politicians from both parties, and leaders of business, the church, and labor.[35] Though guests offered different prescriptions for peace (for instance, union leader Samuel Gompers thought that "an international court . . . presided over by lawyers," was less important than resolving conflicts between labor and capital), all agreed on the need for a new world organization.[36] Thanks to the LEP and other like-minded groups in Europe, by the war's end there was broad public support for some international institutional mechanism to prevent war and enforce the dictates of law and morality.[37] But agreement on the precise nature of that mechanism remained elusive.

Dissenting Legalists

Before 1915, James Brown Scott's court advocacy had seemed the vanguard of internationalism.[38] He saw no need to alter it. "I am bitterly opposed to a world state, or anything approaching it," he wrote to Dutch scholar Jan de Louter shortly after the war began.[39] The outbreak of war proved "that *something more is needed than talk*," but Scott believed that a permanent international court represented that "something more."[40] He remained optimistic. Wars often left in their wake a fertile soil for the growth of law. Had not Grotius written his masterpiece amid the wreckage of the Thirty Years War?[41] The task at hand was to convince world opinion to put an international court at the center of the postwar order. To prove the feasibility of the plan, Scott again invoked America's founding. Modern states faced the same problems as the erstwhile North American colonies after 1783, he contended.[42] What made for peace between the American states was not a coercive central government but the US Supreme Court, which "is in reality an international court."[43] Even though it lacked enforcement power, the Supreme Court had in "three score suits and more" successfully resolved conflicts between states solely through the sanction of public opinion.[44] If international society adopted this "judicial union," it too could experience domestic bliss (the Civil War did not feature prominently in Scott's analysis). "What thirteen sovereign, free, and independent States have done, forty-four sovereign, free and independent States may do," he promised.[45]

Scott's vision for postwar order clung tightly to his prewar agenda. In a 1917 article for the *Advocate of Peace*, he presented a ten-point plan containing all his familiar proposals: a continuation and elaboration of The Hague process, a council of conciliation similar to that advocated by William Jennings Bryan's peace treaties, the use of arbitration for nonjusticiable disputes, and of course, the creation of a permanent court and the education of public opinion.[46]

Scott dismissed the LEP's innovations. "The sheriff did not antedate the judge," he claimed. He is a later creation, if not an afterthought."[47] But the LEP argued that the judge was helpless without the sheriff. It thus posed a direct challenge to the judicialist project. If law was not self-enforcing, the international court became a marginal innovation rather than the centerpiece of global reform. Put on the defensive, Scott fought back. He reached for any argument that might undercut the LEP. The league was impractical. States would not accept any centralized authority over their sovereignty.[48] (By contrast, the chief appeal of a court was precisely its voluntariness). And even if states *would* accept such oversight, they *should not*. "[T]he use of force cannot safely be trusted to any nation or group of nations," he contended.[49] The so-called League to Enforce Peace was really a "League to Create War."[50]

As support for the LEP grew, Scott's arguments became increasingly desperate. The LEP rested ultimately on an *agreement* to use force, he pointed out. Why should one expect that agreement to hold? As soon as a treaty conflicted with a nation's interests, "there are diplomats and there are lawyers shrewd enough to prove to the unwary and to the layman and to the world at large that the nation is not bound by the terms of the treaty."[51] In adopting the dismissive tone of the international law skeptic, however, Scott undermined his own advocacy. If the sole purpose of the internationalist was the long-term education of public opinion, and the arrival of that enlightened public opinion lay far in the future, why waste time creating an international court in the present? Indeed, why prefer legalism to pacifist preaching in the first place?

Scott's argument turned on the assertion that the legal process itself—the act of an international court issuing rulings that established precedent—would reassure states and create trust in law.[52] "My suggestion always has been, and my suggestion still is, to start on the lowest possible plane that marks progress," he explained.[53] Such an approach had more appeal before the war when its achievement seemed both certain and proximate. Now more substantive action seemed warranted. "It is hard to be a mere passive spectator when one would like to help even a wee bit in one's short lifetime," pleaded Frederic Coudert.[54]

The imperative to act did convince many legalists. Although, according to historian David Patterson, only a "minority" of them had joined the LEP, it was not an insignificant minority.[55] Eight members of the ASIL leadership joined the league officially in 1915, and at least four more expressed support for its ideas.[56] John Hays Hammond and Theodore Marburg, past presidents of the ASJSID, also joined.

The LEP's official publication also listed John Bassett Moore as a vice president, but Moore vehemently, and with increasing annoyance, rejected the association.[57] He had attended the LEP's first public meeting but renounced any affiliation with the group when it refused to abandon the "glib" language of enforcement in article 3.[58] If Lowell depicted the LEP as a mature, pragmatic response to the Great War, Moore argued that the collective punishment of aggression was impractical. Proponents seemed to believe the ridiculous proposition that the offending nation "was to be as summarily arrested and confined as an individual who attempted an affray in the street in Boston."[59] The Napoleonic wars had shown how difficult it was even for a united force of nations to punish a motivated offender.[60] And how would the league know for sure who the "aggressor" was in any given situation? History abounded with conflicts of uncertain precipitation; America's wars with England in 1812 and Mexico in 1846 were two examples.[61] To require that nations go to war to punish an aggressor "forthwith," as the program did, would give the accused no time to mount a defense. The application of force in the absence of government was not "enforced law" at all: "Execution without trial, upon an apparent fact . . . is known in our domestic affairs as lynching," Moore protested.[62]

In analogizing the LEP not to the sheriff but the lynch mob, Moore suggested that the proposed league would enforce anarchy, not peace. Violence would only end when human nature changed, and the Great War would not be as transformative in this regard as some supposed. When the conflict ended, Moore predicted in 1916, "we shall find ourselves dealing, not with a new heaven and a new earth, but with the same terrestrial globe and the same firmament, and with problems which, because they inhere in human activities, are as old as man himself."[63] In such a world, arbitration and the law of neutrality continued to offer the best path forward. They limited wars, provided a way for nations to compromise and save face, and served as a civilizing force for cultivating amicable relations and solidarity.[64]

Thus at a crucial moment, key international lawyers fundamentally disagreed on how international law was to bring peace to the world. As adherents of competing legalist visions struggled against each other to gain the allegiance of policymakers and the public, they opened space for competing alternatives.

Struggles Intellectual and Institutional

Scott's pro-court advocacy faced increasing challenges as the LEP's vision of enforcement gained popularity. In 1916, the Lake Mohonk Conference on International Arbitration focused on the LEP's proposals instead of on refining proposals for an international court, much to Scott's consternation.[65] Scott's critics poked holes in his claims that the American experience proved the need for an international court. If anything, the travails of the Early Republic demonstrated the need for "international government."[66] LEP member Talcott Williams argued that "obedience to the law" reflected not the rise of reason but the establishment of a "central power."[67] At the ASIL's 1917 annual meeting, the young diplomat Stanley Hornbeck challenged Scott directly:

> Does Dr. Scott believe that the Supreme Court of the United States would have had that eminently successful history which it has had, had there not been organized ... an administrative and legislative body ...? ... Might I ask Dr. Scott whether he will show us in history any place or system in which law and order have been established without there being behind the law the sanction of some variety of force?[68]

Before anyone could speak, Scott's friend Charles Henry Butler interjected, and Scott, as the chairman of the session, embraced the change of subject, leaving Hornbeck's questions unanswered.

The notion of self-enforcing law also ran contrary to a growing militarist sensibility being espoused by those who argued that the European war required expanding the American military. A. Lawrence Lowell noted, in 1916, that "in the earlier days of the movement we were fighting to keep the word 'enforce' in the title; now we almost have to fight to keep the word 'peace' in."[69] Theodore Roosevelt revived his masculine-honor-based critique of unlimited adjudication: he would not submit an event like the sinking of the *Lusitania* to an international tribunal "any more than I would appeal to some outside tribunal if, when I were walking with my wife, someone slapped her face."[70] The centrality of the threat of violence inhered in a cartoon that accompanied the official LEP publication. (See Figure 7.1) It featured a helmeted man, shirtless and rippling with muscles, toting a lengthy broadsword embossed with the words "justice" and "power."[71] The contrast with the Lady Justice logo of the ASIL or the stern, yet gentle judge of the ASJSID could not have been more striking. The sense of self-restrained manliness that underlay judicialists' prewar appeals seemed out of place in an age of martial masculinity.

Nevertheless, Scott maintained considerable institutional power and used it to undermine the LEP. He still ran the *AJIL* (which remained largely silent on the LEP from 1915 to 1919), and directed the Carnegie Endowment's Division of International Law. Harnessing his resources, Scott moved to quash the LEP and promote his judicialist vision. With the support of Nicholas Murray Butler and Elihu Root, the Endowment steered such groups as the American Peace Society, New York Peace Society, and World's Court League away from the LEP, toward a judicialist position, and, after 1917 encouraged them to support the US war effort.[72] This alienated a growing wing of the internationalist movement, which both embraced international institutions and questioned America's military actions. Such critics turned to groups like the Women's Peace Party and the

LEAGUE TO ENFORCE PEACE

Figure 7.1 A cartoon commemorating the first meeting of the League to Enforce Peace. The depiction of the muscled figure, sharply hewn rocks, and sword (which combines "Power" with "Justice") lends the organization a much more aggressive air than the ASIL or ASJSID. Source: League to Enforce Peace, *Independence Hall Conference Held in the City of Philadelphia, Bunker Hill Day (June 17th), 1915, Together with the Speeches Made at a Public Banquet in the Bellevue-Stratford Hotel on the Preceding Evening* (New York: League to Enforce Peace, 1915).

American Union Against Militarism.[73] The LEP's directors, meanwhile, were furious with the Endowment. William Howard Taft wrote a friend that "Scott answers to the description of 'a snake in the grass' as well as anybody I know."[74] Theodore Marburg, reacting in 1917 to a rumor that Scott was to be commissioned to travel to Europe as a political officer, warned President Wilson that Scott was "the most formidable opponent in this country of the project of a League of Nations." Because Scott knew European diplomats and legal advisers so well, "he can and will do much harm" if sent abroad.[75]

Marburg was correct to note that Scott's access to transnational networks of international lawyers provided avenues of influence. Pan Americanism offered one such opportunity. Scott had founded the American Institute of International Law (AIIL) along with Chilean jurist Alejandro Álvarez in 1912. Both men envisioned it as a Western Hemisphere version of the Institut de droit international that would assemble experts from the United States and Latin America. Álvarez hoped it might develop so-called American international law as a check on US power, while Scott envisioned it providing a Latin American endorsement of just such power (power that Scott optimistically interpreted as leadership). Despite these conflicting missions, the AIIL met for the first time at the Second Pan American Scientific Congress in Washington in the winter of 1915–16.[76] There Scott presented the "Declaration of the Rights and Duties of Nations" to the AIIL. Although it made some concessions to Latin American sensibilities, the declaration seemed mainly to reproduce Scott's vision of global order. It was modeled directly on the US Declaration of Independence, with the rights to "life, liberty, and the pursuit of happiness" internationalized as the rights to "exist" as a state, to sovereignty over national territory, and to juridical equality. Rulings by both the British and US Supreme Courts provided evidence of the existence of these rights.[77] "[T]he law made by judges," Scott asserted, "is better and more satisfactory than the law made by legislatures."[78] Though nominally Pan-American in scope, US legal precedents took pride of place in the declaration. The few citations to Latin American jurists seem hastily added to mollify their countrymen, and Scott mentioned neither Carlos Calvo or Andres Bello in his lengthy opening address to the AIIL. More importantly, the declaration did not limit or prohibit intervention, unlike the various proposals put forward by Latin American international lawyers.[79]

Despite the declaration's US-centric approach, the AIIL's overwhelmingly Latin American membership adopted it unanimously and without discussion.[80] Scott's control over the spending power of the Carnegie Endowment may have accounted for their enthusiasm. The Endowment subsidized the travel of all the Latin American delegates to the meeting.[81] John Bassett Moore alleged that "the members of the Second Pan American Scientific Congress who voted through a previously prepared ticket for the 'American Institute of International Law' . . .

whispered it about that they felt they could do nothing else under the circumstances."[82] At the AIIL's second meeting, in 1917 in Havana, Scott convinced the delegates—by institutional pressure or otherwise—to unanimously adopt what came to be called the "Recommendations of Havana." The list of ten "recommendations" was virtually identical to the manifesto for postwar order that Scott had published in the *Advocate of Peace* earlier the same month. Focused on The Hague process and an international court, it made no mention of enforced peace.[83] A proposal to discuss in more detail proposals for postwar international organization was tabled until after the war.[84]

International lawyers and their allies undermined each other, by failing to agree on a single legalist proposal. Still, the continued influence of law is striking. Indeed, as historian Stephen Wertheim argues, the LEP's "legalist-sanctionist" view of world order, one that combined judicial machinery with a commitment to enforce the law, nearly triumphed. Had a different man been president it is likely that the US government would have promoted a legalist-sanctionist league in 1919.[85] But Woodrow Wilson occupied the White House as the war came to a close, and that made all the difference.

The Anti-Legalist League of Nations

Support for some form of international organization spanned the political spectrum, from pacifist socialists to conservative militarists. The issue in 1919 was therefore not a debate between "internationalists" and "isolationists," but a struggle to define a mutually acceptable internationalism. Because Wilson occupied the White House, his vision took center stage.[86] Wilson had first publicly voiced support for a postwar league at the LEP's 1916 meeting, but offered no specifics. Over the next two years he reaffirmed his support for the creation of "some definite concert of power," and in his famous Fourteen Points address of January 1918 he proposed a "general association of nations . . . for the purpose of affording mutual guarantees of political independence and territorial integrity."[87] The president kept the precise details of this postwar association—its organization, its reach, and its powers—vague. This was good politics. Wilson did not want to hand his opponents any specifics around which to mobilize. Not until the middle of 1918 did he develop anything approaching a concrete plan, even in private. Still, the essential outlines of his vision were clear. In place of the balance of power he advocated a general alliance of nations in which each pledged to guarantee the territorial integrity of the others. The alliance could use force to maintain this guarantee. New states would be constituted based on the self-determination of local peoples. International agreements "openly arrived at" would ensure free travel and trade, and a league council would solve problems cooperatively through deliberative discourse. By removing selfish imperialism and competition among the Great Powers, which Wilson understood as the causes of war, the world would be made safe for progressive development.[88]

Wilson's vision of world order departed not only from the "old diplomacy" of power politics but also from the mainstream of prewar internationalist thought.[89] Wilsonianism suggested a new epistemology of foreign affairs, one that required new forms of expertise. At the conferences at The Hague in 1907 and London in 1908–9, the external relationships between states constituted the object of study. Military knowledge mattered, but legal expertise was more important.[90] The State Department treasured its lawyers; and ad hoc organizations, such as the Joint Neutrality Board, had provided the sort of legal expertise required to deal with the questions of wartime neutrality. But building a "scientific peace" after World War I required new reserves of expert knowledge. Charged with redrawing the map of Europe, peace commissioners would need knowledge about the *internal* characteristics of states, especially relating to populations and geography. This required ethnographers, geographers, economists, and historians, which the State Department could not supply. It was these sorts of men who populated the Inquiry, the proto–think tank that the Wilson administration created to study the issues and prepare for the peace conference negotiations. The Inquiry retained few international lawyers (though several offered their services), but managed to become the leading source of information for American policymakers in Paris.[91] The outcome of the Paris negotiations turned ultimately on diplomatic negotiations rather than academic research, but the Inquiry's personnel illustrated the extent to which Wilsonianism devalued legal expertise.

The covenant of the League of Nations that emerged from the negotiations between Wilson, David Lloyd George of Great Britain, and Georges Clemenceau of France created an unprecedented international organization with the power and the duty to act collectively in the interest of international security. In Article X, the signatories pledged to protect each other's "territorial integrity and existing political independence" in case of "aggression." The article did not specify what measures would be taken, but most understood the pledge to rest ultimately on the threat and use of military force. The League Covenant relegated law to a minor position. True, the final version included articles on arbitration and one calling for the creation of an international court (despite Wilson's continued opposition). But these evinced little engagement with prewar legalist thought. They hardly represented an advance over the resolutions of the 1907 Hague Conference, complained French delegate Léon Bourgeois.[92] Arbitration remained voluntary, and there was no provision for codification conferences or concrete plans or a timetable for establishing the court. As Elihu Root complained, "The scheme practically abandons all effort to promote or maintain anything like a system of international law."[93]

Famously, the US Senate balked at ratifying the Treaty of Versailles, and the United States did not join the League. Legalism had played an important role in this outcome. It represented an alternative internationalism and a reservoir of arguments against Wilson's covenant, for use both by opponents acting in good faith and those seeking to fulfill partisan or personal goals. Elihu Root was a central figure throughout the ratification debate. At nearly seventy-five years of age he remained one of the nation's leading internationalists and a powerful figure in the Republican Party. The war had not dislodged his faith in law. "[T]he establishment of adequate law is the essential of every proposal for a new condition of international affairs better than the old," he had explained to Lassa Oppenheim in 1915.[94] Only a court and legal code could provide the necessary certainty of rights and duties on which states could base cooperation, he continued to argue. But Root did reconsider his prewar conviction that public opinion alone would be sufficient to enforce the law.[95] As he explained to the ASIL in December 1915, "Laws to be obeyed must have sanctions behind them; that is to say, violations of them must be followed by punishment."[96]

But despite frequent entreaties from LEP leaders, Root had refused to join the group. He provided a statement generally supporting the LEP's efforts, but did not endorse its specific proposals. [97] He found the LEP's program too schematic and restrictive. It permitted miscreant nations to commit all manner of "acts of international aggression except war" because they would not have to fear "the national right of protective war."[98] Unlike some other legalists, Root also worried about what might happen should an international court rule against the United States on a sensitive matter. He opposed allowing a court to determine which issues were "justiciable." This would remove from the nations themselves the ability to exempt certain issues from adjudication. "There are some questions each country must decide for itself," he argued to A. Lawrence Lowell. "If, for example, a court were to decide that our right to exclude Orientals is a justiciable question or that our right to maintain the Monroe Doctrine is a justiciable question, the United States would not submit to the judgment of a court. It would break forty treaties rather than submit to such a judgment, and nothing can be worse than to make a treaty that you are not going to live up to."[99] Root favored only lesser revisions to prewar legalism: a permanent international court, a council of conciliation to negotiate nonjusticiable disputes, a changed conceptualization of international law (it ought to be thought of as criminal law, he said, so that every nation would have an interest and a right to punish violations of law even where it was not the victim), and a loose commitment to punish lawbreakers, but only after a diplomatic conference.[100] This position was closer to the LEP than to Scott's judicialist approach, but Root's reluctance to throw his considerable political weight behind the former would hurt the LEP's attempts to gain unanimous support for its program.

Thus, in 1919, the Senate did not vote on the LEP platform but on whether or not to confirm ratification of the Treaty of Versailles and the League covenant. Republican Senators were divided. Some supported signing the treaty without changes. Others, the so-called "irreconcilables," such as Senator William E. Borah (R-ID), opposed the League entirely and pledged to vote against it. Finally, an important group proposed joining Wilson's league only with reservations and amendments. These "reservationists" included Henry Cabot Lodge and, eventually, Taft.[101] Hoping to forge some kind of consensus, party chairman Will Hays asked Root to issue a public statement. Root drafted a letter, dated March 29, 1919, to be published in five thousand newspapers and mailed to one million people.[102] Its text reveals the continuing power of legalism in Root's thought, yet also the limits to his internationalism.

Although Article X had become central to debate over the League, Root's letter hardly addressed the matter.[103] Instead, it focused on the lack of international law in the covenant. War resulted from two kinds of problems, Root explained. Problems of policy could be settled through diplomatic conferences, and he praised Wilson's covenant for creating a mechanism for performing such actions. But legal problems—"controversies about rights under the law of nations and under treaties"—constituted "by far" the largest number of disputes. And Wilson's plan overturned all the progress that had been made toward arbitration and adjudication, threw The Hague Conventions "upon the scrap heap," and disregarded "the judgment of three generations of the wisest and best of American statesmen." Root thus proposed, as his "first change" to the covenant, making it obligatory to submit "justiciable" disputes to an international court. He carefully defined "justiciable" questions as those related to the interpretation of treaty rights and duties, excluding "all questions of policy." Root went on to explain precisely what he had in mind: the League should have no jurisdiction over US immigration policy or the Monroe Doctrine.[104] In essence, it should not apply to the Western Hemisphere. Root had outlined a legalism founded on unilateralism and hemispheric domination.[105]

Root's criticisms helped to weaken support for the treaty, but they did not create a movement for a positive alternative. The terms of the debate had been structured by Wilson's proposal, after all. Root's failure also reflected the divisions within the legalist movement. The LEP favored joining the League.[106] Although Taft and other LEP Republicans disliked Wilson, they believed that Article X fulfilled the LEP's central goal: it provided a mechanism to bring collective forces to bear against those who threatened the peace of the world. The LEP stumped hard for the League. Its roughly 300,000 members across the country wrote letters, lobbied senators, and gave public speeches—an estimated 12,000 a day in May 1919.[107] This contributed to the popularity of the League with the American public. The Carnegie Endowment, however, remained on the sidelines.[108]

In June, Root wrote a second public letter, this one addressed to Senator Lodge. Recognizing that "you will probably be unable to do anything now" about the covenant's dismissal of international law, Root instead went on the offensive against Article X. Collective security was "not an essential or even an appropriate part of the provisions for a League of Nations," he claimed.[109] Because Root had previously embraced Article X on a temporary basis (primarily to protect central Europe against the "barbarous races" of the former Central Powers and the "Bolsheviki"), his detractors condemned the switch as the basest partisanship.[110] No doubt Root did have politics on his mind. The 1920 elections loomed; both Root and Lodge sought to deny the Democrats a victory on a key issue. But it is significant that Root's criticisms fit squarely within his pre-war judicialist outlook.[111] In reality, he had never reconciled the tension between sovereignty and collective security, nor had he fully come to terms with the limits of public opinion to enforce the law.[112] The problem with Wilson's version of a League, he claimed, was that it "rests the hope of the whole world for future peace in a government of men, and not of laws."[113]

Root may have been sincere. But others merely deployed judicialist arguments as rhetorical tools to support unilateralist agendas. Lodge did so.[114] So did David Jayne Hill, who, as assistant secretary of state in 1899, had been vital in putting the international court on The Hague agenda in the first place.[115] Although Hill maintained his support for the court, he became an inveterate opponent of the League of Nations. He couched his complaints in judicialist terms but flung so many arguments at the League and at Wilson that it becomes difficult to separate his support for judicialism from his intense opposition to the Democratic Party and what he saw as creeping socialism in the United States. For Hill, mobilizing legal arguments against the League of Nations facilitated an easy pivot to invoking the Constitution to argue against social-democratic reforms. Root, too, seemed animated by the need to preserve US separation and freedom of action. He feared that the "irresponsible majority" of the League "would protect Mexico in permitting our citizens to be killed in her territory" and "would protect Germany in establishing a naval base in the Caribbean commanding the Panama Canal."[116] And he worried that entanglement in European affairs would spark "dissension and hatred among our own inhabitants of foreign origin."[117] In this context, the primary value of the international court seemed to be that it was not the League. Rather than offering a utopian hope for a future world at peace, proposing an international court became valuable as a political tactic, a way to demonstrate that one was not an isolationist while still resisting a more thorough internationalist program.

When the treaty finally came to a vote in November, the Senate remained fatally split. Most non-irreconcilable Republicans (backed, by this time, by the leaders of the LEP) voted to ratify the treaty with reservations; whereas most

Democrats would support only Wilson's version of the covenant. When the two sides tried to reach a compromise in March 1920, a few more Democrats voted with reservationist republicans, but a revised treaty fell seven votes short of confirming ratification.[118] Competing internationalisms had helped set back internationalism itself.

The "New" International Law and the Eclipse of Judicialist Legalism

Amid the rise and stumbles of Wilsonian internationalism, James Brown Scott continued to mobilize his resources to push his judicialist agenda. During the war, he began devising plans to enlist the Institut de droit international in his efforts.[119] The war had dealt the Institut a grievous blow. Not only did the group cease operations but its membership splintered along national lines.[120] Erstwhile colleagues penned bitter denunciations of their enemies. "You can have no idea whatever of the extent to which even scientific circles are permeated with hatred," lamented Hans Wehberg. The German members, he noted, vowed to "never again sit around the same table with French and English scholars."[121] When the Institut finally gathered again, for an extraordinary session in Paris, in 1919, it excluded Germans and Austrians and issued a statement condemning "the premeditated violation" of Belgian neutrality.[122] Three Germans resigned in protest.[123] The remaining members eventually patched up their hurt feelings, but the Institut itself had sustained a gaping wound: between its last prewar meeting in 1913 and first full postwar session in 1921, forty-five members died—more than a third of its membership.[124]

Scott offered American support. He wanted the Institut to convene in Washington—a city "far away from the war, materially as well as spiritually"— in conjunction with American law societies.[125] "Through such association," he mused at an ASIL executive council meeting in 1918, "a very wide, broad world movement could be inaugurated."[126] Elihu Root cut Scott's daydreaming short—"So far as we can see into the future now, any such meeting would have to be provided with machine guns" so "the thing to address ourselves to now is the killing of more Germans"—but Scott, undeterred, revived the issue at the Institut's 1919 planning session in Paris.[127] He presented Washington to his European colleagues as "*serein et calme*," untouched by the "*devastations de la guerre*." America promised a new beginning to a damaged Europe.[128] Edouard Rolin-Jaequemyns—whose father had founded the Institut some forty-five years before—sensed this point of transition as well: Washington's time had arrived.[129] The assembled members accepted Scott's invitation and chose Elihu Root as president of the Institut for the coming year.[130]

In addition to American hospitality, Scott offered American ideas as a basis for postwar renewal. He convinced delegates at the Institut's 1919 *session extraordinaire* to agree to study the Declaration of Rights and Duties of Nations, and to place it on the agenda for an adoption vote at the next full meeting.[131] In effect this would put the Institut on record as endorsing Scott's agenda for international law. He then lobbied Albert de Lapradelle, whom the Institut had chosen to prepare a report on the topic. The planned Washington meeting offered a chance to adopt "a common platform," and it was vital that the Institut give its support to the declaration, Scott argued.[132] A few critics griped about Scott's attempt to determine the Institut's direction. Edwin Borchard complained to John Bassett Moore that the sole purpose of the Paris meeting "was doubtless to put the Institute's stamp of approval upon the 'Declaration of the Rights of Nations.' "[133] Borchard mournfully concluded, "The whole account makes it look as if the Institute had now become an appendage of the Carnegie Endowment under the baton of J. B. Scott."[134]

Scott's plans did not bear fruit, however. When the Institut finally held its full postwar meeting in 1921 (despite the earlier agreement to come to Washington in 1920, the cost, in time and money, of rebuilding after the war meant that no meeting was held that year), it declined to endorse Scott's declaration.[135] Lapradelle deemed it "tinged with too much *regionalism*," and Boris Noldé of Russia dismissed it, noting that it was based on US jurisprudence.[136] Even Alejandro Álvarez, Scott's AIIL cofounder, and thus presumably a supporter of the declaration, refused to defend it.[137] Andre Mandelstam attacked the declaration's federalist basis. Rather than create a declaration for *states*, the lawyers ought to develop one for *individuals*.[138] Ultimately, the Institut followed Mandelstam's path and endorsed an international Declaration of the Rights of Man.[139] The world wanted not a declaration of independence but a plan for *inter*dependence.

This sensibility reflected the emergence of a new approach to international law after World War I. Sometimes described as "modern" or "modernist" international law, as opposed to the "classical" nineteenth-century variety, this new international law emphasized communal solidarity over nationalist sovereignty.[140] Law should not merely be a set of precedents regulating the behavior of atomistic states, but should animate the constitution of a connected global community, crowned by meaningful multilateral institutions. Nicolas Politis, a Greek lawyer who had taught in Paris from 1910 to 1914 before becoming Greece's foreign minister in 1918, summed up the "New Aspects of International Law" for an American audience in 1928. International jurists were beginning to put international law in step with modern life, he explained. This meant "the definitive abnegation of the dogma of sovereignty" and the recognition that states derived their rights from their membership in an international community. The quest for international "solidarity" should shape the path of international law. And since states were merely "collective fictions," individuals must become the proper subjects of international law, able to call on it for protection even as they would face criminal sanctions for violating it.[141] The influence of this sensibility reached widely: Germans Hans Wehberg, Walter Schücking, and Ottfried Nippold, along with the Chilean Álvarez, came to support the League of Nations and collective enforcement of the law.[142] French lawyers, including Leon Duguit and George Scelle, developed a "solidarist" model that placed international law above the state and based its legitimacy on sociological facts rather than state consent.[143] Meanwhile, lawyers across Britain and the Continent began working together in the new League and other multilateral institutions, forming a new transnational and autonomous international legal profession.[144]

In the United States, disillusion with the limitations of prewar international law combined with Wilson's influence and the changes happening in domestic legal thought to produce a new generation of international lawyers. Self-styled reformers, led by Charles Fenwick, Manley Hudson, and Quincy Wright, captured the mainstream of the profession. They advocated joining the League of Nations and called for new approaches to studying and developing the law.[145] The world could not depend on court precedents, for, as Fenwick noted, "[t]he process of extending international law by judicial decision is very slow."[146] International lawyers must incorporate sociological and philosophical insights, just as domestic American lawyers did, in order to adapt the law to modern conditions.[147] Nor should international lawyers concentrate solely on "law" at the expense of "policy," for the line between the two was so thin as to be invisible. Some traditionalists protested. "This is the American Society of International *Law*!" complained Philip Marshall Brown in 1933.[148] But Brown was swimming against the tide. In fields as diverse as history, art, and theoretical physics, practitioners were undermining old verities and advocating more flexible approaches.[149] Advocates of the "new" international law followed suit. In 1925 the ASIL sponsored a second Conference of Teachers of International Law. Whereas the first, in 1914, had promoted the case method, eleven years later, Manley Hudson expressed the dominant sentiment when he called on lawyers to incorporate "international social science."[150] To meet the needs of a global society, new multidisciplinary studies—for example, Quincy Wright's magnum opus, *A Study of War*—were incorporating insights from law, social science, morality, and politics.[151] Disciplinary pluralism did not fatally split the profession. Scott, Borchard, and George Grafton Wilson all worked with Hudson on the latter's projects to codify international law.[152] But by the mid-1920s, advocates of the judicialist approach no longer set the profession's agenda.

Even James Brown Scott abandoned his attachment to judicialist legalism. Gradually ceding his leadership of the ASIL, in the 1930s Scott embraced a re-sacralized natural law. "Law and morality shall be one and inseparable," he argued in 1934, and he found his guide to morality in the sixteenth-century writings of the Spanish scholastic philosophers.[153] In such works as *The Spanish Origins of International Law* (1934) and *The Catholic Conception of International Law* (1934), Scott argued that Francisco de Vitoria was the real father of international law.[154] Only by returning to the Spaniard's writings could the "intercourse of nations" be made "both moral and Christian."[155] While Scott's praise of Vitoria proved popular in Franco's Spain and parts of Latin America, he ultimately failed to convince the mainstream of international legal scholarship.[156]

Mirages of Interwar Legalism

The eclipse of the judicialist project did not mean the disappearance of international law from American foreign relations. The foreign policy establishment merged the technocrats of the Inquiry with the prewar cadre of conservative bankers and lawyers.[157] The Republican presidential administrations of the 1920s reasserted the prominence of Eastern conservatives.[158] Henry Stimson followed in the footsteps of his mentor, Elihu Root, as a leading lawyer-policy-maker and "wise man," while Charles Evans Hughes carried on Root's legacy by simultaneously serving as secretary of state and president of the ASIL.[159] In 1932, the State Department's new Office of the Legal Advisor (which the previous year had replaced the position of solicitor) had twenty-three attorneys on staff.[160] But if lawyers remained prominent, the fate of legalism as a project for global order was more complicated. The loss of faith in "civilization" as a connective transatlantic phenomenon helped to ensure that the United States would never join the League of Nations, and also to turn its seeming support for other international legal initiatives into a mirage.

In 1921, a permanent international court finally came into being. However, the Permanent Court of International Justice (PCIJ) did not end up fulfilling the judicialist dream. The PCIJ's American supporters did initially portray it as a logical outgrowth of the efforts of James Brown Scott and his allies. They often called it the "Root court," since Elihu Root had played an important role on the Advisory Committee of Jurists (ACJ), the body tasked by the League of Nations with drafting a blueprint for the court.[161] There were important continuities with the prewar legalist project. The ACJ's members were determined to design "a true court of justice."[162] Its proposed court was permanent; relied on judges "of high moral character" chosen according to their expertise and reputation; featured obligatory jurisdiction; and produced rulings based on treaties, customary law, judicial precedents, and "[t]he general principles of law recognized by civilized nations."[163] It solved the riddle of judicial selection that had stymied efforts at The Hague in 1907 by arranging for joint election by both the League of Nations Assembly (where all states had one vote) and the League Council (where the great powers had permanent seats), thereby balancing between the equal rights of nations and the political interests of great powers.[164]

But, though the PCIJ in many ways resembled the ideal court that men like James Brown Scott had proposed before the war, it was not a purely independent legal body. Rather, as historian Michael Dunne argues, it formed a node in the League's broader system of collective security. As League Council chair Léon Bourgeois explained, "[W]hat would be the reality of a sentence of justice, if it did not find in a strong organisation of international institutions . . . the executor of these decisions?"[165] Advocates of the "new" international law in the United States celebrated this connection.[166] But conservative legalists, including Chandler P. Anderson, David Jayne Hill, and Philander Knox, attacked the court as too innovative, too political, and too closely connected to collective security.[167] Moreover, the League had amended the ACJ's draft proposal, in the process significantly trimming the new court's judicialist features. Scott—who had accompanied Root to the ACJ as a technical delegate—complained that the League had "mutilated" the ACJ draft.[168] He gave verbal support to joining the PCIJ, but he refused to authorize the spending of Carnegie Endowment funds in its defense. More damagingly, he supported calls for a third Hague Conference and for the creation of a new independent, alternative international court.[169] Indeed, Scott helped President Warren G. Harding and Senator Henry Cabot Lodge craft speeches and resolutions rejecting the PCIJ in favor of this vague alternative—which, since it had no possibility of being enacted, amounted in practice to no court at all.[170]

Scott's tepid reaction to the PCIJ is revealing, for it illuminates how changing notions of American identity made embracing international law—but not the League—a way to ensure American political non-entanglement. After all, the same developments that produced an expanded internationalism in lawyers like Manley Hudson enhanced nationalistic feelings in others. Mobilization for war at home had generated a commitment to "100 percent Americanism" and a fear of outsiders. German-Americans and war resisters were targets of prejudice and occasional violence.[171] The popularity of the Ku Klux Klan peaked in 1924, which was also the year Congress drastically restricted immigration.[172] Surveys of public and editorial opinion consistently found majority support for joining the League and other multilateral institutions; however, opponents in the Senate managed to leverage the minority's strongly held views against adherence.[173]

Opposing the new international law created strange bedfellows. Conservatives associated "internationalism" with the rise of Bolshevism. "Internationalism would destroy us at home," Philander Knox argued. "Nationalism will save us at home. If there is anything through which we can do good to the world it is our

Americanism."[174] These conservative opponents of the League forged an awkward alliance with Midwestern progressives like Senator William Borah. Borah opposed closer cooperation with Europe, not for fear of the spread of socialism, but because of his opposition to imperialism. The League was a servant of the imperial status quo, in his eyes. For the United States to get involved would mean being conscripted into the nefarious plotting of the European powers.[175]

The notion of international civilization held little appeal for these groups. The United States, in their estimation, was not one among a larger group of "civilized" powers, but a pure exception in a world of fallen states and fallen men. The carnage of the European war seemed to support this interpretation. The notion of a singular, unidirectional civilization came under attack from many angles. Oswald Spengler famously predicted the "Decline of the West," while others suggested that the world was made up of multiple civilizations rather than a singular one.[176] Colonial peoples seeking recognition from the League of Nations did not claim to have satisfied the Western "standard of civilization"; rather, they held up their own, separate civilizations as being equally valid while simultaneously arguing that the barbarity of colonialism undermined Europe's claims on "civilization" in the first place.[177]

Meanwhile, anti-imperialist attitudes took greater hold in the United States, especially among Progressives. In 1926, the Women's International League for Peace and Freedom dispatched a delegation to investigate the US occupation of Haiti, and the US press became more skeptical of Caribbean occupations.[178] Progressives called for a reinterpretation of international law along lines similar to what Carlos Calvo had advocated. Senator Borah suggested that Americans who invested overseas would have to abandon any hope for military intervention on their behalf.[179] Even the scientific basis of "race" was challenged, as the multiculturalist arguments of such anthropologists as Franz Boas began to spread—albeit slowly—through academic and, eventually, broader learned circles.[180] The idea of engaging in a shared civilizing mission rested on increasingly brittle foundations.

In this atmosphere, those who invoked international law often did so in order to evade, not embrace, closer international ties. For instance, as President Harding gradually withdrew his support for the League of Nations, he called for the creation of an "association of nations" linked through a court and international law.[181] Harding never gave a detailed accounting of this association, leading some to wonder whether his proposal was serious or merely political theater. Yet, even if it was the latter, this still suggests the enduring currency of law in American politics and society. Appealing to international law nodded to international cooperation while insulating against more serious commitments. This helps to explain the puzzling fact that men like Borah—a vehement opponent of the League often derided as an isolationist—offered frequent rhetorical support for international law. The law these men supported was not grounded in an assumption of shared civilization.[182] Before the war, James Brown Scott could successfully imply a coincidence between American values and international law. But if the League was going to shape and apply international law—as the "new" international law implied—this assumption was more difficult to sustain.

The PCIJ fell victim to this set of circumstances. In the Senate, opponents complained that joining the court opened a "backdoor to the League." By invoking "advisory jurisdiction," they warned, the League could force the PCIJ to rule on issues that the United States was not prepared to submit to outside oversight, such as the Monroe Doctrine or immigration.[183] Especially to the Midwestern progressives, who were the PCIJ's harshest critics, the League represented a legacy of foreign imperialism that threatened to pollute an innocent United States. Senator Henrik Shipstead (R/FL-MN) alleged that the court's purpose was "to decide that loot acquired as a result of the last war has been legally acquired" while Senator George Norris (R-NE) feared submitting disputes to a court made up of "men who have grown up under a different civilization."[184] James Reed (D-MO) charged that judges were "aliens in tongue, and in every instance aliens in allegiance."[185] Squaring this outlook with an engaged international law was difficult indeed. Surveys of public opinion as a whole consistently showed support for joining the court. But proponents could never achieve enough political momentum to overcome hardline opponents.[186] The gap between those who envisioned international law as part of an apparatus through which the international community enforced proper behavior and those who saw in it a refuge from international jurisdiction was too large. Pro-PCIJ forces could never convince unilateralists like Borah that the United States could join the PCIJ without subjecting itself to broader League supervision.[187]

The only initiatives that could satisfy both supporters of the new international law and those favoring a constricted, quasi-isolationist version were those that guaranteed very little. The Kellogg-Briand Pact is the clearest example. Passed by the Senate 85–1 in 1928 and eventually endorsed by sixty-four nations, the signers of the pact renounced war "as an instrument of national policy," and pledged to settle all disputes by "pacific means."[188] The pact emerged from the "Outlawry of War" movement proposed by Chicago lawyer Salmon Levinson. Levinson's initial plan, formulated during WWI and submitted to the Senate in 1919, declared war a "public crime" and called for the creation of an international court and the codification of international law. "It seeks to apply the tried and effective methods of civilization"—that is, law—"to international relations," he wrote.[189] Though many legalists doubted the efficacy of merely declaring war illegal, the plan's emphasis on a court and codification were broadly consistent with prewar legalist notions.

Yet the reason the movement grew in popularity was not its legalism but the fact that it presented an alternative to Wilson's League of Nations that both liberal internationalists and unilateralists could embrace. It drew "the strangest conglomeration of bed-fellows I have ever known," Levinson recalled.[190] These included the conservative legalist Philander Knox and the liberal philosopher John Dewey; the latter supported outlawry as a means of concentrating public opinion on the problem of war.[191] Liberal international groups, such as the Women's Peace Union and the Women's International League for Peace and Freedom, offered enthusiastic support.[192] Irreconcilable senator William Borah was outlawry's leading proponent for most of the 1920s, although, much to Levinson's frustration, Borah's active promotion of the cause tended to occur only when the country seemed dangerously close to joining the PCIJ, or when doing so promoted his political aspirations.[193]

The outlawry movement made little political headway until James Shotwell, a Columbia University professor and director of the Carnegie Endowment's Division of Economics and History, convinced French foreign minister Aristide Briand to call for a bilateral agreement to ban war in 1927. Briand wanted a security pact to ensure America's military cooperation against the renewal of German militarism. Shotwell—a strong League supporter—sought to bring the United States into closer cooperation with Europe. The US secretary of state, Frank Kellogg, and president, Calvin Coolidge, spurned Briand's initial proposal but were forced to act when the public expressed overwhelming support for the pact (Kellogg alone received some 50,000 letters).[194] By substituting a vague multilateral initiative for Briand's proposed bilateral security pact, the new pact received overwhelming support in large part because it did very little. "Conservatives favored its standpat substance, progressives hungered for its millennialist promise, and all appreciated its unflinching nationalism," explains historian Charles DeBenedetti.[195] By taking the leading position in creating the pact, the United States had reinforced its self-image as a leading promoter of peace, even as it avoided any obligations and created no actual machinery for peace. Shotwell and other internationalist proponents of the pact hoped it would be the starting point for closer cooperation in world politics, but it remained little more than a "sort of international kiss," in the dismissive words of Senator James Reed.[196]

Signing the Kellogg-Briand Pact did not signal a newfound openness to multilateral engagement. In the 1930s, the rise of Nazi Germany, the Italian invasion of Ethiopia, and the Spanish civil war generated renewed debate over American neutrality. How should the nation respond to foreign wars? Should it decide who bore responsibility and then punish the aggressor by cutting off all intercourse? Advocates of the new international law favored this approach. The notion of collective security, after all, left no room for neutrality: all nations had a responsibility to take sides against an aggressor.[197] Of course, the United States was not a member of the League, but as a signatory of the Kellogg-Briand Pact, it seemed to embrace such a responsibility to take sides.[198] Indeed, in 1932, secretary of state Henry Stimson cited the pact when he announced that the United States would no longer recognize any territorial gains taken by armed force.[199] Two years later, the International Law Association endorsed what had come to be called the Stimson Doctrine.[200] If war was illegal, traditional neutrality seemed impossible.[201] "I had thought that the idea of neutrality was pretty well dead," said Charles Fenwick in 1933.[202]

But defenders of traditional neutrality refused to give up. John Bassett Moore led the charge, assisted by Edwin Borchard.[203] They trumpeted the continuing relevance of traditional approaches. There would always be war, Moore suggested, for "the human propensity to get excited and to like excitement" was inherent to the species.[204] By sticking to well-established rules of law and encouraging a judicial habit of mind, these conflicts could be limited in number and severity. "I think it much safer for mankind, if these diseases do break out," Borchard explained, "to confine their ravages as narrowly as possible."[205]

Congress chose neither collective security nor traditional neutrality. Instead, it renounced traditional neutral rights in an attempt to turn the Atlantic Ocean into a defensive moat. For those who supported this position, World War I demonstrated the folly of neutrality in the modern world of submarines and mass industrial production. Should the United States sell arms to belligerents, it would necessarily end up supporting one side and thereby antagonizing the other. The solution, then, was not to stick up for neutral rights but to preemptively prevent engagement. Thus the Neutrality Act of 1935 prohibited loans or the sale of "arms, ammunition or implements of war" to both sides in any war.[206] The country remained divided, but those who saw in domestic law a means of maintaining America's insulation from the world's problems had the upper hand.[207]

The outbreak of World War II in Europe altered this calculus. With Nazi Germany overrunning Paris and threatening London, president Franklin D. Roosevelt argued for revising the neutrality statutes. The United States must become the "arsenal of democracy" in order to defend freedom. Humanitarian concerns recommended it. National security considerations demanded it. The Japanese attack on Pearl Harbor in December 1941 crystallized these opinions.[208] International law had neither prevented the outbreak of war nor insulated the United States from it. Shapers of the next world order would not forget this.

World War I undermined the assumptions that had made the legalist project seem desirable and achievable. No longer able to envision the inevitable progress of civilization, the vanguard of internationalism pressed for formal mechanisms of law enforcement, from the LEP's alliance of states to Wilson's League of Nations. These commitments frightened others, for whom the lesson of the war was the need to insulate an exceptionalist America from the militaristic and imperialist Europeans. Though James Brown Scott marshaled the resources of the CEIP during the war, the internationalist split made a revival of the prewar legalist project impossible. One could no longer plausibly assert that international law would civilize the world without imposing any real costs on the United States. Recognizing that advancing international law would require commitment to suprasovereign institutions, the nation split between those eager to embrace such a commitment and those unwilling to do so. It is a testament to the influence of law in American society that each side continued to invoke the language of law. Combined with the continuing need for legal expertise in the administration of foreign policy, this ensured that international law would remain a part of global politics even in the dawning age of American superpower.

Conclusion

In the chaotic aftermath of the Al-Qaeda attacks of September 11, 2001, President George W. Bush had war on his mind. When secretary of defense Donald Rumsfeld cautioned that international law permitted war for self-defense but not for retribution, Bush reportedly replied: "I don't care what the international lawyers say, we are going to kick some ass."[1] Over the next few years, the Bush administration operationalized this sentiment. The United States went to war in Afghanistan. It detained and sometimes tortured hundreds of alleged militants at the American military base at Guantánamo Bay, Cuba, and various "black sites" around the world.[2] In 2003 Washington launched a war against Iraq that in the eyes of most non-American observers violated international law.[3]

Administration officials dismissed international law as undemocratic, Europhilic, outdated, and anti-American. Attorney General Alberto Gonzales asserted that the new conditions of war rendered key portions of the Geneva Conventions "obsolete" and "quaint."[4] Other administration lawyers contended that practices such as waterboarding did not constitute torture.[5] John Bolton, who served as US ambassador to the United Nations between 2005 and 2006, denied that international law was law at all. To claim that it represented anything beyond "a series of political and moral arrangements" was "simply theology and superstition masquerading as law."[6] Along with other lawyers who moved between academia, private practice, and government, Bolton developed intellectual and legal arguments for why the United States should ignore international law whenever it was convenient. Dubbed the "New Sovereigntists" by legal scholar Peter Spiro, these lawyers maintained that international law had no real "legal" content and that therefore states had no obligation to obey international laws that did not advance their immediate interests.[7]

These arguments formed part of a larger defense of the exercise of American power unbound by international rules. For the first time since Theodore Roosevelt and his allies justified the annexation of the Philippines, some American officials argued that the United States was in fact an empire and that this constituted cause for celebration. "We're an empire now, and when we act, we create our own reality," a senior adviser to the president bragged.[8] By forthrightly embracing its imperial identity, some commenters promised, the nation would bestow a Pax Americana on the world.[9]

If in 1900 the architects of empire had asserted that becoming a Great Power meant embracing international law, a century later it appeared that the resurgence of empire might destroy law altogether. Some international lawyers responded by finding ways to reconcile international law with the exercise of American power. There would be no need to violate the law if the law permitted most of what the nation wanted to do anyway.[10] Others condemned the Bush administration's actions by appealing to history. Torture and illegal war were un-American and ran counter to the country's traditions, these critics argued. America's past support for arbitration and international courts revealed the existence of a tradition of compliance and demonstrated the possibility of reviving it.[11] Because of how this debate has been framed, it has become conventional to think about exceptionalism and empire, on one hand, and compliance with international law, on the other, as mutually exclusive. More international law means less empire; more exceptionalism means less international law.[12]

Legalist Empire has contended that history does not support such a binary interpretation. The first two decades of the twentieth century simultaneously represented a legalist age and an imperial one, and this was no coincidence. Law did much to make empire possible. Leading imperial officials were often also leading proponents of international law. Lawyers provided policymakers with arguments to justify the annexation of the Philippines and US control over Panama. When formal empire lost its luster, they advocated the spread of international legal institutions as a means of enforcing a basic standard of treatment for American overseas capital.

Legal discourse and appeals to professional expertise could never fully silence the critics of American foreign policy. But arguments based in law always possessed a built-in legitimacy, especially in the United States, and lawyers' technical skill in facilitating diplomacy and relationships between capital and the state ensured that they remained essential to policymakers. Institutionally and ideologically, lawyers helped the United States project power overseas.

These observations have important implications for understanding the function of law, the legal profession, and the role of the United States in the world. Legal philosophy and legal doctrine did matter, insofar as they shaped the approaches of international lawyers and bounded the kinds of arguments that could be made about international law. Yet categories of legal "formalism" and "realism" are too austere to capture the political and cultural meanings that infused international legal thought and the legalist agenda in this period. The internalizing of the concept of "civilization," the way that legalists instinctively felt its truth, the way it appeared as inevitable as it was desirable: these were essential to the legalist mindset. The assumption that states could civilize themselves—through the proper education of public opinion by international law professionals—underwrote the judicialist sensibility. International law did not need a direct enforcement mechanism because states would come to police themselves once they understood their true interests.

In turn, this notion of civilization made sense to professional international lawyers because of how it intersected with their own self- and professional identities. International lawyers presented themselves as embodying notions of responsible manhood and enlightened yet pragmatic statesmanship. Both the agenda of the international law profession and its appeal to policymakers make sense only in light of the fact that elite networks shared these values and were therefore predisposed to extend their political and financial support to legalism. The notion of civilization that underlay the advocacy of empire also infused the creation and plausibility of the international law profession.

Thus, to understand the working of international law it is necessary to understand the mental worlds and professional networks of the foreign policy establishment. By taking careful notice of individual actors and institutions within the state, explaining the cultural, intellectual, and power contexts that make certain groups more amenable to international law than others, and exploring why such groups predominate at particular moments, we gain insight into the role of law in the shaping of foreign policy.[13]

Linking international law and empire also undermines the apparent dichotomies between exceptionalism and international law, and between idealism and power. Exceptionalism did not make legalism impossible in the early twentieth century. If anything, it encouraged the promotion of international law. An international court would not threaten American power, legalists argued, because it was in essence the expression of American values abroad. Hence the nonstop comparisons between an international court and the US Supreme Court. And, the argument went, the United States had little to fear from international institutions because the United States was a uniquely law-abiding nation.

This was an optimistic prediction, one that did not come true. But, though tempting, it would be wrong to dismiss early twentieth-century legalists as hopeless idealists. Their visions of world order relied on sunny forecasts of human and state behavior, but these were formulated to be compatible with the extension of American power. Indeed, creating a world of law *was* the projection of power.

From San Francisco to Baghdad

How, then, has the United States come to offer such a prominent challenge to international law in the early twenty-first century? Does this represent the culmination of inherent tendencies or the abandonment of a tradition of legalism? *Legalist Empire* suggests both deep continuities and important divergences. It shows that neither an exceptionalist DNA nor the nation's relative power is sufficient to explain attitudes toward international law. Rather, it suggests, Washington embraces international law when its policymaking elite believes that doing so is consistent with national interests and compatible with national values. Since "interests" and "values" are neither static nor objective, it is vital to understand how social, cultural, and political conditions shape them.

In San Francisco, in 1945, Americans presided over the creation of the United Nations. Along with the International Court of Justice, the World Bank, and the International Monetary Fund, the UN formed the nucleus of an expanded international order. As it had done after the War of 1898, a victorious United States suggested that power and law could coexist. Although the America of 1900 was one power among many, by 1945 it had become far and away the world's superpower.[14] Although one could still find paeans to "civilization" in the postwar years, World War II had crippled faith in its natural and inevitable triumph. American policymers were convinced that the proper functioning of international law required that institutions explicitly reserve a place for the direct exercise of American power. The UN thus represented not the rebirth of judicialist legalism or even the continuation of Wilsonian internationalism but, rather, as a British diplomat noted at the time, "an Alliance of the Great Powers embedded in a universal organization."[15] The UN Security Council gave special rights to the Great Powers, and granted them the authority to use force, not only against misbehaving members of the organization, but also against any country in the world that threatened "international peace and security."[16] Even the Nuremberg war crimes trials, which convicted Nazi leaders of crimes against humanity and aggression and thereby suggested that an international criminal law could help to maintain world order, counseled punishment as the protector of civilization.[17] Although some hoped that the UN might become a champion of human rights by enforcing laws designed to protect individuals from despotic states, by the 1950s the emergence of the Cold War had obscured international law's claims of universal reason.[18]

Over the next three decades, two trends eroded the popularity of international law among US policymakers. First, decolonization swelled the ranks of the United Nations in the 1950s and 1960s as new states emerged from the collapse of empire in Asia and Africa. These states increasingly challenged US international priorities. For instance, they called for a New International Economic Order to rebalance the global economy, and they demanded economic sanctions against apartheid in South Africa, an American Cold War ally.[19] Early twentieth-century legalists had conceptualized the "international" as the realm of "civilization" and believed that the United States shared fundamental values with this civilized world. One could trust the international because it looked like oneself—white and Christian. Decolonization changed this calculus. As "the international" took on a darker hue, American elites were less likely to imagine it as the natural extension of the American essence.

Shifts in the makeup of global society magnified longstanding concerns that international institutions might challenge domestic racial segregation or grant enhanced economic or social rights.[20] In 1949, the president of the American Bar Association, a Utah conservative named Frank Holman, called on the West and South to join forces against the East to "save us from becoming a completely Socialized State at home and a puppet state in a world-wide hegemony."[21] This fear motivated the near-adoption of the so-called Bricker amendment, which would have obliterated the *Paquete Habana* judgment (the Supreme Court's ruling that international law was "part of our law") by changing the Constitution so that treaties would apply only if Congress explicitly adopted them. Subsequent reservations to human rights treaties have accomplished nearly the same thing.[22]

Second, changes in the foreign policy establishment diminished cooperation with international institutions. The Atlanticist elite led by such men as Elihu Root survived both world wars but became a casualty of the Cold War.[23] Between 1900 and 1970, this group could be relied on to support international law in theory if not always in practice. And who could be more "American" than these high-minded and well-connected public servants? But during the anti-communist Red Scare, these men came under attack precisely for their transnational connections. In the eyes of Senator Joseph McCarthy and his allies, international lawyer-diplomats, such as Dean Acheson, were fundamentally un-American: East Coast striped-pants elitists, parlor pinks, and unwitting if not active members of a global communist conspiracy.[24] To be an internationalist was to be an ally of un-American forces. A case in point is Philip C. Jessup, a protégé (and the biographer) of Elihu Root, a professor of international law at Columbia, and an ambassador-at-large in the Truman administration. In 1950, these credentials made Jessup an inviting target for McCarthy. Though both State Department and congressional committees cleared Jessup of McCarthy's charge of "an unusual affinity for communist causes," the message was clear: the sort of people who populated the establishment, who were comfortable with international law, were of suspect loyalty. By the time the Atlantic establishment finally broke down under simultaneous attacks from the left and the right in the wake of the Vietnam War, there was no longer a strong conservative voice for international law, excepting business lobbies concerned with particular trade regimes. This helps to explain the present-day portrayals of nationalism and internationalism as incompatible opposites.[25]

The conditions that had once made legalism a viable political project have been further eroded in the United States over the last four decades. "Civilization" has lived on, but as a contested and vulnerable concept that requires defending by a strong United States, acting unilaterally if necessary. The United States intervenes to defend civilization from barbarism or savagery, rather than to promote its development.[26] The result has been a series of high-profile rejections of international law and international legal institutions. In the 1980s, facing an adverse judgment from the World Court over America's support for antigovernment guerrillas in Nicaragua, the Reagan administration withdrew its acceptance of the court's jurisdiction. The United States also refused to join the International Criminal Court in 1998 and has often been one of only a handful of states unwilling to ratify international treaties, such as the Convention on the Rights of the Child or the Convention on the Elimination of All Forms of Discrimination against Women. The open contempt for international law expressed by some in the George W. Bush administration was more extreme than the previous criticism, but it represented a difference of degree more than a dramatic break with the past.[27]

A Future for Legalism and Legalists?

The second half of the twentieth century thus witnessed a disenchantment with international law and an increasing repudiation of it by the United States. Among foreign policy intellectuals and academics, the discipline of international relations—with an emphasis on power and contestation—supplanted international law as the dominant mode of interpreting world politics. Lawyers who imagined law as emancipation from the reality of power politics became outsider critics, and American officials viewed plans for world order with increasing skepticism.[28]

Yet international lawyers did not vanish; in fact, they multiplied. Recent counts turn up more than 170 attorney-advisers in the Department of State Office of the Legal Adviser, and an astounding ten thousand lawyers in the Department of Defense.[29] The number of legal instruments that regulate global affairs has grown, and the United States continues to be an enthusiastic promoter of international economic institutions.[30] Even purportedly "lawless" places, such as the prison at Guantánamo, as legal scholar David Kennedy points out, are in fact highly regulated; "it is simply that different rules apply and different rules do not apply."[31] The need to navigate such rules has made government lawyers more necessary than ever.

Thus, even as its ability to inspire dreamers has waned, international law's centrality to foreign policy has persisted. Even the most unilateralist officials frequently find it necessary to defend their actions in legal terms—no matter how contorted such legal reasoning might become as a result. The second George

W. Bush administration attempted to ground the use of force more firmly in legal interpretation, an approach that his successor, Barack Obama, has followed.[32] The combination of the importance of law to American governance, the continued ideological power of the rule of law, and the value of crystallizing and legitimizing global order in legal rules has ensured the continued importance of international lawyers. The Bush administration's anti-law rhetoric might be read as a reaction to the fact that international law has attained as much as it has.

When American officials chafe at rules that constrain their freedom of action, they can cast some blame on their legalist predecessors—including James Brown Scott, John Bassett Moore, and Elihu Root—who did their best to tie the nation into the ambit of emerging legal institutions. However, if modern officials consider that these predecessors imagined the expansion of American power going hand in hand with the expansion of international law, they might find the current international legal order more congenial. For the rest of the world, the lesson might instead be the need to reshape legal order instead of focusing on holding Washington to current rules.

Utopia lies no closer today than it did a hundred years ago; perhaps, it seems farther in the distance. But many international lawyers have not lost their faith; nor have their opponents gone silent. America has heard these debates before. So long as a dream of achieving peace through law remains, they assuredly will be heard again.

ABBREVIATIONS USED IN NOTES

AJIL	*American Journal of International Law*
Annuaire	*Annuaire de l'Institut de Droit International*
ASIL	American Society of International Law
ASJSID	American Society for Judicial Settlement of International Disputes
CEIP	Carnegie Endowment for International Peace
CEIPP	Carnegie Endowment for International Peace Papers, Columbia University
CPA	Chandler P. Anderson Papers, Library of Congress
FRUS	*Foreign Relations of the United States*
JBM, LC	John Bassett Moore Papers, Library of Congress
JBM, CLS	John Bassett Moore Papers, Columbia Law School
JBS	James Brown Scott Papers, Georgetown University
LC	Library of Congress, Manuscripts Division
LEP	League to Enforce Peace
NA	State Department Records, RG59 (unless otherwise noted), National Archives II, College Park, MD
NYT	*New York Times*
RGDIP	*Revue Générale de Droit International Public*
RL	Robert Lansing Papers, Library of Congress
WFP	Woolsey Family Papers, Yale University

NOTES

Introduction

1. Quoted in "Root Heads New Body on International Law," *NYT*, January 13, 1906.
2. Lieutenant John Hood, quoted in Richard D. Challener, *Admirals, Generals, and American Foreign Policy, 1898-1914* (Princeton, NJ: Princeton University Press, 1973), 12; *Chicago Record-Herald*, quoted in Bartholomew Sparrow, *The Insular Cases and the Emergence of American Empire* (Lawrence: University of Kansas Press, 2006), 100; William Levere, quoted in Kristin L. Hoganson, *Fighting for American Manhood: How Gender Politics Provoked the Spanish-American and Philippine-American Wars* (New Haven, CT: Yale University Press, 1998), 157.
3. Mary Ann Heiss, "The Evolution of the Imperial Idea and U.S. National Identity," *Diplomatic History* 26, no. 4 (2002): 511–40; Edward P. Crapol, "Coming to Terms with Empire: The Historiography of Late-Nineteenth-Century American Foreign Relations," *Diplomatic History* 16, no. 4 (1992): 573–97; Joseph A. Fry, "Phases of Empire: Late Nineteenth-Century U.S. Foreign Relations," in *The Gilded Age: Essays on the Origins of Modern America*, ed. Charles W. Calhoun (Wilmington, DE: SR Books, 1996), 261–88. On the existence of a "maritime empire" in the nineteenth century, see Brian Rouleau, *With Sails Whitening Every Sea: Mariners and the Making of an American Maritime Empire* (Ithaca, NY: Cornell University Press, 2014).
4. Mary Ellen O'Connell, *The Power and Purpose of International Law* (New York: Oxford University Press, 2008), 14. For a critique of this framing, see Samuel Moyn, "From Antiwar Politics to Antitorture Politics," in *Law and War*, ed. Austin Sarat, Lawrence Douglas, and Martha Merril Umphrey (Stanford, CA: Stanford University Press, 2014), 158–60.
5. Michael H. Hunt, *The America Ascendancy: How the United States Gained and Wielded Global Dominance* (Chapel Hill: University of North Carolina Press, 2007), 2.
6. Fareed Zakaria, *From Wealth to Power: The Unusual Origins of America's World Role* (Princeton, NJ: Princeton University Press, 1998), 45–47.
7. Eric Love, *Race over Empire: Racism and U.S. Imperialism, 1865-1900* (Chapel Hill: University of North Carolina Press, 2004).
8. A 1990 review of all of the American historiography of US-Caribbean relations mentions international law not a single time. David M. Pletcher, "Caribbean 'Empire,' Planned and Improvised," *Diplomatic History* 14, no. 3 (1990): 447–60.
9. Jackson Lears, *Rebirth of a Nation: The Making of Modern America, 1877-1920* (New York: Harper Collins, 2009), 2; Robert A. Divine, et al., *The American Story* (New York: Penguin, 2013), 776.
10. Serge Ricard, "The Exceptionalist Syndrome in U.S. Continental and Overseas Expansionism," in *Reflections on American Exceptionalism*, ed. David K. Adams and Cornelius A. van Minnen (Staffordshire, UK: Keele University Press, 1994), 73–82; Brian Loveman, *No Higher*

Law: American Foreign Policy and the Western Hemisphere since 1776 (Chapel Hill: University of North Carolina Press, 2010).

11. On this as a "legalist" period in United States foreign relations, see Jonathan Zasloff, "Law and the Shaping of American Foreign Policy: From the Gilded Age to the New Era," *New York University Law Review* 78 (April 2003): 240–373; Francis Anthony Boyle, *Foundations of World Order: The Legalist Approach to International Relations, 1898-1922* (Durham, NC: Duke University Press, 1999).

12. Zasloff, "Law and the Shaping," 241; ASIL *Proceedings* 1 (1907). Two exceptions were Robert Bacon, who served as secretary of state for only slightly over a month in 1909, and William Jennings Bryan, a lawyer who only joined the ASIL (as an honorary vice president) in 1913.

13. On the idea of a foreign policy establishment, see Yves Dezalay and Bryant G. Garth, "Law, Lawyers, and Empire," in *The Cambridge History of Law in America*, ed. Christopher Tomlins and Michael Grossberg (New York: Cambridge University Press, 2008), 3:718–58; Godfrey Hodgson, "The Foreign Policy Establishment," in *Ruling America: A History of Wealth and Power in a Democracy*, ed. Steve Fraser and Gary Gerstle (Cambridge, MA: Harvard University Press, 2005), 215–49. Though a true establishment did not emerge until at least the interwar period, a "proto-establishment" can be identified after 1900.

14. Judith N. Shklar, *Legalism: Law, Morals, and Political Trials* (Cambridge, MA: Harvard University Press, 1964), 1. Of course, this viewpoint is not exclusive to lawyers, nor is rule-following the sole moral consideration for lawyers.

15. James P. Piscatori, "Law, Peace, and War in American International Legal Thought," in *American Thinking about Peace and War: New Essays on American Thoughts and Attitudes*, ed. Ken Booth and Moorhead Wright (New York: Barnes and Noble, 1978), 135–36.

16. A note on terminology: *judicialism* and *judicialists* constituted a subset of *legalism* and *legalists*, respectively. The former was always also the latter, but the reverse was not necessarily true. Henceforth, I use *judicialism* to refer to the ideological and political project that imagined international law as self-enforcing and promoted the creation of an international court above all; whereas *legalism* will refer to the broader commitment of those who advocated an increased recourse to international law, even if not all shared judicialists' faith in the power of judicial institutions.

17. On the legal content of WWI-era debates, see John W. Coogan, *The End of Neutrality: The United States, Britain, and Maritime Rights, 1899-1915* (Ithaca, NY: Cornell University Press, 1981), 15; Isabel V. Hull, *A Scrap of Paper: Breaking and Making International Law during the Great War* (Ithaca, NY: Cornell University Press, 2014).

18. E.g., Daniel Abebe and Eric A. Posner, "The Flaws of Foreign Affairs Legalism," *Virginia Journal of International Law* 51, no. 3 (2011): 525; Mark Janis, *America and the Law of Nations, 1776-1939* (New York: Cambridge University Press, 2010), chap. 9.

19. Robert Lansing, *The Peace Negotiations: A Personal Narrative* (Boston: Houghton Mifflin, 1921), 107.

20. Elizabeth Borgwardt, *A New Deal for the World: America's Vision for Human Rights* (Cambridge, MA: Harvard University Press, 2005); David L. Bosco, *Five to Rule Them All: The UN Security Council and the Making of the Modern World* (Oxford: Oxford University Press, 2009); John F. Murphy, *The United States and the Rule of Law in International Affairs* (Cambridge: Cambridge University Press, 2004); Greg Grandin, "The Liberal Traditions in the Americas: Rights, Sovereignty, and the Origins of Liberal Multilateralism," *American Historical Review* 117, no. 1 (2012): 91; Michael Ignatieff, ed., *American Exceptionalism and Human Rights* (Princeton, NJ: Princeton University Press, 2005).

21. David Kennedy, *Of War and Law* (Princeton, NJ: Princeton University Press, 2006).

22. Mary L. Dudziak, *Cold War Civil Rights: Race and the Image of American Democracy* (Princeton, NJ: Princeton University Press, 2000); John F. Witt, *Lincoln's Code: The Laws of War in American History* (New York: Free Press, 2012).

23. Warren F. Kuehl, *Seeking World Order: The United States and International Organization to 1920* (Nashville, TN: Vanderbilt University Press, 1969); David S. Patterson, *Toward a Warless World: The Travail of the American Peace Movement, 1887-1914* (Bloomington: Indiana University Press, 1976); C. Roland Marchand, *The American Peace Movement and Social Reform 1898-1918.* (Princeton, NJ: Princeton University Press, 1972). See also Sondra

Herman, *Eleven against War: Studies in American Internationalist Thought, 1898-1921* (Stanford, CA: Hoover Institution Press, 1969); Michael A. Lutzker, "The 'Practical' Peace Advocates: An Interpretation of the American Peace Movement, 1898-1917" (PhD diss., Rutgers University, 1969); Calvin DeArmond Davis, *The United States and the First Hague Peace Conference* (Ithaca, NY: Cornell University Press, 1962); Davis, *The United States and the Second Hague Peace Conference: American Diplomacy and International Organization 1899-1914* (Durham, NC: Duke University Press, 1975).

24. Peter Maguire, *Law and War: An American Story* (New York: Columbia University Press, 2000); Zasloff, "Law and the Shaping." See also George F. Kennan, *American Diplomacy* (Chicago: University of Chicago Press, 1951).

25. Erez Manela, "The United States in the World," in *American History Now*, ed. Eric Foner and Lisa McGirr (Philadelphia: Temple University Press, 2011), 213; Clara Altman, "The International Context: An Imperial Perspective on American Legal History," in *A Companion to American Legal History*, ed. Salley E. Hadden and Alfred L. Brophy (New York: Wiley, 2013), 543–61. Examples focusing on events from later in the twentieth century include Borgwardt, *New Deal for the World*; Barbara J. Keys, *Reclaiming American Virtue: The Human Rights Revolution of the 1970s* (Cambridge, MA: Harvard University Press, 2014).

26. Sparrow, *Insular Cases*; Kal Raustiala, *Does the Constitution Follow the Flag? The Evolution of Territoriality in American Law* (New York: Oxford University Press, 2009); Daniel S. Margolies, *Spaces of Law in American Foreign Relations: Extradition and Extraterritoriality in the Borderlands and Beyond, 1877-1898* (Athens: University of Georgia, 2011); Katherine Unterman, "Boodle over the Border: Embezzlement and the Crisis of International Mobility, 1880-1890," *Journal of Gilded Age and Progressive Era* 11, no. 2 (2012): 151–89; Eileen P. Scully, *Bargaining with the State from Afar: American Citizenship in Treaty Port China, 1844-1942* (New York: Columbia University Press, 2001); Christina Duffy Burnett [Ponsa], "Contingent Constitutions: Empire and Law in the Americas" (PhD diss., Princeton University, 2010); Sally Engle Merry, *Colonizing Hawaii: The Cultural Power of Law* (Princeton, NJ: Princeton University Press, 2000).

27. Dezalay and Garth, "Law, Lawyers, and Empire."

28. On an earlier manifestation, see Teemu Ruskola, "Canton Is Not Boston: The Invention of American Imperial Sovereignty," *American Quarterly* 57, no. 3 (2005): 859–84.

29. Alfred McCoy and Francisco Scarano, eds., *Colonial Crucible: Empire in the Making of the Modern American State* (Madison: University of Wisconsin Press, 2009); Walter LaFeber, *The New Empire: An Interpretation of American Expansion, 1860-1898* (Ithaca, NY: Cornell University Press, 1998); Richard H. Collin, *Theodore Roosevelt's Caribbean: The Panama Canal, the Monroe Doctrine, and the Latin American Context* (Baton Rouge: Louisiana State University Press, 1990).

30. On race, gender, and US foreign relations, see among others Hoganson, *Fighting for American Manhood*; Mary Renda, *Taking Haiti: Military Occupation and the Culture of U.S. Imperialism, 1915-1940* (Chapel Hill: University of North Carolina Press, 2001); Michael H. Hunt, *Ideology and U.S. Foreign Policy* (New Haven, CT: Yale University Press, 1987); Paul Kramer, *The Blood of Government: Race, Empire, the United States, and the Philippines* (Chapel Hill: University of North Carolina Press, 2006).

31. Louis Henkin, *How Nations Behave*, 2nd ed. (New York: Columbia University Press, 1979), 47; italics in the original.

32. A useful overview of the international law and international relations literature is Jeffrey L. Dunoff and Mark A. Pollack, "International Law and International Relations: Introducing an Interdisciplinary Dialogue," in *Interdisciplinary Perspectives on International Law and International Relations: The State of the Art*, ed. Dunoff and Pollack (Cambridge: Cambridge University Press, 2013), 3–32. For the role of liberal ideology, see Gary J. Bass, *Stay the Hand of Vengeance: The Politics of War Crimes Tribunals* (Princeton, NJ: Princeton University Press, 2000). Sociological approaches include Ryan Goodman and Derek Jinks, *Socializing States: Promoting Human Rights through International Law* (Oxford: Oxford University Press, 2013); Gillaume Sacriste and Antoine Vauchez, "The Force of International Law: Lawyers' Diplomacy on the International Scene in the 1920s," *Law and Social Inquiry* 32, no. 1 (2007): 83–107. On law as self-interest, see Jack L. Goldsmith and Eric Posner, *The Limits*

of International Law (New York: Oxford University Press, 2005) and compare with review essays in *Georgia Journal of International and Comparative Law* 34, no. 2 (2006): 253–484; and Jens David Ohlin, *The Assault on International Law* (New York: Oxford University Press, 2015). On the internalization of international law, see Harold Hongju Koh, "Why Do Nations Obey International Law?" *Yale Law Journal* 106, no. 8 (1997): 2599–659. The idea of international law as a coordinating mechanism traces back to neoliberal institutionalism, which sought to explain international cooperation in terms of rational incentives and transaction costs. Classic exemplars of these approaches are Stephen Krasner, *International Regimes* (Ithaca, NY: Cornell University Press, 1983) and Robert Keohane, *International Institutions and State Power: Essays in International Relations Theory* (Boulder: University of Colorado, 1989). Later scholars bridging international relations and international law modified these frameworks to take into account the specifically "legal" aspects of the law, to mixed success. See particularly Anne-Marie Slaughter Burley, "International Law and International Relations Theory: A Dual Agenda," *AJIL* 87, no. 2 (1993): 205–39; Beth A. Simmons and Richard H. Steinberg, eds., *International Law and International Relations* (Cambridge: Cambridge University Press, 2006).

33. G. John Ikenberry, *After Victory: Institutions, Strategic Restraint, and the Rebuilding of Order after Major Wars* (Princeton, NJ: Princeton University Press, 2001); David A. Lake, *Hierarchy in International Relations* (Ithaca, NY: Cornell University Press, 2009).

34. Harold Hongju Koh, "Bringing International Law Home," *Houston Law Review* 35, no. 3 (1998): 647.

35. Nathaniel Berman, *Passion and Ambivalence: Colonialism, Nationalism, and International Law* (Boston: Martinus Nijhoff, 2012), 55.

36. Martti Koskenniemi, "The Subjective Dangers of Projects of World Community," in *Realizing Utopia: The Future of International Law*, ed. Antonio Cassese (Oxford: Oxford University Press, 2012), 3–13; Eric A. Posner, *The Perils of Global Legalism* (Chicago: University of Chicago Press, 2009).

37. Gerry Simpson, *Great Powers and Outlaw States: Unequal Sovereigns in the International Legal Order* (Cambridge: Cambridge University Press, 2004); Martti Koskenniemi, "International Law and Hegemony: A Reconfiguration," *Cambridge Review of International Affairs* 17, no. 2 (2004): 197–218.

38. Martti Koskenniemi, *From Apology to Utopia: The Structure of International Legal Argument*, (1989; reissued by Cambridge: Cambridge University Press, 2005); China Miéville, *Between Equal Rights: A Marxist Theory of International Law* (Boston: Brill, 2005).

39. The classic modern exemplar of this tendency is Arthur Nussbaum, *A Concise History of the Law of Nations* (1947; repr. New York: MacMillan, 1962). More recent examples include Boyle, *Foundations*; Arthur Eyffinger, *The 1899 Hague Peace Conference: "The Parliament of Man, the Federation of the World"* (The Hague: Kluwer Law International, 2000); Janis, *America and the Law of Nations.* Stephen Neff offers admirably clear profiles of major thinkers across centuries. Stephen C. Neff, *Justice among Nations: A History of International Law* (Cambridge, MA: Harvard University Press, 2014). A criticism of this approach is Randall Lesaffer, "International Law and Its History: The Story of an Unrequited Love," in *Time, History and International Law*, ed. Matthew Craven, Malgosia Fitzmaurice, and Maria Vogiatzi (Leiden: Martinus Nijhoff, 2007), 27–41.

40. Naz K. Modirzadeh, "Folk International Law: 9/11 Lawyering and the Transformation of the Law of Armed Conflict to Human Rights Policy and Human Rights Law to War Governance," *Harvard National Security Journal* 5, no. 1 (2014): 229. For more on "folk" law, see Brian Z. Tamanaha, "What Is Law?" (Washington University in Saint Louis School of Law Legal Studies Research Paper Series no. 15-01-01, January 17–18, 2015).

41. Some scholars argue that the field is currently experiencing a "contextual turn." Martti Koskenniemi, "Histories of International Law: Significance and Problems for a Critical View," *Temple International and Comparative Law Journal* 27, no. 2 (2014): 215; Matthew Craven, "Introduction: International Law and Its Histories," in Craven, Fitzmaurice, and Vogiatzi, *Time, History and International Law*, 1–25. Pioneering works include Martti Koskenniemi, *The Gentle Civilizer of Nations: The Rise and Fall of International Law 1870-1960* (Cambridge: Cambridge University Press, 2002); Antony Anghie, *Imperialism, Sovereignty*

and the Making of International Law (Cambridge: Cambridge University Press, 2004); David Kennedy, "International Law and the Nineteenth Century: History of an Illusion," *Quinnipiac Law Review* 17 (1998): 99–138; Arnulf Becker Lorca, *Mestizo International Law: A Global Intellectual History, 1850-1950* (Cambridge: Cambridge University Press, 2014); Casper Sylvest, "International Law in Nineteenth-Century Britain," *British Yearbook of International Law 2004* 75 (2005): 9–70. Broad histories of internationalism include Mark Mazower, *Governing the World: The History of an Idea, 1815 to the Present* (New York: Penguin, 2012); Glenda Sluga, *Internationalism in the Age of Nationalism* (Philadelphia: University of Pennsylvania Press, 2013). Two evocative yet brief studies of US international lawyers are Carl Landauer, "The Ambivalences of Power: Launching the *American Journal of International Law* in an Era of Empire and Globalization," *Leiden Journal of International Law* 20, no. 2 (2007): 325–58; and Martti Koskenniemi, "The Ideology of International Adjudication" (paper presented at The Hague, September 7, 2007).

42. Richard Olney to Thomas Bayard, July 20, 1895, in *FRUS* (1895), 556–57.
43. Lauren Benton, *A Search for Sovereignty: Law and Geography in European Empires, 1400-1900* (New York: Cambridge University Press, 2010).
44. David Armitage, *The Declaration of Independence: A Global History* (Cambridge, MA: Harvard University Press, 2007).
45. Paul Kramer has called this an "international empire": an empire "in which order was produced through the coordination of multiple, 'legitimate' nation-states, the promotion, management, and disciplining of flows and connections between them, and disproportionate power within multilateral bodies." Paul A. Kramer, "Power and Connection: Imperial Histories of the United States in the World," *American Historical Review* 116, no. 5 (2011): 1366.
46. William J. Novak, "The Myth of the 'Weak' American State," *American Historical Review* 113, no. 3 (2008): 752–72; Stephen Skowronek, *Building a New American State: The Expansion of National Administrative Capacities, 1877-1920* (New York: Cambridge University Press, 1982); Morton Keller, *Affairs of State: Public Life in Late Nineteenth Century America* (Cambridge, MA: Harvard University Press, 1977).
47. Kermit Hall, *The Magic Mirror: Law in American History* (New York: Oxford University Press, 1989), chaps. 11–12; Richard Hofstadter, *The Age of Reform: From Bryan to F.D.R.* (New York: Vintage, 1955), 157–64.
48. Robert H. Wiebe, *The Search for Order, 1877-1920* (New York: Hill and Wang, 1967).
49. Brooks Adams, *The Law of Civilization and Decay: An Essay on History* (New York: Macmillan and Co., 1895); Josiah Strong, *Our Country: Its Possible Future and Its Present Crisis*, rev. ed (1891; repr. Cambridge, MA: Harvard University Press, 1963); Strong, *Expansion under New World-Conditions* (New York: Baker and Taylor Company, 1900); John Fiske, "Manifest Destiny," *Harper's Monthly Magazine*, March 1885, 578–90.
50. Edward Keene, *Beyond the Anarchical Society: Grotius, Colonialism and Order in World Politics* (Cambridge: Cambridge University Press, 2002).
51. On the legal and ideological import of "war" as a conceptual category, see Mary L. Dudziak, *War Time: An Idea, Its History, Its Consequences* (New York: Oxford University Press, 2012).
52. Robert R. Davis, Jr. "Diplomatic Plumage: American Court Dress in the Early National Period," *American Quarterly* 20, no. 2 (1968): 164–79.
53. Richard A. Johnson, *The Administration of United States Foreign Policy* (Austin: University of Texas Press, 1971), 55.
54. Nicole M. Phelps, *U.S.-Habsburg Relations from 1815 to the Paris Peace Conference: Sovereignty Transformed* (Cambridge: Cambridge University Press, 2013).
55. Cushing Strout, *The American Image of the Old World* (New York: Harper and Row, 1963), 143.
56. Daniel Rodgers, *Atlantic Crossings: Social Politics in a Progressive Age* (Cambridge, MA: Harvard University Press, 1998); Christopher Endy, "Travel and World Power: Americans in Europe, 1890-1917," *Diplomatic History* 22, no. 4 (1998): 579; Stuart Anderson, *Race and Rapprochement: Anglo-Saxonism and Anglo-American Relations, 1895-1904* (London: Associated University Presses, 1981); Paul Kramer, "Empires, Exceptions, and Anglo-Saxons: Race and Rule between the British and United States Empires, 1880-1910," *Journal of American History* 88, no. 4 (2002): 1315–53; Julian Go, *Patterns of Empire: The British and American Empires, 1688 to the Present* (New York: Cambridge University Press, 2011).

57. Charles Lipson, *Standing Guard: Protecting Foreign Capital in the Nineteenth and Twentieth Centuries* (Berkeley: University of California Press, 1985)

58. On the United States as a satisfied, status quo power, see Robert E. Hannigan, *The New World Power: American Foreign Policy, 1898-1917* (Philadelphia: University of Pennsylvania Press, 2002).

Chapter 1

1. S. E. Crowe, *The Berlin West African Conference, 1884-1885* (London: Longmans, Green, 1942), 11–91.

2. Critiques of isolationism are abundant but the periodic need to reassert them suggests just how seductive the label remains. A sampling: William Appleman Williams, "The Legend of Isolationism in the 1920's," *Science and Society* 18, no. 1 (1954): 6–7; Andrew Johnstone, "Isolationism and Internationalism in American Foreign Relations," *Journal of Transatlantic Studies* 9, no. 1 (2011): 7–20; Christopher McKnight Nichols, *Promise and Peril: America at the Dawn of a Global Age* (Cambridge, MA: Harvard University Press, 2011); Brooke L. Blower, "From Isolationism to Neutrality: A New Framework for Understanding American Political Culture, 1919-1941," *Diplomatic History* 38, no. 2 (2014): 345–76.

3. Nussbaum, *Concise History*, 225–26.

4. U.S. Congress, Senate, *Report from the Secretary of State relative to affairs of the independent State of Congo*, 49th Cong., 1st sess., 1886, Senate Ex. Doc. 196, 7-12 (hereinafter cited as "Independent State of Congo").

5. A useful introduction is Neff, *Justice among Nations*, 158–66.

6. Benton, *Search for Sovereignty*, 128–37.

7. Nussbaum, *Concise History*, 1–39.

8. Keene, *Beyond the Anarchical Society*, 98–99.

9. F. H. Hinsley, *Power and the Pursuit of Peace: Theory and Practice in the History of Relations Between States* (Cambridge: Cambridge University Press, 1963), 13–32.

10. Daniel Goffman, "The Ottoman Empire," in *The Renaissance World*, ed. John Jeffries Martin (New York: Routledge, 2007), 347–63; Lauren Benton, "Legal Spaces of Empire: Piracy and the Origins of Ocean Regionalism," *Comparative Studies in Society and History* 47, no. 4 (2005): 700–724.

11. Anghie, *Imperialism, Sovereignty*, 27; Nussbaum, *Concise History*, 79–84; David Kennedy, "Primitive Legal Scholarship," *Harvard International Law Journal* 27, no. 1 (1986): 13–40. On Vitoria as the father of international law, see James Brown Scott, *The Catholic Conception of International Law* (Washington, DC: Georgetown University Press, 1934).

12. In practice, it has in modern times been difficult to argue solely from either positive or natural law principles, and so the discourse of international law tends to oscillate between the two. Martti Koskenniemi, *From Apology to Utopia*.

13. Neff, *Justice among Nations*, 143, 165.

14. Nussbaum, *Concise History*, 156–64.

15. For basic definitions, see Barry E. Carter, Phillip R. Trimble, and Allen S. Weiner, *International Law*, 5th ed. (Austin, TX: Wolters Kluwer, 2007), 1–3.

16. Hidemi Suganami, "A Note on the Origin of the Word 'International,'" *British Journal of International Studies* 4, no. 3 (1978): 226–32; Manfred Lachs, *The Teacher in International Law: Teachings and Teaching*, 2nd ed. (Boston: Martinus Nijhoff, 1987), 161–65; *Annuaire de l'Institut de droit international* (1878): 344–56.

17. Koskenniemi, *Gentle Civilizer*, 11–12; Neff, *Justice among Nations*, 265; David Dudley Field, *Outlines of an International Code*, 2nd ed. (New York: Baker, Voorhis & Company, 1876); Patterson, *Toward a Warless World*, 100.

18. Albéric Rolin, *Les Origines de L'Institut de Droit International, 1873-1923: Souvenirs d'un Témoin* (Belgium, 1923); Institut de droit international, *Livre du Centenaire, 1873-1973: Evolution et Perspectives du Droit International* (Basel: Editions S. Karger, 1973), 3–121; F. S. L. Lyons, *Internationalism in Europe, 1815-1914* (Leyden: A. W. Sythoff, 1963), 218.

19. Nussbaum, *Concise History*, 232; Neff, *Justice among Nations*, chap. 6; Carl Schmitt, *The Nomos of the Earth in the International Law of the Jus Publicum Europaeum*, trans. G. L. Ulmen (1950;

repr. New York: Telos Press, 2003); Koskenniemi, *Gentle Civilizer*, 20–22. See also James Q. Whitman, *The Verdict of Battle: The Law of Victory and the Making of Modern War* (Cambridge, MA: Harvard University Press, 2012).

20. Fritz Münch, "L'institut De Droit Internacional: Ses Debuts Comme Organe Collectif De La Doctrine," in *Estudios De Derecho Internacional Homenaje a D. Antonio De Luna* (Madrid: CSIC, 1968), 386–87; Koskenniemi, *Gentle Civilizer*, 20; C. A. Bayly, *The Birth of the Modern World, 1780-1914: Global Connections and Comparisons* (Malden, MA: Blackwell, 2004), 312–20; Nussbaum, *Concise History*, 232; Kennedy, "History of an Illusion," 121; Sylvest, "International Law in Nineteenth-Century Britain," 53.

21. Sylvest, "International Law in Nineteenth-Century Britain," 30.

22. Koskenniemi, *Gentle Civilizer*, 4.

23. D. H. N. Johnson, *The English Tradition in International Law: Lecture at the London School of Economics and Political Science, 20 November 1961* (London: G. Bell and Sons, 1962), 37; Nussbaum, *Concise History*, 294; *The Collected Papers of John Westlake on Public International Law*, ed. Lassa Oppenheim (Cambridge: Cambridge University Press, 1914), xi; Koskenniemi, *Gentle Civilizer*, 20, 69–70.

24. Lachs, *Teacher in International Law*, 75; T. J. Lawrence, "The Evolution of Peace," in *Essays on Some Disputed Questions in Modern International Law*, 2nd ed. (Cambridge: Deighton, Bell, and Co., 1885), 234–77.

25. Casper Sylvest, "The Foundations of Victorian International Law," in *Victorian Visions of Global Order: Empire and International Relations in Nineteenth-Century Political Thought*, ed. Duncan Bell (Cambridge: Cambridge University Press, 2007), 47–48; Sylvest, "International Law in Nineteenth-Century Britain," 29, 41, 57.

26. Alexander Orakhelashvili, "The Idea of European International Law," *European Journal of International Law* 17, no. 2 (2006): 316–17.

27. Frederick Pollock, "The Sources of International Law," *Law Quarterly Review* 18 (1902): 418; italics in the original.

28. Gerrit W. Gong, *The Standard of "Civilization" in International Society* (Oxford: Clarendon Press, 1984). 27. Orakhelashvili highlights references to Christianity in the work of Heffter, Bonfils, and others. Orakhelashvili, "European International Law," 323–24.

29. The word "civilization" seems to have originated in the mid-18th century, likely in France, though it appears soon thereafter in England. Brett Bowden, *The Empire of Civilization: The Evolution of an Imperial Idea* (Chicago: University of Chicago Press, 2009), chap. 2.

30. Kennedy, "International Law and the Nineteenth Century," 123–31.

31. Bowden, *Empire of Civilization*, 55; James Lorimer, *The Institutes of the Law of Nations: A Treatise of the Jural Relations of Separate Political Communities* (Edinburgh: William Blackwood and Sons, 1883), 1:101; Orakhelashvili, "European International Law," 328.

32. Bowden, *Empire of Civilization*, 33.

33. Georg Schwarzenberger, "The Standard of Civilisation in International Law," *Current Legal Problems* 8:1 (1955): 220; Gong, *Standard*, 18, 29.

34. Lorimer, *Institutes*, 1:93; David Clinton, "Francis Lieber, Imperialism, and Internationalism," in *Imperialism and Internationalism in the Discipline of International Relations*, ed. David Long and Brian C. Schmidt (Albany: State University of New York Press, 2005), 28; John Westlake, *International Law* (Cambridge: J. and C. F. Clay, 1904), 1:107.

35. T. E. Holland, *The Elements of Jurisprudence*, 2nd. ed. (Oxford: Clarendon Press, 1882), 295, quoted in Arnulf Becker Lorca, "Sovereignty beyond the West: The End of Classical International Law," *Journal of the History of International Law* 13 (2011): 57.

36. Quoted in Gong, *Standard*, 20.

37. Keene, *Beyond the Anarchical Society*, 98–99; Lorimer, *Institutes*, 1:101–2; Mill is quoted in Schwarzenberger, "Standard of Civilisation," 220–21.

38. Ernest Nys, *The Independent State of the Congo and International Law* (Brussels: J. Lebègue, 1903); Casper Sylvest, " 'Our Passion for Legality': International Law and Imperialism in Late Nineteenth-Century Britain," *Review of International Studies* 34 (2008): 403–23; Koskenniemi, *Gentle Civilizer*, 140, 166.

39. Prasenjit Duara, "The Discourse of Civilization and Pan-Asianism," *Journal of World History*, 12, no. 1 (2001), 100–101.

40. Alice Conklin, *A Mission to Civilize: The Republican Idea of Empire in France and West Africa, 1895-1930* (Stanford, CA: Stanford University Press, 1997); Uday Singh Mehta, *Liberalism and Empire: A Study in Nineteenth-Century British Liberal Thought* (Chicago: University of Chicago Press, 1999); Duncan Bell, "Empire and International Relations in Victorian Political Thought," *The Historical Journal* 49, no. 1 (2006): 281–98; Jennifer Pitts, *A Turn to Empire: The Rise of Imperial Liberalism in Britain and France* (Princeton, NJ: Princeton University Press, 2005); Andrew Fitzmaurice, "Liberalism and Empire in Nineteenth-Century International Law," *American Historical Review* 117, no. 1 (2012): 122–40.

41. Koskenniemi, *Gentle Civilizer*, chap. 2. For a useful guide to theories of imperial expansion see Michael W. Doyle, *Empires* (Ithaca, NY: Cornell University Press, 1986), 19–47.

42. Gong, *Standard*, 5.

43. For some romantic Nationalists, the creation of a strong national state provided the necessary precursor to an international community: both represented a step towards ever larger human collaboration. And, in fact, the building of strong national states overlapped with the emergence of international regimes. Eric Hobsbawm, *Nations and Nationalism since 1780: Programme, Myth, Reality*, 2nd. ed. (Cambridge: Cambridge University Press, 1992), 30–31; Bayly, *Birth of the Modern World*, 247–83.

44. Shogo Suzuki, *Civilization and Empire: China and Japan's Encounter with European International Society* (New York: Routledge, 2009); Pär Kristoffer Cassel, *Grounds of Judgment: Extraterritoriality and Imperial Power in Nineteenth-Century China and Japan* (New York: Oxford University Press, 2012).

45. Arnulf Becker Lorca, "Universal International Law: Nineteenth-Century Histories of Imposition and Appropriation," *Harvard International Law Journal* 51, no. 2 (2010): 475–552.

46. Peter Holquist, "The Russian Empire as a 'Civilized State': International Law as Principle and Practice in Imperial Russia, 1874-1878," National Council for Eurasian and East European Research working paper, Washington, DC, July 2004, http://www.ucis.pitt.edu/nceeer/2004_818-06g_Holquist.pdf.

47. Jesse Siddall Reeves, "The Influence of the Law of Nature upon International Law in the United States," *AJIL* 3 (1909): 552; David Armitage, "The Declaration of Independence and International Law, *William and Mary Quarterly* 59, no. 1 (2002): 49; US Declaration of Independence, at http://www.archives.gov/exhibits/charters/declaration.html.

48. David M. Golove and Daniel J. Hulsebosch, "A Civilized Nation: The Early American Constitution, the Law of Nations, and the Pursuit of International Recognition," *New York University Law Review* 85 (October 2010): 932–1066.

49. Walter Russell Mead, *Special Providence: The American Foreign Policy Tradition* (New York: Routledge, 2002); Walter McDougall, *Promised Land, Crusader State* (Boston: Houghton Mifflin, 1997); Brendan O'Connor, "American Foreign Policy Traditions: A Literature Review," US Studies working paper, University of Sydney, 2009.

50. George Washington, Farewell Address, 1796, hosted by the Avalon Project at avalon.law.yale.edu/18th_century/washing.asp; Thomas Jefferson, First Inaugural Address, March 4, 1801, *The Papers of Thomas Jefferson, Volume 33: 17 February to 30 April 1801*, ed. Barbara B. Oberg (Princeton, NJ: Princeton University Press, 2006), 148–52; Jeffrey J. Malanson, "The Congressional Debate over U.S. Participation in the Congress of Panama, 1825-1826: Washington's Farewell Address, Monroe's Doctrine, and the Fundamental Principles of U.S. Foreign Policy," *Diplomatic History* 30, no. 5 (2006): 813–38; Drew McCoy, *The Elusive Republic: Political Economy in Jeffersonian America* (Chapel Hill: University of North Carolina Press, 1996), 209–35.

51. Jay Sexton, *The Monroe Doctrine: Empire and Nation in Nineteenth-Century America* (New York: Hill and Wang, 2011), 6; Arthur P. Whitaker, *The Western Hemisphere Idea: Its Rise and Decline* (Ithaca, NY: Cornell University Press, 1954).

52. Anders Stephanson, *Manifest Destiny: American Expansion and the Empire of Right* (New York: Hill and Wang, 1995), 42; Hunt, *Ideology and U.S. Foreign Policy*; Amy S. Greenberg, *Manifest Manhood and the Antebellum American Empire* (Cambridge: Cambridge University Press, 2005).

53. Richard Slotkin, *Gunfighter Nation: The Myth of the Frontier in Twentieth-Century America* (Norman: University of Oklahoma Press, 1992).

54. U.S. Congress, Joint Committee on Printing, 49th Cong., 1st sess., S. Rep. 1276 (June 3, 1886).

55. Jules Lobel, "The Rise and Fall of the Neutrality Act: Sovereignty and Congressional War Powers in United States Foreign Policy," *Harvard International Law Journal* 24, no. 3 (1983): 2; John Bassett Moore, *The Principles of American Diplomacy* (New York: Harper and Brothers, 1918), 61; Nils Ørvik, *The Decline of Neutrality 1914-1941, with Special Reference to the United States and the Northern Neutrals,* 2nd ed. (1953; London: Frank Cass, 1971), 18–25; Stephen C. Neff, *The Rights and Duties of Neutrals: A General History* (Manchester, UK: Manchester University Press, 2000), 75–76.

56. Witt, *Lincoln's Code,* 70–77.

57. Neff, *Rights and Duties,* chap. 6. For court decisions, see John Bassett Moore, *A Digest of International Law as Embodied in Diplomatic Discussions. . . .* (Washington, DC: Government Printing Office, 1906), 7:697–739.

58. Moore, *Digest of International Law,* 7:1260–61.

59. Alfred P. Rubin, "The Concept of Neutrality in International Law," in *Neutrality: Changing Concepts and Practices,* ed. Alan T. Leonhard (New York: University Press of America, 1988), 25–26.

60. John Bassett Moore, *The United States and International Arbitration* (Boston: American Peace Society, 1896), 3; Margolies, *Spaces of Law.*

61. Ronald G. Walters, *American Reformers, 1815-1860,* rev. ed. (1978; repr. New York: Hill and Wang, 1997), 115–21; Charles DeBenedetti, *The Peace Reform in American History* (Bloomington: Indiana University Press, 1980), 33–34.

62. William Ladd, *An Essay on a Congress of Nations, For the Adjustment of International Disputes without Resort to Arms,* ed. James Brown Scott (1840; repr. New York: Oxford University Press, 1916), xlix, 77; Hinsley, *Power and the Pursuit,* 94; James Mill, *Essays on Government, Jurisprudence, Liberty of the Press, and Law of Nations* (London: J. Innes, [1825?]).

63. DeBenedetti, *Peace Reform,* 53; Merle Curti, *The American Peace Crusade, 1815-1860* (Durham, NC: Duke University Press, 1929), 58–60; Robert A. Ferguson, *Law and Letters in American Culture* (Cambridge, MA: Harvard University Press, 1984); Novak, "Myth"; Leo Damrosch, *Tocqueville's Discovery of America* (New York: Farrar, Straus, and Giroux, 2010), 102.

64. Paul Laity, *The British Peace Movement, 1870-1914* (Oxford: Clarendon Press, 2001), 14, 127; Sandi E. Cooper, *Patriotic Pacifism: Waging War against War in Europe, 1814-1914* (Oxford: Oxford University Press, 1991), 14–23, 61; Patterson, *Toward a Warless World,* 2; Curti, *American Peace Crusade,* 143–88; Hinsley, *Power and the Pursuit,* 104.

65. James Kent, *Commentaries on American Law,* vol. 1 (New York: O. Halstead, 1826), 1–200; Henry Wheaton, *Elements of International Law,* ed. George Grafton Wilson (1836; Oxford: Clarendon Press, 1936); Janis, *America and the Law of Nations,* chap. 3; Gong, *Standard,* 26–27; Lydia H. Liu, *The Clash of Empires: The Invention of China in Modern World Making* (Cambridge, MA: Harvard University Press, 2004), 121.

66. DeBenedetti, *Peace Reform,* 55; Francis A. Lieber, *Instructions for the Government of Armies of the United States in the Field* (New York: D. Van Nostrand, 1863); Witt, *Lincoln's Code,* 170–284.

67. Howard Jones, *Blue and Gray Diplomacy: A History of Union and Confederate Foreign Relations* (Chapel Hill: University of North Carolina Press, 2010), 200; Amanda Foreman, *A World on Fire: Britain's Crucial Role in the American Civil War* (New York: Random House, 2010), 801; Jackson H. Ralston, *International Arbitration from Athens to Locarno* (Stanford, CA: Stanford University Press, 1929), 197–200.

68. Laity, *British Peace Movement,* 105–11; 131; Moore, *United States and International Arbitration*; International American Conference, *Report of Committees and Discussions Thereon* (Washington, DC: Government Printing Office, 1890), 1:8; "Unratified Olney-Pauncefote Treaty of Arbitration between the United States and Great Britain," *AJIL* 5, no. 2 (1911): 88–93.

69. Alan Tzvika Nissel, "The Turn to Technique: American Professionalization of International Arbitration (1870-1898)" (2011, unpublished manuscript in the author's possession), 55; John Bassett Moore, *History and Digest of the International Arbitrations to*

Which the United States Has Been a Party (Washington, DC: Government Printing Office, 1898), 2:1320.

70. Ralston, *International Arbitration*, 203–4; Thomas R. Hietala, *Manifest Design: American Exceptionalism and Empire*, rev. ed (1985; Ithaca, NY: Cornell University Press, 2003); Amy S. Greenberg, *A Wicked War: Polk, Clay, Lincoln, and the 1846 U.S. Invasion of Mexico* (New York: Vintage Books, 2012); John M. Dobson, *America's Ascent: The United States Becomes a Great Power, 1880-1914* (DeKalb: Northern Illinois University Press, 1978), 49–50; Theodore S. Woolsey, "Responsibility for the 'Maine,'" in *America's Foreign Policy: Essays and Addresses* (New York: The Century Co., 1898), 53–57; José Martí, "The Washington Pan-American Congress," in *Inside the Monster: Writings on the United States and American Imperialism*, ed. Philip S. Foner (New York: Monthly Review Press, 1975), 355; "The American Theory of International Arbitration," *AJIL* 2, no. 2 (1908): 387.

71. Jesse Siddall Reeves, "The International Beginnings of the Congo Free State," John Hopkins University Studies in Historical and Political Science, 12th series, vol. 11–12 (Baltimore: Johns Hopkins Press, 1894); Tim Jeal, Stanley: The Impossible Life of Africa's Greatest Explorer (New Haven, CT: Yale University Press, 2007), 133–38.

72. "Independent State of Congo," 63–64; Crowe, *Berlin Conference*, 97–98; Curti, *Peace or War*, 176.

73. Institut de droit international, "Liberté de navigation sur le Congo," 1883, www.idi-iil.org/idiF/resolutionsF/1883_mun_02_fr.pdf; Reeves, "International Beginnings of Congo," 61–66; *General Act of the Berlin Conference*, in "Independent State of Congo," 297–305; Eric D. Weitz, "From the Vienna to the Paris System: International Politics and the Entangled Histories of Human Rights, Forced Deportations, and Civilizing Missions," *American Historical Review* 113, no. 5 (2008): 1320.

74. Crowe, *Berlin Conference*, 103–4, 133–34, 150–56, 176–91; Adam Hochschild, *King Leopold's Ghost: A Story of Greed, Terror, and Heroism in Colonial Africa* (Boston: Houghton Mifflin, 1998).

75. Nys, *Independent State of the Congo*, 25; David M. Pletcher, *The Awkward Years: American Foreign Relations under Garfield and Arthur* (Columbia: University of Missouri Press, 1962), 308–16.

76. Pletcher, *Awkward Years*, 321–24.

77. Joseph Conrad, *Heart of Darkness*, 3rd Norton critical ed. (New York: W. W. Norton, 1988); Matthew Rubery, *The Novelty of Newspapers: Victorian Fiction after the Invention of the News* (Oxford: Oxford University Press, 2009), 141–58.

78. On the Prize bar, see Witt, *Lincoln's Code*, 82.

79. Virginia Kays Veenswijk, *Coudert Brothers: A Legacy in Law: The History of America's First International Law Firm, 1853-1993* (New York: Truman Talley Books, 1994).

80. Theodore S. Woolsey, "International Law, 1701-1901," in *Two Centuries' Growth of American Law, 1701-1901* (1901; repr. Buffalo, NY: William S. Hein, 1980), 491–520; Barbara J. Frischholz and John M. Raymond, "Lawyers Who Established International Law in the United States, 1776-1914," *AJIL* 76, no. 4 (1982): 817–18.

81. John Bassett Moore, "Boyhood," n.d., box 206, JBM, LC.

82. Richard Megargee, "Realism in American Foreign Policy: The Diplomacy of John Bassett Moore" (PhD diss., Northwestern University, 1963), 10.

83. Megargee, "Diplomacy of John Bassett Moore," 12–14.

84. Edwin Borchard, "Moore's Memoirs, Ch. 1," n.d., 1, in box 217, JBM, LC.

85. Borchard, "Moore's Memoirs, Ch. 1," 1.

86. Borchard, "Moore's Memoirs, Ch. 1," 2.

87. Julius Goebel Jr., *A History of the School of Law, Columbia University* (New York: Columbia University Press, 1955), 168.

88. *Official Register of the United States*, vol. 1 (Washington, DC: Government Printing Office, 1885), 20. See also Johnson, *Administration*, 55–56.

89. Borchard, "Moore's Memoirs Ch. 1," 4; Megargee, "Diplomacy of John Bassett Moore," 120; Moore, "The Disputed Boundary between Venezuela and British Guayana," 14 July 1885, box 164, JBM, LC; for Hawaii (which came during his second stint with the department, in 1898), see Moore to John Pine, 22 October 1910, box 295, JBM, LC.

90. John Bassett Moore, *A Treatise on Extradition and Interstate Rendition* (Boston: The Boston Book Company, 1891), v. For more on the context surrounding Moore's book, see Margolies, *Spaces of Law.*

91. John Bassett Moore, "Renault—1891," n.d., box 207, JBM, LC; Borchard, "Moore's Memoirs, Ch. 1," 7.

92. R. Gordon Hoxie, et. al., *A History of the Faculty of Political Science, Columbia University.* (New York: Columbia University Press, 1955), 48; Neff, *Justice among Nations*, 304.

93. Moore spent these years vacationing in North Carolina and traveling in Europe. Borchard, "Moore's Memoirs, Ch. 6," 1, box 217, JBM, LC; Moore to A. W. Sewall, 5 March 1908, box 13, JBM, CLS; Nicholas Murray Butler to Moore, 21 February 1910, box 16, JBM, LC.

94. See, e.g., Borchard, "Moore's Memoirs Ch. 5," p. 1, box 217, JBM, LC.

95. Borchard, "Moore's Memoirs Ch. 1," 7; Moore to William L. Putnam, 21 December 1906, box 12, JBM, LC. Moore's private dealings, and the implications thereof, are discussed further in chapters 4 and 6. Moore's historical writings included *American Diplomacy: Its Spirit and Achievements* (New York: Harper and Brothers, 1905), and he edited *The Works of James Buchanan*, 12 vols. (Philadelphia: J. B. Lippincott Company, 1908–1911).

96. Moore, "Offer of a Chair of International Law & Political Science at Princeton, 1899," n.d., box 214, JBM, LC; Moore to William R. Day, 15 February 1900, box 7, JBM, LC; Borchard, "Moore's Memoirs Ch. 5," 8; Walter S. Penfield to Moore, 8 November 1912, box 18, JBM, LC.

97. Moore to William Howard Taft, 17 February 1914, box 28, JBM, LC; Alfred T. Mahan to Moore, 1 March 1904, box 10, JBM, LC; Samuel Gompers to Moore, 6, May 1911, box 16, JBM, LC.

98. "John Bassett Moore Expected to Be Made President of University of Virginia," *The State* (Columbia, SC), June 3, 1903.

99. Megargee, "Diplomacy of John Bassett Moore."

100. This is the understanding shared largely by Lassa Oppenheim and many other lawyers who identified themselves as "positivists." See Lassa Oppenheim, "The Science of International Law: Its Task and Method," *AJIL* 2, no. 2 (1908): 313–56.

101. John Bassett Moore, *Four Phases of American Development: Federalism—Democracy—Imperialism—Expansion* (Baltimore: John Hopkins Press, 1912; repr. New York: Da Capo Press, 1970), 51.

102. Moore's mentor, State Department solicitor Francis Wharton, had written the first American digest of international law in 1886. Despite his fondness for Wharton, Moore complained that its "gravest defect" was "the fact that it merely told what was said by only one of the parties to the debate but not what was eventually done." Moore, "Digest of International Law," memorandum, 26 April 1943, box 207, JBM, LC. See also Francis M. Wharton, ed., *A Digest of the International Law of the United States, Taken from Documents Issued by Presidents and Secretaries of State, and from Decisions of Federal Courts and Opinions of Attorneys-General* (Washington, DC: Government Printing Office, 1886).

103. John Bassett Moore, *History and Digest of the International Arbitrations to Which the United States Has Been a Party, together with Appendices Containing the Treaties Relating to Such Arbitrations, and Historical and Legal Notes on Other International Arbitrations Ancient and Modern, and on the Domestic Commissions of the United States for the Adjustment of International Claims*, 6 vols. (Washington, D.C.: Government Printing Office, 1898).

104. Moore, *Digest of International Law*, 8 vols.

105. Department of State, *A Short Account of the Department of State of the United States* (Washington, DC: Government Printing Office, 1922), 30.

106. Moore, *Principles of American Diplomacy*, viii–ix.

107. Moore, *American Diplomacy*, 251–53.

108. "Theodore Salisbury Woolsey: October 22, 1852–April 24, 1929," *American Journal of International Law* 23, no. 3 (1929): 616–17.

109. "Theodore Dwight Woolsey," *Proceedings of the American Academy of Arts and Sciences* 25 (1889–90): 343–46; Theodore S. Woolsey to B. W. Austin, 28 Oct. 1892, box 31, WFP; Woolsey, "The Decadence of this Republic: Notes for a Colby Club Paper," box 47, WFP.

110. Theodore S. Woolsey, "Our Foreign Policy, and Its Relations to Domestic Problems," (1897), and "The United States and the Declaration of Paris," (1894), in *America's Foreign Policy*, 1–21, 273–82.

111. Theodore S. Woolsey, "An Inquiry Concerning Our Foreign Relations," (1892), in *America's Foreign Policy*, 169–91.

112. "An Interoceanic Canal in the Light of Precedent," (1895), in *America's Foreign Policy*, 133–49.

113. Woolsey to Archibald M. Howe, box 31, WFP. On the relationship between war and trade, see "An Inquiry Concerning Our Foreign Relations" (1892), in *America's Foreign Policy*, 188–89.

Chapter 2

1. Elihu Root, "The Lawyer of Today, Address before the New York Country Lawyers Association, New York City, March 13, 1915," in *Addresses on Government and Citizenship*, ed. Robert Bacon and James Brown Scott (Cambridge, MA: Harvard University Press, 1916), 503–4. For context, see Philip C. Jessup, *Elihu Root* (New York: Dodd, Mead and Company, 1938), 1:215–22.

2. Robert C. Hilderbrand, *Power and the People: Executive Management of Public Opinion in Foreign Affairs, 1897-1921* (Chapel Hill: University of North Carolina Press, 1981); LaFeber, *New Empire*; Bonnie M. Miller, *From Liberation to Conquest: The Visual and Popular Cultures of the Spanish-American War of 1898* (Amherst: University of Massachusetts Press, 2011); John L. Offner, *An Unwanted War: The Diplomacy of the United States and Spain over Cuba, 1895-1898* (Chapel Hill: University of North Carolina Press, 1992); Louis A. Pérez, Jr., *The War of 1898: The United States and Cuba in History and Historiography* (Chapel Hill: University of North Carolina Press, 1998).

3. A summary of the treaty is in John Bassett Moore to John Hay, 10 December 1898, in *FRUS* (1898), 965.

4. Frank Ninkovich, *The United States and Imperialism* (Malden, MA: Blackwell, 2001), 10.

5. Root, "Lawyer of Today," 504; Maguire, *Law and War*; Dezalay and Garth, "Law, Lawyers, and Empire."

6. Elmer Plischke, *U.S. Department of State: A Reference History* (Westport, CT: Greenwood Press, 1999), 190–91; George Grafton Wilson to Moore, 19 July 1898, box 214, JBM, LC; John Bassett Moore, "Maritime Law in the War with Spain," *Political Science Quarterly* 15, no. 3 (1900): 399–425; *The Paquete Habana* (1900), 175 U.S. 677.

7. William Appleman Williams, *Empire as a Way of Life* (New York: Oxford University Press, 1982); Ninkovich, *United States and Imperialism*; Fry, "Phases of Empire"; Crapol, "Coming to Terms with Empire."

8. Heiss, "Evolution of the Imperial Idea," 527; Raymond Esthus, "Isolationism and World Power," *Diplomatic History* 2, no. 2 (1978): 117–18; Adams quoted in Bradford Perkins, *The Great Rapprochement: England and the United States, 1895-1914* (New York: Atheneum, 1968), 89.

9. Mark Twain, "To the Person Sitting in Darkness" (1901), in *Mark Twain's Weapons of Satire: Anti-Imperialist Writings on the Philippine-American War*, ed. Jim Zwick (Syracuse, NY: Syracuse University Press, 1992), 22–39; Alan McPherson, "Americanism against American Empire," in *Americanism: New Perspectives on the History of an Ideal*, ed. Michael Kazin and Joseph A. McCartin (Chapel Hill: University of North Carolina Press, 2006), 176.

10. Matthew Frye Jacobson, *Barbarian Virtues: The United States Encounters Foreign Peoples at Home and Abroad, 1876-1917* (New York: Hill and Wang, 2000), 229–33; Benjamin R. Tillman, address to Senate, Reported in 32 Cong. Rec. Part 2, 7 February 1899, 1531–32; William Graham Sumner, "The Predominant Issue" (1900), in *War and Other Essays* (New Haven, CT: Yale University Press, 1911), 345–46.

11. Walter L. Williams, "United States Indian Policy and the Debate over Philippine Annexation: Implications for the Origins of American Imperialism," *Journal of American History* 66, no. 4 (1980): 820.

12. Fry, "Phases of Empire," 263–64; Jacobson, *Barbarian Virtues*, 222; LaFeber, *New Empire*; Challener, *Admirals, Generals*, chap. 1.

13. Ninkovich, *United States and Imperialism*, 40–41.
14. Eric Hobsbawm, *The Age of Empire, 1875-1914* (New York: Vintage Books, 1987), 56–59; Chamberlain is quoted in Wolfgang J. Mommsen, *Theories of Imperialism*, trans. P. S. Falla (German lst ed. 1977; repr. New York: Random House, 1980), 6.
15. Stephanson, *Manifest Destiny*, 67.
16. *The Foreign Policy of the United States: Political and Commercial. Addresses and Discussion at the Annual Meeting of the American Academy of Political and Social Science, April 7-8, 1899* (Philadelphia: American Academy of Political and Social Science, 1899), 22, 47.
17. Kramer, "Empires, Exceptions, and Anglo-Saxons"; Susan K. Harris, *God's Arbiters: Americans and the Philippines, 1898-1902* (New York: Oxford University Press, 2011), 140.
18. Albert J. Beveridge, "The Star of Empire" (September 25, 1900), in *The Meaning of the Times and Other Speeches* (Indianapolis, IN: Bobbs-Merrill Co., 1908), 118–43.
19. "Sixto Lopez on the Philippine Question," *The Outlook*, April 13, 1901, 846.
20. My emphasis here differs from other recent studies. Fabian Hilfrich argues that exceptionalism pervaded both sides of the empire debate, but acknowledges the presence of expansionist appeals to common imperial identity. Susan Harris sees pro-imperialists as espousers of a kind of Christian exceptionalism and minimizes the way this discourse was connected to broader transatlantic arguments for empire. Fabian Hilfrich, *Debating American Exceptionalism: Empire and Democracy in the Wake of the Spanish-American War* (New York: Palgrave Macmillan, 2012); Harris, *God's Arbiters*.
21. Joseph M. Siracusa, "Progressivism, Imperialism, and the Leuchtenberg Thesis, 1952-1974: An Historiographical Appraisal," *Australian Journal of Politics and History* 20 (December 1974): 312–25.
22. Ninkovich, *United States and Imperialism*, 40–41; Stephanson, *Manifest Destiny*, xiv; Strong, *Expansion under New World Conditions*, 270, 288.
23. Harris, *God's Arbiters*, 23.
24. Olney to Frederick Bayard, 20 July 1895, in *FRUS* (1895), 545–62.
25. Gerald G. Eggert, *Richard Olney: Evolution of a Statesman* (University Park: Pennsylvania State University Press, 1974); Olney to Bayard, 20 July 1895; Sexton, *Monroe Doctrine*, 159.
26. Richard Olney, "International Isolation of the United States," *Atlantic Monthly*, May 1898, 577–88; Richard Olney, "Growth of Our Foreign Policy," *Atlantic Monthly*, March 1900, 289–301.
27. Walter Wellman, "Shall the Monroe Doctrine Be Modified?" *North American Review*, December 1901, 832–44; An American Business Man, "Is the Monroe Doctrine a Bar to Civilization?" *North American Review* , April 1903, 518–29; Gretchen Murphy, *Hemispheric Imaginings: The Monroe Doctrine and Narratives of U.S. Empire* (Durham, NC: Duke University Press, 2005), chap. 4.
28. Carman F. Randolph, "Constitutional Aspects of Annexation," *Harvard Law Review* 12, no. 5 (1898): 291.
29. Quoted in Sparrow, *Insular Cases*, 1.
30. US Const., art. IV, sec. 3; Raustiala, *Does the Constitution Follow the Flag?*, 33–34; Sarah H. Cleveland, "Powers Inherent in Sovereignty: Indians, Aliens, Territories, and the Nineteenth Century Origins of Plenary Power in Foreign Affairs," *Texas Law Review* 81, no. 1 (2002): 164–72; Sparrow, *Insular Cases*, chap. 1.
31. *Ker v. Illinois* (1886), 119 U.S. 436; *In re Ross* (1891), 140 U.S. 453, at 462, 464; Margolies, *Spaces of Law*, 330; Raustiala, *Does the Constitution Follow the Flag?*, 63–64.
32. "Government of Territories and Colonies," *Harvard Law Review* 12, no. 3 (1898): 205–6.
33. Randolph, "Constitutional Aspects."
34. Simeon E. Baldwin, "The Constitutional Questions Incident to the Acquisition and Government by the United States of Island Territory," *Harvard Law Review* 12, no. 6 (1899): 412–13.
35. Raustiala, *Does the Constitution Follow the Flag?*, 84.
36. C. C. Langdell, "The Status of Our New Territories," *Harvard Law Review*, 12:6 (1899): 365–392; James Bradley Thayer, "Our New Possessions," *Harvard Law Review* 12, no. 7 (1899): 464–85.
37. Sam Erman, "Constitutional Storm Rising: U.S. Expansion Resumes, 1898-1900," unpublished manuscript in author's possession (2014).
38. Baldwin, "Constitutional Questions," 415.

39. *Foreign Policy of the United States,* 67–68, 70–72.

40. Sparrow, *Insular Cases,* 101–2.

41. Quoted in Sparrow, *Insular Cases,* 108.

42. Thomas A. Bailey questions the centrality of the empire issue to the election results. Bailey, "Was the Presidential Election of 1900 a Mandate on Imperialism?" *Mississippi Valley Historical Review* 24, no. 1 (1937): 43–52.

43. *Downes v. Bidwell* (1901), 182 U.S. 244, at 279, 282, 286.

44. *Downes v. Bidwell,* at 306, 308; Sparrow, *Insular Cases,* 93; Roger P. Alford, "International Law as an Interpretive Tool in the Supreme Court, 1901-1945," in *International Law in the U.S. Supreme Court: Continuity and Change,* ed. David Sloss, Michael D. Ramsay, and William S. Dodge (Cambridge: Cambridge University Press, 2011), 270–72.

45. *Downes v. Bidwell,* at 369, 380; Sparrow, *Insular Cases,* 97; Cleveland, "Powers Inherent," 228.

46. Abbot Lawrence Lowell, "The Status of Our New Possessions: A Third View," *Harvard Law Review* 13, no. 3 (1899): 155–76

47. *Downes v. Bidwell,* at 341–42; 373; *Dorr v. United States* (1904), 138, at 140; Cleveland, "Powers Inherent," 238.

48. Moore, *American Diplomacy,* viii. Moore, "Congress of Arts and Sciences, St. Louis Exhibition, 1905," n. d. *c.*1940, box 215, JBM, LC; Megargee, "John Bassett Moore."

49. Theodore S. Woolsey, "The Future of the Philippines," (1898), in *America's Foreign Policy,* 105, 107.

50. David J. Silbey, *A War of Frontier and Empire: The Philippine-American War, 1899-1902* (New York: Hill and Wang, 2007), 126.

51. Christopher Capozzola, "Constabulary Duty: Policing the Philippines, 1901-1904," unpublished manuscript in author's possession (2009); Brian McAllister Linn, *The Philippine War, 1899-1902* (Lawrence: University Press of Kansas, 2000), 315; Max Boot, *The Savage Wars of Peace: Small Wars and the Rise of American Power* (New York: Basic Books, 2002), 120; Kramer, *Blood of Government,* 144–45.

52. Hoganson, *Fighting for American Manhood,* chap. 8; Daniel E. Bender, *American Abyss: Savagery and Civilization in the Age of Industry* (Ithaca, NY: Cornell University Press, 2009), 40–68; Ian Tyrrell, *Reforming the World: The Creation of America's Moral Empire* (Princeton, NJ: Princeton University Press, 2010), chap. 6; Twain, "Person Sitting in Darkness," 39.

53. Silbey, *War of Frontier and Empire,* 156–57; Maguire, *Law and War,* 50.

54. Maguire, *Law and War,* 8.

55. Elihu Root, "The United States and the Philippines in 1900, Address at Canton, Ohio, October 24, 1900," in *The Military and Colonial Policy of the United States: Addresses and Reports,* ed. Robert Bacon and James Brown Scott (Cambridge, MA: Harvard University Press, 1916), 27–64; Root to Scott, 18 August 1916, box 7, JBS.

56. Root, "U.S. and the Philippines," 35.

57. Root, "U.S. and the Philippines," 36.

58. On the uses of this justification, see Kramer, *Blood of Government.*

59. Root, "U.S. and the Philippines," 44.

60. David J. Brewer, "Growth of the Judicial Function," 7 July 1898, *Report of the Organization and First Annual Meeting of the Colorado Bar Association* (1898), 88; Mark S. Weiner, "Teutonic Constitutionalism: The Role of Ethno-Juridical Discourse in the Spanish-American War," in *Foreign in a Domestic Sense: Puerto Rico, American Expansion, and the Constitution,* ed. Christina Duffy Burnett [Ponsa] and Burke Marshall (Durham, NC: Duke University Press, 2001), 65.

61. A graduate of Yale and the Cincinnati Law School, Taft became a federal judge in the US Sixth Circuit court in 1892. David Burton, *William Howard Taft: Confident Peacemaker* (New York: Fordham University Press, 2004), 1–9; Ralph E. Minger, *William Howard Taft and United States Foreign Policy: The Apprenticeship Years, 1900-1908* (Urbana: University of Illinois Press), 8–9, 14–15. Root is quoted in Minger, *Apprenticeship,* 102. The newspaper profile of Taft is in Lars Schoultz, *Beneath the United States: A History of U.S. Policy toward Latin America* (Cambridge, MA: Harvard University Press, 1998), 205.

62. Minger, *Apprenticeship,* 75; Paul D. Hutchcroft, "The Hazards of Jeffersonianism: Challenges of State Building in the United States and Its Empire," in McCoy and Scarano, *Colonial*

Crucible, 387; Peter W. Stanley, *A Nation in the Making: The Philippines and the United States, 1899-1921* (Cambridge, MA: Harvard University Press, 1974), 65.

63. Theodore S. Woolsey, "The Government of Dependencies," in *Foreign Policy of the United States,* 3–18; Theodore S. Woolsey, "The Legal Aspects of Aguinaldo's Capture," *The Outlook,* April 13, 1901, 855–56.

64. "On Keeping the Fourth of July," *Atlantic Monthly,* July 1902, 4.

65. Silbey, *War of Frontier and Empire,* 205–6.

66. Lester D. Langley, *The United States and the Caribbean in the Twentieth Century,* 4th ed. (Athens: University of Georgia Press, 1989), 30. On whether or not Roosevelt actually boasted of "taking" the canal zone, see James F. Vivian, "The Taking of the Panama Canal Zone: Myth and Reality," *Diplomatic History* 4, no. 1 (1980): 95–100.

67. David McCullough, *The Path between the Seas: The Creation of the Panama Canal, 1870-1914* (New York: Simon and Schuster, 1977), 254–55; Challener, *Admirals, Generals,* 35–36; Edmund Morris, *Theodore Rex* (New York: Random House, 2001), 241–42. Fear of Germany's naval power also factored into the equation. See Carl Cavanagh Hodge, "A Whiff of Cordite: Theodore Roosevelt and the Transoceanic Naval Arms Race, 1897-1909," *Diplomacy and Statecraft* 19, no. 4 (2008): 712–31.

68. Dwight C. Miner, *The Fight for the Panama Route: The Story of the Spooner Act and the Hay-Herrán Treaty* (New York: Columbia University Press, 1940); Jeffrey A. Engel, "The Democratic Language of American Imperialism: Race, Order, and Theodore Roosevelt's Personifications of Foreign Policy Evil," *Diplomacy and Statecraft* 19, no. 4 (2008): 682. Text of the Hay-Herrán Treaty is in Miner, *Panama Route,* app. C, 413–26.

69. John Bassett Moore, "1903," [c.1932], box 207, JBM, LC; Loomis to Moore, 12 August 1903, box 134, JBM, LC; Loomis to Moore 15 August 1903, reel 3, FBLP. See discussion in Miner, *Panama Route,* 341n15. Note that Loomis told Moore that Roosevelt had requested the memo; but when forwarding the memo to Roosevelt on August 15, Loomis intimated that he (Loomis) had requested it of Moore.

70. Text of the memorandum can be found in Miner, *Panama Route,* app. D, 427–32; and in John Bassett Moore, *The Collected Papers of John Bassett Moore* (New Haven, CT: Yale University Press, 1945), 3:102–7.

71. Quoted in Miner, *Panama Route,* 428.

72. The treaty was actually with New Granada, which later became Colombia.

73. Roosevelt to John Hay, 19 August 1903, quoted in Miner, *Panama Route,* 345.

74. Moore to Dwight Miner, 20 October 1939, cited in Miner, *Panama Route,* 345.

75. Moore, "1903."

76. Collin, *Roosevelt's Caribbean,* 242, 244.

77. Miner, *Panama Route,* 352.

78. See the notes on pp. 665–66 in Morris, *Theodore Rex,* for a discussion of a meeting between Roosevelt and Bunau-Varilla in which the president hinted at his support. Moore's role was more indirect: Bunau-Varilla was visiting William Burr, an engineering professor at Columbia, when Burr mentioned a conversation he'd had with Moore about Panama. Bunau-Varilla arranged a meeting, and talk turned to an article Bunau-Varilla had published in *Le Matin* that made a claim similar to the one Moore had made in his memo to Roosevelt. According to Bunau-Varilla, when Moore claimed he could not talk about the issue, the Frenchmen intuited that Moore had written a memo to Roosevelt about Panama. Moore, on the other hand, believed that someone—my guess would be Loomis, though Collin suggests it was Burr—had leaked the memo to Bunau-Varilla. See Philippe Bunau-Varilla, *Panama: The Creation, Destruction, and Resurrection* (New York: McBride, Nast and Company, 1914), 295–97; Moore, "Bunau-Varilla," undated memorandum, box 207, JBM, LC; Collin, *Roosevelt's Caribbean,* 254, 302.

79. LaFeber, *Panama Canal,* 26; John Major, *Prize Possession: The United States and the Panama Canal, 1903-1979* (New York: Cambridge University Press, 1993), 41.

80. John Major, "Who Wrote the Hay–Bunau-Varilla Convention?" *Diplomatic History* 8, no. 2 (1984): 115–23.

81. Moore, "1903"; Loomis to Moore, 25 November 1903, reel 3, FBLP.

82. Collin suggests that Moore played a more direct role by passing on Bunau-Varilla's arguments to Roosevelt. But I can find no direct evidence of this. Instead, Loomis seems to have

been Bunau-Varilla's conduit to the White House. Collin, *Roosevelt's Caribbean*, 254–55; Morris, *Theodore Rex*, 665; Major, *Prize Possession*, 58. Moore's legal rationales did circulate widely in the press. Collin, *Roosevelt's Caribbean*, 251.

83. Morris, *Theodore Rex*, 295, 302.

84. Quoted in Eggert, *Olney*, 291.

85. "The Right of Secession," *New York Times*, January 1, 1904.

86. A comprehensive review of the press and congressional reaction is in Terence Graham, *The "Interests of Civilization"? Reaction in the United States against the "Seizure" of the Panama Canal Zone, 1903-1904*, Lund Studies in International History 19 (Lund, Sweden: Esselte Studium, 1983). Overall, of the 137 newspapers that Graham surveyed, 58 (42%) opposed TR and 79 (58%) supported him.

87. *FRUS* (1903), xxxii–xlii.

88. Moorfield Storey, *The Recognition of Panama: Address Delivered at Massachusetts Reform Club, December 5, 1903* (Boston: Geo. H. Ellis Co., 1904), 18; Theodore S. Woolsey, "The Recognition of Panama and Its Results," *Green Bag* 16 (1904): 10–11; Woolsey, "General Political Developments, 1910," box 47, WFP.

89. Moore, "Amendments of and Additions to Roosevelt's Draft of His Special Message to Congress of January 4, 1904," box 134, JBM, LC.

90. Theodore Roosevelt, "Message from the President of the United States Transmitting a Statement of Action in Executing the Act Entitled 'An Act to Provide for the Construction of a Canal Connecting the Waters of the Atlantic and Pacific Oceans,' Approved June 28, 1902," January 4, 1904, *FRUS* (1903), 260.

91. Moore, "1903."

92. For the full text of Moore's suggestions, see "Amendments of & Additions to Pres. Roosevelt's draft," box 134, JBM, LC. In the following paragraphs, I cite the finished document, since the wording is the same.

93. TR to Moore, January 6, 1904, in *The Letters of Theodore Roosevelt*, ed. Elting E. Morison (Cambridge, MA: Harvard University Press, 1951), 3:689–90. Loomis told Moore that the president "was exceedingly grateful" and "highly pleased with your presentation of the various points which you discussed." Loomis to Moore, 29 December 1903, reel 3, Francis B. Loomis Papers.

94. Roosevelt, "Message from the President," 273.

95. Collin, *Roosevelt's Caribbean*, 297; Edwin C. Hoyt, "National Policy and International Law: Case Studies from American Canal Policy," Monograph Series in World Affairs, vol. 4, no. 1, 1966–67 (Denver, CO: Social Science Foundation and Graduate School of International Studies, University of Denver, 1966); Loveman, *No Higher Law*, 184.

96. LaFeber, *Panama Canal*, 32.

97. For critical analysis of Moore's legal arguments, see Thomas D. Schoonover, "Morality and Political Purpose in Theodore Roosevelt's Actions in Panama in 1903," in *The United States in Central America, 1860-1911: Episodes of Social Imperialism and Imperial Rivalry in the World System* (Durham, NC: Duke University Press, 1991), 99–104.

98. Roosevelt, "Message from the President," 274.

99. Jessup, *Root*, 1:403.

100. Roosevelt, "Message from the President," 275; italics mine.

101. On how alternative forms of intervention applied to nominally "civilized" but less powerful regions, see Lorca, "Universal International Law."

102. William Cullen Dennis, "The Panama Situation in the Light of International Law: The Treaty of 1846 between the United States and New Granada," *American Law Register* 52, no. 5 (1904): 300.

103. Graham, *Interests of Civilization*, 76–79.

104. David Axeen, "'Heroes of the Engine Room': American 'Civilization' and the War with Spain," *American Quarterly* 36, no. 4 (1984): 481–502; Michael Adas, *Dominance by Design: Technological Imperatives and America's Civilizing Mission* (Cambridge, MA: Harvard University Press, 2006), 129–216.

105. Richard Olney, "The Development of International Law," *AJIL* 1, no. 2 (1907): 426.

106. James William Park, *Latin American Underdevelopment: A History of Perspectives in the United States, 1870-1965* (Baton Rouge: Louisiana State University Press, 1995); Fredrick B. Pike, *The United States and Latin America: Myths and Stereotypes of Civilization and Nature* (Austin: University of Texas Press, 1992).

107. E. Berkeley Tompkins, *Anti-Imperialism in the United States: The Great Debate, 1890-1920* (Philadelphia: University of Pennsylvania Press, 1970), 257–61.

108. LaFeber, *Panama Canal,* 32–33.

109. Moore, *Digest of International Law.*

110. Moore, *Digest of International Law,* 3:48–78.

111. Mahan to Moore, 1, June 1912, box 18, JBM, LC.

Chapter 3

1. Ralph Dingman Nurnberger, "James Brown Scott: Peace through Justice" (PhD diss., Georgetown University, 1975), 23, 32–35; Robert Stevens, *Law School: Legal Education in America from the 1850s to the 1980s* (Chapel Hill: University of North Carolina Press, 1983), 78.

 2. Winton U. Solberg, *The University of Illinois, 1894-1904: The Shaping of a University* (Urbana: University of Illinois Press, 2000), 226.

 3. Solberg, *University of Illinois,* 85.

 4. Solberg, *University of Illinois,* 85.

 5. "Luncheon of Executive Council and Board of Editors," ASIL *Proceedings* 25 (1931): 242–43.

 6. Solberg, *University of Illinois,* 86.

 7. James Brown Scott, "International Arbitration: Address of Mr. James Brown Scott before the Sunset Club, Los Angeles, California, 1897," MS1207, Harvard Law School Library Special Collections, 1897. The manuscript is dated 1897, and several scholars have since used that date, but contemporary publications indicate that the address was in fact delivered in 1896. Fred L. Alles, "The Sunset Club," *The Land of Sunshine: A Southern California Magazine* 5, no. 3 (1896): 127.

 8. Lutzker, "'Practical' Peace Advocates."

 9. DeBenedetti, *Peace Reform in American History,* 69.

10. Laity, *British Peace Movement,* 132.

11. Andrew C. Imbrie, "Lectures on Law by Prof. Woodrow Wilson 1894-1895," box 59, Lecture Notes Collection, Mudd Library, Princeton University.

12. International Law—Fourth Monthly Test, 9 March 1904, box 49, WFP.

13. American Diplomatic History—Final Exam, 17 May 1904, box 49, WFP.

14. John Bassett Moore, *International Law Situations with Solutions and Notes* (Washington, DC: Government Printing Office, 1901).

15. Brian C. Schmidt, *The Political Discourse of Anarchy: A Disciplinary History of International Relations* (Albany, NY: State University of New York Press, 1998), 100.

16. W. W. Willoughby, "The Legal Nature of International Law," *AJIL* 2, no. 2 (1908): 361.

17. John Austin, *Lectures on Jurisprudence,* 4th ed. (London: John Murray, 1873), 2:780; Mark W. Janis, *The American Tradition of International Law: Great Expectations 1789-1914* (Oxford: Oxford University Press, 2004), chap. 1.

18. See, e.g., Ohlin, *Assault on International Law,* 22–23.

19. E. Anthony Rotundo, *American Manhood: Transformations in Masculinity from the Revolution to the Modern Era* (New York: Basic Books, 1993); Michael Kimmel, *Manhood in America: A Cultural History* (New York: Free Press, 1996); Gail Bederman, *Manliness and Civilization: A Cultural History of Gender and Race in the United States, 1880-1917* (Chicago: University of Chicago Press, 1995).

20. Rotundo, *American Manhood,* 234.

21. Bederman, *Manliness and Civilization,* chap. 5; Sarah Watts, *Rough Rider in the White House: Theodore Roosevelt and the Politics of Desire* (Chicago: University of Chicago Press, 2003); Patricia O'Toole, *When Trumpets Call: Theodore Roosevelt after the White House* (New York: Simon and Schuster, 2004).

22. Hoganson, *Fighting for American Manhood,* 71.

23. Hoganson, *Fighting for American Manhood*, 18–21; Judith Papachristou, "American Women and Foreign Policy, 1898-1905: Exploring Gender in Diplomatic History," *Diplomatic History* 14, no. 4 (1990): 493–509.

24. Hoganson, *Fighting for American Manhood*, 20. For the popularity of the war, see Miller, *From Liberation to Conquest*.

25. On the membership of these groups, see Robert Beisner, *Twelve against Empire: The Anti-Imperialists, 1898-1900* (New York: McGraw-Hill, 1968); Kuehl, *Seeking World Order*.

26. Kevin P. Murphy, *Political Manhood: Red Bloods, Mollycoddles, and the Politics of Progressive Era Reform* (New York: Columbia University Press, 2008), 15–17.

27. Rotundo, *American Manhood*, 170–73.

28. James Brown Scott to Johnkheer J. Loudon, 27 February 1914, vol. 260, CEIPP.

29. Samuel Eliot Morison, *Three Centuries of Harvard, 1636-1936* (Cambridge, MA: Harvard University Press, 1963), 326.

30. Jerold S. Auerbach, *Unequal Justice: Lawyers and Social Change in Modern America* (New York: Oxford University Press, 1976), 76.

31. Bruce A. Kimball, *The Inception of Modern Professional Education: C. C. Langdell, 1826-1906* (Chapel Hill: University of North Carolina Press, 2009).

32. Thomas C. Grey, "Langdell's Orthodoxy," *University of Pittsburgh Law Review* 45, no. 1 (1983–84): 13; Kimball, *Inception of Modern Professional Education*, 6.

33. Hugh C. MacGill and R. Kent Newmyer, "Legal Education and Legal Thought, 1790-1920," in *The Cambridge History of Law in America*, vol. 2: *The Long Nineteenth Century (1789-1920)*, ed. Michael Grossberg and Christopher Tomlins (Cambridge: Cambridge University Press, 2008), 50–51.

34. Dorothy Ross, *The Origins of American Social Science* (New York: Cambridge University Press, 1991).

35. Kimball, *Inception of Modern Legal Education*, 269, 310.

36. William R. Johnson, *Schooled Lawyers: A Study in the Clash of Professional Cultures* (New York: New York University Press, 1978), 101.

37. Macgill and Newmyer, "Legal Education," 51.

38. Grey, "Langdell's Orthodoxy," 34.

39. Stevens, *Law School*, 40.

40. Macgill and Newmyer, "Legal Education," 54; "Ernst Freund: Pioneer of Administrative Law," *University of Chicago Law Review* 29, no. 4 (1962): 763.

41. Frischholz and Raymond, "Lawyers Who Established International Law," 817.

42. Wiebe, *Search for Order*, 121; Dee Garrison, *Apostles of Culture: The Public Librarian and American Society, 1876-1920* (New York: Free Press, 1979), 3; John A. Matzko, "'The Best Men of the Bar': The Founding of the American Bar Association," in *The New High Priests: Lawyers in Post–Civil War America*, ed. Gerard W. Gawalt (Westport, CT: Greenwood Press, 1984), 75; Peter Novick, *That Noble Dream: The "Objectivity Question" and the American Historical Profession* (Cambridge: Cambridge University Press, 1988), 48; Schmidt, *Political Discourse of Anarchy*, 81.

43. Wiebe, *Search for Order*, 144–50.

44. Robert L. Church, "Economists as Experts: The Rise of an Academic Profession in the United States, 1870-1920," in *The University in Society*, ed. Lawrence Stone (Princeton, NJ: Princeton University Press, 1974), 571–609.

45. Robert W. Gordon, "The American Legal Profession, 1870-2000," in Grossberg and Tomlins, *Cambridge History of Law in America*, 3:73–126.

46. Justice David Brewer, quoted in Russell G. Pearce, "Lawyers as America's Governing Class: The Formation and Dissolution of the Original Understanding of the American Lawyer's Role," *University of Chicago Law School Roundtable* 8 (2001): 396.

47. Matzko, "Best Men of the Bar," 75–97; Auerbach, *Unequal Justice*, 48.

48. Auerbach, *Unequal Justice*, 24–25.

49. Gordon, "American Legal Profession," 73.

50. Michael Grossberg, "Institutionalizing Masculinity: The Law as a Masculine Profession," in *Meanings for Manhood: Constructions of Masculinity in Victorian America*, ed. Mark C. Carnes and Clyde Griffen (Chicago: University of Chicago Press, 1990), 141, 149; Virginia

G. Drachman, *Sisters in Law: Women Lawyers in Modern American History* (Cambridge, MA: Harvard University Press, 1998), 2.

51. Stevens, *Law School*, 84.
52. Kimball, *Inception of Modern Professional Education*, 289.
53. Stevens, *Law School*, 54; Grossberg, "Institutionalizing Masculinity," 144.
54. Joseph Beale, quoted in Macgill and Newmyer, "Legal Education," 54.
55. Auerbach, *Unequal Justice*, 32–35.
56. For an extended argument to this point, see John Hepp, "James Brown Scott and the Rise of Public International Law," *Journal of the Gilded Age and Progressive Era* 7, no. 2 (2008): 151–79.
57. James Brown Scott, "The Place of International Law in Legal Education," *Annual Report of the American Bar Association* 26 (1903): 587–88; James Brown Scott, "The Place of International Law in American Jurisprudence," *Green Bag* 15 (1903): 164–73; James Brown Scott, "The Legal Nature of International Law," 5 *Columbia Law Review* (1905): 124–52.
58. James Brown Scott, ed., *Cases on International Law: Selected from Decisions of English and American Courts* (Boston: Boston Book Company, 1902), v.
59. Scott, "Place of International Law," 588.
60. James Brown Scott to Charles W. Ames, 12 June 1914, box 77, JBS. Scott's *Cases* began as a second edition of Freeman Snow's *Cases and Opinions on International Law* (Boston: Boston Book Company 1893). Scott had been a student of Snow's at Harvard, but Snow had taught international law in the faculty of History and Government, not for the law school. Morison, *Three Centuries of Harvard*, 349, 376.
61. James Brown Scott, "The Study of the Law," *American Law School Review* 2, no. 1 (1906): 1–10; Finch, "Biography," 21.
62. Manley O. Hudson, "Twelve Casebooks on International Law," *AJIL* 32, no. 3 (1938): 447–48.
63. Hepp, "James Brown Scott," 167; Nurnberger, "James Brown Scott," 46.
64. Scott, "Place of International Law," 591.
65. Scott, "Place of International Law," 592.
66. Patterson, *Toward a Warless World*, 129.
67. DeBenedetti, *Peace Reform*, 79; Lutzker, "'Practical' Peace Advocates," 3.
68. "History of the Organization of the American Society of International Law," ASIL *Proceedings* 1 (1907): 23.
69. "History of the Organization," 27–31; James Brown Scott, "American Society of International Law Preliminary Organization," box 1, ASIL Papers; "Root Heads New Body on International Law," *NYT*, January 13, 1906.
70. "Editorial Comment," *AJIL* 1, no. 1 (1907): 129.
71. "History of the Organization," 24.
72. "Constitution," *AJIL* 1, no. 1 (1907): 133.
73. Frederic Kirgis, *The American Society of International Law's First Century 1906-2006* (Boston: Martinus Nijhoff, 2006), 45.
74. Multiple methods exist for measuring wealth across eras. I have compared the figures as a share of income (GDP/capita), which I think is the most appropriate measure considering the role of the Endowment. Alternative methods give a wide range of values: for instance, when compared to the Consumer Price Index, $10 million in 1910 equals "only" $257 million in 2014; but when analyzed as a share of GDP, it equals over $5 billion. I calculated these numbers using Samuel H. Williamson, "Six Ways to Compute the Relative Value of a U.S. Dollar Amount, 1790 to Present," MeasuringWorth, 2008, http://www.measuring-worth.com/uscompare/. The average wage figure comes from Susan B. Carter et al., eds., *Historical Statistics of the United States*, millennial ed. (New York: Cambridge University Press, 2006), 2:265.
75. "The American Institute of International Law," *AJIL* 6, no. 4 (1912): 949. On the American Institute of International Law, see Burnett [Ponsa], "Contingent Constitutions"; Grandin, "Liberal Traditions."
76. "Je ne veux pas exagérer, mais en toute sincérité je pense qu'une nouvelle ère s'ouvre pour le Droit International." Scott to Renault, 1 June 1912, box 10, JBS.
77. Sluga, *Internationalism in the Age of Nationalism*, chap. 1.
78. "First Meeting of Board of Trustees," box 12, CEIPP.

79. Kuehl, *Seeking World Order*, 112.

80. On Marburg, see Nancy Jean Duke, "Theodore Marburg: An Internationalist's Place in History" (PhD diss., Florida State University, 1995). Marburg called the meeting that established the ASJSID, but, according to John Bassett Moore, Scott founded the organization "mainly for the purpose of getting into the pocket of Theodore Marburg." Moore, "Memorandum," 12 May 1913, box 91, JBM, LC.

81. Talcott Williams, quoted in ASJSID *Proceedings* (1915): 97; Elihu Root quoted in John Hays Hammond, *The Autobiography of John Hays Hammond* (New York: Farrar and Rinehart, 1935), 2:613.

82. "The American Society for the Judicial Settlement of International Disputes," *AJIL* 4, no. 4 (1910): 930–32. See also ASJSID *Proceedings*, 1910-1916, and the pamphlet series *Judicial Settlement of International Disputes*.

83. On idealism, see Zasloff, "Law and the Shaping"; Patterson, *Toward a Warless World*, 158. For the critique of conservatism, see Hatsue Shinohara, *US International Lawyers in the Interwar Years: A Forgotten Crusade* (Cambridge: Cambridge University Press, 2012), 35–36. David Kennedy criticizes the assumption that prewar international lawyers were obsessed with sovereignty. Kennedy, "History of an Illusion."

84. Scholars employ various terms to describe late nineteenth century jurisprudence: "classical legal thought," "classical orthodoxy," and "formalism," among others. I will use "classical" and "classicism" for sake of clarity and conciseness. On the entire period as one of "Classical legal thought," see Duncan Kennedy, *The Rise and Fall of Classical Legal Thought* (1975; repr. Washington, DC: Beard Books, 2006). "Legal realism" did not exist as such until the 1920s, but scholars have identified various "proto-realists" before then.

85. [Oliver Wendell Holmes Jr.], review of *A Selection of Cases on the Law of Contracts*, by Christopher C. Langdell, *American Law Review* 14, no. 3 (1880): 234.

86. Roscoe Pound, "The Need of a Sociological Jurisprudence," *Green Bag* 19 (1907): 612.

87. Neil Duxbury, *Patterns of American Jurisprudence* (Oxford: Oxford University Press, 1995), 66.

88. Kermit L. Hall, "The Courts, 1790-1920," in Grossberg and Tomlins, *Cambridge History of Law in America*, 2:116, 130–31; Lawrence M. Friedman, *A History of American Law*, 2nd ed. (New York: Simon and Schuster, 1985), 344–45.

89. Kermit L. Hall and Peter Karsten, *The Magic Mirror: Law in American History*, 2nd ed. (New York: Oxford University Press, 2009), 263–64.

90. For a defense of *Lochner* from a libertarian position, see David E. Bernstein, *Rehabilitating Lochner: Defending Individual Rights against Progressive Reform* (Chicago: University of Chicago Press, 2011).

91. For one, there was broad diversity among jurists of the time. Classical jurisprudence did not begin and end with Langdell, and it is more accurate to speak of a classical "intellectual tendency" than a rigid school of thought. Duxbury, *Patterns of American Jurisprudence*, 68–69. For diverse expressions of classicism, see Stephen A. Siegel, "Joel Bishop's Orthodoxy," *Law and History Review*, 13, no. 2 (1995): 217; Siegel, "Francis Wharton's Orthodoxy: God, Historical Jurisprudence, and Classical Legal Thought," *American Journal of Legal History* 46, no. 4 (2004): 422–46; Lewis A. Grossman, "Langdell Upside-Down: James Coolidge Carter and the Anticlassical Jurisprudence of Anticodification," *Yale Journal of Law and the Humanities* 19 (2007): 149–219.

92. Stephen A. Siegel, "Lochner Era Jurisprudence and the American Constitutional Tradition," *North Carolina Law Review* 70 (1991): 1–111.

93. David M. Rabban, *Law's History: American Legal Thought and the Transatlantic Turn to History* (Cambridge: Cambridge University Press, 2014).

94. Richard A. Cosgrove, *Our Lady the Common Law: An Anglo-American Legal Community, 1870-1930* (New York: New York University Press, 1987), 170.

95. Rabban, *Law's History*, 6.

96. For a denial of any meaningful differences between classical jurists and legal realists, see Brian Z. Tamanaha, *Beyond the Formalist-Realist Divide: The Role of Politics in Judging* (Princeton, NJ: Princeton University Press, 2010). On the limitations of Tamanaha's analysis, see Alfred L. Brophy, "Did Formalism Never Exist?" *Texas Law Review* 92 (2013): 383–411.

97. William M. Wiecek, *The Lost World of Classical Legal Thoughts: Law and Ideology in America, 1886-1937* (New York: Oxford University Press, 1998), 5.

98. Kennedy, *Rise and Fall of Classical Legal Thought.*

99. Kunal Parker, *Common Law, History, and Democracy in America, 1790-1900* (Cambridge: Cambridge University Press, 2013).

100. Daniel R. Ernst, "Free Labor, the Consumer Interest, and the Law of Industrial Disputes, 1885-1900," *American Journal of Legal History* 36, no. 1 (1992): 19–37; Wiecek, *Lost World of Classical Legal Thought*, 7–11.

101. Owen M. Fiss, *Troubled Beginnings of the Modern State, 1888-1910* (Cambridge: Cambridge University Press, 1993).

102. James Brown Scott, "The Evolution of a Permanent International Judiciary," *AJIL* 6, no. 2 (1912): 320; Edwin M. Borchard, "The Legal Evolution of Peace," *American Law Review* 45 (1911): 710. See also Frederick Pollock, "The Sources of International Law," *Law Quarterly Review* 18 (1902): 418–29.

103. Denys P. Myers, "Legal Basis of the Rules of Blockade in the Declaration of London," *AJIL* 4, no. 3 (1910): 572.

104. Willoughby, "Legal Nature of International Law."

105. E.g., Henry G. Crocker, "Chronicle of International Events," *AJIL* 2, no. 3 (1908): 649–65.

106. Amos S. Hershey, "History of International Law Since the Peace of Westphalia," *AJIL* 6, no. 1 (1912): 30–69; David J. Bederman, "Appraising a Century of Scholarship in the American Journal of International Law," *AJIL* 100, no. 1 (2006): 52.

107. See chapter 4 for the US role at The Hague.

108. Martti Koskenniemi refers to the "sensibility" of international lawyers as something that "connotes both ideas and practices but also involves broader aspects of the political faith, image of self and society, as well as the structural constraints within which international law professionals live and work." Koskenniemi, *Gentle Civilizer*, 2.

109. Borchard, "Legal Evolution of Peace," 708.

110. Scott to Leon C. Prince, 4 June 1913, box 1, ASIL Papers.

111. Shinohara, *US International Lawyers*, 35.

112. Richard Olney, "The Development of International Law," *AJIL* 1, no. 4 (1907): 429; Alpheus H. Snow, "International Law and Political Science," *AJIL* 7, no. 2 (1913): 316; Paul S. Reinsch, "International Administrative Law and National Sovereignty," *AJIL* 3, no. 1 (1909): 13.

113. Scott, "Legal Nature," 844.

114. Zasloff, "Law and the Shaping," 256.

115. Elihu Root, "The Need of Popular Understanding of International Law," *AJIL* 1, no. 1 (1907): 2.

116. James Brown Scott, Review of *World Organization*, by Raymond L. Bridgman and *The Federation of the World*, by Benjamin F. Trueblood, *AJIL* 2, no. 3 (1908): 727.

117. Paul S. Reinsch, "International Administrative Law and National Sovereignty," *AJIL* 3, no. 1 (1909): 18.

118. Lassa Oppenheim, "The Science of International Law: Its Task and Method" *AJIL* 2, no. 2 (1908): 313–56; Boyle, *Foundations of World Order*, 11.

119. Oppenheim to Scott, 19 February 1907 and 8 November 1907, box 6, JBS. On Oppenheim, see Benedict Kingsbury, "Legal Positivism as Normative Politics: International Society, Balance of Power and Lassa Oppenheim's Positive International Law" *European Journal of International Law* 13 (April 2002): 401–36; Mathias Schmoeckel, "The Internationalist as a Scientist and Herald: Lassa Oppenheim," *European Journal of International Law* 11, no. 3 (2000): 699–712; Amanda Perreau-Saussine, "A Case Study on Jurisprudence as a Source of International Law: Oppenheim's Influence," in Craven, Fitzmaurice, and Vogiatzi *Time, History and International Law*, 91–117.

120. Oppenheim, "Science of International Law," 318, 330.

121. Oppenheim, "Science of International Law," 314, 317, 322, 356.

122. Jackson H. Ralston, "Should Any National Dispute Be Reserved from Arbitration?" *Advocate of Peace* 70, no. 7 (1908): 160.

123. Scott to W. Kaufmann, 26 January 1912, vol. 256, CEIPP; Scott to Amos Hershey, 4 November 1912, box 77, JBS.

124. Scott to W. Kaufmann, 26 January 1912, vol. 256, CEIPP.

125. Elihu Root, "The Real Questions under the Japanese Treaty and the San Francisco School Board Resolution," *AJIL* 1, no. 2 (1907): 273–74.

126. Elihu Root, "Address at a Conference of Teachers of International Law," in *Addresses on International Subjects*, ed. Robert Bacon and James Brown Scott (Cambridge, MA: Harvard University Press, 1916), 128.

127. Quoted in Richard W. Leopold, *Elihu Root and the Conservative Tradition* (Boston: Little, Brown, 1954), 20.

128. Weekly polls of public opinion were uncommon until the mid-1930s, and remained controversial into the 1940s. George Gallup, *A Guide to Public Opinion Polls* (Princeton, NJ: Princeton University Press, 1944), v.

129. Nicholas Murray Butler, *The International Mind: An Argument for the Judicial Settlement of International Disputes* (New York: Charles Scribner's Sons, 1912), x.

130. Borchard, "Legal Evolution of Peace," 717.

131. Landauer, "Ambivalences of Power"; Patterson, *Toward a Warless World*, 156.

132. Gerald W. McFarland, "Partisan of Non-Partisanship: Dorman B. Eaton and the Genteel Reform Tradition," *Journal of American History* 54 (1968): 806–22.

133. John G. Sproat, *"The Best Men": Liberal Reformers in the Gilded Age* (New York: Oxford University Press, 1968).

134. James Brown Scott, *The American Institute of International Law: Its Declaration of the Rights and Duties of Nations* (Washington, DC: American Institute of International Law, 1916), 76; McFarland, "Partisan of Non-Partisanship."

135. Novick, *That Noble Dream*, 3.

136. Oppenheim to James Brown Scott, 12 September 1918, vol. 270, CEIPP.

137. Simeon Baldwin, "The New Era of International Courts," *Judicial Settlement of International Disputes*, no. 1 (August 1910): 4.

138. Quoted in James Brown Scott, "Aim and Purpose of the American Society for Judicial Settlement of International Disputes," *Judicial Settlement of International Disputes*, no. 2a (November 1910): 5.

139. Alona E. Evans and Carol Per Lee Plumb, "Notes and Comments: Women and the American Society of International Law," *AJIL* 68, no. 2 (1974): 290–99.

140. Thomas Haskell, *The Emergence of Professional Social Science* (Urbana: University of Illinois Press, 1977), 220. By depicting both intimacy and conflict within an exclusively male space, the ASJSID image might be read to suggest instabilities in the discourse of responsible manhood itself. The judge, after all, turns to a combination of physical touch and written display to dissuade the workman. His goal, preventing the shell from entering the cannon in the middle of a homosocial encounter, could suggest anxieties about penetration and the destabilization of strictly defined gender roles.

141. Scott to Walther Schücking, 15 July 1912, vol. 256, CEIPP.

142. Scott to Alfred H. Fried, 17 June 1912, box 10, JBS.

143. James Brown Scott, *The Status of the International Court of Justice* (New York: Oxford University Press, 1916), 52.

144. Ralston, *International Arbitration from Athens to Locarno*, 174–89.

145. Jackson H. Ralston, *International Arbitral Law and Procedure, Being a Resume of the Proccedure and Practice of International Commissions, and Including the Views of Arbitrators Upon Questions Arising under the Law of Nations* (Boston: Ginn and Co., 1910), 17–18.

146. Patterson, *Toward a Warless World*, 108–9.

147. Scott, "Aim and Purpose," 13.

148. Ernest Nys, "The Necessity of a Permanent Tribunal," *Judicial Settlement of International Disputes*, no. 2 (November 1910): 18; James Brown Scott, "Aim and Purpose," 3.

149. Simeon E. Baldwin, "New Era of International Courts," 3.

150. James Brown Scott, in "Discussion," *ASJSID Proceedings* 4 (1913): 241.

151. Politis, "The Work of the Hague Court," *Judicial Settlement of International Disputes*, no. 6 (November 1911): 14.

152. Scott, "Aim and Purpose," 8–9.
153. Eugene Wambaugh, "Why the Growth of Law Is Aided by Courts More Than by Commissions," ASJSID *Proceedings* (1910): 141–42.
154. Scott, "Discussion," 294.
155. Simeon E. Baldwin, "New Era of International Courts," 8.
156. Elihu Root, "The Importance of Judicial Settlement," *Judicial Settlement of International Disputes*, no. 3 (February 1911): 7.
157. Patterson, *Towards a Warless World*, 154.
158. Address of President William Howard Taft, ASJSID *Proceedings*, no. 1 (1910): 352.
159. Nys, "Necessity of a Permanent Tribunal," 26.
160. James Brown Scott, "The Evolution of a Permanent International Judiciary," *AJIL* 6, no. 2 (1912): 319.
161. Charles N. Gregory, "The Proposed International Prize Court," *AJIL* 2, no. 3 (1908): 475.
162. [James Brown Scott], "The American Society for Judicial Settlement of International Disputes," in *Judicial Settlement of International Disputes*, no. 1 (August 1910): 27.
163. William H. Short, "Certain Permanent Values in the Arbitral Method," ASJSID *Proceedings* 4 (1913): 250–61.
164. John Bassett Moore, "Law and Organization: Presidential Address to the Eleventh Annual Meeting of the American Political Science Association," *American Political Science Review* 9, no. 1 (1915): 10.
165. Moore to Thomas Willing Balch, 26 June 1920, box 295, JBM, LC.
166. Omer Hershey, "Covenants without the Sword," *Green Bag* 21, no. 10 (1909): 508.
167. Examples include R. Floyd Clarke, "A Permanent Tribunal of International Arbitration: Its Necessity and Value," *AJIL* 1, no. 2 (1907): 342–408; "The Growth of International Law under a Permanent Court of Arbitration," *AJIL* 1, no. 3 (1907): 730–34; Elihu Root, "The Relations between International Tribunals of Arbitration and the Jurisdiction of National Courts," *AJIL* 3, no. 3 (1909): 529–36; "Proposal to Modify the International Prize Court and to Invest it as Modified with the Jurisdiction and Functions of a Court of Arbitral Justice," *AJIL* 4, no. 1 (1910): 163–66; "The American Society for the Judicial Settlement of International Disputes," *AJIL* 4, no. 4 (1910): 930–32.
168. "Preliminary Report of the Committee of the American Society of International Law on the Codification of the Principles of Justice in Times of Peace between Nations, Appointed under the Resolution of the Society of April 24, 1909," ASIL *Proceedings* 4 (1910): 197–227.
169. Carnegie Endowment for International Peace, *Report on the Teaching of International Law in the Educational Institutions of the United States, April 18, 1913* (Washington, DC: CEIP, 1913).
170. *Proceedings of the Conference of American Teachers of International Law Held at Washington, DC, April 23-25, 1914* (Washington, DC: Byron S. Adams, 1914), 42–43; American Bar Association, Section of International Law, *The ABA Section of International Law: Leading the World's International Lawyers since 1878* (Chicago: ABA Section of International Law, 2008), 7.
171. "Minutes of the Meeting of the Standing Committee on the Study and Teaching of International Law," 27 April 1916, box "Executive Council Minutes," ASIL Papers.
172. *Conference of American Teachers*, 42; Shinohara, *US International Lawyers*, 20–21.
173. Barry Friedman, "The History of the Countermajoritarian Difficulty, Part Three: The Lesson of *Lochner*," *New York University Law Review* 76 (2001):1387.
174. Elihu Root, "The Arizona Constitution and the Recall of Judges," in *Addresses on Government and Citizenship*, ed. Robert Bacon and James Brown Scott (Cambridge, MA: Harvard University Press, 1916), 387–404.
175. Marchand, *American Peace Movement*, 63.
176. Herman, *Eleven against War*, chap. 2.
177. Marchand, *American Peace Movement*, 50.
178. Church, "Economists as Experts," 571–72.
179. Quoted in Cosgrove, *Our Lady the Common Law*, 67.
180. Borchard to Jackson H. Ralston, 26 August 1925, carton 1, Ralston Papers, Bancroft Library, University of California, Berkeley.
181. Nurnberger, "James Brown Scott," 48.

182. Scott to Louis Renault, 18 May 1914, vol. 261, CEIPP; James Brown Scott, "Review of President Roosevelt's Administration," *The Outlook*, February 13, 1909.
183. Elihu Root, *Miscellaneous Addresses*, ed. James Brown Scott and Robert Bacon (Cambridge, MA: Harvard University Press, 1917), viii–ix.
184. Scott to Louis Renault, 29 March 1911, box 10, JBS.
185. James Brown Scott to David Jayne Hill, 28 January 1907, box 37, JBS; James Brown Scott to Oscar S. Straus, 12 December 1908, box 1, ASIL Papers; Kirgis, *First Century*, 25, 45.
186. CEIP, *Year Book for 1913-1914*, 184–85.
187. Tunstall Smith to CEIP Trustees, 15 December 1913, vol. 258, CEIPP; CEIP, *Year Book for 1915*, 47–50.
188. Scott to Scott, 5 June 1913, vol. 257, CEIPP.
189. Various authors, "L'Institut américain de droit international," *RGDIP* 19, no. 3 (1912): 329–44 and *RGDIP* 20, no. 1 (1913): 101–11. See also Albert de Lapradelle, "L'Institut américain de droit international," *RGDIP* 19, no. 1 (1912): i–xi, and Paul Fauchille, "La Fondation de l'institut américain de droit international," *RGDIP* 20, no. 1 (1913): 74–88.
190. Vesnitch to Scott, 4 April 1913, box 8, JBS. I could not find any letter in which Scott tells Fauchille to kill the article, but Vesnitch mentions that he had instructed Fauchille to share his letter with Scott before publishing it, and since it did not appear in the *RGDIP*, it appears Scott persuaded Fauchille not to print it.
191. Borchard to Moore, 17 April 1919, box 40, JBM, LC; Borchard to Moore, 13 December 1915, box 29, JBM, LC.
192. Stowell to John Bassett Moore, 24 November 1909, box 23, Ellery C. Stowell Papers.
193. George Winfield Scott to John Bassett Moore, 13 January 1910, box 15, JBM, LC; Ellery C. Stowell to John Bassett Moore, 9 March 1910, box 15, JBM, LC; Joseph Chamberlain, Review of *The Hague Conferences of 1899 and 1907*, by James Brown Scott, *Columbia Law Review* 10, no. 3 (1910): 277–78. At the urging of Dean Kirchwey, the *Columbia Law Review* published a retraction. "Book Reviews," *Columbia Law Review* 10 (1910): 374. For a letter defending Scott, see Chandler P. Anderson [?] to George Kirchwey, 15 March 1910, box 10, JBS.
194. Frank W. Fox, *J. Reuben Clark: The Public Years* (Provo, UT: Brigham Young University Press, 1980), 83–86.
195. Ernest Nys, review of *The Hague Conferences of 1899 and 1907. A series of lectures delivered before the Johns Hopkins University in the year 1908*, by J. B. Scott, *Revue de Droit International et de Législation Comparée* 2nd Series,16, no. 4 (1909): 608; Albert de Lapradelle, review of *The Hague Conferences of 1899 and 1907. A Series of lectures delivered before the Johns Hopkins University in the year 1908*, by James Brown Scott, *RGDIP* 16, no. 4 (1909): 514–15. The book also received approving reviews in the *Harvard Law Review* (by A.R.G., 23, no. 4 (1910): 319–20) and *American Political Science Review* (by Simeon Baldwin, 3, no. 3 (1909): 460–62).
196. Quoted in Solberg, *University of Illinois*, 228.
197. Mark T. Berger, *Under Northern Eyes: Latin American Studies and US Hegemony in the Americas 1898-1990* (Bloomington: Indiana University Press, 1995), 35; Courtney Johnson, "Understanding the American Empire: Colonialism, Latin Americanism, and Professional Social Science, 1898-1920," in McCoy and Scarano, *Colonial Crucible*, 175–90; Paul S. Reinsch, *Colonial Government* (New York: Macmillan, 1902); Paul S. Reinsch, *Colonial Administration* (New York: Macmillan, 1905); Alpheus Henry Snow, *The Administration of Dependencies: A Study of the Evolution of the Federal Empire, with Special Reference to American Colonial Problems* (New York: G. P. Putnam's Sons, 1902); *Proceedings of the American Political Science Association* (Lancaster, PA: Wickersham Press, 1905), 25–26.
198. Robert Vitalis, "Birth of a Discipline," in *Imperialism and Internationalism in the Discipline of International Relations*, ed. David Long and Brian C. Schmidt (Albany: State University of New York Press, 2005), 159–81.
199. Reinsch, *Colonial Government*, 70; Paul S. Reinsch, "International Unions and Their Administration," *AJIL* 1, no. 3 (1907): 579–623; Paul S. Reinsch, "International Administrative Law and National Sovereignty," *AJIL* 3, no. 1 (1909): 1–45; Paul S. Reinsch, *Public International Unions: Their Work and Organization* (Boston: Ginn and Company,

1911); Noel H. Pugach, *Paul S. Reinsch: Open Door Diplomat in Action* (Millwood, NY: KTO Press, 1979).

200. Landauer, "Ambivalences of Power," 327–28.

201. Lori Fisler Damrosch, "The 'American' and the 'International' in the American Journal of International Law," *AJIL* 100, no. 1 (2006): 7–10; Bederman, "Appraising a Century of Scholarship," 28; Landauer, "Ambivalences of Power," 343.

202. James Brown Scott to Beekman Winthrop, 20 January 1910, box 1, ASIL Papers; Kirgis, *First Century*, 25.

203. Scott to George Grafton Wilson, 26 October 1910, box 37, JBS; Scott to Theodore S. Woolsey, 26 October 1910, JBS.

204. James Echols, "Jackson Ralston and the Last Single Tax Campaign," *California History* 58, no. 3 (1979): 256–63; Jackson H. Ralston, *Study and Report for American Federation of Labor upon Judicial Control Over Legislatures as to Constitutional Questions* (Washington, DC: Law Reporter Printing Company, 1919).

205. Ralston, "Autobiography: Adventures in Life of a Washington City Lawyer"; "Abstract of Remarks Made by Mr. Jackson H. Ralston before the Commonwealth Club's Section on International Relations, March 26, 1925," cartons 4–5, Ralston Papers.

206. Jackson H. Ralston and W. T. Sherman Doyle, *Venezuelan Arbitrations of 1903* (Washington, DC: Government Printing Office, 1904); Ralston, *International Arbitral Law and Procedure*.

207. Ralston, "National Dispute," 160.

208. Lipson, *Standing Guard*, 57.

209. William C. Dennis to Candelaria Gold and Silver Mining Co., 26 March 1925; miscellaneous business records; in cartons 2–3, Ralston Papers. See also "Autobiography" at this location.

210. Brian S. McBeth, *Gunboats, Corruption, and Claims: Foreign Intervention in Venezuela, 1899-1908* (Westport, CT: Greenwood Press, 2001), 189; *Venezuelan Claims: Letter of Messrs. Ralston & Siddons and George N. Baxter to Hon. S. M. Cullom, Chairman of the Committee on Foreign Relations of the Senate of the United States* (Washington, DC, 1908).

211. Harold F. Peterson, *Diplomat of the Americas: A Biography of William I. Buchanan (1852-1909)* (Albany: State University of New York Press, 1977), 333.

212. Robert Gordon, "'The Ideal and the Actual in the Law': Fantasies and Practices of New York City Lawyers, 1870-1910," in Gawalt, *New High Priests*, 53.

213. "The Annexation of Korea to Japan," *AJIL* 4:4 (1910): 923–25; Alpheus Henry Snow, "Neutralization Versus Imperialism," *AJIL* 2, no. 3 (1908): 562–90.

214. Quoted in Tompkins, *Anti-Imperialism*, 264–65.

215. Duke, "Marburg," 41.

216. Here I use the term *American exceptionalism* to suggest the belief that the United States is not only unique but superior, and that it occupies a world-historical position as the "indispensable" nation in the redemption of humanity. On the complicated history and meanings of the term (and why it should not be used as a descriptor of reality, but only an ideological signifier), see Daniel Rodgers, "Exceptionalism," in *Imagined Histories: American Historians Interpret the Past*, ed. Anthony Molho and Gordon S. Wood (Princeton, NJ: Princeton University Press, 1998), 21–40; Mary Nolan, "Against Exceptionalisms," *American Historical Review* 102, no. 3 (1997): 769–74; Michael Kammen, "The Problem of American Exceptionalism: A Reconsideration," *American Quarterly*, 45, no. 1 (1993): 1–43.

217. Ernest Lee Tuveson, *Redeemer Nation: The Idea of America's Millennial Role* (Chicago: University of Chicago Press, 1968).

218. George W. Wickersham, "The Supreme Court of the United States: A Prototype of a Court of Nations," *ASJSID Proceedings* 3 (1912): 17–43. The ASJSID devoted its sixth conference to the "Supreme Court of the United States." *ASJSID Proceedings* 6 (1916).

219. James Brown Scott, *The United States of America: A Study in International Organization* (Washington, DC: CEIP, 1920), 467–68.

220. Recent scholarship has rehabilitated some of Scott's claims by emphasizing the "international" aspects of the early federal union. Alison L. LaCroix, *The Ideological Origins of American Federalism* (Cambridge, MA: Harvard University Press, 2010), chap. 5; David C. Hendrickson, *Peace Pact: The Lost World of the American Founding* (Lawrence: University

Press of Kansas, 2003); Peter Onuf and Nicholas Onuf, *Federal Union, Modern World: The Law of Nations in an Age of Revolutions, 1776-1814* (Madison, WI: Madison House, 1993); Daniel Deudney, "The Philadelphia System: Sovereignty, Arms Control, and Balance of Power in the American States-Union, Circa 1787-1861," *International Organization* 49, no. 2 (1995): 191–228.

221. "Prospectus," *AJIL* 1, no. 1 (1907): 130.
222. Scott to Henry Goudy, 9 March 1912, vol. 256, CEIPP.

Chapter 4

1. *Proceedings at the Laying of a Wreath on the Tomb of Hugo Grotius in the Nieuwe Kerk, in the City of Delft, July 4th 1899 by the Commission of the United States of America to the International Peace Conference of The Hague* (The Hague: Martinus Nijhoff, 1899), 6–7, 12, 16, 30.
2. Davis, *First Hague,* 23–38; James Brown Scott, ed., *Instructions to the American Delegates to The Hague Peace Conferences and Their Official Reports* (New York: Oxford University Press, 1916), 1–2.
3. Joseph Choate remarked on the overlap of the "Spanish War" and the "World's Peace Conference." Joseph Choate, *The Two Hague Conferences* (Princeton, NJ: Princeton University Press, 1913), 3.
4. Davis, *First Hague,* 70–77.
5. Convention for the Pacific Settlement of International Disputes, 29 July 1899, and Laws and Customs of Wars on Land, 29 July 1899, available from the Avalon Project, http://avalon.law. yale.edu/subject_menus/lawwar.asp (accessed 3 July 2015); Scott Andrew Keefer, "Building the Palace of Peace: The Hague Conference of 1899 and Arms Control in the Progressive Era," *Journal of the History of International Law* 8 (2006): 13; David Caron, "War and International Adjudication: Reflections on the 1899 Peace Conference," *AJIL* 94, no. 1 (2000): 4–30.
6. Davis, *First Hague,* 147–64.
7. Davis, *First Hague,* 176–79.
8. Martha Finnemore, *The Purpose of Intervention: Changing Beliefs About the Use of Force* (Ithaca, NY: Cornell University Press, 2003), 41–42; "Peace of World Called a Dream," *Chicago Daily Tribune,* June 16, 1907; John W. Foster, *Diplomatic Memoirs* (Boston: Houghton Mifflin, 1909), 2:212.
9. Davis, *Second Hague,* 259; "Andrew Carnegie's Gift for Temple of Peace," *NYT,* April 26, 1903; Fredrik Sterzel, *The Inter-Parliamentary Union* (Stockholm: P. A. Norstedt and Söner, 1968), 26; *FRUS* (1904), 10–13; "America and the Hague Conference," *The Times* (London), October 24, 1907. Roosevelt ultimately allowed Nicholas to again claim official responsibility for calling the conference, but America's role was widely recognized (delegates at the first meeting in June officially thanked Roosevelt along with Nicholas and the Netherlands' Queen Wilhelmina). "Second Peace Congress Open," *NYT,* June 16, 1907; Davis, *Second Hague,* 123–24, 184, 193.
10. "Meeting of the American Commission to the Second Hague Conference, Held April 20, 1907, in the Diplomatic Room of the Department of State," box 20, Choate Papers, LC.
11. Howard K. Beale, *Theodore Roosevelt and the Rise of America to World Power* (Baltimore: Johns Hopkins University Press, 1956), 340.
12. *FRUS* (1905), xxx.
13. Robert B. Charles, "Legal Education in the Late Nineteenth Century, through the Eyes of Theodore Roosevelt," *American Journal of Legal History* 37, no. 3 (1993): 233–72; Roosevelt to Leonard Wood, quoted in James R. Holmes, *Theodore Roosevelt and World Order: Police Power in International Relations* (Washington, DC: Potomac Books, 2006), 23.
14. Beale, *Roosevelt and the Rise of America,* 354; *FRUS,* (1906), lv.
15. Fiske, "Manifest Destiny," 578–79.
16. Theodore Roosevelt, *The Winning of the West* (New York: G. P. Putnam's Sons, 1896), 1:1; *FRUS* (1904), xli; Beale, *Roosevelt and the Rise of America,* 353
17. Roosevelt to Henry White, August 14, 1906, in *Letters of Theodore Roosevelt,* 5:359.
18. *FRUS* (1904), xl.
19. *FRUS* (1906), lv.
20. Lewis L. Gould, *The Presidency of Theodore Roosevelt* (Lawrence: University Press of Kansas, 1991), 267. See also Hodge, "Whiff of Cordite."

21. *FRUS* (1902), xx.

22. Roosevelt to Oscar S. Straus, 15 June 1905, box 4, Oscar S. Straus Papers, LC.

23. Beale, *Roosevelt and the Rise of America*, 349.

24. Frank Ninkovich, "Theodore Roosevelt: Civilization as Ideology," *Diplomatic History* 10, no. 3 (1986): 231.

25. Larry L. Fabian, *Andrew Carnegie's Peace Endowment: The Tycoon, the President, and Their Bargain of 1910* (Washington, DC: CEIP, 1985), 55.

26. Davis, *Second Hague*, 115; Roosevelt to Root, September 14, 1905, in *Letters of Theodore Roosevelt*, 5:26.

27. TR knew, however, that the notorious corporate lawyer would face a difficult political campaign, and Root did not desire the White House. Jessup, *Root*, 2:123.

28. James Brown Scott, ed., *The Proceedings of the Hague Peace Conferences* (New York: Oxford University Press, 1921), 2:1015–16; US Department of State, *Instructions to the American Delegates to The Hague Conference* (Washington, Government Printing Office, 1907).

29. "Second Peace Congress Open," *NYT*, June 16, 1907; Martin Ceadel, *Semi-Detached Idealists: The British Peace Movement and International Relations, 1854-1945* (New York: Oxford University Press, 2001), 166.

30. Frederick C. Hicks, ed. *Arguments and Addresses of Joseph Hodges Choate* (St. Paul, MN: West Publishing, 1926); Davis, *Second Hague*, 261.

31. Scott, *Proceedings*, 2:313–16; "Choate's Plea for Permanent Court," *NYT*, August 2, 1907.

32. Scott, *Proceedings*, 2:316–25.

33. "Proposals at Hague," *NYT*, July 9, 1907; "A Permanent Court," *Chicago Daily Tribune*, August 4, 1907; *The Times* (London), August 5, 1907.

34. Scott, *Proceedings*, 2:354.

35. Simpson, *Great Powers and Outlaw States*, 145; Becker Lorca, "Sovereignty beyond the West," 24–35.

36. Scott, *Proceedings*, 2:321–25, 612–14; Davis, *Second Hague*, 265–68.

37. Simpson, *Great Powers and Outlaw States*, 135.

38. Scott, *Proceedings,* 2:623.

39. Davis, *Second Hague,* 272; Charles W. Turner, *Ruy Barbosa: Brazilian Crusader for the Essential Freedoms* (New York: Abingdon-Cokesbury Press, 1945), 42, 105.

40. Homero Pires, *Anglo-American Political Influences on Rui Barbosa*, trans. Sylvia Medrado Clinton (Río de Janeiro: Casa de Rui Barbosa, 1949), 53; Scott, *Proceedings*, 2:343, 647; Becker Lorca, "Sovereignty beyond the West," 25–26.

41. Scott, *Proceedings*, 2:619–21; Becker Lorca, "Sovereignty beyond the West," 24n46.

42. Scott, *Proceedings*, 2:629, 700.

43. Scott, *Proceedings*, 2:625, 683–87, 701; Davis, *Second Hague*, 275–76.

44. "The Hague Fiasco," *The Times* (London), October 19, 1907; "See Gain for Peace at Hague," *Chicago Daily Tribune*, October 20, 1907; "End of the 'Peace Comedy,'" *Literary Digest*, October 26, 1907; "'Posturing and Mouthing' at The Hague," *The Outlook* November 9, 1907; Davis, *Second Hague*, 296; Jessup, *Root*, 2:82.

45. Scott, *Status of the International Court*, 39; Patterson, *Warless World*, 160–61; Eyffinger, "Critical Moment," 222; Denys P. Myers, "The Origin of The Hague Arbitral Courts," *AJIL* 10, no. 2 (1916): 270–327.

46. Scott, *Proceedings*, 2:145, 690.

47. Scott, *Proceedings*, 2:600–601, 649–51, 660, 692.

48. Scott, *Proceedings*, 2:599–600.

49. Shinohara, *US International Lawyers*, 36.

50. Elihu Root, "Nobel Peace Prize Address" (1914), in *Addresses on International Subjects*, 157; John F. Witt, *Patriots and Cosmopolitans: Hidden Histories of American Law* (Cambridge, MA: Harvard University Press, 2007), 178–79.

51. Herman, *Eleven against War*, 31.

52. Herman, *Eleven against War*, 30–31.

53. Elihu Root, "The Real Monroe Doctrine" (1914), in *Addresses on International Subjects*, 113; Root, "The Relations between International Tribunals of Arbitration and the Jurisdiction of National Courts" (1909), in *Addresses on International Subjects,* 39–40.

54. *NYT*, quoted in "What Was Done at The Hague," *Literary Digest*, October 26, 1907.

55. For instance, Scott attempted to broaden the International Prize Court into a full international court. When the Prize Court failed, he proposed a court that would at first be made up of a small number of Great Powers. This, too, failed to come to fruition. See Benjamin A. Coates, "Transatlantic Advocates: American International Law and U.S. Foreign Relations, 1898–1919" (PhD diss., Columbia University, 2010), 214–18; James Brown Scott to Nicholas Murray Butler, 27 November and 16 December 1912, box 10, JBS.

56. Elihu Root, "The Function of Private Codification in International Law," 1911, in *Addresses on International Subjects*, 57–72.

57. Root, "Function of Private Codification," 67.

58. Münch, "L'Institut de droit internacional," 391–92.

59. Sluga, *Internationalism*, 12–13; Emily S. Rosenberg, "Transnational Currents in a Shrinking World," in *A World Connecting, 1870-1945*, ed. Emily S. Rosenberg (Cambridge, MA: Harvard University Press, 2012), 831–34.

60. Root, "Function of Private Codification"; Münch, "L'Institut de droit international," 391–92.

61. Rodgers, *Atlantic Crossings*; Eric Rauchway, *Blessed among Nations: How the World Made America* (New York: Hill and Wang, 2006); Fabian, *Peace Endowment*, 4; Oppenheim to James Brown Scott, 22 January 1915, vol. 262, CEIPP.

62. James Kloppenberg, *Uncertain Victory: Social Democracy and Progressivism in European and American Thought, 1870-1920* (New York: Oxford University Press, 1986), 3. For intellectual collaboration, see Richard Kleen to John Bassett Moore, 19 February 1898, box 214, JBM, LC (asking Moore to review his book on neutrality); John Bassett Moore, review of *Chapters on the Principles of International Law*, by John Westlake, *Political Science Quarterly* 10 (1895): 550–51; Max Hüber, "The Intercantonal Law of Switzerland (Swiss Interstate Law)," *AJIL* 3, no. 1 (1909): 62–98; Thomas Willing Balch, "La question des pêcheries de l'Atlantique. Un différend entre les États-Unis et l'Empire britannique," *Revue de Droit International et Legislation Comparée* 16, no. 4 (1909): 415–34; James Brown Scott to Max Huber, 6 January 1912, vol. 256, CEIPP (requesting copies of Huber's writings); Lassa Oppenheim to James Brown Scott, 19 April 1907, box 6, JBS (requesting to receive State Department publications); Raymond Weeks to John Bassett Moore, 5 August 1913, box 24, JBM, LC (in which Moore promises to speak to the Senate to oppose a proposed 15 percent tariff on books). The *AJIL* regularly reviewed European works. For a European review of Scott's work, see *RGDIP* 16, no. 4 (1909): 514–15. On the Anglo-American common law connection, see Cosgrove, *Our Lady the Common Law*.

   For Scott's relations with Europeans, see Oppenheim to Scott, 31 July 1911, box 6, JBS; Albert de Lapradelle, *Maitres et doctrines du droit des gens* (Paris: Les Éditions Internationales, 1950), 265, 405; Scott to Francis Hagerup, 7 October 1920, box 8, JBS; Renault to Scott, 21 May 1911, box 6, JBS; Schücking to Scott, 14 October 1912, vol. 256, CEIPP; Nurnberger, "James Brown Scott," 298. Scott also spoke German fluently. He later learned Spanish as well. Nurnberger, "James Brown Scott," 28.

   For Moore, see Mr. Wollerson to Moore, 10 May 1915, box 40, JBM, CLS; Moore to John Adams Moore, 9 April 1908, box 14, JBM, LC; Moore to Huber, 23 January 1913, box 21, JBM, LC; Oppenheim to Moore, 24 January 1910, box 15, JBM, LC. Recalling Westlake, Moore reminisced about "clambering with him over the rocks of his native Cornwall." Moore to Frederic Coudert, 20 January 1911, box 16, JBM, LC.

   On portraits, see George A. Finch, "Biography of James Brown Scott"; Louis Renault to Scott, 21 May 1911, box 6, JBS; Oppenheim to Moore, 24 January 1910, box 15, JBM, LC. Elihu Root filled his office with "engravings of great English lawyers." Jessup, *Root*, 1:278. This might be considered as an early version of what Oscar Schachter called the "invisible college." Schachter, "The Invisible College of International Lawyers," *Northwestern University Law Review* 72, no. 2 (1977): 217–26.

63. Moore to Col. William Warfield, 22 November 1920, box 20, JBM, CLS; Edwin Borchard to Moore, 13 December 1920, box 42, JBM, LC; Moore to C. Van Eeckhaute, 26 July 1913, box 20, JBM, LC; Lawrence to Moore, 23 June 1908, box 14, JBM, LC; Moore to Seth Low, 30 August 1911, box 16, JBM, LC; James Brown Scott, "To the Electors for the Chichele Professorship of International Law and Diplomacy in the University of Oxford," 19 October 1910, box 57, JBS.

64. "Proceedings of a Meeting of the Board of Trustees," box 12, CEIPP; *Annuaire* (1911): 7; Scott to Clunet, 22 November 1911, vol. 252, CEIPP. The franc-dollar exchange rate of 5:1, listed in Carter et. al., *Historical Statistics*, 5:567. $4 in 1912 is equivalent to roughly $101 in 2014, http://www.measuringworth.com/uscompare/relativevalue.php.

65. Scott to Albéric Rolin, 27 June 1912, box 10, JBS; *Annuaire* (1912), 556–71. The Comité's advice did sometimes make a difference. For instance, whereas Scott had earlier rejected proposals to subsidize journals of *private* international law, after the Comité advised otherwise, Scott extended aid to the Société de législation comparée and the *Journal du Droit International Privé et de la Jurisprudence Comparée*, among others. Scott to Renault, 28 October 1912, vol. 255, CEIPP; CEIP, *Year Book for 1913-1914* (Washington, DC: CEIP, 1914), 101, 119, 151–52.

66. Simpson, *Great Powers and Outlaw States*, 136; CEIP, *Year Book for 1912*, 120–22; *Annuaire* (1912), 608; Moore to Edwin Borchard, 17 November 1920, box 42, JBM, LC.

67. James Brown Scott, "Survey of answers received from the various governments with regard to the project of the creation of an Academy of International Law at The Hague," 1913, vol. 257, CEIPP; CEIP, *Year Book for 1911*, 109–15, 145–55; Scott to J. Loudon, 27 February 1914, vol. 260, CEIPP; Scott to Louis Renault, 17 March 1914, vol. 261, CEIPP; Scott to Loudon, 21 October 1913, vol. 257, CEIPP; Scott to Root, 16 January 1914, vol. 259, CEIPP; Scott to Albéric Rolin, 26 June 1914, vol. 260, CEIPP; CEIP, *Year Book for 1915*, 131. The academy was eventually opened in 1923. As Giles Scott-Smith observes, beginning in the 1950s, it became "involved in a broad strategy begun by the Eisenhower administration to ensure a smooth transition from a colonial to a postcolonial world order." It was then funded by the Ford and Rockefeller Foundations, and Americans hoped that the academy would inculcate respect for Western order among Third World leaders. In a move that surely would have gratified James Brown Scott, the academy even introduced Harvard's case method in the 1960s. Scott-Smith argues that the academy became a "strategic institution" in which foundations linked their giving to America's foreign policy goals and its posture toward the Third World between 1956 and 1972. In fact, the academy was from the beginning linked to American conceptions of world order. Giles Scott-Smith, "Attempting to Secure an 'Orderly Evolution': American Foundations, The Hague Academy of International Law and the Third World," *Journal of American Studies* 41, no. 3 (2007): 509–32.

68. CEIP, *Year Book for 1912*, 138–43; and *Year Book for 1913-1914*, 147–48, 164

69. Edouard Clunet to James Brown Scott, 28 April 1912, vol. 256, CEIPP.

70. Scott to F. Meyer, 31 March 1913, vol. 254, CEIPP; Edouard Clunet to Scott, 28 April 1912, vol. 256, CEIPP; Marquis de Olivart to Scott, 10 September 1912, vol. 255, CEIPP. Scott did eventually agree to allow Olivart to distribute a supplement along with the *AJIL*. Scott to Olivart, 30 October 1912, vol. 255; 6 November 1913, vol. 257, CEIPP.

71. "Coastwise" referred to local trade from one American port to another. But the canal was not contiguous with the United States, so in practice it would allow for trade from New York to California, giving a boost to American shippers.

72. Section 11 of the act forbids railroad-owned ships from using the canal to skirt this competition. For wording of the relevant portions of the act, see "Panama Canal Act: 'An Act to provide for the opening, maintenance, protection, and operation fo the Panama Canal, and the sanitation and government of the Canal Zone,'" *FRUS* (1912), 472–73. Pertinent sections of the Democratic and Progressive Party platforms for 1912 can be found in Hon. Joseph R. Knowland, ed., *Panama Canal Tolls: Symposium of Views Protesting against a Surrender of American Rights and Upholding the Side of the United States in the Toll Controversy* (Washington DC, Government Printing Office, 1913), 5. Taft's motivation is in Donald F. Anderson, *William Howard Taft: A Conservative's Conception of the Presidency* (Ithaca, NY: Cornell University Press, 1968), 241.

73. Art. III, no. 1.

74. A. Mitchell Innes to Secretary of State, 8 July 1912, *FRUS* (1912), 469–70; "Panama Canal Act: Protest by the British Government," *Canadian Law Times* 33 (1913): 79. For a detailed development of this argument, see Lassa Oppenheim, *The Panama Canal Conflict between Great Britain and the United States of America* (Cambridge: Cambridge University Press, 1913).

75. *FRUS* (1912), 476–77.

76. Among prominent legalists, those who believed that the treaty forbade toll exemption included James Brown Scott, Elihu Root, Eugene Wambaugh, John Westlake, Amos Hershey, Crammond Kennedy, Charles Stockton, and Talcott Williams. Those who supported Taft's position included Chandler P. Anderson, John Bassett Moore, Richard Olney, and Thomas Baty. Eugene Wambaugh, "Exemption from Panama Tolls," *AJIL* 7, no. 2 (1913): 233–44; "American Society of International Law," *Green Bag* 25 (1913): 285–87; Chandler P. Anderson, *Panama Canal Tolls: An Address on the Issues between the United States and Great Britain in Regard to Panama Canal Tolls, as Raised in the Recent Diplomatic Correspondence*, 63rd Cong., 1st sess., 1913, S. Doc 32; "Free Tolls Justified, Contention of Moore," *Washington Herald*, March 7, 1914, in box 93, JBM, LC; Richard Olney, "The Canal Tolls Legislation and the Hay-Pauncefote Treaty," *The Lawyer and Banker and Southern Bench and Bar Review* 6 (June 1913): 164–71.

77. "Convention concerning Arbitration between the United States and Great Britain," supplement, *AJIL* 2, no. 3 (1908): 299.

78. "The ABC of the Panama Canal Controversy," *International Conciliation* 2 (1913): 13.

79. CEIP, *Year Book for 1913–1914*, 80.

80. Scott to Eliot, 2 January 1913, box 10, JBS.

81. Scott to Oppenheim, 1 February 1913, box 10, JBS.

82. Jessup, *Root*, 2:264.

83. Jessup, *Root*, 2:266; Finch, "Biography of James Brown Scott."

84. In a 1904 speech, Root defended Roosevelt's Panama policy by appealing to this sense of moral obligation. Elihu Root, "The Ethics of the Panama Question: An Address before the Union League Club of Chicago, February 22, 1904," in *Addresses on International Subjects*, 175–206; Jessup, *Root*, 2:265–66.

85. Elihu Root, "The Obligations of the United States as to Panama Canal Tolls: An Address in the Senate, January 21, 1913," in *Addresses on International Subjects*, 224.

86. Root, "Obligations," 224–25; italics mine.

87. Elihu Root, "Panama Canal Tolls: An Address in the Senate, May 21, 1914," in *Addresses on International Subjects*, 302.

88. Root, "Obligations," 232–33

89. Root, "Canal Tolls," 302.

90. Root, "Obligations," 238.

91. Harold F. White, "Legal Aspects of the Panama Canal," *Illinois Law Review* 8 (1913): 461.

92. CEIP, *Year Book for 1913-1914*, 38, 79–82. See also Simeon E. Baldwin to James Brown Scott, 23 December 1912, vol. 256, CEIPP.

93. Neither Scott nor Root had uttered any public criticism of Roosevelt's policy at the time. Root later attempted to patch up relations with Colombia, but not until 1923 did the two nations finally settle the matter. Scott, "Review of President Roosevelt's Administration," *The Outlook*, February 13, 1913, 351; David Healy, *Drive to Hegemony: The United States in the Caribbean, 1898-1917* (Madison: University of Wisconsin Press, 1988), 246; Schoultz, *Beneath the United States*, 257.

94. Root, "Obligations," 208.

95. John Westlake to James Brown Scott, 14 March 1913, box 9, JBS; Scott to Wilhelm Kaufmann, 3 February 1913, vol. 258, CEIPP; "Statement of Oscar Straus," in *Panama Canal Tolls: Hearings before the Committee on Interoceanic Canals*, United States Senate, 63rd Cong., 2nd sess., 1914, H.Rep. 14385, 237. French publicist Ernest Nys wrote that the United States should not even bother to arbitrate, for "il a tort, absolument tort & quand une affaire est claire, on ne la soumet pas à la décision d'un arbiter ou d'un juge." Scott to Elihu Root, 30 March 1913, box 10, JBS.

96. Scott to Butler, 19 December 1912. Quoted in Nurnberger, "James Brown Scott," 211–12.

97. Warren Kuehl writes "From 1905 to 1920 . . . American citizens assumed the leadership in efforts to organize the world." Kuehl, *Seeking World Order*, 74. Calvin Davis notes, "In no other countries were arbitration advocates more confident that the advance of international judicial methods could reduce armed conflict." Davis, *First Hague*, 16.

98. Moore, *Four Phases*, 198–99.

99. Many agreed with John Bassett Moore that the latter represented "the greatest treaty of arbitration the world had yet seen." Moore, "The United States and International Arbitration," (1891), in *Collected Papers*, 1:113, and, for an overview of American arbitrations, 120.

100. For instance, James Brown Scott argued that the 1910 North Atlantic Fisheries arbitration (which ended a nearly century-long conflict between the United States and Britain over fishing rights) resolved serious "questions of internal and external sovereignty." But if a hundred years had passed without violence, it seems unlikely the issue would have led to war in the future. James Brown Scott, ed., *Argument of the Honorable Elihu Root on behalf of the United States before the North Atlantic Fisheries Arbitration Tribunal, at The Hague, 1910* (New York: World Peace Foundation, 1912), cii.

101. Nicolas Politis, "The Work of The Hague Court," *Judicial Settlement of International Disputes* 6 (1911): 8. See also Davis, *Second Hague*, 58–62.

102. All figures are from CEIP, "Arbitrations and Diplomatic Settlements of the United States," pamphlet no. 1 (Washington, DC: CEIP, 1914).

103. Otis Cartwright, Memorandum for Dr. Scott, 17 February 1914, vol. 259, CEIPP.

104. Hannigan, *New World Power*, 144–45.

105. Quoted in Kuehl, *Seeking World Order*, 157.

106. Kuehl, *Seeking World Order*, 41–42, 61; Boyle, *Foundations of World Order*, 31–33

107. "Text of the Anglo-American Treaty of Arbitration Signed at Washington D.C., August 3, 1911," *Advocate of Peace* (Sept. 1911): 196–98; William Howard Taft, *The United States and Peace* (New York: Charles Scribner's Sons, 1914), 115.

108. John P. Campbell, "Taft, Roosevelt, and the Arbitration Treaties of 1911," *Journal of American History* 53, no. 2 (1966): 280.

109. *Taft and Roosevelt: The Intimate Letters of Archie Butt, Military Aide* (Garden City, NY: Doubleday, Doran, 1930), 765; Davis, *Second Hague*, 325.

110. Davis, *Second Hague*, 321; Fabian, *Carnegie's Peace Endowment*, 27, 52–59.

111. Lewis L. Gould, *Helen Taft: Our Musical First Lady* (Lawrence: University Press of Kansas, 2010), 126.

112. *Intimate Letters of Archie Butt*, 635–36.

113. John E. Noyes, "William Howard Taft and the Arbitration Treaties," *Villanova Law Review* 56 (2011): 536–37; Kirgis, *First Century*, 24; Address of President William Howard Taft," ASJSID *Proceedings* (1910): 351–57; Taft, *United States and Peace*, 181.

114. Andrew Carnegie, "Peace versus War: The President's Solution," *Century Magazine*, June 1910, 308; "President Taft on International Peace," *AJIL* 5 (1911): 723; Anderson, *Taft*, 281; Taft, *United States and Peace*, 116, 132.

115. Roosevelt to Arthur Lee, August 22, 1911, quoted in Jessup, *Root*, 2:274.

116. Ninkovich, "Civilization as Ideology," 231; Bederman, *Manliness and Civilization*, chap. 3; George M. Beard, *American Nervousness: Its Causes and Consequences* (New York: G. P. Putnam's Sons, 1881); Jessup, *Root*, 2:272; Theodore Roosevelt, "The Arbitration Treaty with Great Britain," *The Outlook*, May 20, 1911, 97–98; Theodore Roosevelt, "The Peace of Righteousness," *The Outlook*, September 9, 1911, 66–70; Campbell, "Arbitration Treaties of 1911," 285.

117. Campbell, "Arbitration Treaties of 1911," 281; Frank S. Gardner to Elihu Root, 28 December 1911, box 78, Root Papers, LC; *Intimate Letters of Archie Butt*, 732.

118. W. Stull Holt, *Treaties Defeated by the Senate* (Baltimore: Johns Hopkins Press, 1933), 233; David Nasaw, *Andrew Carnegie* (New York: Penguin, 2006), 755; Jessup, *Root*, 2:276; Davis, *Second Hague*, 325. On the arbitration treaties as a cause and consequence of the Taft-Roosevelt split, see O'Toole, *When Trumpets Call*, 126–41.

119. Wambaugh, "Exemption from Panama Canal Tolls," *AJIL* 7, no. 2 (1913): 233–44.

120. J. Michael Hogan, *The Panama Canal in American Politics: Domestic Advocacy and the Evolution of Policy* (Carbondale: Southern Illinois University Press, 1986), 44–53.

121. John M. Latané, "The Panama Canal Act and the British Protest, *AJIL* 7, no. 1 (1913): 20.

122. *Panama Canal Tolls: Hearings*, 441–42; 450–51.

123. "From a Speech of Hon. James O'Gorman, of New York, in the Senate of the United States, January 22, 1913," in *Symposium of Views*, ed. Knowland, 11–12.

124. "From a Speech of Hon. James O'Gorman," 11–12.

125. Arthur S. Link, *Wilson: The New Freedom* (Princeton, NJ: Princeton University Press, 1956), 306.

126. Perkins, *Great Rapprochement*, 303. The article was Latané, "Panama Canal Act."

127. Charles Seymour, ed., *The Intimate Papers of Colonel House* (Boston: Houghton Mifflin Co., 1926), 1:192–93.

128. Jessup, *Root*, 2:265.

129. Link, *New Freedom*, 311.

130. Quotes are from Woodrow Wilson, "Address to a Joint Session of Congress on Panama Canal Tolls," March 5, 1914, in The American Presidency Project, online, ed. John T. Woolley and Gerhard Peters, http://www.presidency.ucsb.edu/ws/?pid=65375 (accessed June 2010). The substance of Wilson's remarks became clear soon after when he amicably resolved a brewing dispute with England over Mexico.

131. William Coker asserts that Wilson was motivated primarily by an idealistic belief in the need to uphold the Hay-Pauncefote Treaty. William S. Coker, "The Panama Canal Tolls Controversy: A Different Perspective," *Journal of American History* 55, no. 3 (1968): 555–64.

Chapter 5

1. Healy, *Drive to Hegemony*, 135.

2. Dana Munro, *Intervention and Dollar Diplomacy in the Caribbean, 1900-1921* (Princeton, NJ: Princeton University Press, 1964), 13–16.

3. Schoultz, *Beneath the United States*, 191.

4. Janet Penrose Trevelyan, *The Life of Mrs. Humphry Ward* (New York: Dodd, Mead, 1923), 211; Warren Zimmerman, *First Great Triumph: How Five Americans Made Their Country a World Power* (New York: Farrar, Straus and Giroux, 2002), 142. I thank James Barefield for bringing Trevelyan to my attention.

5. Jessup, *Root*, 1:183.

6. Jessup, *Root*, 2:431; conversion as a ratio of the purchasing power index, via measuringworth. com

7. Leopold, *Root*, 16–17.

8. Zimmerman, *First Great Triumph*, 141.

9. Jessup, *Root*, 1:133.

10. Gordon, "American Legal Profession," 3:96.

11. Jessup, *Root*, 1:133.

12. Leopold, *Root*, 50.

13. Boyle, *Foundations of World Order*, 86–87; Hepp, "James Brown Scott," 1.

14. Finnemore, *Purpose of Intervention*, 44–48.

15. For a broader exploration of this theme, see Ikenberry, *After Victory*.

16. See, especially, Scully, *Bargaining with the State*; Ruskola, "Canton Is Not Boston."

17. Christopher May, *The Rule of Law: The Common Sense of Global Politics* (Northampton, MA: Edward Elgar, 2014), xi–xii; Jeremy Waldron, "The Concept and the Rule of Law," *Georgia Law Review* 43, no. 1 (2008): 1–61.

18. George B. Davis, Address, ASIL *Proceedings* 1 (1907): 91–92.

19. E.g., Walter LaFeber, *The New Cambridge History of American Foreign Relations, Volume 2: The American Search for Opportunity, 1865-1913* (New York: Cambridge University Press, 2013).

20. Orray E. Thurber, *Castro and the Asphalt Trust* (New York, 1907), 21–31; William Maurice Sullivan, "The Rise of Despotism in Venezuela: Cipriano Castro, 1899-1908" (PhD diss., University of New Mexico, 1974), 257–58; McBeth, *Gunboats, Corruption, and Claims*, 67–70, 74–75; Judith Ewell, *Venezuela and the United States: From Monroe's Hemisphere to Petroleum's Empire* (Athens: University of Georgia Press, 996), 101.

21. Noel Maurer, *The Empire Trap: The Rise and Fall of U.S. Intervention to Protect American Property Overseas, 1893-1976* (Princeton, NJ: Princeton University Press, 2013), 83–85; United Kingdom, *Correspondence respecting the affairs of Venezuela* (London: HMSO, 1903); Nancy Mitchell, "The Height of the German Challenge: The Venezuela Blockade, 1902–1903," *Diplomatic History* 20, no. 2 (1996): 185–209; McBeth, *Gunboats*, 92–93.

22. Schoultz, *Beneath the United States*, 180.

23. Munro, *Intervention and Dollar Diplomacy*, 71.

24. McBeth, *Gunboats*, 92–93.

25. James Brown Scott, ed., *The Hague Court Reports* (New York: Oxford University Press, 1916), 55–61; Kevin Anderson, "The Venezuelan Claims Controversy at the Hague, 1903," *Historian* 57, no. 3 (1995): 525–36.

26. Healy, *Drive to Hegemony*, 106.

27. Roosevelt, "Message of the President to the Senate and the House of Representatives," 6 December 1904, *FRUS* (1904), xli.

28. Sexton, *Monroe Doctrine*, 229–30.

29. Douglas R. Gow, "How Did the Roosevelt Corollary Become Linked to the Dominican Republic?" *Mid-America* 58, no. 3 (1976): 159–65; J. Fred Rippy, "Antecedents of the Roosevelt Corollary of the Monroe Doctrine," *Pacific Historical Review* 9, no. 3 (1940): 267–79.

30. Veeser, *World Safe for Capitalism*, 10–101; Maurer, *Empire Trap*, 60–63.

31. Moore's Departmental confidants included assistant secretary of state Francis B. Loomis and second assistant secretary of state Alvey Adee. Loomis to Moore, 3 June 1903, box 10, JBM, LC; Adee to Moore, 1 November 1905, box 11, JBM, CLS.

32. Edwin Borchard, *The Diplomatic Protection of Citizens Abroad, or The Law of International Claims* (New York: Banks Law Publishing Company, 1915); Alan Nissel, "The Duality of State Responsibility," *Columbia Human Rights Law Review* 44, no. 3 (2013): 797–99. On how this practice could give rise to military intervention, see Maurer, *Empire Trap*.

33. Cyrus Veeser, *A World Safe for Capitalism: Dollar Diplomacy and America's Rise to Global Power* (New York: Columbia University Press, 2002), 108, 113.

34. "Arbitration of the Claim of the San Domingo Improvement Company Against the Dominican Republic," *FRUS* (1904), 271.

35. Veeser, *World Safe*, 118.

36. Veeser, *World Safe*, 112.

37. "Award of the Commission of Arbitration Under the Provisions of the Protocol of January 31, 1903, between the United States of America and the Dominican Republic, for the Settlement of the Claims of the San Domingo Improvement Company of New York and its Allied Companies," *FRUS* (1904), 274–77.

38. Veeser, *World Safe*, 121, 124.

39. Schoultz, *Beneath the United States*, 185–87.

40. Healy, *Drive to Hegemony*, 121–23.

41. Maurer, *Empire Trap*, 74.

42. Veeser, *World Safe*, 141.

43. Maurer, *Empire Trap*, 72–73.

44. Emily Rosenberg, *Financial Missionaries to the World: The Politics and Culture of Dollar Diplomacy, 1900-1930* (Durham, NC: Duke University Press, 2003), 46.

45. Nikita Harwich Vallenilla, *Asfalto y Revolución: la New York & Bermudez Company* (Caracas, Venezuela: Monte Avila Editores, 1992), chap. 13; Avery D. Andrews to John Bassett Moore, 3 January 1905, box 62, JBM, CLS.

46. For details, see Benjamin A. Coates, "Securing Hegemony Through Law: Venezuela, the U.S. Asphalt Trust, and the Uses of International Law, 1904-1909," *Journal of American History* 102, no. 2 (2015): 380–405.

47. For Moore's arguments, see esp. letters of 24 August 1904, 26 August, 1904, 8 September 1904, 20 September 1904, 28 November 1904, box 63, JBM, CLS; and 23 January 1905 and 18 March 1905, box 62, box 63, JBM, CLS.

48. Moore to Hay, 20 September 1904, box 63, JBM, CLS.

49. For other citations to European authorities, see, for example, "A Short Memorandum List of the Best Later Works on International Law," 1897, entry 744, "Reports of Clerks and Bureau Officers," Records of the State Department, RG 59, NA.

50. Mark Janis sees Moore's work as an attempt to put international law on a scientific footing through the identification and organization of diplomatic precedent. Janis, *American Tradition*, 124. Moore's work for the NY&B suggests that collecting precedents could prove just as useful for corporate lobbyists as academic modernizers.

51. Moore to Hay, 20 September 1904, box 63, JBM, CLS.

52. Moore to Secretary of State, 23 January 1904, box 62, JBM, CLS.
53. Moore to Brown, 26 August 1904, box 63, JBM, CLS.
54. McBeth, *Gunboats*, 118. A copy of Moore's draft protocol is in box 63, JBM, CLS.
55. McBeth, *Gunboats*, 46–47; John Hay, Diary Entry, 17 February 1905, reel 1, Hay Papers, LC.
56. Borchard, *Diplomatic Protection*, 284, sec. 114; Wharton, *Digest of the International Law of the United States*, 660; Ministro de Relaciones Exteriores, *Libro Amarillo de la República Venezuela* (Caracas, 1905), xxxiv; J. Gillis Wetter, "Diplomatic Assistance to Private Investment: A Study of the Theory and Practice of the United States During the Twentieth Century," *University of Chicago Law Review* 29 (1961–62): 310–16.
57. John Hay, Diary Entries, 6 December and 30 December 1904, reel 1, Hay Papers, LC; Moore to Lindsay, 24 February 1905, box 62, JBM, CLS.
58. Hay to Bowen, 10 March 1905, box 63, JBM, CLS.
59. McBeth, *Gunboats*, 123.
60. Schoultz, *Beneath the United States*, 178.
61. *New York Evening Post*, December 24, 1904, cited in Vallenilla, *Asfalto*, 365.
62. McBeth, *Gunboats*, 118; U.S. Department of State, *In the Matter of the Charges of Mr. Herbert W. Bowen* (Washington, DC: Government Printing Office, 1905).
63. Schoultz, *Beneath the United States*, 191.
64. John Mabry Matthews, *The Conduct of American Foreign Relations* (New York: Century Co., 1922), 47.
65. Richard Hume Werking, *The Master Architects: Building the United States Foreign Service, 1890-1913* (Lexington: University of Kentucky Press, 1977), 1–15; Graham Stuart, *The Department of State: a History of its Organization, Procedure, and Personnel* (New York: MacMillan, 1949), 194; Francis M. Huntington Wilson, *Memoirs of an Ex-Diplomat* (Boston: Bruce Humphries, 1945), 47–48.
66. Molly Wood, "'Commanding Beauty' and 'Gentle Charm': American Women and Gender in the Early Twentieth-Century Foreign Service," *Diplomatic History* 31, no. 3 (2007): 505; Wilson, *Memoirs*, 136–37.
67. Plischke, *Department of State*, 207.
68. Werking, *Master Architects*, 121–70.
69. Department of State, *Outline of Work*, 28–30.
70. The State Department archives do not contain separate records for the office of the solicitor, so a precise determination of all legal work throughout this period is impossible. However, there is a card index beginning in 1910 purporting to include all of the correspondence with the solicitor's office. Though it is not, in fact, comprehensive, it does permit a rough accounting. The largest category of correspondence, if not the absolute majority in all years, involved the protection of US financial interests abroad. See Solicitor Name Card Index, available by requesting 59/250/16/24 "Decimal File 1910-1929 Source Card Index Solicitor," box 1346, NA.
71. "Meeting of the American Commission to the Second Hague Conference, Held April 20, 1907, in the Diplomatic Room of the Department of State," box 20, Choate Papers, LC.
72. Amos S. Hershey, "The Calvo and Drago Doctrines," *AJIL* 1, no. 1 (1907): 43–44; David J. Bederman, "The Glorious Past and Uncertain Future of International Claims Tribunals," in *International Courts for the Twenty-First Century*, ed. Mark Weston Janis (Boston: Martinus Nijhoff, 1992), 168–69.
73. Scully, *Bargaining with the State*, 105–7.
74. Borchard, *Diplomatic Protection*, 653–57.
75. Stuart, *Department of State*, 204; James Brown Scott to Elihu Root, 30 December 1905, box 7, JBS.
76. Nurnberger, "James Brown Scott," 132.
77. These figures come from the *Register of the Department of State* (Washington, DC: Government Printing Office, 1900, 1906, 1910).
78. Department of State, *Short Account of the Department of State*.
79. Department of State, *Outline of the Organization and Work of the Department of State* (Washington, DC: Government Printing Office, 1911). This represented slightly more than 10 percent of the department's total work force.

80. *Register of the Department of State* (1910); Stuart, *Department of State*, 219.

81. A. C. Bedford to Moore, 24 April 1914, box 49, JBM, CLS.

82. Werking, *Master Architects*, 150.

83. "Report of the Committee on International Law," *Annual Report of the American Bar Association* 34 (1911): 407.

84. Frederick Van Dyne, *Our Foreign Service: The "A B C" of American Diplomacy* (Rochester, NY: Lawyers Co-Operative Publishing Company, 1909), 205.

85. Van Dyne, *Our Foreign Service*, 197–206. These included John Bassett Moore's *Digest of International Law* and his works on arbitration and extradition; James Brown Scott's *Casebook of International Law*; works by Halleck, Oppenheim, Snow, Lawrence, and Woolsey; and the *AJIL*. Robert D. Schulzinger, *The Making of the Diplomatic Mind: The Training, Outlook, and Style of United States Foreign Service Officers, 1908-1931* (Middletown, CT: Wesleyan University Press, 1975), 54, 171fn14.

86. Wilson, *Memoirs*, 61–62, 163; Werking, *Master Architects*, 89; Francis M. Huntington Wilson to Ellery C. Stowell, 31 March 1907, box 13, Stowell Papers, LC.

87. Werking, *Master Architects*, 123, 155.

88. Marchand, *Peace Movement*, 70.

89. Pérez Jr., *War of 1898*, 21.

90. Art. III.

91. Quoted in Burnett [Ponsa], "Continent Constitutions," 185.

92. Zasloff, "Law and the Shaping," 288–91.

93. Burnett [Ponsa], "Contingent Constitutions," 139.

94. "Constitution of the Republic of Panama," February 13, 1904, text from Comparative Constitutions Project, http://portal.clinecenter.illinois.edu/cgi-bin/rview?REPOSID=1&ID=7909 (accessed July 23, 2014).

95. Healy, *Drive to Hegemony*, 133.

96. Boyle, *Foundations*, 32–33.

97. Thomas L. Karnes, *The Failure of Union: Central America, 1824-1960* (Chapel Hill: University of North Carolina Press, 1961), 185–86.

98. *FRUS* (1907), 2:614–15.

99. For minutes of the meetings, see *FRUS* (1907), 2:665–74. See also Thomas M. Leonard, *Central America and the United States: The Search for Stability* (Athens: University of Georgia Press, 1991), 59–60.

100. "Convention for the Establishment of a Central American Court of Justice," *AJIL* Supp., 2, no. 1 (1908): 231–43.

101. Luis Anderson, "The Peace Conference of Central America," *AJIL* 2, no. 1 (1908): 144, 146.

102. Karnes, *Failure of Union*, 193.

103. *FRUS* (1907), 2:689–90.

104. *FRUS* (1907), 2:688.

105. Karnes, *Failure of Union*, 194.

106. Grandin, "Liberal Traditions in the Americas."

107. Whitaker, *Western Hemisphere Idea*, chap. 2.

108. Liliana Obregón, "Regionalism Constructed: A Short History of 'Latin American International Law,'" European Society of International Law Conference Paper Series, No. 5 (2012), 7.

109. Arturo Ardao, *Génesis de la Idea y el Nombre de América Latina* (Caracas, Venezuela: Centro de Estudios Latinoamericanos Rómulo Gallegos, 1980), 82–83, 186–99; Aims McGuinness, "Searching for 'Latin America': Race and Sovereignty in the Americas in the 1850s," in *Race and Nation in Modern Latin America*, ed. Nancy P. Applebaum, Anne S. Macpherson, and Karin Alejandra Rosemblatt (Chapel Hill: University of North Carolina Press, 2003), 88.

110. Donald R. Shea, *The Calvo Clause: A Problem of Inter-American and International Law and Diplomacy* (Minneapolis: University of Minnesota Press, 1955), 19.

111. Shea, *Calvo Clause*, 27–32, 33–34.

112. Luis M. Drago to Margin García Mérou, 29 December 1902, in *FRUS* (1903), 1–5. An expanded version of the argument is in Luis M. Drago, "State Loans in Their Relation to

International Policy," *AJIL* 1, no. 3 (1907): 692–726; Drago, "Les Emprunts d'État et leurs Rapports avec la politique internationale" *RGDIP* 19 (1907): 251–87.

113. Edward Ames to John Hay, 5 May 1903, *FRUS* (1903), 6.
114. Walter Penfield, quoted in Hannigan, *New World Power*, 64.
115. Carlos Calvo, quoted in Burnett [Ponsa], "Contingent Constitutions," 299–300.
116. Becker Lorca, "Universal International Law."
117. William Eleroy Curtis, *The Capitals of Spanish America* (New York: Harper and Brothers, 1888), 472, 542; Sexton, *Monroe Doctrine*, 237. Roosevelt is quoted in Ricardo Salvatore, "The Making of a Hemispheric Intellectual-Statesman: Leo S. Rowe in Argentina (1906–1919)," *Journal of Transnational American Studies* 2, no. 1 (2010): 10–11.
118. Quoted in Schoultz, *Beneath the United States*, 191.
119. *Speeches Incident to the Visit of Secretary Root to South America, July 4 to September 30, 1906* (Washington, DC: Government Printing Office: 1906), 9–13.
120. "Meeting of the American Commission."
121. Juan Pablo Scarfi, "In the Name of the Americas: the Pan-American Redefinition of the Monroe Doctrine and the Emerging Language of American International Law in the Western Hemisphere, 1898–1933," *Diplomatic History*, 40, no. 2 (2016): 204.
122. Elihu Root, "The Monroe Doctrine" (1904), in *Addresses on Miscellaneous Subjects*, 268.
123. Elihu Root, "The Relations between International Tribunals of Arbitration and the Jurisdiction of National Courts" (1909), in *Addresses on International Subjects*, 35.
124. *Speeches Incident to the Visit of Secretary Root*, 157–58.
125. Elihu Root, "The Basis of Protection to Citizens Residing Abroad" (1910), in *Addresses on International Subjects*, ed. Bacon and Scott, 48.
126. *FRUS* (1906), 2:1205. Thanks to Max Paul Friedman for bringing this quote to my attention.
127. Hershey, "Calvo and Drago Doctrines," 26–45.
128. James Brown Scott, ed., *The Hague Conventions and Declarations of 1899 and 1907* (New York: Oxford University Press, 1918), 89.
129. Shea, *Calvo Clause*, 15. Since the Drago doctrine referred only to "public" or bond debts, the Porter resolution in some ways represented an expanded restriction. Edwin M. Borchard, "International Contractual Claims and Their Settlement," *Judicial Settlement of International Disputes*, no. 13 (August 1913): 51–52.
130. Scott, *Hague Conventions*, 92–95.
131. Scott, *Proceedings*, 1:589.
132. Paul W. Kahn, *The Reign of Law: Marbury v. Madison and the Construction of America* (New Haven, CT: Yale University Press, 1997), 22.
133. Koskenniemi, "International Law and Hegemony."
134. Michael Mann contrasts the acceptance of modern structural adjustment programs with the need to use violence to enforce the dollar diplomacy of this era. Michael Mann, *Sources of Social Power*, vol. 3: *Global Empires and Revolution, 1890-1945* (New York: Cambridge University Press, 2012), 94.
135. See Moore to Secretary of State, 19 December 1905; and Root to Moore, 22 December 1905, box 62, JBM, CLS.
136. *Correspondence relating to Wrongs Done to American Citizens by the Government of Venezuela*, 60 Cong., 1 sess., 1908, S. Doc. 413, 154.
137. Embert J. Hendrickson, "Root's Watchful Waiting and the Venezuelan Controversy," *The Americas* 23, no. 2 (1966): 115–29.
138. John V. Lombardi, *Venezuela: The Search for Order, the Dream of Progress* (New York: Oxford University Press, 1982), 205.
139. Coates, "Securing Hegemony."
140. http://www.nobelprize.org/nobel_prizes/peace/laureates/1912/; James C. Knarr, *Uruguay and the United States, 1903-1929: Diplomacy in the Progressive Era* (Kent, OH: Kent State University Press, 2012); Salvatore, "Hemispheric Intellectual"; Johnson, "Understanding the American Empire"; *Speeches Incident to the Visit of Philander Chase Knox, Secretary of State of the United States of America, to the Countries of the Caribbean*

(Washington, DC: Government Printing Office, 1913), 49, 72; Healy, *Drive to Hegemony*, 143–44; Schoultz, *Beneath the United States*, 196.

141. Quoted in Richard H. Steinberg and Jonathan Zasloff, "Power and International Law," *AJIL* 100, no. 1 (2006): 67–68.

142. Walter V. Scholes and Marie V. Scholes, *The Foreign Policies of the Taft Administration* (Columbia: University of Missouri Press, 1970), 1–10.

143. Wilson, *Memoirs*, 212.

144. Arturo Alessandri, quoted in Frederick B. Pike, *Chile and the United States, 1880-1962* (Notre Dame, IN: University of Notre Dame Press, 1963), 142.

145. The claim dated back to the 1870s, and originated in contracts between an American-owned firm based in Chile, and the Bolivian government. As part of the settlement of the War of the Pacific, in which Chile annexed part of Bolivia, the former country agreed to take responsibility for outstanding claims against the latter. But Chile steadfastly claimed that since the Alsop company was incorporated in Chile, it was a Chilean entity, and that therefore the company's claims should be subject to Chilean justice, not international adjudication. Henry F. Munro and Ellery C. Stowell, *International Cases: Arbitrations and Incidents Illustrative of International Law as Practised by Independent States* (Boston: Houghton-Mifflin, 1916), 326–34; Pike, *Chile and the United States*, 141.

146. Pike, *Chile and the United States*, 141–142; Munro and Stowell, *Cases*.

147. Pike, *Chile and the United States*, 142.

148. Scholes and Scholes, *Foreign Policies*, 12.

149. There are no references to this conflict in Scott's personal papers or in the biographies by Nurnberger, Finch, or Hepp. I found some oblique references to it in letters from Ellery Stowell (who was a clerk at the time) to Moore, but the bulk of the evidence is preserved in the papers of J. Reuben Clark, an assistant solicitor. Frank Fox, a biographer of Clark, discusses it at length. See Stowell to Moore, 16 January 1910 and 9 March 1910, box 15, JBM, LC; Fox, *Clark*, chaps. 2–4; Huntington Wilson, *Memoirs*, 165.

150. Fox, *Clark*, 32–42; 231. Clark grew up in Utah before attending Columbia, where he also studied with John Bassett Moore. He went on to serve as ambassador to Mexico, and eventually became a leader in the Mormon Church.

151. The paper is described in Fox, *Clark*, 91.

152. Healy, *Drive to Hegemony*, 146.

153. Rosenberg, *Financial Missionaries*, 1–3.

154. Maurer, *Empire Trap*, chap. 4. On Nicaragua, see Michel Gobat, *Confronting the American Dream: Nicaragua Under U.S. Imperial Rule* (Durham, NC: Duke University Press, 2005).

155. Alan McPherson, *The Invaded: How Latin Americans and Their Allies Fought and Ended U.S. Occupations* (New York: Oxford University Press, 2014), 13–21.

156. Friedman, "History of the Countermajoritarian Difficulty," 1434; Auerbach, *Unequal Justice*, 32–33.

157. Rosenberg, *Financial Missionaries*, 79.

158. Robert David Johnson, *The Peace Progressives and American Foreign Relations* (Cambridge, MA: Harvard University Press, 1995), 37.

159. Woodrow Wilson, "A Statement on Relations with Latin America" (12 March 1913), *Papers of Woodrow Wilson*, 27:172.

160. Wilson to Charles Talcott, December 31, 1879, quoted in John M. Mulder, *Woodrow Wilson: The Years of Preparation* (Princeton, NJ: Princeton University Press, 1978), 63; John Milton Cooper, Jr., *Woodrow Wilson: A Biography* (New York: Alfred A. Knopf, 2009), 35.

161. John M. Mulder, "'A Gospel of Order': Woodrow Wilson's Religion and Politics," in *The Wilson Era: Essays in Honor of Arthur S. Link*, ed. John Milton Cooper, Jr. and Charles Neu (Arlington Heights, IL: Harland Davidson, 1991), 229.

162. Mulder, *Years of Preparation*, chap. 1.

163. Woodrow Wilson, "The Interpreter of English Liberty," in *Mere Literature and Other Essays* (Boston: Houghton, Mifflin, 1900), 158.

164. Trygve Throntveit, "'Common Counsel': Woodrow Wilson's Pragmatic Progressivism, 1885-1913," in *Reconsidering Woodrow Wilson: Progressivism, Internationalism, War, and Peace*, ed. John Milton Cooper, Jr. (Baltimore: Johns Hopkins University Press, 2008), 25–56.

165. Woodrow Wilson, "The Law and the Facts," Presidential Address, Seventh Annual Meeting of the American Political Science Association, *American Political Science Review* 5, no. 1 (1911): 1.

166. N. Gordon Levin Jr. is right to locate Wilsonianism as an alternative between revolution and imperialism. It is worth pointing out, however, that by the time Wilson entered the White House, his "liberal capitalist" vision incorporated a healthy role for the state, as his domestic reforms reveal. N. Gordon Levin, Jr., *Woodrow Wilson and World Politics: America's Response to War and Revolution* (New York: Oxford University Press, 1968); Throntveit, "Common Counsel"; Link, *New Freedom*, chaps. 5–8; Elizabeth Sanders, *Roots of Reform: Farmers, Workers, and the American State, 1877-1917* (Chicago: University of Chicago Press, 1999), chaps. 6–11.

167. Wilson, "Law and the Facts," 6–10.

168. Cooper, *Woodrow Wilson*, 328–30.

169. David H. Burton, *Taft, Wilson, and World Order* (Madison, NJ: Fairleigh Dickenson University Press, 2003), 15–19.

170. Scott to Lansing, 9 April 1917, box 2, ASIL Papers.

171. Woodrow Wilson, *The State: Elements of Historical and Practical Politics* (1889; repr. Boston: D. C. Heath, 1898), 604–5.

172. Quoted in Auerbach, *Unequal Justice*, 34.

173. Link, *New Freedom*, 95.

174. Paolo Coletta, *William Jennings Bryan, Volume II: Progressive Politician and Moral Statesman, 1909-1915* (Lincoln: University of Nebraska Press, 1969), 103.

175. James Brown Scott, ed., *Treaties for the Advancement of Peace between the United States and Other Powers Negotiated by the Honourable William Jennings Bryan* (New York: Oxford University Press, 1920), 146.

176. Coletta, *Bryan*, chap. 9.

177. Scott to Hüber, 14 May 1914, vol. 261, CEIPP.

178. Healy, *Drive to Hegemony*, 187.

179. Hannigan, *New World Power*, 46; Healy, *Drive to Hegemony*, 168.

180. Woodrow Wilson, "An Address on Latin American Policy in Mobile, Alabama, 27 October 1913," in *Papers of Woodrow Wilson*, 28:450.

181. Diary of Josephus Daniels, 11 March 1913, *Papers of Woodrow Wilson*, 27:169; Woodrow Wilson, "A Statement on Relations with Latin America," 12 March 1913, *Papers of Woodrow Wilson*, 27:172–73.

182. Healy, *Drive to Hegemony*, 165.

183. Coletta, *Bryan*, 110.

184. House to Wilson, 8 March 1913, *Papers of Woodrow Wilson*, 27:163. The quote comes from "The Real Counsellor," *Vancouver Province*, 1913, copy in box 93, JBM, LC.

185. Moore to Frederic Coudert, 21 March 1913, box 20, JBM, LC.

186. Megargee, "Diplomacy of John Bassett Moore," 10–14; Cooper, *Woodrow Wilson*, 33; Moore, memorandum, 1899, box 7, JBM, LC; Moore, memorandum, 27 June 1913, box 92, JBM, LC.

187. Moore to Bryan, 13 March 1913, box 19, JBM, LC.

188. Stuart, *Department of State*, 226.

189. Megargee, "Diplomacy of John Bassett Moore," 168–69.

190. Moore, Memorandum, 7 July 1913; and Memorandum 21 October 1913, box 92, JBM, LC.

191. Coletta, *Bryan*, 110.

192. Lloyd C. Gardner, "Woodrow Wilson and the Mexican Revolution," in *Woodrow Wilson and a Revolutionary World, 1913-1921*, ed. Arthur S. Link (Chapel Hill: University of North Carolina Press, 1982), 5; Mark T. Gilderhus, *Diplomacy and Revolution: U.S.-Mexican Relations under Wilson and Carranza*. (Tucson: University of Arizona Press, 1977), 1.

193. John Mason Hart, *Revolutionary Mexico: The Coming and Process of the Mexican Revolution* (Berkeley: University of California Press, 1987).

194. Friedrich Katz, *The Secret War in Mexico: Europe, the United States and the Mexican Revolution* (Chicago: University of Chicago Press, 1981), 3–49.

195. Henry Lane Wilson refused to intervene to save the former president, and gave Huerta the impression that he would not mourn Madero's execution. Katz, *Secret War*, 92–112.

196. Scholes and Scholes, *Foreign Policies of the Taft Administration*, 101–4.

197. Hart, *Revolutionary Mexico*, 284–85.

198. Moore, Memorandum, 18 August, 1913, box 92, JBM, LC.

199. Mark Benbow, *Leading Them to the Promised Land: Woodrow Wilson, Covenant Theology, and the Mexican Revolution, 1913-1915* (Kent, OH: Kent State University Press, 2010), 12, 25–44.

200. On the stages of Wilson's policy, see Kendrick A. Clements, "Woodrow Wilson's Mexican Policy, 1913-15," *Diplomatic History* 4, no. 2 (1980): 113–36.

201. Woodrow Wilson, "An Address on Latin American Policy in Mobile, Alabama" (October 27, 1913), in *Papers of Woodrow Wilson*, 28:448–53. See also Knock, *To End all Wars*, 26.

202. The phrase "self-determination," so identified with Wilson in the popular memory, actually originated with Vladimir Lenin. For an account of how Wilson later came to adopt it, see Erez Manela, *The Wilsonian Moment: Self-Determination and the International Origins of Anticolonial Nationalism* (New York: Oxford University Press, 2007), 37–43.

203. Moore, Memorandum, 18 August 1913, box 92, JBM, LC.

204. "A Statement on Relations with Latin America," March 12, 1913, in *Papers of Woodrow Wilson*, 27:172–73.

205. Moore, Memorandum, 22 August 1913, box 92, JBM, LC. Bryan claimed that "[t]he reference to gov't by the consent of the governed was put in at my suggestion." Bryan, handwritten note on "Statement with Regard to Latin America," in box 29, Bryan Papers, LC.

206. Moore to Nicholas Murray Butler, 17 February 1914, box 25, JBM, LC. Of course, Wilson was no racial democrat. He reneged on promises to black leaders who had supported his candidacy and oversaw the segregation of federal agencies. He also doubted that "Mexican peons are at present as capable of self-government as other people," but expected them eventually to progress to that position. Benbow, *Leading Them to the Promised Land*, 8.

207. Moore, Memorandum, 18 August 1913, box 92, JBM, LC.

208. Moore, Memorandum, 15 June 1913, box 92, JBM, LC.

209. Peter V. N. Henderson, "Woodrow Wilson, Victoriano Huerta, and the Recognition Issue in Mexico," *The Americas* 41, no. 2 (1984): 151–76; Joseph B. Kelly, "John Bassett Moore's Concept of Recognition," *Journal of the John Bassett Moore Society of International Law* 2 (1961–62): 21.

210. Mikulas Fabry, *Recognizing States: International Society and the Establishment of New States Since 1776* (New York: Oxford University Press, 2010).

211. Moore, *Digest of International Law*, 1:124. Haiti was an important exception to this rule. Fearing the effects on its own enslaved population of recognizing a "black republic," the United States refused to recognize Haiti until 1863.

212. Schoultz, *Beneath the United States*, 236; Gilderhus, *Diplomacy and Revolution*, 2.

213. Moore, Memorandum, 14 May 1913, box 92, JBM, LC.

214. Scholes and Scholes, *Foreign Policies of the Taft Administration*, 17.

215. A copy of the proposed telegram is in *Papers of Woodrow Wilson*, 28:453. See Megargee, "Diplomacy of John Bassett Moore," 231–35, for an account of this episode.

216. Moore to Wilson, 28 October 1913, box 24, JBM, LC.

217. He thereby almost surely prevented a serious diplomatic controversy. Megargee, "Diplomacy of John Bassett Moore," 231–35; Perkins, *Great Rapprochement*, 203.

218. Clements, "Wilson's Mexican Policy," 118.

219. Around the same time, Edward M. House reported that Wilson planned to declare war but carry it out via blockade rather than invasion. Lloyd C. Gardner, *Safe for Democracy: The Anglo-American Response to Revolution, 1913-1923* (New York: Oxford University Press, 1984), 56.

220. Moore, Memorandum, 31 October 1913, box 92, JBM, LC. The original passage appears as a single paragraph. I have inserted line breaks here for ease of comprehension.

221. Moore, Memorandum, 31 October 1913.

222. Moore, Letter of Resignation (unsent), November 1913, box 93, JBM, LC.

223. Wilson's about-face likely resulted from a meeting with Senator Augustus Bacon, who informed the president that there was no public support for war. Clements, "Wilson's Mexican Policy," 118.

224. Moore, Memorandum, 18 August 1913, box 92, JBM, LC.
225. Moore, Memorandum, 18 August 1913, and Memorandum, 31 October 1913, box 92, JBM, LC.
226. Schoultz, *Beneath the United States*, 246
227. Knock, *To End All Wars*, 27.
228. Benbow, *Leading Them to the Promised Land*, 99–124.
229. He left after a year, as promised. "Moore Out as Protest," *Boston Evening Transcript*, March 5, 1914.
230. Clipping in box 93, JBM, LC.
231. Quoted in "Moore out as Protest," *Boston Evening Transcript*, March 5, 1914.
232. Daniel Malloy Smith, *Robert Lansing and American Neutrality, 1914-17* (Berkeley: University of California Press, 1958), 1; Elihu Root to Woodrow Wilson, March 11, 1914, *in Papers of Woodrow Wilson*, 29:331.
233. Stuart, *Department of State*, 238.
234. The biggest exception, aside from Mexico, was the attempt to make amends to Colombia for the US role in Panamanian independence. Bryan negotiated a treaty that would have apologized to Colombia and paid it $25 million. Theodore Roosevelt's allies interpreted this as a slap in the face, and successfully prevented ratification until the 1920s. Link, *New Freedom*, 321–22.
235. Edward S. Kaplan, *U.S. Imperialism in Latin America* (Westport, CT: Greenwood Press, 1998), 28.
236. Link, *New Freedom*, 336.
237. Schoultz, *Beneath the United States*, 230–33; Laurent Dubois, *Haiti: The Aftershocks of History* (New York: Picador, 2012), 204–64; Rosenberg, *Financial Missionaries*, 87.
238. Carter, et. al., *Historical Statistics*, 5:536.
239. Schoulz, *Beneath the United States*, 252.
240. Link, *New Freedom*, 330.
241. Wilson critic David Healy and Wilson supporter Arthur Link more or less agree on this point. See Healy, *Drive to Hegemony*, chap. 10; and Link, *New Freedom*, chap. 10. On how this applied to Haiti, see Maurer, *Empire Trap*, 121–22.
242. Rosenberg, *Financial Missionaries*, 92.
243. John Milton Cooper, Jr., "'An Irony of Fate': Woodrow Wilson's Pre-World War I Diplomacy," *Diplomatic History* 3, no. 4 (1979): 425–37.
244. Quoted in Schoultz, *Beneath the United States*, 222.

Chapter 6

1. Oppenheim to James Brown Scott, 17 August 1914, vol. 259, CEIPP.
2. Schücking to James Brown Scott, 21 August 1914, box 7, JBS.
3. Scott to Heinrich Lammash, 8 October 1914, vol. 260, CEIPP.
4. Scott to Root, 1 September 1914, vol. 261, CEIPP.
5. Theodore S. Woolsey, "Retaliation and Punishment," ASIL *Proceedings* 9 (1915): 62.
6. Elihu Root, "The Outlook for International Law," ASIL *Proceedings* 9 (1915): 4.
7. Louis Renault, "War and the Law of Nations in the Twentieth Century," *AJIL* 9, no. 1 (1915): 16.
8. George Grafton Wilson, in ASIL *Proceedings* 10 (1916): 105.
9. Joint Committee on Printing, *Moore's Digest of International Law*, 64th Cong., 2nd sess., 1917, H. Rep. 1447. This was issued on February 9, 1917.
10. Finch to John Bassett Moore, 14 November 1917, box 35, JBM, LC. For an example, see Edward L. Bacon to Theodore S. Woolsey, 28 June 1914, box 31, WFP.
11. Nicholas Murray Butler to John Bassett Moore, 2 January 1918, box 37, JBM, LC; "Northwestern University announcement of Popular International Law Course to be given by Charles Cheney Hyde," 1916, box 2, ASIL Papers.
12. Moore to Alvey Adee, 29 August 1916, box 29, JBM, CLS. Business records are in JBM, CLS.
13. Anderson, Diary Entries, 9 and 10 June 1915, roll 1, CPA.

14. Plischke, *Department of State,* 289. See also Rachel West, *The Department of State on the Eve of the First World War* (Athens: University of Georgia Press, 1978).

15. Alice M. Morrissey, *The American Defense of Neutral Rights, 1914–1917* (Cambridge, MA: Harvard University Press, 1939), 21–22.

16. *Boston Evening Transcript,* 15 February 1915, in roll 1, CPA.

17. Wambaugh served as "Special Counsel" between 10 August 1914, and 26 September 1914, providing over forty opinions during that period. See Eugene Wambaugh, "Official Memoranda Filed by Me as Special Counsel for the Department of State," 1914, copy in Harvard Law School Library Special Collections. Anderson was in Europe at the war's outbreak, and initially remained in London to advise the American ambassador. When he returned to the United States in February 1915, Lansing convinced him to stay in Washington as an adviser. Benjamin T. Harrison, *Dollar Diplomat: Chandler Anderson and American Diplomacy in Mexico and Nicaragua, 1913-1928* (Pullman: Washington State University Press, 1988), 13–18. Scott was a special adviser. Arthur S. Link, *Wilson: The Struggle for Neutrality, 1914–1915* (Princeton, NJ: Princeton University Press, 1960), 48–49.

18. Sandra Taylor Caruthers, "The Work of the Joint State-Navy Neutrality Board, 1914–1917" (MA thesis, University of Colorado, 1963), 1–2.

19. Robert W. Tucker, *Woodrow Wilson and the Great War: Reconsidering America's Neutrality, 1914–1917* (Charlottesville: University of Virginia Press, 2007). The most detailed development of this argument is Coogan, *End of Neutrality.* See also Charles Callan Tansill, *America Goes to War* (Boston: Little, Brown, 1938); Edwin Montefiore Borchard and William Potter Lage, *Neutrality for the United States* (New Haven, CT: Yale University Press, 1937). For a comparative perspective, see Ørvik, *Decline of Neutrality.*

20. Arthur Link contends that American policy was in fact strictly neutral, while Ernest May terms it "benevolent neutrality." Link, *Struggle for Neutrality*; Ernest R. May, *The World War and American Isolation, 1914–1917* (Cambridge, MA: Harvard University Press, 1959). Others absolve Wilson by contending that strict adherence to neutrality under international law was virtually impossible under new conditions of warfare. Ross Gregory, *The Origins of American Intervention in the First World War* (New York: W. W. Norton, 1971). Patrick Devlin also focuses on the breakdown of international law, but implies that Wilson's actions were driven more by ideological and psychological factors in any case. Patrick Devlin, *Too Proud to Fight: Woodrow Wilson's Neutrality* (New York: Oxford University Press, 1975).

21. The historiography on Wilsonian foreign policy is vast. For a sampling, see John Milton Cooper, Jr., *The Warrior and the Priest: Woodrow Wilson and Theodore Roosevelt* (Cambridge, MA: Harvard University Press, 1983); Gardner, *Safe for Democracy*; Lloyd Ambrosius, *Wilsonian Statecraft: Theory and Practice of Liberal Internationalism during World War I* (Wilmington, DE: SR Books, 1991). An overview is David Steigerwald, "The Reclamation of Woodrow Wilson?" *Diplomatic History* 23, no. 1 (1999): 79–99; John A. Thompson, "Woodrow Wilson and World War I: A Reappraisal," *Journal of American Studies* 19, no. 3 (1985): 325–48.

22. Tucker, *Wilson,* 81. For a historiographical overview, see Tucker, *Wilson,* chap. 3.

23. See, esp., Coogan, *End of Neutrality,* 193; Morrissey, *American Defense of Neutral Rights.*

24. Rubin, "Concept of Neutrality in International Law," 23–25.

25. Moore, *Principles of American Diplomacy,* 61; Coogan, *End of Neutrality,* 17.

26. Janice E. Thomson, *Mercenaries, Pirates, and Sovereigns: State-Building and Extraterritorial Violence in Early Modern Europe* (Princeton, NJ: Princeton University Press, 1994), 81–83.

27. Ørvik, *Decline,* 73.

28. McDougall, *Promised Land, Crusader State,* 42; Robert W. Tucker and David C. Hendrickson, *Empire of Liberty: The Statecraft of Thomas Jefferson* (New York: Oxford University Press, 1990), chap. 6.

29. Neff, *Rights and Duties,* chap. 6; Moore, *Digest of International Law,* 7:697–739.

30. Moore, *Digest of International Law,* 7:1260–61.

31. Coogan, *End of Neutrality,* 25–28; Jürg Martin Gabriel, *The American Conception of Neutrality after 1941* (New York: Palgrave MacMillan, 2002), chap 1.

32. In most neutrality literature, "impartiality" refers to equal assistance to belligerents, rather than to judgment. See, e.g., Gabriel, *American Conception,* 11; Tucker, *Wilson,* 59. My meaning

here is closer to that used by Pål Wrange, who describes impartiality as "independent engagement . . . based on an assessment of the facts in the light of norms." Pål Wrange, "Impartial or Uninvolved? The Anatomy of 20th Century Doctrine on the Law of Neutrality" (PhD diss., University of Stockholm, 2007), 1047.

33. Wrange, "Impartial or Uninvolved," 243. For an American citation of this strand of thought, see Philip Marshall Brown, "Munitions and Neutrality," ASIL *Proceedings* 10 (1916): 40.
34. Alfred Thayer Mahan, quoted in Coogan, *End of Neutrality,* 57.
35. Coogan, *End of Neutrality,* 57–69; Davis, *Second Hague,* 139–40.
36. Joseph Choate, quoted in Davis, *Second Hague,* 171–72.
37. James Brown Scott, "The International Court of Prize," *AJIL* 5, no. 2 (1911): 305.
38. Elihu Root, "The Real Significance of the Declaration of London," *AJIL* 6, no. 3 (1912): 591–93.
39. Moore, "Contraband of War," *Proceedings of the American Philosophical Society* 51, no. 203 (1912): 39.
40. Neff, *Rights and Duties,* 100.
41. Neff, *Rights and Duties,* 64; Moore, *Digest of International Law,* 7:685–87.
42. Moore, "Contraband," 39.
43. Moore, "Contraband," 40–1.
44. Charles G. Fenwick, *The Neutrality Laws of the United States* (Washington, DC: Carnegie Endowment for International Peace, 1913).
45. CEIP, *Year Book for 1912,* 130.
46. James Brown Scott, introduction to Fenwick, *Neutrality Laws,* iii–iv.
47. Scott to Henry S. Drinker, 4 May 1914, vol. 259, CEIPPP.
48. James F. Willis, *Prologue to Nuremberg: The Politics and Diplomacy of Punishing War Criminals of the First World War* (Westport, CT: Greenwood Press, 1982), 74.
49. Smith, *Robert Lansing and American Neutrality,* 8. Note that Smith uses "legalist" in the sense of proceduralist pedant, rather than a believer in promoting international law.
50. Ørvik, *Decline of Neutrality,* 82.
51. Smith, *Robert Lansing,* 1; "Pleads for Venezuela; John W. Foster Argues against Government Aiding Claimants," *New York Times,* April 16, 1908.
52. Lansing to Henry Purcell, 4 February 1913, RL; Hodgson, "Foreign Policy Establishment," 229.
53. Lansing, memorandum, December 1916, 763.72111/4332½, NA.
54. Lansing, memorandum, 3 May 1915; and "Materialism and Patriotism," June 1915, reel 1, RL.
55. Robert Lansing, "Notes on Sovereignty in a State" *AJIL* 1, no. 1 (1907): 107.
56. Lansing, "Notes on Sovereignty in a State," 110; italics in the original. See also Robert Lansing, "Notes on Sovereignty in a State" *AJIL* 1, no. 2 (1907): 320.
57. Robert Lansing, "The Relation of International Law to Fundamental Rights" ASJSID *Proceedings* 3 (1912): 239.
58. Lansing, "Relation of International Law to Fundamental Rights," 240.
59. Smith, *Lansing,* 8.
60. Scott to Robert Lansing, 4 Feb. 1915, box 13, JBS.
61. Scott, "The Right of Neutrals to Protest Against Violations of International Law" *AJIL* 10, no. 2 (April 1916): 343.
62. Elihu Root, "The Outlook for International Law," ASIL *Proceedings* 9 (1915): 9.
63. Scott to M. G. Gram, 2 May 1915, box 14, JBS.
64. Scott to Louis Renault, 7 May 1915, box 11, JBS. See also Wambaugh to Lansing, 18 Sept. 1914, no. 35 in Wambaugh, "Official Memoranda," 190–96.
65. Jesse Reeves, in ASIL *Proceedings* 10 (1916): 60.
66. For proposals of neutral alliance, see Theodore S. Woolsey, "Retaliation and Punishment," ASIL *Proceedings* 9 (1915): 62–69; Edward A. Harriman, "What Means Should Be Provided and Procedure Adopted for Authoritatively Determining Whether The Hague Conventions or Other General International Agreements, or the Rules of International Law, Have Been Violated?" ASIL *Proceedings* 9 (1915): 69–77; Heinrich Lammasch, "Unjustifiable War and the Means to Avoid It," *AJIL* 10, no. 4 (1916): 689–705.
67. Lansing, Memorandum of Meeting with Swedish Minister, 1 Dec. 1914, 763.72111/4331½, RG59, NA; Ørvik, *Decline,* 114–15. Ørvik sees this as an explicitly anti-neutral move; I suggest it reflects a different conception of neutrality.

68. Lansing to Woodrow Wilson, 10 Oct. 1914, 763.72112/133½, NA.
69. Gregory, *Origins*, 43; Adam Tooze, *The Deluge: The Great War, America and the Remaking of the Global Order, 1916–1931* (New York: Viking, 2014), 34–40.
70. Moore, *Digest of International Law*, 7:955–73; "Convention Concerning the Rights and Duties of Neutral Powers in Naval War," Art. 7, Oct. 18, 1907, in James Brown Scott, ed., *The Hague Peace Conferences of 1899 and 1907* (Baltimore: Johns Hopkins Press, 1909), 2:511.
71. During the Franco-Prussian War, Belgium, Switzerland, and Japan prevented the shipment of arms. Neff, *Rights and Duties*, 106. During WWI, Brazil, China, Denmark, the Netherlands, Norway, Spain, and Sweden prohibited the exportation of munitions. Carlton Savage, *Policy of the United States toward Maritime Commerce in War* (Washington, DC: Government Printing Office, 1936), 2:43. For arguments against changing the law, see Lansing to Wilson, 10 Dec. 1914, 763.72111/1332½, NA.
72. Johann von Bernstorff to Lansing, 15 Sept. 1914, in *FRUS* (1914), Supp., 572–73.
73. William Jennings Bryan to Walter Hines Page, 6 Aug. 1914, *FRUS* (1914), Supp., 216.
74. *FRUS* (1914), Supp., lxii.
75. Walter Hines Page to Secretary of State, recd. 26 Aug. 1914, *FRUS* (1914), Supp., 218–20.
76. Coogan, *End of Neutrality*, 154–68.
77. Seymour, *Intimate Papers of Colonel House*, 1:307–8.
78. Walter Hines Page to Secretary of State, 15 Mar. 1915, in *FRUS* (1915), Supp., 143–45.
79. Neff, *Rights and Duties*, 151–53; Hull, *Scrap of Paper*, 185–92.
80. Coogan, *End of Neutrality*, chap. 9–10.
81. Link, *Struggle for Neutrality*, 352.
82. Too much fealty to American special interests could be detrimental. In 1915, Lansing told Anderson he needed him to remain an official department adviser because Solicitor Cone Johnson "was so much under the influence of the cotton interests" that he required close supervision. Memorandum by Anderson, 8 Sept. 1915, roll 1, CPA.
83. Caruthers, "Neutrality Board," 61–62; Wambaugh, "Official Memoranda."
84. Wambaugh to Lansing, 9 Sept. 1914, no. 26 in Wambaugh, "Official Memoranda," 149–51.
85. Lansing to Page, 26 Sept. 1914, 763.72112/126, NA.
86. Neutrality Board, Memorandum no. 75, 18 Mar. 1915, M367-173, NA
87. Neutrality Board, Memoranda nos. 71 and 71bis, 6 Mar. 1915, M367-173, NA.
88. Coogan, *End of Neutrality*, 234.
89. Coogan, *End of Neutrality*, 254.
90. Memorandum by Anderson, 20 Mar. 1915, CPA; Tucker, *Wilson*, 105-6.
91. Wambaugh to Lansing, 8 Sept. 1914, in Wambaugh, no. 24 in "Official Memoranda," 139–40; Smith, *Lansing*, 20. See also Lansing to Walter Hines Page, 28 Sept. 1914, *FRUS* (1914), Supp., 232–33.
92. Smith, *Lansing*, 46–47.
93. Wambaugh to Lansing, 9 Sept. 1914, no. 26 in Wambaugh, "Official Memoranda," 149–51. Anderson omitted even the formal protest. See Anderson, "Memorandum of reasons why the United States should acquiesce without protest," 21 Oct. 1914, CPA.
94. Neutrality Board, Memorandum no. 71bis.
95. Neutrality Board, Memorandum no. 137, 15 May, 1916, M367-176, NA.
96. Cited in Caruthers, "Neutrality Board," 88.
97. Smith, *Lansing*, 50–51; Savage, *Maritime Commerce*, 2:56–57; Caruthers, "Neutrality Board," 90.
98. Devlin, *Too Proud*, 206.
99. Smith, *Lansing*, 142.
100. Paul Vincent, *The Politics of Hunger: The Allied Blockade of Germany, 1915-1919* (Athens: Ohio University Press, 1985), 137–45; A. C. Bell, *A History of the Blockade of Germany* (1937; London: HMSO, 1961), 671–72; Hull, *Scrap of Paper*, 169.
101. Memorandum by Anderson, 3 May 1915, CPA.
102. Lansing, "Consideration and Outline of Policies," 11 July 1915, RL.
103. Scott to Louis Renault, 26 May 1917, box 11, JBS.
104. Tansill, *America Goes to War*, 168.
105. CEIP, *Year Book for 1913–1914*, 43–44.

106. E.g., Albéric Rolin to Scott, 28 Sept. 1914, box 10, JBS. Although exaggerated by the Allies, widespread German atrocities did occur. See John Horne and Alan Kramer, *German Atrocities, 1914: A History of Denial* (New Haven, CT: Yale University Press, 2000). "Barbarians" is from Fernand Daguin to James Brown Scott, 27 August 1915, vol. 263, CEIPP.
107. Oppenheim to James Brown Scott, 20 September 1915, box 6, JBS; John Pawley Bate to James Brown Scott, 17 August 1914, vol. 260, CEIPP.
108. See e.g., Rolin to Scott, 28 September 1914, box 10, JBS. See also Louis Renault to James Brown Scott, 1 July 1915, box 6, JBS.
109. Hans Wehberg to James Brown Scott, 4 September 1914, box 9, JBS.
110. Karl Strupp to James Brown Scott, 25 August 1914, box 7, JBS; Heinrich Lammasch to Scott, 15 September 1914, vol. 260, CEIPP.
111. See, e.g., Scott to Jules Jean Prudhommeaux, 7 August 1914, vol. 260, CEIPP.
112. Justus D. Doenecke, *Nothing Less than War: A New History of America's Entry into World War I* (Lexington: University Press of Kentucky, 2011), 111.
113. Lutzker, " 'Practical' Peace Advocates," 322–25. See also Priscilla Roberts, "Paul D. Cravath, the First World War, and the Anglophile Internationalist Tradition," *Australian Journal of Politics and History* 51, no. 2 (2005): 194–215.
114. Doenecke, *Nothing Less Than War*, 40.
115. According to Philip Jessup, "There is no evidence that Root ever came to realize that the British had violated international law in their treatment of American vessels." Jessup, *Root*, 2:320. This seems hard to believe, considering his frequent conversations with Scott and Chandler Anderson. If Root did admit British violations, though, certainly he deemed them much less serious than those of Germany.
116. The best account of this is Hull, *Scrap of Paper*, chaps. 5–6.
117. Jessup, *Root*, 2:chap. 30.
118. Jessup, *Root*, 2:310.
119. Amos S. Hershey, "Germany: The Main Obstacle to the World's Peace," *Independent*, 66 (May 20, 1909): 1071–76. Cited in Daniel M. Smith, "National Interest and American Intervention, 1917: An Historiographical Appraisal," *Journal of American History* 52, no. 1 (1965): 11.
120. CEIP, *Year Book for 1915*, 105.
121. Hull, *Scrap of Paper*, 42–44.
122. James Harris Vickery, "The Problem of the 'German Professor,' " *International Law Notes* 1, no. 7 (1916): 103–5.
123. Ellery C. Stowell, *The Diplomacy of the War of 1914: The Beginnings of the War* (Boston: Houghton Mifflin Co., 1915), 515.
124. Charles Cheney Hyde, review of *Belgium's Case: A Juridical Enquiry*, by Charles de Visscher, *AJIL* 11, no. 3 (1917): 737–39.
125. Members of the Oxford Faculty of Modern History, *Why We Are at War: Great Britain's Case* (Oxford: Oxford at the Clarendon Press, 1914), 108–17.
126. On the similarities between German and American naval strategies, see Dirk Bönker, *Militarism in a Global Age: Naval Ambitions in Germany and the United States before World War I* (Ithaca, NY: Cornell University Press, 2012).
127. Nicoletta F. Gullace, "Sexual Violence and Family Honor: British Propaganda and International Law during the First World War," *American Historical Review* 102, no. 3 (1997): 714–47.
128. Elihu Root, "The Effect of Democracy on International Law," ASIL *Proceedings* 11 (1917): 7.
129. Tucker, *Wilson*, 34.
130. "Consideration and Outline of Policies," 11 July 1915, reel 1, RL.
131. "Consideration and Outline of Policies."
132. "What Will the President Do?" 3 December 1916, reel 1, RL.
133. Smith, "National Interest," 5–24.
134. Caruthers, "Neutrality Board," 27–28; Wambaugh to Lansing, 22 September 1914, no. 40, in Wambaugh, "Official Memoranda," 223–26.
135. Department of State, "The Status of Armed Merchant Vessels," 19 Sept. 1914, *FRUS* (1914), Supp., 611–12.

136. Johan den Hertog, "Dutch Neutrality and the Value of Legal Argumentation," in *Caught in the Middle: Neutrals, Neutrality and the First World War*, ed. Johan den Hertog and Samuël Kruizinga (Amsterdam: Aksant Academic Publishers, 2010), 23–42; *AJIL Supplement*, 12, no. 3 (1918): 196–203.

137. Tucker, *Wilson*, 132–33.

138. Borchard and Lage, *Neutrality*, 43.

139. Neutrality Board, Memorandum no. 41, 22 Oct. 1914, M367–172, NA.

140. Rodney Carlisle, *Sovereignty at Sea: U.S. Merchant Ships and American Entry into World War I* (Gainesville: University Press of Florida, 2009), 27.

141. Tucker, *Wilson*, 136–39.

142. Hull, *Scrap of Paper*, 257–58, 265–66. Hull argues that submarines *could* in fact successfully interdict shipping while complying with the rules of cruiser warfare. Nevertheless, many German officials believed otherwise.

143. Tucker, 136–39; Devlin, *Too Proud*, 283–84. See also discussion in ASIL *Proceedings* 9 and 10 (1915–16).

144. Hull, *Scrap of Paper*, 268.

145. Alice Morrissey McDiarmid, "The Neutrality Board and Armed Merchantmen, 1914–1917," *AJIL* 69, no. 2 (1975): 377–78.

146. Caruthers, "Neutrality Board," 28.

147. Tansill, *American Goes to War*, 259–60.

148. "President Wilson's Letter to Senator Stone Announcing His Stand on Armed Liner Issue," *NYT*, February 25, 1916.

149. Lester H. Woolsey, "Memorandum—House Resolution 147," 1916, Lester H. Woolsey Papers.

150. "The President's Letter of February 24, 1916, Asserting the Right of American Citizens to Travel on Armed Merchant Ships," in *FRUS* (1916), Supp., 177–78.

151. For an example, see William R. Manning to George Finch, 11 June 1918, vol. 269, CEIPP.

152. Root, "Effect of Democracy," 10–11.

153. James Brown Scott to Elihu Root, 4 February 1918, box 2, ASIL Papers. See also "Minutes of the Meeting of the Committee on Annual Meeting," 2 February 1918, box: "Executive Council Minutes," ASIL Papers. For the committee's public statement, see "International Law and the War," *AJIL* 12, no. 2 (1918): 338–40.

154. Clarke to James Brown Scott, 3 April 1918, box 2, ASIL Papers. Clarke ended his letter: "With heartfelt wishes for your and Mrs. Scott's health and prosperity, and with a fervent 'D— the Kaiser.'"

155. Coudert to James Brown Scott, 3 April 1918, box 2, ASIL Papers.

156. James Brown Scott to Robert Lansing, 21 April 1917, vol. 270, CEIPP; Excerpt from Minutes of Board of Trustees, 18 April 1919, box 36, JBS; ASIL *Proceedings* 11 (1917): 25; Nurnberger, "James Brown Scott," 255–56.

157. Arthur I. Andrews to James Brown Scott, 28 May 1917, box 2, ASIL Papers.

158. Nurnberger, "James Brown Scott," 255–56.

159. Charles Cheney Hyde to George Finch, 17 May 1918, box 2, ASIL Papers; Lutzker, "Practical Peace Advocates," 339.

160. Nicholas Murray Butler to James Brown Scott, 13 August 1918; and Scott to Butler, 14 August 1918, in vol. 271, CEIPP; James Brown Scott, "The Dawn in Germany: The Lichnowsky and other Disclosures," *AJIL* 12, no. 2 (1918): 386–402.

161. Randolph Bourne understood better than most how the war would warp intellectual inquiry and argument. Bourne, *War and the Intellectuals: Collected Essays, 1915–1919*, ed. Carl Resek (1964; Indianapolis, IN: Hackett Publishing Co., 1999).

Chapter 7

1. From $598 billion (in 2009 dollars) to $744 billion from 1914 to 1918. "Graphing Various Historical Economic Series: Real GDP, 1790–Present," Measuringworth, 2015, https://www.measuringworth.com.

2. Tooze, *The Deluge*, 211.

3. Kennan, *American Diplomacy*, 95–103.
4. Mark W. Janis, "North America: American Exceptionalism in International Law," in *The Oxford Handbook of the History of International Law*, ed. Bardo Fassbender and Anne Peters (Oxford: Oxford University Press, 2012), 549.
5. Borchard to Moore, 26 August 1919, box 40, JBM, LC.
6. Stephen G. Craft, "John Bassett Moore, Robert Lansing, and the Shandong Question," *Pacific Historical Review* 60, no. 2 (1997): 233.
7. Lansing, *Peace Negotiations*, 107; James Brown Scott, "Work in the Field of International Law: Memorandum of Progress," box 47, JBS.
8. Margaret MacMillan, *Paris 1919: Six Months That Changed the World* (New York: Random House, 2003), 149; John Milton Cooper, Jr., *Warrior and the Priest*, 338; Thomas J. Knock, *To End All Wars: Woodrow Wilson and the Quest for a New World Order* (Princeton, NJ: Princeton University Press, 1992), 205.
9. Lawrence Gelfand, *The Inquiry: American Preparations for Peace, 1917-1919* (New Haven, CT: Yale University Press, 1963), 51–52.
10. Thomas Parkinson to John Bassett Moore, 22 April 1914, box 27, JBM, LC.
11. Kuehl, *Seeking World Order*, 261–62.
12. Charles Repington, quoted in David Reynolds, *The Long Shadow: The Legacies of the Great War in the Twentieth Century* (New York: W. W. Norton, 2014), 178.
13. Casper Sylvest, "Continuity and Change in British Liberal Internationalism, c. 1900-1930," *Review of International Studies* 31 (2005): 263–83; Laity, *British Peace Movement*, 234; Antoine Pillet, "La guerre actuelle et le droit des gens," *RGDIP* 23, no. 1 (1916): 5–31.
14. Ruhl J. Bartlett, *The League to Enforce Peace* (Chapel Hill: University of North Carolina Press, 1944), 28–37.
15. Historians have offered conflicting characterizations of the relationship between international lawyers and the LEP. Lawrence Gelfand argues that legal scholars opposed the LEP "because of its alleged incompatibility with national sovereignty," while Warren Kuehl lumps Root, Scott, and Moore together as "pacifists" opposed to the "internationalists" who backed the LEP. Stephen Wertheim characterizes the LEP as favoring a "legalist-sanctionist" path. Sondra Herman notes that "legalists, like James Brown Scott, Nicholas Murray Butler, and Elihu Root," opposed the LEP because they "feared that Americans were unprepared to accept the obligations of membership in any organization that pledged automatic sanctions." Gelfand, *Inquiry*, 37; Kuehl, *Seeking World Order*, 208–13; Stephen Wertheim, "The League That Wasn't: American Designs for a Legalist-Sanctionist League of Nations and the Intellectual Origins of International Organization, 1914-1920," *Diplomatic History* 35, no. 5 (2011): 797–836; Herman, *Eleven against War*, 57–58. See also Patterson, *Toward a Warless World*, 249–53.
16. The program is in LEP, *Enforced Peace: Proceedings of the First Annual National Assemblage of the League to Enforce Peace, Washington, May 26-27, 1916* (New York: LEP, 1916), 189–90.
17. Martin David Dubin, "Toward the Concept of Collective Security: The Bryce Group's 'Proposals for the Avoidance of War,' 1914-1917," *International Organization* 24, no. 2 (1970): 300; Viscount Bryce and others, *Proposals for the Prevention of Future Wars* (London: George Allen and Unwin, 1917).
18. LEP, *Enforced Peace*, 189–90.
19. LEP, *Independence Hall Conference Held in the City of Philadelphia, Bunker Hill Day (June 17th), 1915, Together with the Speeches Made at a Public Banquet in the Bellvue-Stratford Hotel on the Preceding Evening* (New York: League to Enforce Peace, 1915), 13–19. On Taft's initial skepticism of "enforcement," see Bartlett, *League*, 36.
20. LEP, *Independence Hall Conference*, 17.
21. A. Lawrence Lowell, "A League to Enforce Peace," *Atlantic Monthly*, September 1915, 393; LEP, *Independence Hall Conference*, 10.
22. Wertheim, "League That Wasn't," 809.
23. Lowell, "League to Enforce Peace," 392; Herman, *Eleven against War*, chap. 3.
24. See, e.g., LEP, *Enforced Peace*, 5–6, 20, 165.
25. LEP, *Independence Hall Conference*, 62.
26. Lowell, "League to Enforce Peace," 394; LEP, *Enforced Peace*, 22–23.

27. LEP, *Enforced Peace*, 53; William H. Short, *Program and Policies of the League to Enforce Peace: A Handbook for Officers, Speakers, and Editors* (New York: League to Enforce Peace, 1916), 43–44.

28. Lowell, "League to Enforce Peace," 393–94; Kuehl, *Seeking World Order*, 212.

29. LEP, *Enforced Peace*, 16–17, 27.

30. LEP, *Enforced Peace*, 56.

31. Theodore Marburg, Minutes, 25 January 1915, box 48, WFP.

32. Marburg, Minutes; Herman, *Eleven against War*, 75–77.

33. Herman, *Eleven against War*, 74.

34. Short, *Program and Policies*, 24.

35. LEP, *Enforced Peace*; Bartlett, *League*, 49.

36. LEP, *Enforced Peace*, 110–11.

37. Bartlett, *League*, 60; Sally Marks, *The Illusion of Peace: International Relations in Europe, 1918-1933*, 2nd ed. (New York: Palgrave Macmillan, 2003), 7–8.

38. Kuehl, *Seeking World Order*, 203.

39. Scott to de Louter, 11 March 1914, vol. 261, CEIPP.

40. Scott to Oppenheim, 8 September 1914, vol. 259, CEIPP; emphasis mine.

41. Scott, "The Nature and Form of the Agreement for the Submission of Justiciable Disputes to an International Court," ASIL *Proceedings* 9 (1915): 87; Scott to Michel Kebedgy, 2 May 1915, box 11, JBS.

42. Scott elaborated this argument most fully in *United States of America: A Study in International Organization*.

43. CEIP, *Year Book for 1916*, 150.

44. James Brown Scott, "The Organization of International Justice," *Advocate of Peace* 79, no. 1 (1917): 17; James Brown Scott, "Suits Between States" *AJIL* 12, no. 3 (1918): 619–27; CEIP, *Year Book for 1917*, 146.

45. Scott, "Organization of International Justice," 13, 15.

46. Scott, "Organization of International Justice."

47. Scott, "Organization of International Justice," 16.

48. Scott, "Organization of International Justice," 16.

49. Scott to John Wesley Hill, 8, June 1915, box 11, JBS.

50. Nurnberger, "James Brown Scott," 243. Scott quoted in Martin David Dubin, "The Carnegie Endowment for International Peace and the Advocacy of a League of Nations, 1914-1918," *Proceedings of the American Philosophical Society* 123, no. 6 (1979): 349.

51. Scott, "International Organization," 104.

52. Scott, "Project of an International Court," 14.

53. ASJSID *Proceedings* 9 (1915): 44–45.

54. Coudert to John Bassett Moore, 23 March 1916, box 33, JBM, LC.

55. David Patterson, "The United States and the Origins of the World Court," *Political Science Quarterly* 91, no. 2 (1987): 288.

56. LEP members included George Gray (who later withdrew), George Grafton Wilson, Oscar Straus, Theodore Woolsey, Richard Olney, Jacob M. Dickinson, William Howard Taft, and Leo Rowe. They constituted three out of seven members of the executive committee, two out of the nine on the AJIL editorial board, and five of fifteen vice presidents. Those who supported the LEP but did not join officially included Amos Hershey, Everett P. Wheeler, Richard Bartholdt, and John Latané. Short, *Program and Policies of the LEP*, 50–53; ASIL *Proceedings* 8 (1914): v–vi.

57. LEP, *Independence Hall Conference*, 58–62; Moore to William H. Short, 10 August 1916, box 161, JBM, LC.

58. William H. Short to Moore, 15 May 1915, box 161, JBM, LC; Moore to Short, 15, May 1915, box 161, JBM, LC.

59. Moore to Edwin Borchard, 7 April 1916, box 32, JBM, LC.

60. Moore to Alpheus H. Snow, 26 April 1916, box 295, JBM, LC.

61. Moore to William H. Short, 3 July 1915, box 161, JBM, LC. John Bassett Moore, "The Peace Problem," Address on the Peace Problem, delivered at the Twentieth Celebration of Founder's Day, held at Carnegie Institute, in Pittsburgh, PA, on April 27, 1916," reprinted

from *Columbia University Quarterly*, 18, no. 3 (1916); 64th Cong., 2nd sess., S. Doc. 700. (30 Jan. 1917), 9–10.

62. Moore to Edward L. Conn, 23, June 1916, box 46, JBS. Conn was a reporter at the *Washington Times*. He forwarded this letter to James Brown Scott, in whose papers it is preserved.

63. Moore, "Peace Problem," 3.

64. Moore, "Peace Problem," 11–12.

65. *Report of the Twenty-Second Annual Lake Mohonk Conference on International Arbitration, May 17th, 18th and 19th, 1916* (Lake Mohonk Conference on International Arbitration, NY, 1916); Cecilie Reid, "American Internationalism: Peace Advocacy and International Relations 1895-1916" (PhD diss., Boston College, 2005), 241–55.

66. ASIL *Proceedings* 11 (1917): 119–20.

67. ASJSID *Proceedings* 9 (1915): 83. Williams was a member of the LEP.

68. ASIL *Proceedings* 11 (1917): 123–24.

69. Lowell to Leo S. Rowe, 15 March 1916, box 114, A. Lawrence Lowell Papers, Harvard University

70. Quoted in Wertheim, "League That Wasn't," 811.

71. A copy of the image is in the frontispiece to LEP, *Independence Hall Conference*.

72. Dubin, "CEIP and the Advocacy of a League."

73. On wartime progressive internationalists, see Knock, *To End All Wars*; Herman, *Eleven against War*, chap. 5; Patterson, *Toward a Warless World*, 247–50; Alan Dawley, *Changing the World: American Progressives in War and Revolution* (Princeton, NJ: Princeton University Press, 2003), 92–96; Jane Addams, *Peace and Bread in Time of War* (New York: MacMillan, 1922).

74. Taft to H. S. Houston, 30 April 1918, quoted in Dubin, "CEIP and the Advocacy of a League," 367.

75. Theodore Marburg to Woodrow Wilson, 20 May 1917, case 4004, reel 360, Wilson Papers, LC.

76. On the American Insitute of International Law, see Burnett [Ponsa], "Contingent Constitutions," chap. 4.

77. Scott, *American Institute of International Law: Its Declaration of the Rights and Duties of Nations*, 11.

78. Scott, *American Institute of International Law*, 15.

79. Lorca, *Mestizo International Law*, 328.

80. L'Institut Américain de Droit International, *Procés-Verbaux*, 89.

81. CEIP, *Year Book for 1916*, 18.

82. Moore to Edwin Borchard, 17 November 1920, box 42, JBM, LC.

83. "Final Act of the Havana Meeting of the American Institute of International Law," supplement, *AJIL* 11, no. 2 (1917): 47–49. See also Scott, "Organization of International Justice."

84. Amos S. Hershey, "Projects Submitted to the American Institute of International Law," *AJIL* 11, no. 2 (1917): 392.

85. Wertheim, "League That Wasn't," 833.

86. Ross A. Kennedy, *The Will to Believe: Woodrow Wilson, World War I, and America's Strategy for Peace and Security* (Kent, OH: Kent State University Press, 2009); Knock, *To End All Wars*.

87. Woodrow Wilson, "Conditions of Peace" (January 22, 1917) and "Fourteen Conditions of Peace" (January 8, 1918), in *Selected Addresses and Public Papers of Woodrow Wilson*, ed. Albert Bushnell Hart (New York: Modern Library, 1918), 172, 249.

88. Knock, *To End All Wars*, 148–54; Manela, *Wilsonian Moment*, 41–43.

89. Kuehl, *Seeking World Order*, 285–87, 340–44; Patterson, *Toward a Warless World*, 254. David Steigerwald calls Root and other legalists "Wilsonians," arguing that the dispute between conservatives and progressive internationalists reflected "means, not ends." My argument here is that the difference in means was significant; certainly, it seemed so at the time. David Steigerwald, *Wilsonian Idealism in America* (Ithaca, NY: Cornell University Press, 1994), 41.

90. On lawyers' dominance at the 1907 Hague Peace Conference, see Finnemore, *Purpose of Intervention*, 39–40.

91. Gelfand, *Inquiry*, 29–30, 179; Neil Smith, *American Empire: Roosevelt's Geographer and the Prelude to Globalization* (Berkeley: University of California Press, 2003), 146. Among those offering their services in vain were Chandler P. Anderson, Charles Cheney Hyde, and Charles N. Gregory. Gelfand, *Inquiry*, 73; Hyde to House, 2 October 1917, Records of the Inquiry, RG

256/350, folder "C. C. Hyde," NA; Gregory to House 11 October 1917, entry 2, box 22, RG 256, folder "C. C. Hyde," NA. The one active Inquiry member associated with international law was Manley Hudson, who went on to earn a great deal of renown in the field but was in 1919 still a junior figure.

92. Davis, *Second Hague*, 352–55.
93. Elihu Root, "Letter of Honorable Elihu Root to Honorable Will H. Hays Regarding the Covenant of the League of Nations," *AJIL* 13, no. 3 (1919): 587.
94. Root to Oppenheim, 6 March 1915, quoted in Martin David Dubin, "Elihu Root and the Advocacy of a League of Nations, 1914-1917," *Western Political Quarterly* 19, no. 3 (1966): 445.
95. Dubin, "Root and the Advocacy of a League," 444–48.
96. Elihu Root, "The Outlook for International Law" ASIL *Proceedings* 9 (1915): 5.
97. Lowell to Root, 28 July 1915, 5 January 1916, box 114, Lowell Papers; Root to Lowell, 10 February 1916, box 114, Lowell Papers.
98. Root to A. Lawrence Lowell, 14 January 1916, box 114, Lowell Papers.
99. Root to Lowell, 9 August 1915, box 114, Lowell Papers.
100. Root, "Outlook for International Law," 9–10; Dubin, "Root and the Advocacy of a League," 451.
101. Bartlett, *League to Enforce Peace*, 144.
102. Root, "Letter to Hays"; Wertheim, "League That Wasn't," 822.
103. Herman, *Eleven against War*, 81.
104. Root, "Letter to Hays."
105. Herman, *Eleven against War*, 48–49.
106. Bartlett, *League to Enforce Peace*, 113–67.
107. Bartlett, *League to Enforce Peace*, 127–28.
108. Kuehl, *Seeking World Order*, 323.
109. Elihu Root, "Letter of the Honorable Elihu Root to Senator Henry Cabot Lodge Regarding the Covenant of the League of Nations," *AJIL* 13, no. 3 (1919): 600.
110. Root, "Letter to Hays," 592–93. Herman, *Eleven against War*, 49–50, stresses the fear of Communism. On detractors, see Bartlett, *League to Enforce Peace*, 138–39.
111. In 1921, Root addressed the ASIL and gave a similar take: he appreciated that the League created a permanent forum for negotiation, but continued to believe that the future of peace required the development of law and judicial institutions. Elihu Root, Opening Address, ASIL *Proceedings* 15 (1921): 1–13.
112. Dubin, "Root and the Advocacy of a League," 455.
113. Root, "Letter to Lodge," 597.
114. Bartlett, *League to Enforce Peace*, 175.
115. David Jayne Hill, *Americanism: What It Is* (1916; New York: D. Appleton and Company, 1919), 187; Aubrey Parkman, *David Jayne Hill and the Problem of World Peace* (Lewisburg, PA: Bucknell University Press, 1974), chaps. 9–11.
116. Quoted in Dubin, "CEIP and the Advocacy of a League," 352.
117. Quoted in Dawley, *Changing the World*, 278–79.
118. John Milton Cooper, Jr., *Breaking the Heart of the World: Woodrow Wilson and the Fight for the League of Nations* (Madison: University of Wisconsin Press, 2001), 266–69, 362–70; Bartlett, *League to Enforce Peace*, 167–204.
119. CEIP, *Year Book for 1915*, 130–31.
120. CEIP, *Year Book for 1913-1914*, 102.
121. Wehberg to James Brown Scott, 29 April 1915, vol. 263, CEIPP.
122. *Annuaire* 27 (1919), 341–44; Koskenniemi, *Gentle Civilizer*, 293.
123. Albéric Rolin to Scott, 23 June 1920, vol. 278, CEIPP.
124. Philip Marshall Brown to Scott, 6 October 1921, vol. 282, CEIPP; *Annuaire* 28 (1921), viii.
125. Scott to Francis Hagerup, 2 May 1915, box 14, JBS; Scott to Albéric Rolin, 2 May 1915, vol. 263, CEIPP.
126. "Annual Meeting of the Executive Council of the American Society of International Law," 27 April 1918, box "American Society of International Law Executive Council—1918," ASIL Papers.

127. "Annual Meeting of the Executive Council," 27 April 1918, ASIL Papers.
128. This was a common theme in the immediate postwar years as American philanthropic societies extended humanitarian and reconstruction aid in Europe. Merle Curti, *American Philanthropy Abroad: A History* (New Brunswick, NJ: Rutgers University Press, 1963), chap. 10; Julia F. Irwin, "Nation Building and Rebuilding: The American Red Cross in Italy During the Great War," *Journal of the Gilded Age and Progressive Era* 8, no. 3 (2009): 407–39.
129. ". . . l'année prochaine est l'époque la meilleure qu'on puise choisir pour se rendre en Amérique."
130. *Annuaire* (1919): 324–40.
131. *Annuaire* (1919): 322.
132. Scott to Lapradelle, 30 September 1919, box 11, JBS.
133. Borchard to Moore, 14 May 1919, box 40, JBM, LC.
134. Borchard to Moore, 15 November 1920, box 42, JBM, LC.
135. James Brown Scott, "The Institute of International Law," *AJIL* 16, no. 2 (April 1922): 245.
136. *Annuaire* (1921): 205, 215 ("teintée de trop de *régionalisme*"; emphasis in the original).
137. *Annuaire* (1921): 218; Nathaniel Berman, "'But the Alternative Is Despair': European Nationalism and the Modernist Renewal of International Law," *Harvard Law Review* 106, no. 8 (1993): 1803, fn 48.
138. *Annuaire* (1921): 219–22.
139. The Institut considered the question of a Declaration of Rights and Duties of States again in 1925 but never formally endorsed one. *Annuaire* (1925): 238–45.
140. Becker Lorca, *Mestizo International Law*, 200; Berman, "But the Alternative Is Despair."
141. Nicolas Politis, *The New Aspects of International Law* (Washington, DC: CEIP, 1928).
142. Wrange, "Impartial or Uninvolved," 217; Shinohara, *US International Lawyers*, 37–43; Becker Lorca, *Mestizo International Law*, chaps. 6–7.
143. Nussbaum, *Concise History*, 279; Neff, *Justice among Nations*, 373–78; Koskenniemi, *Gentle Civilizer*, 297–316.
144. Sacriste and Vauchez, "Force of International Law."
145. Shinohara, *US International Lawyers*, 35; Neff, *Justice among Nations*, 371–73.
146. Shinohara, *US International Lawyers*, 31.
147. Hall, *Magic Mirror*, 2nd. ed., 291–94.
148. Shinohara, *US International Lawyers*, 126.
149. Novick, *That Noble Dream*, 149.
150. Shinohara, *US International Lawyers*, 54–55.
151. Shinohara, *US International Lawyers*, 45; Quincy Wright, *A Study of War*, 2nd ed. (1942; repr. Chicago: University of Chicago Press, 1964); Clinton F. Fink and Christopher Wright, "Quincy Wright on War and Peace: A Statistical Overview and Selected Bibliography," *Journal of Conflict Resolution* 14, no. 4 (1970): 543–54.
152. James T. Kenny, "Manley O. Hudson and the Harvard Research in International Law, 1927-1940," *International Lawyer* 11, no. 2 (1977): 319–29.
153. James Brown Scott, *The Spanish Origins of International Law: Francisco de Vitoria and His Law of Nations* (Oxford: Oxford University Press, 1934), 11a.
154. Scott, *Catholic Conception of International Law*.
155. Quoted in Christopher Rossi, *Broken Chain of Being: James Brown Scott and the Origins of Modern International Law* (The Hague: Kluwer Law International, 1998), 86.
156. Nussbaum, *Concise History*, Appendix II. On Scott's appropriation of Vitoria and his attempt to spread his vision to Latin American jurists, see Juan Pablo Scarfi, *El Imperio de la Ley: James Brown Scott y la Construcción de un Orden Jurídico Interamericano* (Buenos Aires: Fondo de Cultura Económica de Argentina, 2014), 181–207.
157. Robert Schulzinger, *The Wise Men of Foreign Affairs: The History of the Council on Foreign Relations* (New York: Columbia University Press, 1984).
158. Alex Goodall, "US Foreign Relations under Harding, Coolidge, and Hoover: Power and Constraint," in *A Companion to Warren G. Harding, Calvin Coolidge, and Herbert Hoover*, ed. Katherine A. S. Sibley (New York: Wiley-Blackwell, 2014), 56–58.
159. Jonathan Zasloff, "Law and the Shaping of American Foreign Policy: The Twenty Years' Crisis," *Southern California Law Review* 77 (2004): 583–682.

160. Department of State, *Register of the Department of State, January 1, 1932* (Washington, DC: Government Printing Office, 1932), 3.
161. Michael Dunne, *The United States and the World Court, 1920-1935* (London: Pinter Publishers, 1988), 29, 47, 57. On the ACJ, see in addition to Dunne: Patterson, "Origins of the World Court," 290, 293–94; James Brown Scott, *The Project of a Permanent Court of International Justice and Resolutions of the Advisory Committee of Jurists* (Washington: CEIP, 1920); Ole Spiermann, "'Who Attempts Too Much Does Nothing Well': The 1920 Advisory Committee of Jurists and the Statute of the Permanent Court of International Justice," *British Year Book of International Law 2002* 73 (2003): 187–260. Root traveled to The Hague for the ACJ's meetings on a $50,000 budget provided by the CEIP. Elihu Root, untitled report on board meeting, 1920, vol. 280, CEIPP.
162. Antoine Vauchez, "The Making of the International Professional: The Drafting of the first World Court and the Genesis of the International Way of Expertise," unpublished manuscript in author's possession, 14.
163. Articles 2, 33–34, 35. A copy of the ACJ draft in French and English is in Scott, *Project of a Permanent Court*, 149–68.
164. Manley O. Hudson, *A Treatise on the Permanent Court of International Justice* (New York: MacMillan, 1934), 235. The League would vote on judges from a list of nominees selected by judges to the PCA.
165. Quoted in Dunne, *United States and the World Court*, 31.
166. Joining the court, explained Manley Hudson, meant successfully jumping a "hurdle" on the way to joining the League. Dunne, *United States and the World Court*, 157.
167. Chandler P. Anderson, "Anderson Replies to Wickersham," *NYT*, May 12, 1924; Warren F. Kuehl and Lynne K. Dunn, *Keeping the Covenant: American Internationalists and the League of Nations, 1920-1939* (Kent, OH: Kent University Press, 1997), 113; Johnson, *Peace Progressives*, 208.
168. James Brown Scott, "The Permanent Court of International Justice," *AJIL* 15, no. 2 (1921): 265; James Brown Scott to Ake Hammarskjöld, December 10, 1920, vol. 280, CEIPP.
169. Charles DeBenedetti, *Origins of the Modern American Peace Movement, 1915-1929* (Millwood, NY: KTO Press, 1978), 54.
170. Dunne, *United States and the World Court*, 89, 94.
171. Christopher Capozzola, *Uncle Sam Wants You: World War I and the Making of the Modern American Citizen* (New York: Oxford University Press, 2008); Knock, *To End All Wars*, chap. 8.
172. Leonard Moore, *Citizen Klansmen: The Ku Klux Klan in Indiana, 1921-1928* (Chapel Hill: University of North Carolina Press, 1991), 184–86; John Higham, *Strangers in the Land: Patterns of American Nativism, 1860-1925* (New Brunswick, NJ: Rutgers University Press, 2002), 234–330; Mae Ngai, *Impossible Subjects: Illegal Aliens and the Making of Modern America* (Princeton, NJ: Princeton University Press, 2004), 21–55.
173. On the political power of the irreconcilables in the 1920s, see Kuehl and Dunn, *Keeping the Covenant*, chaps. 1, 4.
174. Nichols, *Promise and Peril*, 314.
175. Robert James Maddox, *William E. Borah and American Foreign Policy* (Baton Rouge: Louisiana State University Press, 1969), 50–64; Johnson, *Peace Progressives*, 87–99.
176. Duara, "Discourse of Civilization," 102–5; Reynolds, *Long Shadow*, 215.
177. Becker Lorca, *Mestizo International Law*, 239–58.
178. DeBenedetti, *Origins*, 172; McPherson, *Invaded*, 194–95; Renda, *Taking Haiti*, 264–70.
179. Johnson, *Peace Progressives*, 132.
180. Elazar Barkan, *The Retreat of Scientific Racism: Changing Concepts of Race in Britain and the United States Between the World Wars* (Cambridge: Cambridge University Press, 1992), 334.
181. Kuehl and Dunn, *Keeping the Covenant*, 9, 30.
182. DeBenedetti, *Origins*, 148.
183. Dunne, *United States and the World Court*, 86–116. Ironically, the man who brought this issue to the attention of Senate opponents was the United States' sole judge on the PCIJ— none other than John Bassett Moore. On Moore's complex view of the court, see Borchard,

"Moore's Memoirs Chapter 9," box 217, JBM, LC; Moore to Thomas Willing Balch, March 24, 1921, box 295, JBM, LC; Borchard, "Moore's Memoirs Chapter 10," box 217, JBM, LC.

184. Johnson, *Peace Progressives*, 171–72, 307.

185. Johnson, *Peace Progressives*, 259; Dunne, *United States and the World Court*, 129.

186. Kuehl and Dunn, *Keeping the Covenant*, 107–8, 122–23. In 1925 the House voted 301–28, and the Senate 76–17 to join the PCIJ but only with significant reservations, which Europeans balked at ratifying. A subsequent compromise was reached in 1929, but the Senate did not vote on it until 1935, at which time the resolution fell seven votes shy of the necessary two-thirds majority. Dunne, *United States and the World Court*, 146–47, 177–88; Kuehl and Dunn, *Keeping the Covenant*, 118, 122.

187. Dunne, *United States and the World Court*, 261; Maddox, *Borah*, 168–69.

188. Warren I. Cohen, *Empire without Tears: America's Foreign Relations 1921-1933* (New York: Alfred A. Knopf, 1987), 61; "Treaty between the United States and other Powers providing for the renunciation of war as an instrument of national policy," http://avalon.law.yale.edu/20th_century/kbpact.asp (accessed August 25, 2014).

189. Salmon O. Levinson, *Outlawry of War* (Chicago: American Committee for the Outlawry of War, 1921), 11–12, 22–23.

190. DeBenedetti, *Origins*, 62.

191. John Dewey, "What Outlawry of War Is Not," *New Republic*, October 3, 1923, 149–52; Dewey, "War and a Code of Law," *New Republic*, October 24, 1923, 224–26; Charles F. Howlett, "John Dewey and the Crusade to Outlaw War," *World Affairs* 138, no. 4 (1976): 336–55.

192. Harriet Hyman Alonso, *The Women's Peace Union and the Outlawry of War, 1921-1942* (Knoxville: University of Tennessee Press, 1989).

193. Maddox, *Borah*, 136–72.

194. Cohen, *Empire without Tears*, 60–62.

195. DeBenedetti, *Origins*, 75.

196. David C. DeBoe, "Secretary Stimson and the Kellogg-Briand Pact," in *Essays on American Foreign Policy*, ed. Margaret F. Morris and Sandra L. Myres (Austin: University of Texas Press, 1974), 31–53; Harold Josephson, "Outlawing War: Internationalism and the Pact of Paris," *Diplomatic History* 3, no. 4 (1979): 377–90; Nichols, *Promise and Peril*, 308.

197. Lobel, "Rise and Fall of the Neutrality Act," 48.

198. Quincy Wright, "The Meaning of the Pact of Paris," *AJIL* 27, no. 1 (1933): 59–61.

199. DeBoe, "Secretary Stimson and the Kellogg-Briand Pact."

200. Neff, *Justice among Nations*, 393.

201. Blower, "From Isolationism to Neutrality."

202. Shinohara, *US International Lawyers*, 125.

203. Megargee, "Diplomacy of John Bassett Moore," 313; Moore, " New Isolation," *AJIL* 27, no. 4 (1933): 607–29; Justus D. Doenecke, "Edwin M. Borchard, John Bassett Moore, and Opposition to American Intervention in World War II," *Journal of Libertarian Studies* 6, no. 1 (1982): 1–34.

204. Moore, "Why We Have Not Seen the Last of War" (1930), in *Collected Papers*, 6:338.

205. Shinohara, *US International Lawyers*, 138–39.

206. Justus D. Doenecke and John E. Wilz, *From Isolation to War, 1931-1941*, 3rd ed. (Wheeling, IL: Harlan Davidson, 2003), 58–59.

207. On ideological divisions, see Blower, "From Isolationism to Neutrality."

208. David Reynolds, *From Munich to Pearl Harbor: Roosevelt's America and the Origins of the Second World War* (Chicago: Ivan R. Dee, 2001).

Conclusion

1. Richard A. Clarke, *Against All Enemies: Inside America's War on Terror* (New York: Free Press, 2004), 24.

2. Senate Select Committee on Intelligence, *Committee Study of the Central Intelligence Agency's Detention and Interrogation Program*, December 13, 2012, Available at http://www.intelligence.senate.gov/sites/default/files/press/executive-summary_0.pdf (accessed July 8, 2015).

3. Philippe Sands, *Lawless World: America and the Making and Breaking of Global Rules from FDR's Atlantic Charter to George W. Bush's Illegal War* (New York: Viking, 2005), 1–3.

4. Alberto R. Gonzales, Memorandum for the President, 25 January 2002, 2. Available at https://www2.gwu.edu/~nsarchiv/NSAEBB/NSAEBB127/02.01.25.pdf (accessed June 4, 2015).

5. David Cole, *The Torture Memos: Rationalizing the Unthinkable* (New York: New Press, 2009).

6. John R. Bolton, "Is There Really 'Law' in International Affairs?" *Transnational Law and Contemporary Problems* 10, no. 1 (2000): 48.

7. Peter J. Spiro, "The New Sovereigntists: American Exceptionalism and Its False Prophets," *Foreign Affairs* 79, no. 6 (2000): 9–15; Goldsmith and Posner, *Limits of International Law*; Posner, *Perils of Global Legalism*; Ohlin, *Assault on International Law*, chaps. 1–2.

8. Ron Suskind, "Faith, Certainty, and the Presidency of George W. Bush," *New York Times Magazine*, October 17, 2004.

9. Niall Ferguson, *Colossus: The Price of America's Empire* (New York: Penguin Press, 2004).

10. Goldsmith, *Power and Constraint*; Ohlin, *Assault on International Law*, chap. 5; Harold Hongju Koh, "The Obama Administration and International Law" (speech at the Annual Meeting of the American Society of International Law, March 25, 2010).

11. Mary Ellen O'Connell, "Arbitration and Avoidance of War: The Nineteenth-Century American Vision," in *The Sword and the Scales: The United States and International Courts and Tribunals*, ed. Cesare P. R. Romano (Cambridge: Cambridge University Press, 2009), 30–45.

12. Natsu Taylor Saito, *Meeting the Enemy: American Exceptionalism and International Law* (New York: New York University Press, 2010).

13. Michael P. Scharf, "International Law in Crisis: A Qualitative Empirical Contribution to the Compliance Debate," *Cardozo Law Review* 31, no. 1 (2009): 93.

14. Geir Lundestad, "Empire by Invitation? The United States and Western Europe, 1945-1952," *Journal of Peace Research* 23, no. 3 (1986): 264.

15. Mazower, *Governing the World*, 209; Paul Kennedy, *The Parliament of Man: The Past, Present, and Future of the United Nations* (New York: Random House, 2006), 27–30; Robert C. Hilderbrand, *Dumbarton Oaks: The Origins of the United Nations and the Search for Postwar Security* (Chapel Hill: University of North Carolina Press, 1990); Robert Osgood, "Woodrow Wilson, Collective Security, and the Lessons of History," in *The Philosophy and Policies of Woodrow Wilson*, ed. Earl Latham (Chicago: University of Chicago Press, 1958), 187–98. For an argument that American support for multilateralism reflected instead the triumph of an optimistic pragmatism birthed by the New Deal, see Borgwardt, *New Deal for the World*.

16. UN Charter, 2, sec. 6.

17. Nazi crimes were so severe, said chief American prosecutor Robert H. Jackson, that "civilization cannot tolerate their being ignored." Robert H. Jackson, "Opening Address for the United States" (November 21, 1945), in *The Nuremberg War Crimes Trial 1945-46: A Documentary History*, ed. Michael R. Marrus (New York: Bedford/St. Martin's, 1997), 79.

18. Mary Ann Glendon, *A World Made New: Eleanor Roosevelt and the Universal Declaration of Human Rights* (New York: Random House, 2001); Samuel Moyn, *The Last Utopia: Human Rights in History* (Cambridge, MA: Harvard University Press, 2010), chap. 2.

19. Mazower, *Governing the World*, 311–17; Vanessa Ogle, "State Rights against Private Capital: The 'New International Economic Order' and the Struggle over Aid, Trade, and Foreign Investment, 1962-1981," *Humanity* 5, no. 2 (2014): 211–34; Ryan M. Irwin, *Gordian Knot: Apartheid and the Unmaking of the Liberal World Order* (New York: Oxford University Press, 2012).

20. Duane Tananbaum, *The Bricker Amendment Controversy: A Test of Eisenhower's Political Leadership* (Ithaca, NY: Cornell University Press, 1988), 7.

21. Tananbaum, *Bricker Amendment*, 9.

22. Louis Henkin, "U.S. Ratification of Human Rights Conventions: The Ghost of Senator Bricker," *AJIL* 89, no. 2 (1995): 341–50.

23. Hodgson, "Foreign Policy Establishment."

24. See among others, Robert Dean, *Imperial Brotherhood: Gender and the Making of Cold War Foreign Policy* (Amherst: University of Massachusetts Press, 2001).

25. Andreas L. Paulus, "From Neglect to Defiance? The United States and International Adjudication," *European Journal of International Law* 15, no. 4 (2004): 811.
26. Bowden, *Empire of Civilization*, chaps. 7–8.
27. Sands, *Lawless World*, 14.
28. Koskenniemi, *Gentle Civilizer*, 465–85.
29. Michael P. Scharf and Paul R. Williams, *Shaping Foreign Policy in Times of Crisis: The Role of International Law and the State Department Legal Adviser* (Cambridge: Cambridge University Press, 2010), xix; Goldsmith, *Terror Presidency*, 91.
30. Sands, *Lawless World*, 95–142.
31. David Kennedy, "The Mystery of Global Governance," *Ohio Northern University Law Review* 34 (2008): 849.
32. See Goldsmith, *Power and Constraint*.

BIBLIOGRAPHY

Archival Collections

American Society of International Law, Washington, DC
    American Society of International Law Papers
Bancroft Library, University of California, Berkeley
    Jackson H. Ralston Papers
Butler Library, Rare Books and Manuscripts Collection, Columbia University, New York, NY
    Carnegie Endowment for International Peace Papers
Columbia University Law School, New York, NY
    John Bassett Moore Papers
Harvard University Archives, Harvard University, Cambridge, MA
    A. Lawrence Lowell Papers
Harvard University Law School Library, Cambridge, MA
    Eugene Wambaugh, "Official Memoranda filed by me as Special Counsel for the Department of State"
Lauinger Library, Georgetown University, Washington, DC
    James Brown Scott Papers
Library of Congress, Washington, DC
    Chandler P. Anderson Papers
    William Jennings Bryan Papers
    Joseph H. Choate Papers
    John W. Foster Papers
    Philander C. Knox Papers
    Robert Lansing Papers
    William McKinley Papers
    John Bassett Moore Papers [Note: this collection is now housed in the Rare Book & Manuscripts Library, Columbia University]
    Elihu Root Papers
    Ellery C. Stowell Papers
    Oscar S. Straus Papers
    William Howard Taft Papers
    Woodrow Wilson Papers
    Lester H. Woolsey Papers
Mudd Library, Princeton University
    Lecture Notes Collection
    Robert Lansing Papers

National Archives II, College Park, MD
  State Department Records, Record Group 59
  Inquiry Documents, Record Group 256/350
Sterling Memorial Library, Yale University, New Haven, CT
  Woolsey Family Papers
Stanford University Libraries, Special Collections, Stanford, CA
  Francis B. Loomis Papers

International Law Serials

American Journal of International Law (1907–1921)
American Society of International Law *Proceedings* (1907–1921)
American Society for Judicial Settlement of International Disputes *Proceedings* (1910–1916)
Annuaire de l'Institut de droit international (1898–1922)
Carnegie Endowment for International Peace. *Year Book* (1911–1919)
Judicial Settlement of International Disputes. Pamphlet Series (1910–1916)
Reports of the Annual Lake Mohonk Conference on International Arbitration 1–22 (1895–1916)
"Report of the Committee on International Law." In *Annual Report of the American Bar Association*
  (1900–1913)
Revue de Droit International et de Législation Comparée (1898–1919)
Revue Générale de Droit International Public (1898–1922)

Mainstream Periodicals

The Atlantic Monthly
The Nation
The New York Times
The North American Review
The Outlook

Court Records

Dorr v. United States, 195 U.S. 138 (1904).
Downes v. Bidwell, 182 U.S. 244 (1901).
The Paquete Habana, 175 U.S. 677 (1900).
Ker v. Illinois, 119 U.S. 436 (1886).
In re Ross, 140 U.S. 453 (1891).

Government Publications

UNITED KINGDOM

Correspondence Respecting the Affairs of Venezuela. London: Her Majesty's Stationery Office, 1903.

UNITED STATES

Official Register of the United States. Washington, DC: Government Printing Office, 1885.
Department of State. *A Short Account of the Department of State of the United States.* Washington,
  DC: Government Printing Office, 1922.
———. *In the Matter of the Charges of Mr. Herbert W. Bowen.* Washington, DC: Government Printing
  Office, 1905.
———. *Instructions to the American Delegates to the Hague Conference.* Washington, DC: Government
  Printing Office, 1907.
———. *Outline of the Organization and Work of the Department of State.* Washington, DC: Government
  Printing Office, 1911.

——. *Papers Relating to the Foreign Relations of the United States, 1898-1914*. Washington, DC: Government Printing Office, 1901-1922.

——. *Papers Relating to the Foreign Relations of the United States, Supplement: The World War, 1914-1918*. Washington, DC: Government Printing Office, 1928-1933.

——. *Papers Relating to the Foreign Relations of the United States, Supplement: The Lansing Papers*. 2 vols. Washington, DC: Government Printing Office, 1939-1940.

——. *Register of the Department of State*. Washington, DC: Government Printing Office, 1900-1918, 1932.

——. *Speeches Incident to the Visit of Philander Chase Knox, Secretary of State of the United States of America, to the Countries of the Caribbean*. Washington, DC: Government Printing Office, 1913.

——. *Speeches Incident to the Visit of Secretary Root to South America, July 4 to September 30, 1906*. Washington, DC: Government Printing Office, 1906.

U.S. Congress. House. Joint Committee on Printing. *Moore's Digest of International Law*. 64th Cong., 2nd sess., 1917. H. Rep. 1447.

U.S. Congress. Senate. Committee on Interoceanic Canals. *Panama Canal Tolls*. 63rd Cong., 2nd sess., 1914, H Rep. 14385.

U.S. Congress, Senate. *Report from the Secretary of State Relative to Affairs of the Independent State of Congo*, 49th Cong., 1st sess., 1886, Senate Ex. Doc. 196.

——. *A Treaty of Peace between the United States and Spain*. 55th Cong, 3rd sess., 1899. S. Doc. 62.

——. *Correspondence relating to Wrongs Done to American Citizens by the Government of Venezuela*. 60th Cong., 1st sess., 1908. S. Doc. 413.

VENEZUELA

Ministro de Relaciones Exteriores. *Libro Amarillo de la República Venezuela*. Caracas, 1905.

Document Collections

Choate, Joseph Hodges. *Arguments and Addresses of Joseph Hodges Choate*. Edited by Frederick C. Hicks. St. Paul, MN: West Publishing Company, 1926.

House, Edward Mandell. *The Intimate Papers of Colonel House*. Edited by Charles Seymour. 4 vols. Boston: Houghton Mifflin, 1926–28.

Moore, John Bassett. *The Collected Papers of John Bassett Moore*. 7 vols. New Haven, CT: Yale University Press, 1945.

Roosevelt, Theodore. *The Letters of Theodore Roosevelt*. Edited by Elting E. Morison. 8 vols. Cambridge, MA: Harvard University Press, 1951.

Savage, Carlton. *Policy of the United States Toward Maritime Commerce in War*. 2 vols. Washington, DC: Government Printing Office, 1936.

Taft and Roosevelt: The Intimate Letters of Archie Butt, Military Aide. Garden City, NY: Doubleday, Doran, 1930.

Wilson, Woodrow. *The Papers of Woodrow Wilson*. Edited by Arthur S. Link et al. 69 vols. Princeton, NJ: Princeton University Press, 1966–1994.

Printed Primary Sources

Adams, Brooks. *The Law of Civilization and Decay: An Essay on History*. New York: MacMillan, 1895.

"The ABC of the Panama Canal Controversy." *International Conciliation* 2 (1913): 3–14.

Addams, Jane. *Peace and Bread in Time of War*. New York: MacMillan Co., 1922.

Alles, Fred L. "The Sunset Club." *The Land of Sunshine: A Southern California Magazine* 5, no. 3 (1896): 125–28.

American Institute of International Law. *The Recommendations of Habana Concerning International Organization*. New York: Oxford University Press, 1917.

Anderson, Chandler P. *Panama Canal Tolls: An Address on the Issues between the United States and Great Britain in Regard to Panama Canal Tolls, as Raised in the Recent Diplomatic Correspondence.* S. Doc. 32. Washington, DC: GPO, 1913.

"Arbitration of the Panama Canal Dispute," *Green Bag* 25, no. 1 (1913): 91–93.

Austin, John. *Lectures on Jurisprudence.* 4th ed., 2 vols. London: John Murray, 1873.

Balch, Thomas Willing. "La question des pêcheries de l'Atlantique. Un différend entre les États-Unis et l'Empire britannique." *Revue de Droit International et Legislation Comparée* 16, no. 4 (1909): 415–34.

Baldwin, Simeon E. "The Constitutional Questions Incident to the Acquisition and Government by the United States of Island Territory." *Harvard Law Review* 12, no. 6 (1899): 393–416.

Beard, George M. *American Nervousness: Its Causes and Consequences.* New York: G. P. Putnam's Sons, 1881.

Beveridge, Albert J. "The Star of Empire" (September 25, 1900). In *The Meaning of the Times and Other Speeches.* Indianapolis: Bobbs-Merrill Co., 1908, 118–43.

Borchard, Edwin. *The Diplomatic Protection of Citizens Abroad, or The Law of International Claims.* New York: Banks Law Publishing Company, 1915.

——. "The Legal Evolution of Peace." *American Law Review* 45 (1911): 708–17.

Bourne, Randolph. *War and the Intellectuals: Collected Essays, 1915-1919.* Edited by Carl Resek. Indianapolis, IN: Hackett Publishing Co., 1999. Originally published in 1964.

Brewer, David J. "Growth of the Judicial Function." *Report of the Organization and First Annual Meeting of the Colorado Bar Association,* 1898.

Bunau-Varilla, Philippe. *Panama: The Creation, Destruction, and Resurrection.* New York: McBride, Nast & Company, 1914.

Butler, Nicholas Murray. *The International Mind: An Argument for the Judicial Settlement of International Disputes.* New York: Charles Scribner's Sons, 1912.

Bryce, Viscount, and Others. *Proposals for the Prevention of Future Wars.* London: George Allen and Unwin, 1917.

Carnegie, Andrew. "Peace versus War: The President's Solution." *Century Magazine,* June 1910, 307–10.

Carnegie Endowment for International Peace, Division of International Law. *Arbitrations and Diplomatic Settlements of the United States.* Washington, DC: Carnegie Endowment for International Peace, 1914.

——. *Report on the Teaching of International Law in the Educational Institutions of the United States, April 18, 1913.* Washington, DC: Carnegie Endowment for International Peace, 1913.

Chamberlain, Joseph. Review of *The Hague Conferences of 1899 and 1907,* by James Brown Scott. *Columbia Law Review* 10, no. 3 (1910): 276–78.

Choate, Joseph H. *The Two Hague Conferences.* Princeton, NJ: Princeton University Press, 1913.

Clark, J. Reuben. *Right to Protect Citizens in Foreign Countries by Landing Forces.* Washington, DC: Government Printing Office, 1934. Originally published in 1912.

"The Congress of Nations," *Advocate of Peace* 68 (July 1906): 144–45.

Conrad, Joseph. *Heart of Darkness,* 3rd Norton critical ed. New York: W. W. Norton, 1988.

Curtis, William Eleroy. *The Capitals of Spanish America.* New York: Harper & Brothers, 1888.

Dennis, William Cullen. "The Panama Situation in the Light of International Law. The Treaty of 1846 between the United States and New Granada." *American Law Register* 52, no. 5 (1904): 265–306.

Dewey, John. "What Outlawry of War Is Not." *New Republic,* October 3, 1923, 149–52.

——. "War and a Code of Law." *New Republic,* October 24, 1923, 224–26.

Fenwick, Charles G. *The Neutrality Laws of the United States.* Washington, DC: Carnegie Endowment for International Peace, 1913.

Field, David Dudley. *Outlines of an International Code.* 2nd ed. New York: Baker, Voorhis & Company, 1876.

Fiske, John. "Manifest Destiny." *Harper's Monthly Magazine* 70, March 1885, 578–90.

The Foreign Policy of the United States: Political and Commercial. Addresses and Discussion at the Annual Meeting of the American Academy of Political and Social Science, April 7-8, 1899. Philadelphia: American Academy of Political and Social Science, 1899.

Foster, John W. *Diplomatic Memoirs.* 2 vols. Boston: Houghton Mifflin, 1909.

Giddings, Franklin H. "Imperialism?" *Political Science Quarterly* 13, no. 4 (Dec. 1898): 585–605.

"Government of Territories and Colonies." *Harvard Law Review* 12, no. 3 (1898): 205–206.

Gregory, Charles Noble. "The Study of International Law in Law Schools." n.p., 1907.

Hammond, John Hays. *The Autobiography of John Hays Hammond.* 2 vols. New York: Farrar and Rinehart, 1935.

Hershey, Omer. "Covenants without the Sword." *Green Bag* 21, no. 10 (1909): 491–508.

Hill, David Jayne. *Americanism: What It Is.* New York: D. Appleton and Company, 1919. Originally published in 1916.

[Holmes, Oliver Wendell, Jr.] Review of *A Selection of Cases on the Law of Contracts,* by Christopher C. Langdell. *American Law Review* 14, no. 3 (1880): 233–35.

House, Edward M., and Charles Seymour, eds. *What Really Happened at Paris: The Story of the Peace Conference, 1918-1919.* New York: Charles Scribner's Sons, 1921.

Hudson, Manley O. *A Treatise on the Permanent Court of International Justice.* New York: MacMillan, 1934.

Hunt, Gaillard. *The Department of State of the United States: Its History and Functions.* New Haven, CT: Yale University Press, 1914.

Hyde, Charles Cheney. "Intervention in Theory and Practice." *Illinois Law Review* 6, no. 1 (1911): 1–16.

——. "Legal Problems Capable of Settlement by Arbitration." In *Proceedings of the Second National Peace Congress, Chicago, May 2 to 5, 1909,* edited by Charles E. Beals, 221–233. Chicago, 1909.

Institut américain de droit international. *Procés-Verbaux de la Première Session tenue à Washington (29 Décembre 1915 au 8 Janvier 1916).* Washington, DC: Institut américain de droit international, 1916.

Institut de droit international. "Liberté de navigation sur le Congo." 1883. www.idi-iil.org/idiF/resolutionsF/1883_mun_02_fr.pdf.

International American Conference. *Reports of Committees and Discussions Thereon. Rev. under the direction of the Executive Committee by Order of the Conference, Adopted March 7, 1890.* Washington, DC: Government Printing Office, 1890.

International Law Association. *Report of the Eighteenth Conference, Held at Buffalo, U.S.A., August 31-Sept. 2, 1899.* London: West, Newman and Co., 1900.

——. *Report of the Twenty-Fourth Conference, Held at Portland, Maine, U.S.A., August 29-31, 1907.* London: West, Newman & Co., 1908.

Jefferson, Thomas. First Inaugural Address, 4 March 1801. In *The Papers of Thomas Jefferson, Volume 33: 17 February to 30 April 1801,* edited by Barbara B. Oberg, 148–52. Princeton, NJ: Princeton University Press, 2006.

Kent, James. *Commentaries on American Law.* Vol. 1. New York: O. Halstead, 1826.

Knowland, Joseph R. *Panama Canal Tolls: Symposium of Views Protesting against a Surrender of American Rights and Upholding the Side of the United States in the Toll Controversy.* Washington, DC: Government Printing Office, 1913.

Ladd, William. *An Essay on a Congress of Nations, For the Adjustment of International Disputes without Resort to Arms.* Reprinted, with introduction by James Brown Scott. New York: Oxford University Press, 1916. Originally published in 1828.

Langdell, C. C. "The Status of Our New Territories." *Harvard Law Review,* 12:6 (1899): 365–392.

Lansing, Robert. "James Brown Scott." *Green Bag* 24, no. 4 (1912): 169–76.

——. *The Peace Negotiations: A Personal Narrative.* Boston: Houghton Mifflin Co., 1921.

——. *War memoirs of Robert Lansing, Secretary of State.* Indianapolis: Bobbs-Merrill, 1935.

Lapradelle, Albert de, and Ellery C. Stowell. "Latin America at the Hague Conference." *Yale Law Journal* 17 (1907–8), 270–80.

Lawrence, T. J. *Essays on Some Disputed Questions in Modern International Law*. Cambridge: Deighton, Bell and Co., 1885.

League to Enforce Peace. *Enforced Peace: Proceedings of the First Annual National Assemblage of the League to Enforce Peace, Washington, May 26-27, 1916.* New York: League to Enforce Peace, 1916.

——. *Independence Hall Conference held in the City of Philadelphia, Bunker Hill Day (June 17th), 1915, Together with the Speeches Made at a Public Banquet in the Bellvue-Stratford Hotel on the Preceding Evening.* New York: League to Enforce Peace, 1915.

Levinson, Salmon O. *Outlawry of War*. Chicago: American Committee for the Outlawry of War, 1921.

Lieber, Francis A. *Instructions for the Government of Armies of the United States in the Field.* New York: D. Van Nostrand, 1863.

Lorimer, James. *The Institutes of the Law of Nations: A Treatise of the Jural Relations of Separate Political Communities.* Edinburgh: William Blackwood and Sons, 1883.

Lowell, A. Lawrence. "A League to Enforce Peace." *Atlantic Monthly*, September 1915, 392–400.

——. "The Status of Our New Possessions: A Third View." *Harvard Law Review* 13, no. 3 (1899): 155–76.

Lyon-Caen, Charles. "M. Louis Renault." *Journal of Comparative Legislation and International Law* 18, no. 2 (1918): 193–99.

Mahan, Alfred Thayer. *Armaments and Arbitration, or the Place of Force in the International Relations of States.* New York: Harper & Brothers, 1912.

——. *The Interest of America in International Conditions.* London: Sampson, Low, Marston & Company, 1910.

Martí, José. *Inside the Monster: Writings on the United States and American Imperialism.* Edited by Philip S. Foner. New York: Monthly Review Press, 1975.

Members of the Oxford Faculty of Modern History. *Why We Are at War: Great Britain's Case.* Oxford: Oxford at the Clarendon Press, 1914.

Mill, James. *Essays on Government, Jurisprudence, Liberty of the Press, and Law of Nations.* London: J. Innes, [1825?].

Moore, John Bassett. *American Diplomacy: Its Spirit and Achievements.* New York: Harper & Brothers Publishers, 1905.

——. "Contraband of War." *Proceedings of the American Philosophical Society* 51, no. 203 (1912): 18–49.

——. *A Digest of International Law as Embodied in Diplomatic Discussions, Treaties and Other International Agreements, International Awards, the Decisions of Municipal Courts, and the Writings of Jurists, and Especially in Documents, Published and Unpublished, Issued by Presidents and Secretaries of State of the United States, the Opinions of the Attorneys-General, and the Decisions of Courts, Federal and State.* 8 vols. Washington, DC: Government Printing Office, 1906.

——. *Four Phases of American Development: Federalism—Democracy—Imperialism—Expansion.* New York: Da Capo Press, 1970. Originally published in 1912.

——. *History and Digest of the International Arbitrations to Which the United States Has Been a Party.* 6 vols. Washington, DC: Government Printing Office, 1898. Reprint, Buffalo, NY: William S. Hein, 1995.

——. *International Adjudications: Ancient and Modern.* 6 vols. Washington, DC: Carnegie Endowment for International Peace, 1929–1936.

——. *International Law Situations with Solutions and Notes.* Washington, DC: Government Printing Office, 1901.

——. *The Interoceanic Canal and the Hay-Pauncefote Treaty.* Washington, DC: Government Printing Office, 1900.

——. "Law and Organization: Presidential Address the Eleventh Annual Meeting of the American Political Science Association." *American Political Science Review* 9, no. 1 (1915): 1–15.

——. "Maritime Law in the War with Spain." *Political Science Quarterly* 15, no. 3 (1900): 399–425.

——. "The New Isolation," *American Journal of International Law* 27, no. 4 (1933): 607–29.

——. " 'The Peace Problem,' Address on the Peace Problem, delivered at the Twentieth Celebration of Founder's Day, Held at Carnegie Institute, in Pittsburgh, PA, on April 27, 1916." 64th Cong., 2d sess., 1917. S. Doc. 700.

——. *The Principles of American Diplomacy.* 2nd ed. New York: Harper & Brothers, 1918.

——. *Report on Extraterritorial Crime and the Cutting Case.* Washington, DC: Government Printing Office, 1887.

——. Review of *La Diplomatie Francaise et la Ligue des Neutres de 1780*, by Paul Fauchille. *Political Science Quarterly* 10, no. 4 (1895): 701–702.

——. *A Treatise on Extradition and Interstate Rendition.* Boston: Boston Book Company, 1891.

——. *The United States and International Arbitration.* Boston: American Peace Society, 1896.

——. "The Venezuela Decision from the Point of View of Present International Law." *Report of the Annual Meeting of the Lake Mohonk Conference on International Arbitration* 10 (1904), 61–66.

Munro, Henry F., and Ellery C. Stowell. *International Cases: Arbitrations and Incidents Illustrative of International Law as Practised by Independent States.* Boston: Houghton Mifflin Co., 1916.

Nys, Ernest. *The Independent State of the Congo and International Law.* Brussels: J. Lebègue and Co., 1903.

Olney, Richard. "The Canal Tolls Legislation and the Hay-Pauncefote Treaty." *The Lawyer and Banker and Southern Bench and Bar Review* 6 (June 1913): 164–71.

——. "Growth of Our Foreign Policy." *Atlantic Monthly*, March 1900, 289–301

——. "International Isolation of the United States." *Atlantic Monthly,* May 1898, 577–88.

Oppenheim, Lassa. *The Panama Canal Conflict between Great Britain and the United States of America.* New York: Cambridge University Press, 1913.

Payn, F.W. "Intervention among States." *Law Magazine and Review: A Quarterly Review of Jurisprudence* 26 (1900–1901): 106–16.

Politis, Nicolas. *The New Aspects of International Law.* Washington, DC: Carnegie Endowment for International Peace, 1928.

Pollock, Frederick. "The Sources of International Law." *Law Quarterly Review* 18 (1902): 418–29.

Pound, Roscoe. "The Need of a Sociological Jurisprudence." *Green Bag* 19 (1907): 607–15.

Proceedings of the American Political Science Association. Lancaster, PA: Wickersham Press, 1905.

Proceedings of the Conference of American Teachers of International Law held at Washington, DC, April 23-25, 1914. Washington, DC: Byron S. Adams, 1914.

Proceedings at the Laying of a Wreath on the Tomb of Hugo Grotius in the Nieuwe Kerk, in the City of Delft, July 4th 1899 by the Commission of the United States of America to the International Peace Conference of The Hague. The Hague: Martinus Nijhoff, 1899.

Ralston, Jackson H. *International Arbitration from Athens to Locarno.* Stanford, CA: Stanford University Press, 1929.

——. *International Arbitral Law and Procedure.* Boston: Ginn and Company, 1910.

——. "Should Any National Dispute Be Reserved from Arbitration?" *Advocate of Peace* 70, no. 7 (1908): 159–61.

——. *Study and Report for American Federation of Labor upon Judicial Control over Legislatures as to Constitutional Questions.* Washington, DC: Law Reporter Printing Company, 1919.

Ralston Jackson H., and W. T. Sherman Doyle. *Venezuelan Arbitrations of 1903.* Washington: Government Printing Office, 1904.

Randolph, Carman F. "Constitutional Aspects of Annexation." *Harvard Law Review* 12, no. 5 (1898): 291–315.

Reinsch, Paul S. *Colonial Administration.* New York: Macmillan, 1905.

——. *Colonial Government.* New York: Macmillan, 1902.

——. *Public International Unions: Their Work and Organization.* Boston: Ginn and Company, 1911.

Reeves, Jesse Siddall. "The International Beginnings of the Congo Free State." In *John Hopkins University Studies in Historical and Political Science*, 12th series, vol. 11–12. Baltimore: Johns Hopkins Press, 1894.

Rolin, Albéric. *Les Origines de L'Institut de Droit International, 1873-1923: Souvenirs d'un Témoin.* Belgium, 1923.

Roosevelt, Theodore. *The Winning of the West, Vol. 1.* New York: G. P. Putnam's Sons, 1896.

Root, Elihu. *Addresses on Government and Citizenship.* Edited by Robert Bacon and James Brown Scott. Cambridge, MA: Harvard University Press, 1916.

——. *Addresses on International Subjects.* Edited by Robert Bacon and James Brown Scott. Cambridge, MA: Harvard University Press, 1916.

——. *Instructions to the American Delegates to The Hague Conference.* Washington, 1907.

——. *Miscellaneous Addresses.* Edited by Robert Bacon and James Brown Scott. Cambridge, MA: Harvard University Press, 1917.

——. *The Military and Colonial Policy of the United States: Addresses and Reports.* Edited by Robert Bacon and James Brown Scott . Cambridge, MA: Harvard University Press, 1916.

——. "The Panama Canal a Sacred Trust." *The Independent,* February 6, 1913, 285–89.

Schücking, Walther. *The International Union of The Hague Conferences.* Translated by Charles G. Fenwick. New York: Oxford University Press, 1918. German edition published in 1912.

Scott, James Brown, ed. *The American Institute of International Law: Its Declaration of the Rights and Duties of Nations.* Washington, DC: American Institute of International Law, 1916.

——. ed. *Argument of the Honorable Elihu Root on behalf of the United States before the North Atlantic Fisheries Arbitration Tribunal, at The Hague, 1910.* Washington, DC: World Peace Foundation, 1912.

——. ed. *Cases on International Law: Selected from Decisions of English and American Courts.* Boston: Boston Book Company, 1902.

——. ed. *Cases on International Law: Principally Selected from Decisions of English and American Courts.* 2nd ed. American Casebook Series. St. Paul, MN: West Publishing, 1922.

——. *The Catholic Conception of International Law: Francisco de Vitoria, Founder of the Modern Law of Nations, Francisco Suárez, Founder of the Modern Philosophy of Law in General and in Particular of the Law of Nations: A Critical Examination and a Justified Appreciation.* Washington, DC: Georgetown University Press, 1934.

——. "The Duty of Neutrals to Protest." *Advocate of Peace* 79 (March 1917): 82–84.

——. "Elihu Root (February 15, 1845–Feburary 7, 1937), an Appreciation." American Society of International Law *Proceedings* 31 (1937): 1–32.

——. ed. *The Hague Conventions and Declarations of 1899 and 1907.* New York: Oxford University Press, 1918.

——. ed. *The Hague Court Reports.* New York: Oxford University Press, 1916.

——. ed. *The Hague Peace Conferences of 1899 and 1907.* 2 vols. Baltimore: Johns Hopkins Press, 1909.

——. ed. *Instructions to the American Delegates to The Hague Peace Conferences and Their Official Reports.* New York: Oxford University Press, 1916.

——. "International Arbitration: Address of Mr. James Brown Scott before the Sunset Club, Los Angeles, California, 1897." MS 1207, Special Collections, Harvard University Law Library.

——. "International Law in Legal Education." *Columbia Law Review* 4 (June 1904): 409–22.

——. "The Law of Nations and the American Society of International Law." *Report of the Annual Lake Mohonk Conference on International Arbitration* 12 (1906): 145–51.

——. *Law, the State, and the International Community.* 2 vols. New York: Columbia University Press, 1939.

——. "The Legal Nature of International Law." *Columbia Law Review* 5 (1905): 124–52.

——. "The Organization of International Justice." *Advocate of Peace* 79, no. 1 (1917): 10–22.

——. "The Place of International Law in American Jurisprudence." *Green Bag* 15 (1903): 164–73.

——. The Place of International Law in Legal Education." *Annual Report of the American Bar Association* 26 (1903): 583–94.

——. ed. *The Proceedings of The Hague Peace Conferences.* 5 vols. New York: Oxford University Press, 1920-21.

——. *The Project of a Permanent Court of International Justice and Resolutions of the Advisory Committee of Jurists.* Washington, DC: Carnegie Endowment for International Peace, 1920.

——. ed. *Resolutions of the Institute of International Law.* New York: Oxford University Press, 1916.

——. "Review of President Roosevelt's Administration." *The Outlook* 91 (February 13, 1909), 350–57.

——. "Robert Lansing: Counselor for the Department of State." *American Review of Reviews* 51 (April 1915): 426.

——. *The Spanish Origins of International Law: Francisco de Vitoria and His Law of Nations.* Oxford: At the Clarendon Press, 1934.

——. *The Status of the International Court of Justice, with an Appendix of Addresses and Official Documents.* New York: Oxford University Press, 1916.

——. "The Study of the Law." *American Law School Review* 2, no. 1 (1906): 1–10.

——. ed. *Treaties for the Advancement of Peace between the United States and Other Powers Negotiated by the Honourable William Jennings Bryan.* New York: Oxford University Press, 1920.

——. "The Two Institutes of International Law." *American Journal of International Law* 26 (January 1932): 87–102.

——. *The United States of America: A Study in International Organization.* Washington, DC: Carnegie Endowment for International Peace, 1920.

Short, William H. *Program and Policies of the League to Enforce Peace: A Handbook for Officers, Speakers, and Editors.* New York: League to Enforce Peace, 1916.

Snow, Alpheus Henry. *The Administration of Dependencies: A Study of the Evolution of the Federal Empire, with Special Reference to American Colonial Problems.* New York: G. P. Putnam's Sons, 1902.

Snow, Freeman. *Cases and Opinions on International Law with Notes and a Syllabus.* Boston: Boston Book Company, 1893.

Stead, W.T. *The Americanization of the World.* New York: Horace Markley, 1902.

Stimson, Henry. "The Pact of Paris: Three Years of Development." *Foreign Affairs* 11, no. 1 (1933): i–ix.

Storey, Moorfield. *The Recognition of Panama. Address Delivered at Massachusetts Reform Club, December 5, 1903.* Boston: Geo. H. Ellis Co., 1904.

Stowell, Ellery C. *The Diplomacy of the War of 1914: The Beginnings of the War.* Boston: Houghton Mifflin Co., 1915.

Strong, Josiah. *Expansion under New World-Conditions.* New York: Baker and Taylor Company, 1900.

——. *Our Country: Its Possible Future and Its Present Crisis.* Rev. ed. Cambridge, MA: Harvard University Press, 1963. Originally published in 1891.

Sumner, William Graham. "The Predominant Issue" (1900). In *War and Other Essays.* New Haven, CT: Yale University Press, 1911, 337–52.

"Symposium on International Law: Its Origin, Obligation, and Future." *Proceedings of the American Philosophical Society* 60, no. 4 (1912): 291–329.

Taft, William Howard. *The United States and Peace.* New York: Charles Scribner's Sons, 1914.

Thayer, James Bradley. "Our New Possessions." *Harvard Law Review* 12, no. 7 (1899): 464–85.

"Theodore Dwight Woolsey." *Proceedings of the American Academy of Arts and Sciences* 25 (1889–90): 343–46.

Thurber, Orray E. *Castro and the Asphalt Trust.* New York, 1907.

Tillman, Benjamin R. Address to Senate. 32 *Cong. Rec.* Part 2. 7 February 1899, 1531–2.

Trevelyan, Janet Penrose. *The Life of Mrs. Humphry Ward.* New York: Dodd, Mead, and Company, 1923.

Twain, Mark. "To the Person Sitting in Darkness" (1901). In *Mark Twain's Weapons of Satire: Anti-Imperialist Writings on the Philippine-American War*, edited by Jim Zwick, 22–39. Syracuse, NY: Syracuse University Press, 1992.

Van Dyne, Frederick. *Our Foreign Service: The "A B C" of American Diplomacy.* Rochester, NY: Lawyers Co-Operative Publishing Company, 1909.

Venezuelan Claims: Letter of Messrs. Ralston and Siddons and George N. Baxter to Hon. S.M. Cullom, Chairman of the Committee on Foreign Relations of the Senate of the United States. Washington, 1908.

Vickery, James Harris. "The Problem of the 'German Professor.'" *International Law Notes* 1, no. 7 (1916): 103–105.

Washington, George. "Farewell Address" (1796). The Avalon Project. Lillian Goldman Law Library. Yale Law School. http://www.avalon.law.yale.edu/18th_century/washing.asp.

Westlake, John. "The Hague Conferences." In *The Collected Papers of John Westlake on Public International Law*, edited by Lassa Oppenheim, 244–51. Cambridge: Cambridge University Press, 1914.

——. *International Law*. Cambridge: J. and C. F. Clay, 1904.

Wharton, Francis M. *A Digest of the International Law of the United States, Taken from Documents Issued by Presidents and Secretaries of State, and from Decisions of Federal Courts and Opinions of Attorneys-General*. Washington, DC: Government Printing Office, 1886.

Wheaton, Henry. *Elements of International Law*. Edited by George Grafton Wilson. Oxford: Oxford at the Clarendon Press, 1936. Originally published in 1836.

White, Harold F. "Legal Aspects of the Panama Canal." *Illinois Law Review* 8 (1913): 442–61.

Wilson, Francis M. Huntington. *Memoirs of an Ex-Diplomat*. Boston: Bruce Humphries, Inc., 1945.

Wilson, George Grafton. *Class Cases on International Law*. Cambridge, MA: Harvard University Press, n.d.

——. *Handbook of International Law*. St. Paul, MN: West Publishing Co., 1910.

Wilson, Woodrow. "The Ideals of America." *Atlantic Monthly*, December 1902, 721–34.

——. "The Interpreter of English Liberty." In *Mere Literature and Other Essays*. Boston: Houghton Mifflin Co., 1900, 104–60.

——. "'The Law and the Facts,' Presidential Address, Seventh Annual Meeting of the American Political Science Association." *American Political Science Review* 5, no. 1 (1911): 1–11.

——. *The State: Elements of Historical and Practical Politics*. Boston: D. C. Heath, 1898. Originally published in 1889.

Woolsey, Lester H. "The Fallacies of Neutrality." *American Journal of International Law* 30, no. 2 (1936): 256–62.

Woolsey, Theodore Dwight. *Introduction to the Study of International Law*. New York: Charles Scribner & Son, 1871.

Woolsey, Theodore Salisbury. *America's Foreign Policy: Essays and Addresses*. New York: The Century Co., 1898.

——. "International Law, 1701-1901." In *Two Centuries' Growth of American Law, 1701-1901*, 491–520. Buffalo, NY: William S. Hein, 1980. Originally published in 1901.

——. "The Recognition of Panama and Its Results." *Green Bag* 16 (1904): 6–12.

Wright, Quincy. "The Meaning of the Pact of Paris." *American Journal of International Law* 27, no. 1 (1933): 59–61.

——. *A Study of War*. 2nd ed. Chicago: University of Chicago Press, 1964. Originally published in 1942.

Secondary Sources

Abebe, Daniel, and Eric A. Posner, "The Flaws of Foreign Affairs Legalism." *Virginia Journal of International Law* 51, no. 3 (2011): 507–48.

Abrams, Irwin. "The Emergence of the International Law Societies." *Review of Politics* 19, no. 3 (1957): 361–80.

Adas, Michael. *Dominance by Design: Technological Imperatives and America's Civilizing Mission*. Cambridge, MA: Harvard University Press, 2006.

Alford, Roger P. "International Law as an Interpretive Tool in the Supreme Court, 1901-1945." In *International Law in the U.S. Supreme Court: Continuity and Change*, edited by David Sloss, Michael D. Ramsay, and William S. Dodge, 257–84. Cambridge: Cambridge University Press, 2011.

Alonso, Harriet Hyman. *The Women's Peace Union and the Outlawry of War, 1921-1942*. Knoxville: University of Tennessee Press, 1989.

Altman, Clara. "The International Context: An Imperial Perspective on American Legal History." In *A Companion to American Legal History*, edited by Salley E. Hadden and Alfred L. Brophy, 543–61. New York: Wiley, 2013.

American Bar Association, Section of International Law. *The ABA Section of International Law: Leading the World's International Lawyers since 1878*. Chicago, IL: American Bar Association Section of International Law, 2008.

Ambrosius, Lloyd. *Wilsonian Statecraft: Theory and Practice of Liberal Internationalism during World War I*. Wilmington, DE: SR Books, 1991.

Anderson, Donald F. *William Howard Taft: A Conservative's Conception of the Presidency*. Ithaca, NY: Cornell University Press, 1968.

Anderson, Kevin. "The Venezuelan Claims Controversy at The Hague, 1903." *Historian* 57, no. 3 (1995): 525–36.

Anderson, Stuart. *Race and Rapprochement: Anglo-Saxonism and Anglo-American Relations, 1895-1904*. Rutherford, NJ: Fairleigh Dickinson University Press, 1981.

Anghie, Antony. *Imperialism, Sovereignty and the Making of International Law*. Cambridge: Cambridge University Press, 2004.

Ardao, Arturo. *Génesis de la Idea y el Nombre de América Latina*. Caracas, Venezuela: Centro de Estudios Latinoamericanos Rómulo Gallegos, 1980.

Armitage, David. *The Declaration of Independence: A Global History*. Cambridge, MA: Harvard University Press, 2007.

———. "The Declaration of Independence and International Law. *William and Mary Quarterly* 59, no. 1 (2002): 39–64.

Auerbach, Jerold S. *Unequal Justice: Lawyers and Social Change in Modern America*. New York: Oxford University Press, 1976.

Axeen, David. "'Heroes of the Engine Room': American 'Civilization' and the War with Spain." *American Quarterly* 36, no. 4 (1984): 481–502.

Bailey, Thomas A. "Was the Presidential Election of 1900 A Mandate on Imperialism?" *Mississippi Valley Historical Review* 24, no. 1 (1937): 43–52.

Barkan, Elazar. *The Retreat of Scientific Racism: Changing Concepts of Race in Britain and the United States Between the World Wars*. Cambridge: Cambridge University Press, 1992.

Bartlett, Ruhl J. *The League to Enforce Peace*. Chapel Hill: University of North Carolina Press, 1944.

Bass, Gary J. *Stay the Hand of Vengeance: The Politics of War Crimes Tribunals*. Princeton, NJ: Princeton University Press, 2000.

Bayly, C. A. *The Birth of the Modern World, 1780-1914: Global Connections and Comparisons*. Malden, MA: Blackwell, 2004.

Beale, Howard K. *Theodore Roosevelt and the Rise of America to World Power*. Baltimore: Johns Hopkins University Press, 1956.

Becker Lorca, Arnulf. *Mestizo International Law: A Global Intellectual History, 1850-1950*. Cambridge: Cambridge University Press, 2014.

———. "Sovereignty beyond the West: The End of Classical International Law." *Journal of the History of International Law* 13 (2011): 7–73.

———. "Universal International Law: Nineteenth-Century Histories of Imposition and Appropriation." *Harvard International Law Journal* 51, no. 2 (2010): 475–552.

Bederman, David J. "Appraising a Century of Scholarship in the *American Journal of International Law*." *American Journal of International Law* 100, no. 1 (2006): 20–63.

———. "The Glorious Past and Uncertain Future of International Claims Tribunals." In *International Courts for the Twenty-First Century*, edited by Mark Weston Janis, 161–82. Boston: Martinus Nijhoff, 1992.

Bederman, Gail. *Manliness and Civilization: A Cultural History of Gender and Race in the United States, 1880-1917*. Chicago: University of Chicago Press, 1995.

Beisner, Robert. *From the Old Diplomacy to the New, 1865-1900*. 2nd ed. Arlington Heights, IL: Harlan Davidson, 1986. Originally published in 1975.

———. *Twelve against Empire: The Anti-Imperialists, 1898-1900*. New York: McGraw-Hill, 1968.

Bell, A. C. *A History of the Blockade of Germany*. Reprint, London: Her Majesty's Stationery Office, 1961. Originally published in 1937.

Bell, Duncan. "Empire and International Relations in Victorian Political Thought." *Historical Journal* 49, no. 1 (2006): 281–98.

Benbow, Mark. *Leading Them to the Promised Land: Woodrow Wilson, Covenant Theology, and the Mexican Revolution, 1913-1915*. Kent, OH: Kent State University Press, 2010.

Bender, Daniel E. *American Abyss: Savagery and Civilization in the Age of Industry*. Ithaca, NY: Cornell University Press, 2009.

Bender, Thomas. *A Nation among Nations: America's Place in World History*. New York: Hill and Wang, 2006.

Benton, Lauren. "Legal Spaces of Empire: Piracy and the Origins of Ocean Regionalism." *Comparative Studies in Society and History* 47, no. 4 (2005): 700–724.

———. *A Search for Sovereignty: Law and Geography in European Empires, 1400-1900*. New York: Cambridge University Press, 2010.

Berger, Mark T. *Under Northern Eyes: Latin American Studies and US Hegemony in the Americas 1898-1990*. Bloomington: Indiana University Press, 1995.

Berman, Nathanial. "'But the Alternative Is Despair': European Nationalism and the Modernist Renewal of International Law." *Harvard Law Review* 106, no. 8 (1993): 1792–903.

———. *Passion and Ambivalence: Colonialism, Nationalism, and International Law*. Boston: Martinus Nijhoff, 2012.

Bernstein, David E. *Rehabilitating Lochner: Defending Individual Rights Against Progressive Reform*. Chicago: University of Chicago Press, 2011.

Bilder, Richard B. "The Office of the Legal Adviser: The State Department Lawyer and Foreign Affairs." *American Journal of International Law* 56, no. 3 (1962): 633–84.

Bledstein, Burton J. *The Culture of Professionalism: The Middle Class and the Development of Higher Education in America*. New York: W. W. Norton, 1976.

Blower, Brooke L. "From Isolationism to Neutrality: A New Framework for Understanding American Political Culture, 1919-1941." *Diplomatic History* 38, no. 2 (2014): 345–76.

Bolton, John R. "Is There Really 'Law' in International Affairs?" *Transnational Law and Contemporary Problems* 10, no. 1 (2000): 1–48.

Bönker, Dirk. *Militarism in a Global Age: Naval Ambitions in Germany and the United States before World War I*. Ithaca, NY: Cornell University Press, 2012.

Boot, Max. *The Savage Wars of Peace: Small Wars and the Rise of American Power*. New York: Basic Books, 2002.

Borchard, Edwin Montefiore, and William Potter Lage. *Neutrality for the United States*. New Haven, CT: Yale University Press, 1937.

Borgwardt, Elizabeth. *A New Deal for the World: America's Vision for Human Rights*. Cambridge, MA: Harvard University Press, 2005.

Bosco, David L. *Five to Rule Them All: The UN Security Council and the Making of the Modern World*. Oxford: Oxford University Press, 2009.

Bowden, Brett. *The Empire of Civilization: The Evolution of an Imperial Idea*. Chicago: University of Chicago Press, 2009.

Boyle, Francis Anthony. *Foundations of World Order: The Legalist Approach to International Relations, 1898-1922*. Durham, NC: Duke University Press, 1999.

Brophy, Alfred L. "Did Formalism Never Exist?" *Texas Law Review* 92 (2013): 383–411.

Bull, Hedley. *The Anarchical Society: A Study of Order in World Politics*. 3rd ed. London: Palgrave MacMillan, 2002. Originally published in 1977.

Burnett [Ponsa], Christina Duffy. "Contingent Constitutions: Empire and Law in the Americas." PhD diss., Princeton University, 2010.

Burton, David H. *Taft, Wilson, and World Order*. Madison, NJ: Fairleigh Dickenson University Press, 2003.

———. *William Howard Taft: Confident Peacemaker*. New York: Fordham University Press, 2004.

Campbell, John P. "Taft, Roosevelt and the Arbitration Treaties of 1911." *Journal of American History* 53, no. 2 (1966): 279–98.

Capozzola, Christopher. "Constabulary Duty: Policing the Philippines, 1901-1904." Unpublished manuscript.

——. *Uncle Sam Wants You: World War I and the Making of the Modern American Citizen.* New York: Oxford University Press, 2008.

Carlisle, Rodney. *Sovereignty at Sea: U.S. Merchant Ships and American Entry into World War I.* Gainesville: University Press of Florida, 2009.

Caron, David. "War and International Adjudication: Reflections on the 1899 Peace Conference." *American Journal of International Law* 94, no. 1 (2000): 4–30.

Carr, Edward Hallett. *The Twenty Years' Crisis, 1919-1939.* 2nd ed. New York: Harper Collins, 1946. Originally published in 1939.

Carter, Barry E., Phillip R. Trimble, and Allen S. Weiner. *International Law.* 5th ed. Austin: Wolters Kluwer, 2007.

Carter, Susan B., Scott Sigmund Gartner, Michael R. Haines, Alan L. Olmstead, Richard Sutch, Gavin Wright, eds. *Historical Statistics of the United States.* Millennial ed., 5 vols. New York: Cambridge University Press, 2006.

Caruthers, Sandra Taylor. "The Work of the Joint State-Navy Neutrality Board, 1914-1917." MA thesis, University of Colorado, 1963.

Cassel, Pär Kristoffer. *Grounds of Judgment: Extraterritoriality and Imperial Power in Nineteenth-Century China and Japan.* New York: Oxford University Press, 2012.

Ceadel, Martin. *Semi-Detached Idealists: The British Peace Movement and International Relations, 1854-1945.* New York: Oxford University Press, 2001.

Challener, Richard D. *Admirals, Generals, and American Foreign Policy, 1898-1914.* Princeton, NJ: Princeton University Press, 1973.

Charles, Robert B. "Legal Education in the Late Nineteenth Century, through the Eyes of Theodore Roosevelt." *American Journal of Legal History* 37, no. 3 (1993): 233–72.

Chickering, Roger. *Imperial Germany and a World Without War: The Peace Movement and German Society.* Princeton, NJ: Princeton University Press, 1975.

Chickering, Roger, and Stig Förster. *Great War, Total War: Combat and Mobilization on the Western Front, 1914-1918.* Cambridge: Cambridge University Press, 2000.

Church, Robert L. "Economists as Experts: The Rise of an Academic Profession in the United States, 1870-1920." In *The University in Society,* edited by Lawrence Stone, 571–609. Princeton, NJ: Princeton University Press, 1974.

Clarke, Richard A. *Against All Enemies: Inside America's War on Terror.* New York: Free Press, 2004.

Clements, Kendrick A. "Woodrow Wilson's Mexican Policy, 1913-15." *Diplomatic History* 4, no. 2 (1980): 113–36.

Cleveland, Sarah H. "Powers Inherent in Sovereignty: Indians, Aliens, Territories, and the Nineteenth Century Origins of Plenary Power in Foreign Affairs." *Texas Law Review* 81, no. 1 (2002): 1–284.

Clinton, David. "Francis Lieber, Imperialism, and Internationalism." In *Imperialism and Internationalism in the Discipline of International Relations,* edited by David Long and Brian C. Schmidt, 23–42. Albany: State University of New York Press, 2005.

Coates, Benjamin A. "Securing Hegemony through Law: Venezuela, the U.S. Asphalt Trust, and the Uses of International Law, 1904-1909." *Journal of American History* 102, no. 2 (2015): 380–405.

——. "Transatlantic Advocates: American International Law and U.S. Foreign Relations, 1898–1919." PhD diss., Columbia University, 2010.

Cohen, Warren I. *Empire without Tears: America's Foreign Relations 1921-1933.* New York: Alfred A. Knopf, 1987.

Coker, William S. "The Panama Canal Tolls Controversy: A Different Perspective." *Journal of American History* 55, no. 3 (1968): 555–64.

Cole, David. *The Torture Memos: Rationalizing the Unthinkable.* New York: New Press, 2009.

Coletta, Paolo. *William Jennings Bryan.* Vol. 2: *Progressive Politician and Moral Statesman, 1909-1915.* Lincoln: University of Nebraska Press, 1969.

Collin, Richard H. *Theodore Roosevelt's Caribbean: The Panama Canal, the Monroe Doctrine, and the Latin American Context*. Baton Rouge: Louisiana State University Press, 1990.

Conklin, Alice. *A Mission to Civilize: The Republican Idea of Empire in France and West Africa, 1895-1930*. Stanford, CA: Stanford University Press, 1997.

Coogan, John W. *The End of Neutrality: The United States, Britain, and Maritime Rights, 1899-1915*. Ithaca, NY: Cornell University Press, 1981.

Cooper, John Milton, Jr. *Breaking the Heart of the World: Woodrow Wilson and the Fight for the League of Nations*. Madison: University of Wisconsin Press, 2001.

——. "'An Irony of Fate': Woodrow Wilson's Pre-World War I Diplomacy." *Diplomatic History* 3, no. 4 (1979): 425–37.

——. *The Warrior and the Priest: Woodrow Wilson and Theodore Roosevelt*. Cambridge, MA: Harvard University Press, 1983.

——. *Woodrow Wilson: A Biography*. New York: Alfred A. Knopf, 2009.

Cooper, Sandi E. *Patriotic Pacifism: Waging War against War in Europe, 1814-1914*. New York: Oxford University Press, 1991.

Cosgrove, Richard A. *Our Lady the Common Law: An Anglo-American Legal Community, 1870-1930*. New York: New York University Press, 1987.

Craft, Stephen G. "John Bassett Moore, Robert Lansing, and the Shandong Question." *Pacific Historical Review* 60, no. 2 (1997): 231–49.

Crapol, Edward P. "Coming to Terms with Empire: The Historiography of Late-Nineteenth-Century American Foreign Relations." *Diplomatic History* 16, no. 4 (1992): 573–97.

Craven, Matthew. "Introduction: International Law and its Histories." In *Time, History and International Law*, edited by Matthew Craven, Malgosia Fitzmaurice, and Maria Vogiatzi, 1–25. Leiden: Martinus Nijhoff, 2007.

Crowe, S. E. *The Berlin West African Conference, 1884-1885*. London: Longmans, Green, 1942.

Curti, Merle. *The American Peace Crusade, 1815-1860*. Durham, NC: Duke University Press, 1929.

——. *American Philanthropy Abroad: A History*. New Brunswick, NJ: Rutgers University Press, 1963.

Damrosch, Leo. *Tocqueville's Discovery of America*. New York: Farrar, Straus and Giroux, 2010.

Damrosch, Lori F. "The 'American' and the 'International' in the *American Journal of International Law*." *American Journal of International Law* 100, no. 1 (2006): 2–19.

Davis, Calvin DeArmond. *The United States and the First Hague Peace Conference*. Ithaca, NY: Cornell University Press, 1962.

——. *The United States and the Second Hague Peace Conference: American Diplomacy and International Organization 1899-1914*. Durham, NC: Duke University Press, 1975.

Davis, Robert R., Jr. "Diplomatic Plumage: American Court Dress in the Early National Period." *American Quarterly* 20, no. 2 (1968): 164–79.

Dawley, Alan. *Changing the World: American Progressives in War and Revolution*. Princeton, NJ: Princeton University Press, 2003.

Dean, Robert D. *Imperial Brotherhood: Gender and the Making of Cold War Foreign Policy*. Amherst: University of Massachusetts Press, 2001.

DeBenedetti, Charles. *Origins of the Modern American Peace Movement, 1915-1929*. Millwood, NY: KTO Press, 1978.

——. *The Peace Reform in American History*. Bloomington: Indiana University Press, 1980.

DeBoe, David C. "Secretary Stimson and the Kellogg-Briand Pact." In *Essays on American Foreign Policy*, edited by Margaret F. Morris and Sandra L. Myres, 31–53. Austin: University of Texas Press, 1974.

den Hertog, Johan, and Samuël Kruizinga, eds. *Caught in the Middle: Neutrals, Neutrality and the First World War*. Amsterdam: Aksant Academic, 2010.

Deudney, Daniel. "The Philadelphia System: Sovereignty, Arms Control, and Balance of Power in the American States-Union, Circa 1787-1861." *International Organization* 49, no. 2 (1995): 191–228.

Devlin, Patrick. *Too Proud to Fight: Woodrow Wilson's Neutrality*. New York: Oxford University Press, 1975.

Dezalay, Yves, and Bryant G. Garth. "Law, Lawyers, and Empire." In *The Cambridge History of Law in America*. Vol. 3, *The Twentieth Century and After (1920–)*, edited by Michael Grossberg and Christopher Tomlins, 718–58. New York: Cambridge University Press, 2008.

Divine Robert A., T. H. Breen, R. Hal Williams, Ariela J. Gross, and H. W. Brands. *The American Story*. New York: Penguin, 2013.

Dobson, John M. *America's Ascent: The United States Becomes a Great Power, 1880-1914*. DeKalb: Northern Illinois University Press, 1978.

Doenecke, Justus D. "Edwin M. Borchard, John Bassett Moore, and Opposition to American Intervention in World War II." *Journal of Libertarian Studies* 6, no.1 (1982): 1–34.

——. *Nothing Less Than War: A New History of America's Entry into World War I*. Lexington: University Press of Kentucky, 2011.

Doenecke, Justus D., and John E. Wilz. *From Isolation to War, 1931-1941*, 3rd ed. Wheeling, IL: Harlan Davidson, 2003.

Doyle, Michael W. *Empires*. Ithaca, NY: Cornell University Press, 1986.

Drachman, Virginia G. *Sisters in Law: Women Lawyers in Modern American History*. Cambridge, MA: Harvard University Press, 1998.

Duara, Prasenjit. "The Discourse of Civilization and Pan-Asianism." *Journal of World History* 12, no. 1 (2001): 99–130.

Dubin, Martin David. "The Carnegie Endowment for International Peace and the Advocacy of a League of Nations, 1914-1918." *Proceedings of the American Philosophical Society* 123, no. 6 (1979): 344–68.

——. "Elihu Root and the Advocacy of a League of Nations, 1914-1917." *The Western Political Quarterly* 19, no. 3 (1966): 439–55.

——. "Toward the Concept of Collective Security: The Bryce Group's 'Proposals for the Avoidance of War,' 1914-1917." *International Organization* 24, no. 2 (1970): 288–316.

Dubois, Laurent. *Haiti: The Aftershocks of History*. New York: Picador, 2012.

Dudziak, Mary L. *Cold War Civil Rights: Race and the Image of American Democracy*. Princeton, NJ: Princeton University Press, 2000.

——. *War Time: An Idea, Its History, Its Consequences*. New York: Oxford University Press, 2012.

Duke, Nancy Jean. "Theodore Marburg: An Internationalist's Place in History." PhD diss., Florida State University, 1995.

Dunlap, Charles J., Jr. "Lawfare: A Decisive Element of 21st-Century Conflicts?" *Joint Force Quarterly* 54, no. 3 (2009): 34–39.

Dunne, Michael. *The United States and the World Court, 1920-1935*. London: Pinter, 1988.

Dunoff, Jeffrey L., and Mark A. Pollack. "International Law and International Relations: Introducing an Interdisciplinary Dialogue." In *Interdisciplinary Perspectives on International Law and International Relations: The State of the Art*, edited by Jeffrey L. Dunoff and Mark A. Pollack, 3–32. Cambridge: Cambridge University Press, 2013.

Duxbury, Neil. *Patterns of American Jurisprudence*. Oxford: Oxford University Press, 1995.

Echols, James. "Jackson Ralston and the Last Single Tax Campaign." *California History* 58, no. 3 (1979): 256–63.

Eggert, Gerald G. *Richard Olney: Evolution of a Statesman*. University Park: Pennsylvania State University Press, 1974.

Endy, Christopher. "Travel and World Power: Americans in Europe, 1890-1917." *Diplomatic History* 22, no. 4 (1998): 565–94.

Engel, Jeffrey A. "The Democratic Language of American Imperialism: Race, Order, and Theodore Roosevelt's Personifications of Foreign Policy Evil." *Diplomacy and Statecraft* 19, no. 4 (2008): 671–89.

Erman, Sam. "Constitutional Storm Rising: U.S. Expansion Resumes, 1898-1900." Unpublished manuscript in author's possession, 2014.

Ernst, Daniel R. "Free Labor, the Consumer Interest, and the Law of Industrial Disputes, 1885-1900." *American Journal of Legal History* 36, no. 1 (1992): 19–37.

"Ernst Freund: Pioneer of Administrative Law." *University of Chicago Law Review* 29, no. 4 (1962): 755–81.

Esthus, Raymond. "Isolationism and World Power." *Diplomatic History* 2, no. 2 (1978): 117–29.

Eulau, Heinz, and John D. Sprague. *Lawyers in Politics: A Study in Professional Convergence.* Indianapolis, IN: Bobbs-Merrill, 1964.

Evans, Alona E., and Carol Per Lee Plumb. "Notes and Comments: Women and the American Society of International Law." *American Journal of International Law* 68, no. 2 (1974): 290–99.

Ewell, Judith. *Venezuela and the United States: From Monroe's Hemisphere to Petroleum's Empire.* Athens: University of Georgia Press, 1996.

Eyffinger, Arthur. "A Highly Critical Moment: Role and Record of the 1907 Hague Peace Conference." *Netherlands International Law Review* 59, no. 2 (2007): 197–228.

——. *The 1899 Hague Peace Conference: "The Parliament of Man, the Federation of the World."* The Hague: Kluwer Law International, 2000.

Fabian, Larry L. *Andrew Carnegie's Peace Endowment: The Tycoon, The President, and Their Bargain of 1910.* Washington, DC: Carnegie Endowment for International Peace, 1985.

Fabry, Mikulas. *Recognizing States: International Society and the Establishment of New States Since 1776.* New York: Oxford University Press, 2010.

Ferguson, Niall. *Colossus: The Price of America's Empire.* New York: Penguin Press, 2004.

Ferguson, Robert A. *Law and Letters in American Culture.* Cambridge, MA: Harvard University Press, 1984.

Fink, Clinton F., and Christopher Wright. "Quincy Wright on War and Peace: A Statistical Overview and Selected Bibliography." *Journal of Conflict Resolution* 14, no. 4 (1970): 543–54.

Finnemore, Martha. *The Purpose of Intervention: Changing Beliefs about the Use of Force.* Ithaca, NY: Cornell University Press, 2003.

Fiss, Owen M. *Troubled Beginnings of the Modern State, 1888-1910.* Cambridge: Cambridge University Press, 1993.

Fitzmaurice, Andrew. "Liberalism and Empire in Nineteenth-Century International Law." *American Historical Review* 117, no. 1 (2012): 122–40.

Fitzmaurice, Sir Gerald. "The Contribution of the Institute of International Law to the Development of International Law." *Recueil des Cours de l'Académie de Droit Internationale de la Haye* 1 (1973): 203–59.

Foreman, Amanda. *A World on Fire: Britain's Crucial Role in the American Civil War.* New York: Random House, 2010.

Fox, Frank W. *J. Reuben Clark: The Public Years.* Provo, UT: Brigham Young University Press, 1980.

Friedman, Barry. "The History of the Countermajoritarian Difficulty, Part Three: The Lesson of *Lochner.*" *New York University Law Review* 76 (2001): 1383–455.

Friedman, Lawrence M. *A History of American Law.* 2nd ed. New York: Simon and Schuster, 1985.

——. "Lawyers in Cross-Cultural Perspective." In *Lawyers in Society: Comparative Theories,* edited by Richard L. Abel and Philip S. C. Lewis, 1–26. Berkeley: University of California Press, 1989.

Frischholz, Barbara J., and John M. Raymond. "Lawyers Who Established International Law in the United States, 1776-1914." *American Journal of International Law* 76, no. 4 (1982): 802–29.

Fry, Joseph A. "Phases of Empire: Late Nineteenth-Century U.S. Foreign Relations." In *The Gilded Age: Essays on the Origins of Modern America,* edited by Charles W. Calhoun, 261–88. Wilmington, DE: SR Books, 1996.

Gabriel, Jürg Martin. *The American Conception of Neutrality after 1941.* New York: Palgrave MacMillan, 2002.

Gallup, George. *A Guide to Public Opinion Polls.* Princeton, NJ: Princeton University Press, 1944.

Gardner, Lloyd C. *Safe for Democracy: The Anglo-American Response to Revolution, 1913-1923.* New York: Oxford University Press, 1984.

——. "Woodrow Wilson and the Mexican Revolution." In *Woodrow Wilson and a Revolutionary World, 1913-1921,* edited by Arthur Link, 3–48. Chapel Hill: University of North Carolina Press, 1982.

Garrison, Dee. *Apostles of Culture: The Public Librarian and American Society, 1876-1920.* New York: Free Press, 1979.

Gawalt, Gerard W., ed. *The New High Priests: Lawyers in Post-Civil War America.* Westport, CT: Greenwood Press, 1984.

Gelfand, Lawrence. *The Inquiry: American Preparations for Peace, 1917-1919.* New Haven, CT: Yale University Press, 1963.

Gilderhus, Mark T. *Diplomacy and Revolution: U.S.-Mexican Relations under Wilson and Carranza.* Tucson: University of Arizona Press, 1977.

——. *Pan American Visions: Woodrow Wilson in the Western Hemisphere, 1913-1921.* Tucson: University of Arizona Press, 1986.

Glendon, Mary Ann. *A World Made New: Eleanor Roosevelt and the Universal Declaration of Human Rights.* New York: Random House, 2001.

Go, Julian. *Patterns of Empire: The British and American Empires, 1688 to the Present.* New York: Cambridge University Press, 2011.

Gobat, Michel. *Confronting the American Dream: Nicaragua Under U.S. Imperial Rule.* Durham, NC: Duke University Press, 2005.

Goebel Jr., Julius. *A History of the School of Law, Columbia University.* New York: Columbia University Press, 1955.

Goffman, Daniel. "The Ottoman Empire." In *The Renaissance World,* edited by John Jeffries Martin, 347–63. New York: Routledge, 2007.

Goldsmith, Jack L. *Power and Constraint: The Accountable Presidency after 9/11.* New York: W. W. Norton, 2012.

——. *The Terror Presidency: Law and Judgment Inside the Bush Administration.* New York: W. W. Norton, 2007.

Goldsmith, Jack L., and Eric Posner. *The Limits of International Law.* New York: Oxford University Press, 2005.

Golove, David M., and Daniel J. Hulsebosch. "A Civilized Nation: The Early American Constitution, the Law of Nations, and the Pursuit of International Recognition." *New York University Law Review* 85 (October 2010): 932–1066.

Gong, Gerrit W. *The Standard of "Civilization" in International Society.* Oxford: Oxford at the Clarendon Press, 1984.

Goodall, Alex. "US Foreign Relations under Harding, Coolidge, and Hoover: Power and Constraint." In *A Companion to Warren G. Harding, Calvin Coolidge, and Herbert Hoover,* edited by Katherine A. S. Sibley, 53–76. New York: Wiley-Blackwell, 2014.

Goodman, Ryan, and Derek Jinks. *Socializing States: Promoting Human Rights through International Law.* Oxford: Oxford University Press, 2013.

Gordon, Robert W. "The American Legal Profession, 1870-2000." In *The Cambridge History of Law in America, Volume 3: The Twentieth Century and After (1920-),* edited by Michael Grossberg and Christopher Tomlins, 73–126. Cambridge: Cambridge University Press, 2008.

——. "'The Ideal and the Actual in the Law': Fantasies and Practices of New York City Lawyers, 1870-1910." In *The New High Priests: Lawyers in Post–Civil War America,* edited by Gerard W. Gawalt, 51–74. Westport, CT: Greenwood Press, 1984.

——. "Legal Thought and Legal Practice in the Age of American Enterprise, 1870-1920." In *Professions and Professional Ideologies in America,* edited by Gerald L. Geison, 70–110. Chapel Hill: University of North Carolina Press, 1983.

Gould, Lewis L. *Helen Taft: Our Musical First Lady.* Lawrence: University Press of Kansas, 2010.

——. *The Presidency of Theodore Roosevelt.* Lawrence: University Press of Kansas, 1991.

——. *The William Howard Taft Presidency.* Lawrence: University Press of Kansas, 2009.

Gow, Douglas R. "How Did the Roosevelt Corollary Become Linked to the Dominican Republic?" *Mid-America* 58, no. 3 (1976): 159–65.

Graber, D. A. *Crisis Diplomacy: A History of U.S. Intervention Policies and Practices.* Washington, DC: Public Affairs, 1959.

Graham, Terence. *The "Interests of Civilization"? Reaction in the United States against the "Seizure" of the Panama Canal Zone, 1903-1904.* Lund Studies in International History 19. Lund, Sweden: Esselte Studium, 1983.

Grandin, Greg. "The Liberal Traditions in the Americas: Rights, Sovereignty, and the Origins of Liberal Multilateralism." *American Historical Review* 117, no. 1 (2012): 68–91.

Gregory, Ross. *The Origins of American Intervention in the First World War.* New York: W. W. Norton, 1971.

Greenberg, Amy S. *Manifest Manhood and the Antebellum American Empire.* Cambridge: Cambridge University Press, 2005.

——. *A Wicked War: Polk, Clay, Lincoln, and the 1846 U.S. Invasion of Mexico.* New York: Vintage, 2012.

Grewe, Wilhelm G. *The Epochs of International Law.* Translated by Michael Byers. New York: Walter de Gruyter, 2000.

Grey, Thomas C. "Langdell's Orthodoxy." *University of Pittsburgh Law Review* 45, no. 1 (1983–84): 1–53.

Grossberg, Michael. "Institutionalizing Masculinity: The Law as a Masculine Profession." In *Meanings for Manhood: Constructions of Masculinity in Victorian America,* edited by Mark C. Carnes and Clyde Griffen, 133–51. Chicago: University of Chicago Press, 1990.

Grossman, Lewis A. "Langdell Upside-Down: James Coolidge Carter and the Anticlassical Jurisprudence of Anticodification." *Yale Journal of Law and the Humanities* 19 (2007): 149–219.

Gullace, Nicoletta F. "Sexual Violence and Family Honor: British Propaganda and International Law during the First World War." *American Historical Review* 102, no. 3 (1997): 714–47.

Hall, Kermit. *The Magic Mirror: Law in American History.* New York: Oxford University Press, 1989.

——. "The Courts, 1790-1920." In *The Cambridge History of Law in America.* Vol. 2, *The Long Nineteenth Century (1789–1920),* edited by Michael Grossberg and Christopher Tomlins, 106–32. New York: Cambridge University Press, 2008.

Hannigan, Robert E. *The New World Power: American Foreign Policy, 1898-1917.* Philadelphia: University of Pennsylvania Press, 2002.

Harris, Susan K. *God's Arbiters: Americans and the Philippines, 1898-1902.* New York: Oxford University Press, 2011.

Harrison, Benjamin T. *Dollar Diplomat: Chandler Anderson and American Diplomacy in Mexico and Nicaragua, 1913-1928.* Pullman: Washington State University Press, 1988.

Hart, H. L. A. *The Concept of Law.* 2nd ed. New York: Oxford University Press, 1994. Originally published in 1961.

Hart, John Mason. *Revolutionary Mexico: The Coming and Process of the Mexican Revolution.* Berkeley: University of California Press, 1987.

Haskell, Thomas. *The Emergence of Professional Social Science.* Urbana: University of Illinois Press, 1977.

Healy, David. *Drive to Hegemony: The United States in the Caribbean, 1898-1917.* Madison: University of Wisconsin Press, 1988.

Heiss, Mary Ann. "The Evolution of the Imperial Idea and U.S. National Identity." *Diplomatic History* 26, no. 4 (2002): 511–40.

Henderson, Peter V.N. "Woodrow Wilson, Victoriano Huerta, and the Recognition Issue in Mexico." *The Americas* 41, no. 2 (1984): 151–76.

Hendrickson, David C. *Peace Pact: The Lost World of the American Founding.* Lawrence: University Press of Kansas, 2003.

Hendrickson, Embert J. "Root's Watchful Waiting and the Venezuelan Controversy." *The Americas* 23, no. 2 (1966): 115–29.

Henkin, Louis. *How Nations Behave: Law and Foreign Policy.* 2nd ed. New York: Columbia University Press, 1979. Originally published in 1968.

——. "U.S. Ratification of Human Rights Conventions: The Ghost of Senator Bricker." *American Journal of International Law* 89, no. 2 (1995): 341–50.

Hepp, John. "James Brown Scott and the Rise of Public International Law." *Journal of the Gilded Age and Progressive Era* 7, no. 2 (2008): 151–79.

Herman, Sondra. *Eleven Against War: Studies in American Internationalist Thought, 1898-1921.* Stanford, CA: Hoover Institution Press, 1969.

Hietala, Thomas R. *Manifest Design: American Exceptionalism and Empire.* Rev. ed. Ithaca, NY: Cornell University Press, 2003. Originally published in 1985.

Higham, John. *Strangers in the Land: Patterns of American Nativism, 1860-1925.* New Brunswick, NJ: Rutgers University Press, 2002.

Hilderbrand, Robert C. *Dumbarton Oaks: The Origins of the United Nations and the Search for Postwar Security.* Chapel Hill: University of North Carolina Press, 1990.

——. *Power and the People: Executive Management of Public Opinion in Foreign Affairs, 1897-1921.* Chapel Hill: University of North Carolina Press, 1981.

Hilfrich, Fabian. *Debating American Exceptionalism: Empire and Democracy in the Wake of the Spanish-American War.* New York: Palgrave Macmillan, 2012.

Hinsley, F.H. *Power and the Pursuit of Peace: Theory and Practice in the History of Relations Between States.* Cambridge: Cambridge University Press, 1963.

Hobsbawm, Eric. *The Age of Empire, 1875-1914.* New York: Vintage, 1987.

——. *Nations and Nationalism since 1780: Programme, Myth, Reality.* 2d. ed. Cambridge: Cambridge University Press, 1992. Originally published in 1990.

Hochschild, Adam. *King Leopold's Ghost: A Story of Greed, Terror, and Heroism in Colonial Africa.* Boston: Houghton Mifflin, 1998.

Hodge, Carl Cavanagh. "A Whiff of Cordite: Theodore Roosevelt and the Transoceanic Naval Arms Race, 1897-1909." *Diplomacy and Statecraft* 19, no. 4 (2008): 712–31.

Hodgson, Godfrey. "The Foreign Policy Establishment." In *Ruling America: A History of Wealth and Power in a Democracy,* edited by Steve Fraser and Gary Gerstle, 215–49. Cambridge, MA: Harvard University Press, 2005.

Hofstadter, Richard. *The Age of Reform: From Bryan to F.D.R.* New York: Vintage, 1955.

Hogan, J. Michael. *The Panama Canal in American Politics: Domestic Advocacy and the Evolution of Policy.* Carbondale: Southern Illinois University Press, 1986.

Hoganson, Kristin L. *Fighting for American Manhood: How Gender Politics Provoked the Spanish-American and Philippine-American Wars.* New Haven, CT: Yale University Press, 1998.

Holmes, James R. *Theodore Roosevelt and World Order: Police Power in International Relations.* Washington, DC: Potomac Books, 2006.

Holquist, Peter. "The Russian Empire as a 'Civilized State': International Law as Principle and Practice in Imperial Russia, 1874-1878." National Council for Eurasian and East European Research working paper. http://www.ucis.pitt.edu/nceeer/2004_818-06g_Holquist.pdf.

Holt, W. Stull. *Treaties Defeated by the Senate.* Baltimore: Johns Hopkins Press, 1933.

Horne, John and Alan Kramer. *German Atrocities, 1914: A History of Denial.* New Haven, CT: Yale University Press, 2000.

Horwitz, Morton J. *The Transformation of American Law, 1870-1960: The Crisis of Legal Orthodoxy.* New York: Oxford University Press, 1992.

Howlett, Charles F. "John Dewey and the Crusade to Outlaw War." *World Affairs.* 138, no. 4 (1976): 336–55.

Hoxie, R. Gordon , Sally Falk Moore, Joseph Dorfman, Richard Hofstadter, Theodore W. Anderson, Jr., John D. Millett, and Seymour Martin Lipset. *A History of the Faculty of Political Science, Columbia University.* New York: Columbia University Press, 1955.

Hoyt, Edwin C. "National Policy and International Law: Case Studies from American Canal Policy." *Monograph Series in World Affairs,* 4:1. The Social Science Foundation and Graduate School of International Studies, University of Denver, Denver: University of Denver, 1966–67.

Hudson, Manley O. "Twelve Casebooks on International Law." *American Journal of International Law* 32, no. 3 (1938): 447–56.

Hull, Isabel V. *A Scrap of Paper: Breaking and Making International Law during the Great War.* Ithaca, NY: Cornell University Press, 2014.

Hunt, Michael H. *The America Ascendancy: How the United States Gained and Wielded Global Dominance.* Chapel Hill: University of North Carolina Press, 2007.

———. *Ideology and U.S. Foreign Policy.* New Haven, CT: Yale University Press, 1987.

Hutchcroft, Paul D. "The Hazards of Jeffersonianism: Challenges of State Building in the United States and Its Empire." In *Colonial Crucible: Empire in the Making of the Modern American State,* edited by Alfred W. McCoy and Francisco A. Scarano, 375–89. Madison: University of Wisconsin Press, 2009.

Ignatieff, Michael, ed. *American Exceptionalism and Human Rights.* Princeton, NJ: Princeton University Press, 2005.

Ikenberry, G. John. *After Victory: Institutions, Strategic Restraint, and the Rebuilding of Order after Major Wars.* Princeton, NJ: Princeton University Press, 2001.

Institut de droit international. *Livre du Centenaire 1873-1973, Evolution et Perspectives du Droit International.* Basel: Editions S. Karger, 1973.

Iriye, Akira. *From Nationalism to Internationalism: US Foreign Policy to 1914.* Boston: Routledge and Kegan Paul, 1977.

———. *Global Community: The Role of International Organizations in the Making of the Contemporary World.* Berkeley: University of California Press, 2002.

Irwin, Julia F. "Nation Building and Rebuilding: The American Red Cross in Italy During the Great War." *Journal of the Gilded Age and Progressive Era* 8, no. 3 (2009): 407–39.

Irwin, Ryan M. *Gordian Knot: Apartheid and the Unmaking of the Liberal World Order.* New York: Oxford University Press, 2012.

Jacobsen, Matthew Frye. *Barbarian Virtues: The United States Encounters Foreign Peoples at Home and Abroad, 1876-1917.* New York: Hill and Wang, 2000.

Jaeger, Hans-Martin. "'World Opinion' and World Organization: Governmentality, System Differentiation, and the International Public Sphere." PhD diss., Columbia University, 2005.

Janis, Mark W. *America and the Law of Nations 1776-1939.* New York: Oxford University Press, 2010.

———. *The American Tradition of International Law: Great Expectations 1789-1914.* New York: Oxford University Press, 2004.

———. "North America: American Exceptionalism in International Law." In *The Oxford Handbook of the History of International Law,* edited by Bardo Fassbender and Anne Peters, 525–52. Oxford: Oxford University Press, 2012.

Jeal, Tim. *Stanley: The Impossible Life of Africa's Greatest Explorer.* New Haven, CT: Yale University Press, 2007.

Jessup, Philip C. *Elihu Root.* 2 vols. New York: Dodd, Mead & Company, 1938.

Johnson, Courtney. "Understanding the American Empire: Colonialism, Latin Americanism, and Professional Social Science, 1898-1920." In *Colonial Crucible: Empire in the Making of the Modern American State,* edited by Alfred McCoy and Francisco Scarano, 175–90. Madison: University of Wisconsin Press, 2009.

Johnson, D. H. N. *The English Tradition in International Law: Lecture at the London School of Economics and Political Science, 20 November 1961.* London: G. Bell and Sons, 1962.

Johnson, Richard A. *The Administration of United States Foreign Policy.* Austin: University of Texas Press, 1971.

Johnson, Robert David. *The Peace Progressives and American Foreign Relations.* Cambridge, MA: Harvard University Press, 1995.

Johnson, William R. *Schooled Lawyers: A Study in the Clash of Professional Cultures.* New York: New York University Press, 1978.

Johnstone, Andrew. "Isolationism and Internationalism in American Foreign Relations." *Journal of Transatlantic Studies* 9, no. 1 (2011): 7–20.

Jones, Dorothy V. *Toward a Just World: The Critical Years in the Search for International Justice.* Chicago: University of Chicago Press, 2002.

Jones, Howard. *Blue and Gray Diplomacy: A History of Union and Confederate Foreign Relations.* Chapel Hill: University of North Carolina Press, 2010.

Josephson, Harold. "Outlawing War: Internationalism and the Pact of Paris." *Diplomatic History* 3, no. 4 (1979): 377–90.

Kahn, Paul W. *The Reign of Law: Marbury v. Madison and the Construction of America.* New Haven, CT: Yale University Press, 1997.

Kammen, Michael. "The Problem of American Exceptionalism: A Reconsideration." *American Quarterly* 45, no. 1 (1993): 1–43.

Kaplan, Edward S. *U.S. Imperialism in Latin America.* Westport, CT: Greenwood Press, 1998.

Karnes, Thomas L. *The Failure of Union: Central America, 1824-1960.* Chapel Hill: University of North Carolina Press, 1961.

Katz, Friedrich. *The Secret War in Mexico: Europe, the United States and the Mexican Revolution.* Chicago: University of Chicago Press, 1981.

Kazin, Michael. *A Godly Hero: The Life of William Jennings Bryan.* New York: Alfred A. Knopf, 2006.

Keefer, Scott Andrew. "Building the Palace of Peace: The Hague Conference of 1899 and Arms Control in the Progressive Era." *Journal of the History of International Law* 8, no. 1 (2006): 1–17.

Keene, Edward. *Beyond the Anarchical Society: Grotius, Colonialism and Order in World Politics.* Cambridge: Cambridge University Press, 2002.

Keller, Morton. *Affairs of State: Public Life in Late Nineteenth Century America.* Cambridge, MA: Harvard University Press, 1977.

Kelly, Joseph B. "John Bassett Moore's Concept of Recognition." *Journal of the John Bassett Moore Society of International Law* 2 (1961-62): 19–29.

Kennan, George F. *American Diplomacy.* Expanded ed. Chicago: University of Chicago, 1984. Originally published in 1951.

Kennedy, David. "International Law and the Nineteenth Century: History of an Illusion." *Quinnipiac Law Review* 17 (1998): 99–138.

———. "The Mystery of Global Governance." *Ohio Northern University Law Review* 34 (2008): 827–60.

———. *Of War and Law.* Princeton, NJ: Princeton University Press, 2006.

———. "Primitive Legal Scholarship." *Harvard International Law Journal* 27, no. 1 (1986): 13–40.

Kennedy, David M. *Over Here: The First World War and American Society.* New York: Oxford University Press, 1980.

Kennedy, Duncan. *The Rise and Fall of Classical Legal Thought.* Washington, DC: Beard Books, 2006. Originally published in 1975.

———. "Two Globalizations of Law and Legal Thought: 1850-1968." *Suffolk University Law Review* 36, no. 3 (2003): 631–80.

Kennedy, Paul. *The Parliament of Man: The Past, Present, and Future of the United Nations.* New York: Random House, 2006.

Kennedy, Ross A. *The Will to Believe: Woodrow Wilson, World War I, and America's Strategy for Peace and Security.* Kent, OH: Kent State University Press, 2009.

Kenny, James T. "Manley O. Hudson and the Harvard Research in International Law, 1927-1940." *International Lawyer* 11, no. 2 (1977): 319–29.

Keohane, Robert. *International Institutions and State Power: Essays in International Relations Theory.* Boulder: University of Colorado, 1989.

Keys, Barbara J. *Reclaiming American Virtue: The Human Rights Revolution of the 1970s.* Cambridge, MA: Harvard University Press, 2014.

Kimball, Bruce A. *The Inception of Modern Professional Education: C. C. Langdell, 1826-1906.* Chapel Hill: University of North Carolina Press, 2009.

Kimmel, Michael. *Manhood in America: A Cultural History.* New York: Free Press, 1996.

Kingsbury, Benedict. "Legal Positivism as Normative Politics: International Society, Balance of Power, and Lassa Oppenheim's Positive International Law." *European Journal of International Law* 13 (2002): 401–36.

Kirgis, Frederic. *The American Society of International Law's First Century 1906-2006*. Boston: Martinus Nijhoff, 2006.

Kloppenberg, James T. *Uncertain Victory: Social Democracy and Progressivism in European and American Thought, 1870-1920*. New York: Oxford University Press, 1986.

Knarr, James C. *Uruguay and the United States, 1903-1929: Diplomacy in the Progressive Era*. Kent, OH: Kent State University Press, 2012.

Knock, Thomas J. *To End all Wars: Woodrow Wilson and the Quest for a New World Order*. Princeton, NJ: Princeton University Press, 1992.

Koh, Harold Hongju. "Bringing International Law Home." *Houston Law Review* 35, no. 3 (1998): 623–81.

———. "The Obama Administration and International Law." Speech at the Annual Meeting of the American Society of International Law, March 25, 2010. http://www.state.gov/s/l/releases/remarks/139119.htm. Accessed July 11, 2015.

———. "Why Do Nations Obey International Law?" *Yale Law Journal* 106, no. 8 (1997): 2599–659.

Koskenniemi, Martti. "The Ideology of International Adjudication, with Special Reference to the 1907 Hague Conference." Paper Presented at The Hague, September 7, 2007. www.helsinki.fi/eci/Publications/MKHague%201907-puheversio07a.pdf. Accessed March 3, 2009.

———. *From Apology to Utopia: The Structure of International Legal Argument*.Cambridge: Cambridge University Press, 2005.

———. *The Gentle Civilizer of Nations: The Rise and Fall of International Law 1870-1960*. Cambridge: Cambridge University Press, 2002.

———. "Histories of International Law: Significance and Problems for a Critical View." *Temple International and Comparative Law Journal* 27, no. 2 (2014): 215–40.

———. "International Law and Hegemony: A Reconfiguration." *Cambridge Review of International Affairs* 17, no. 2 (2004): 197–218.

———. "The Subjective Dangers of Projects of World Community." In *Realizing Utopia: The Future of International Law*, edited by Antonio Cassese, 3–13. Oxford: Oxford University Press, 2012.

Kramer, Larry D. *The People Themselves: Popular Constitutionalism and Judicial Review*. New York: Oxford University Press, 2000.

Kramer, Paul. *The Blood of Government: Race, Empire, the United States, and the Philippines*. Chapel Hill: University of North Carolina Press, 2006.

———. "Empires, Exceptions, and Anglo-Saxons: Race and Rule between the British and United States Empires, 1880-1910." *Journal of American History* 88, no. 4 (2002): 1315–53.

———. "Power and Connection: Imperial Histories of the United States in the World," *American Historical Review* 116, no. 5 (2011): 1348–91.

Krasner, Stephen. *International Regimes*. Ithaca, NY: Cornell University Press, 1983.

Kuehl, Warren F., ed. *Biographical Dictionary of Internationalists*. Westport, CT: Greenwood Press, 1983.

———. *Seeking World Order: The United States and International Organization to 1920*. Nashville, TN: Vanderbilt University Press, 1969.

Kuehl Warren F., and Lynne K. Dunn. *Keeping the Covenant: American Internationalists and the League of Nations, 1920-1939*. Kent, OH: Kent University Press, 1997.

LaFeber, Walter. *The New Cambridge History of American Foreign Relations, Volume 2: The American Search for Opportunity, 1865-1913*. New York: Cambridge University Press, 2013.

———. *The New Empire: An Interpretation of American Expansion, 1860-1898*. Ithaca, NY: Cornell University Press, 1998 Originally published in 1963.

———. *The Panama Canal: The Crisis in Historical Perspective*. New York: Oxford University Press, 1989 Originally published in 1978.

Lachs, Manfred. *The Teacher in International Law: Teachings and Teaching*. 2nd ed. Boston: Martinus Nijhoff, 1987.

LaCroix, Alison. *The Ideological Origins of American Federalism*. Cambridge, MA: Harvard University Press, 2010.

Laity, Paul. *The British Peace Movement, 1870-1914.* Oxford: Clarendon Press, 2001.

Lake, David A. *Hierarchy in International Relations.* Ithaca, NY: Cornell University Press, 2009.

Landauer, Carl. "The Ambivalences of Power: Launching the American Journal of International Law in an Era of Empire and Globalization." *Leiden Journal of International Law* 20, no. 3 (2007): 325–58.

———. "A Latin American in Paris: Alejandro Álvarez's Le Droit International Américain." *Leiden Journal of International Law* 19 (2006): 957–81.

Lang, Andrew, and Susan Marks. "People with Projects: Writing the Lives of International Lawyers." *Temple International and Comparative Law Journal* 27, no. 2 (2013): 437–53.

Langhorne, Richard. "Arbitration: The First Phase, 1870-1914." In *Diplomacy and World Power,* edited by Michael Dockrill and Brian McKercher, 43–55. Cambridge: Cambridge University Press, 1996.

Langley, Lester D. *The United States and the Caribbean in the Twentieth Century.* 4th ed. Athens: University of Georgia Press, 1989.

Lapradelle, Albert de. *Maitres et doctrines du droit des gens.* 2nd ed. Paris: Les Éditions internationales, 1950.

Lauterpacht, Hersh. "The So-Called Anglo-American and Continental Schools of Thought in International Law." *British Year Book of International Law* 12 (1931): 31–62.

Lears, Jackson. *Rebirth of a Nation: The Making of Modern America, 1877-1920.* New York: Harper Collins, 2009.

Leigh, Monroe, and Cristian DeFrancia. "International Law Societies and the Development of International Law." *Virginia Journal of International Law* 41, no. 4 (2000–2001): 941–51.

Leonard, Thomas M. *Central America and the United States: The Search for Stability.* Athens: University of Georgia Press, 1991.

Leopold, Richard. *Elihu Root and the Conservative Tradition.* Boston: Little, Brown, 1954.

———. "The Problem of American Intervention, 1917: An Historical Retrospect." *World Politics* 2, no. 3 (1950): 405–25.

Lesaffer, Randall. "International Law and Its History: The Story of an Unrequited Love." In *Time, History and International Law,* edited by Matthew Craven, Malgosia Fitzmaurice, and Maria Vogiatzi, 27–41. Leiden: Martinus Nijhoff, 2007.

Levin, N. Gordon, Jr. *Woodrow Wilson and World Politics: America's Response to War and Revolution.* Oxford: Oxford University Press, 1968.

Lindgren, James M. "'The Blow Which Civilization Has Suffered': American Preservationists and the Great War, 1914-1919." *Public Historian* 27, no. 3 (2005): 27–56.

Link, Arthur S. *The Higher Realism of Woodrow Wilson and Other Essays.* Nashville, TN: Vanderbilt University Press, 1971.

———. *Wilson the Diplomatist: A Look at His Major Foreign Policies.* Baltimore: Johns Hopkins Press, 1957.

———. *Wilson: Campaigns for Progressivism and Peace.* Princeton, NJ: Princeton University Press, 1965.

———. *Wilson: Confusions and Crises, 1915-1916.* Princeton, NJ: Princeton University Press, 1964.

———. *Wilson: The New Freedom.* Princeton, NJ: Princeton University Press, 1956.

———. *Wilson: The Struggle for Neutrality, 1914-1915.* Princeton, NJ: Princeton University Press, 1960.

———. ed. *Woodrow Wilson and a Revolutionary World, 1913-1921.* Chapel Hill: University of North Carolina Press, 1982.

Linn, Brian McAllister. *The Philippine War, 1899-1902.* Lawrence: University Press of Kansas, 2000.

Lipson, Charles. *Standing Guard: Protecting Foreign Capital in the Nineteenth and Twentieth Centuries.* Berkeley: University of California Press, 1984.

Liu, Lydia H. *The Clash of Empires: The Invention of China in Modern World Making.* Cambridge, MA: Harvard University Press, 2004.

Lobel, Jules. "The Rise and Fall of the Neutrality Act: Sovereignty and Congressional War Powers in United States Foreign Policy." *Harvard International Law Journal* 24, no. 3 (1983): 1–71.

Lombardi, John V. *Venezuela: The Search for Order, the Dream of Progress.* New York: Oxford University Press, 1982.

Love, Eric. *Race over Empire: Racism and U.S. Imperialism, 1865-1900.* Chapel Hill: University of North Carolina Press, 2004.

Loveman, Brian. *No Higher Law: American Foreign Policy and the Western Hemisphere since 1776.* Chapel Hill: University of North Carolina Press, 2010.

Lundestad, Geir. "Empire by Invitation? The United States and Western Europe, 1945-1952." *Journal of Peace Research* 23, no. 3 (1986): 263–77.

Lutzker, Michael Arnold. "The 'Practical' Peace Advocates: An Interpretation of the American Peace Movement, 1898-1917." PhD diss., Rutgers University, 1969.

Lyons, F. S. L. *Internationalism in Europe, 1815-1914.* Leyden: A. W. Sythoff, 1963.

Macalister-Smith, Peter. "Bio-Bibliographical Key to the Membership of the Institut de Droit International, 1873-2001." *Journal of the History of International Law* 5 (2003): 77–159.

MacGill, Hugh C., and R. Kent Newmyer. "Legal Education and Legal Thought, 1790-1920." In *The Cambridge History of Law in America, Volume 2: The Long Nineteenth Century (1789-1920)*, edited by Michael Grossberg and Christopher Tomlins, 36–66. Cambridge: Cambridge University Press, 2008.

MacMillan, Margaret. *Paris 1919: Six Months That Changed the World.* New York: Random House, 2003.

Maddox, Robert James. *William E. Borah and American Foreign Policy.* Baton Rouge: Louisiana State University Press, 1969.

Maguire, Peter. *Law and War: An American Story.* New York: Columbia University Press, 2000.

Maier, Charles. *Among Empires: American Ascendancy and Its Predecessors.* Cambridge, MA: Harvard University Press, 2006.

Major, John. *Prize Possession: The United States and the Panama Canal, 1903-1979.* New York: Cambridge University Press, 1993.

———. "Who Wrote the Hay-Bunau-Varilla Convention?" *Diplomatic History* 8, no. 2 (1984): 115–23.

Malanson, Jeffrey J. "The Congressional Debate over U.S. Participation in the Congress of Panama, 1825-1826: Washington's Farewell Address, Monroe's Doctrine, and the Fundamental Principles of U.S. Foreign Policy." *Diplomatic History* 30, no. 5 (2006): 813–38.

Manela, Erez. *The Wilsonian Moment: Self-Determination and the International Origins of Anticolonial Nationalism.* New York: Oxford University Press, 2007.

———. "The United States in the World." In *American History Now*, edited by Eric Foner and Lisa McGirr, 201–20. Philadelphia: Temple University Press, 2011.

Mann, Michael. *Sources of Social Power.* Vol. 3: *Global Empires and Revolution, 1890-1945.* New York: Cambridge University Press, 2012.

Marchand, C. Roland. *The American Peace Movement and Social Reform, 1898-1918.* Princeton, NJ: Princeton University Press, 1972.

Margolies, Daniel S. *Spaces of Law in American Foreign Relations: Extradition and Extraterritoriality in the Borderlands and Beyond, 1877-1898.* Athens: University of Georgia, 2011.

Marks, Frederick W.III. "Morality as a Drive Wheel in the Diplomacy of Theodore Roosevelt." *Diplomatic History* 2, no. 1 (1978): 43–62.

Marks, Sally. *The Illusion of Peace: International Relations in Europe, 1918-1933.* 2nd ed. New York: Palgrave Macmillan, 2003. Originally published in 1979.

Marrus, Michael R. *The Nuremberg War Crimes Trial 1945-46: A Documentary History.* New York: Bedford/St. Martin's, 1997.

Matthews, John Mabry. *The Conduct of American Foreign Relations.* New York: The Century Co., 1922.

John A. Matzko. "'The Best Men of the Bar': The Founding of the American Bar Association." In *The New High Priests: Lawyers in Post-Civil War America*, edited by Gerard W. Gawalt, 75–97. Westport, CT: Greenwood Press, 1984.

Maurer, Noel. *The Empire Trap: The Rise and Fall of U.S. Intervention to Protect American Property Overseas, 1893-1976.* Princeton, NJ: Princeton University Press, 2013.

May, Christopher. *The Rule of Law: The Common Sense of Global Politics.* Northampton, MA: Edward Elgar, 2014.

May, Ernest R. *Imperial Democracy: The Emergence of America as a Great Power.* Reprint, Chicago: Imprint Publications, 1991. Originally published in 1961.

———. *The World War and American Isolation, 1914-1917.* Cambridge, MA: Harvard University Press, 1959.

Mazower, Mark. *Governing the World: The History of an Idea, 1815 to the Present.* New York: Penguin, 2012.

———. *No Enchanted Palace: The End of Empire and the Ideological Origins of the United Nations.* Princeton, NJ: Princeton University Press, 2009.

McBeth, Brian S. *Gunboats, Corruption, and Claims: Foreign Intervention in Venezuela, 1899-1908.* Westport, CT: Greenwood Press, 2001.

McCartney, Paul T. *Power and Progress: American National Identity, the War of 1898, and the Rise of American Imperialism.* Baton Rouge: Louisiana State University Press, 2006.

McCoy, Alfred, and Francisco Scarano, eds. *Colonial Crucible: Empire in the Making of the Modern American State.* Madison: University of Wisconsin Press, 2009.

McCoy, Drew. *The Elusive Republic: Political Economy in Jeffersonian America.* Chapel Hill: University of North Carolina Press, 1996.

McCullough, David. *The Path between the Seas: The Creation of the Panama Canal, 1870-1914.* New York: Simon and Schuster, 1977.

McDougall, Walter. *Promised Land, Crusader State: The American Encounter with the World Since 1776.* Boston: Houghton Mifflin, 1997.

McFarland, Gerald W. "Partisan of Non-Partisanship: Dorman B. Eaton and the Genteel Reform Tradition." *Journal of American History* 54 (1968): 806–22.

McGuinness, Aims. "Searching for 'Latin America': Race and Sovereignty in the Americas in the 1850s." In *Race and Nation in Modern Latin America*, edited by Nancy P. Applebaum, Anne S. Macpherson, and Karin Alejandra Rosemblatt, 87–107. Chapel Hill: University of North Carolina Press, 2003.

McPherson, Alan. "Americanism against American Empire." In *Americanism: New Perspectives on the History of an Ideal*, edited by Michael Kazin and Joseph A. McCartin, 169–91. Chapel Hill: University of North Carolina Press, 2006.

———. *The Invaded: How Latin Americans and Their Allies Fought and Ended U.S. Occupations.* New York: Oxford University Press, 2014.

Mead, Walter Russell. *Special Providence: The American Foreign Policy Tradition.* New York: Routledge, 2002.

Megargee, Richard. "Realism in American Foreign Policy: The Diplomacy of John Bassett Moore." PhD diss., Northwestern University, 1963.

Mehta, Uday Singh. *Liberalism and Empire: A Study in Nineteenth-Century British Liberal Thought.* Chicago: University of Chicago Press, 1999.

Merry, Sally Engle. *Colonizing Hawaii: The Cultural Power of Law.* Princeton, NJ: Princeton University Press, 2000.

Miéville, China. *Between Equal Rights: A Marxist Theory of International Law.* Boston: Brill, 2005.

Miller, Bonnie M. *From Liberation to Conquest: The Visual and Popular Cultures of the Spanish-American War of 1898.* Amherst: University of Massachusetts Press, 2011.

Miller, Mark C. *The High Priests of American Politics: The Role of Lawyers in American Political Institutions.* Knoxville: University of Tennessee Press, 1995.

Miner, Dwight C. *The Fight for the Panama Route: The Story of the Spooner Act and the Hay-Herrán Treaty.* New York: Columbia University Press, 1940.

Minger, Ralph Eldin. *William Howard Taft and United States Foreign Policy: The Apprenticeship Years, 1900-1908.* Urbana: University of Illinois Press, 1975.

Mitchell, Nancy. "The Height of the German Challenge: The Venezuela Blockade, 1902-1903." *Diplomatic History* 20, no. 2 (1996): 184–209.

Modirzadeh, Naz K. "Folk International Law: 9/11 Lawyering and the Transformation of the Law of Armed Conflict to Human Rights Policy and Human Rights Law to War Governance." *Harvard National Security Journal* 5, no. 1 (2014): 225–304.

Mommsen, Wolfgang J. *Theories of Imperialism.* Translated by P. S. Falla. New York: Random House, 1980. Originally published in 1977.

Moore, Leonard. *Citizen Klansmen: The Ku Klux Klan in Indiana, 1921-1928.* Chapel Hill: University of North Carolina Press, 1991.

Morison, Samuel Eliot. *Three Centuries of Harvard, 1636-1936.* Cambridge, MA: Harvard University Press, 1963.

Morris, Edmund. *Theodore Rex.* New York: Random House, 2001.

Morrissey, Alice M. *The American Defense of Neutral Rights 1914-1917.* Cambridge, MA: Harvard University Press, 1939.

Morrissey McDiarmid, Alice. "The Neutrality Board and Armed Merchantmen, 1914-1917." *American Journal of International Law* 69, no. 2 (1975): 374–81.

Moyn, Samuel. "From Antiwar Politics to Antitorture Politics." In *Law and War,* edited by Austin Sarat, Lawrence Douglas, and Martha Merril Umphrey, 154–97. Stanford, CA: Stanford University Press, 2014.

——. *The Last Utopia: Human Rights in History.* Cambridge, MA: Harvard University Press, 2010.

Mulder, John M. "'A Gospel of Order': Woodrow Wilson's Religion and Politics." In *The Wilson Era: Essays in Honor of Arthur S. Link,* edited by John Milton Cooper, Jr. and Charles Neu, 223–47. Arlington Heights, IL: Harlan Davidson, 1991.

——. *Woodrow Wilson: The Years of Preparation.* Princeton, NJ: Princeton University Press, 1978.

Münch, Fritz. "L'Institut de droit international: ses debuts comme organe collectif de la doctrine." In *Estudios de Derecho Internacional Homenaje a D. Antonio de Luna,* 385–96. Madrid: CSIC, 1968.

Munro, Dana. *Intervention and Dollar Diplomacy in the Caribbean, 1900-1921.* Princeton, NJ: Princeton University Press, 1964.

Murphy, Gretchen. *Hemispheric Imaginings: The Monroe Doctrine and Narratives of U.S. Empire.* Durham, NC: Duke University Press, 2005.

Murphy, Kevin P. *Political Manhood: Red Bloods, Mollycoddles, and the Politics of Progressive Era Reform.* New York: Columbia University Press, 2008.

Murphy, John F. *The United States and the Rule of Law in International Affairs.* Cambridge: Cambridge University Press, 2004.

Nasaw, David. *Andrew Carnegie.* New York: Penguin, 2006.

Neff, Stephen C. *Justice among Nations: A History of International Law.* Cambridge, MA: Harvard University Press, 2014.

——. *The Rights and Duties of Neutrals: A General History.* Manchester, UK: Manchester University Press, 2000.

Ngai, Mae. *Impossible Subjects: Illegal Aliens and the Making of Modern America.* Princeton, NJ: Princeton University Press, 2004.

Nichols, Christopher McKnight. *Promise and Peril: America at the Dawn of a Global Age.* Cambridge, MA: Harvard University Press, 2011.

Ninkovich, Frank. *Global Dawn: The Cultural Foundation of American Internationalism, 1865-1890.* Cambridge, MA: Harvard University Press, 2009.

——. "Theodore Roosevelt: Civilization as Ideology." *Diplomatic History* 10, no. 3 (1986): 221–45.

——. *The United States and Imperialism.* Malden, MA: Blackwell, 2001.

Nissel, Alan. "The Duality of State Responsibility." *Columbia Human Rights Law Review* 44, no. 3 (2013): 793–858.

——. "The Turn to Technique: American Professionalization of International Arbitration (1870-1898)." Unpublished manuscript in the author's possession.

Nolan, Mary. "Against Exceptionalisms." *American Historical Review* 102, no. 3 (1997): 769–74.

Novak, William J. "The Myth of the 'Weak' American State." *American Historical Review* 113, no. 3 (2008): 752–72.

Novick, Peter. *That Noble Dream: The "Objectivity Question" and the American Historical Profession.* Cambridge: Cambridge University Press, 1988.

Noyes, John E. "William Howard Taft and the Arbitration Treaties." *Villanova Law Review* 56 (2011): 536–37.

Nurnberger, Ralph Dingman. "James Brown Scott: Peace through Justice." PhD diss., Georgetown University, 1975.

Nussbaum, Arthur. *A Concise History of the Law of Nations.* New York: MacMillan, 1947.

O'Connell, Mary Ellen. "Arbitration and Avoidance of War: The Nineteenth-Century American Vision." In *The Sword and the Scales: The United States and International Courts and Tribunals,* edited by Cesare P. R. Romano, 30–45. Cambridge: Cambridge University Press, 2009.

———. *The Power and Purpose of International Law.* New York: Oxford University Press, 2008.

O'Connor, Brendan. "American Foreign Policy Traditions: A Literature Review." US Studies Working Paper, University of Sydney, 2009.

Obregón, Liliana. "Between Civilisation and Barbarism: Creole Interventions in International Law." *Third World Quarterly* 27, no. 5 (2006): 815–32.

———. "Regionalism Constructed: A Short History of 'Latin American International Law.'" European Society of International Law Conference Paper Series. No. 5, 2012.

Offner, John L. *An Unwanted War: The Diplomacy of the United States and Spain over Cuba, 1895-1898.* Chapel Hill: University of North Carolina Press, 1992.

Ogle, Vanessa. "State Rights against Private Capital: The 'New International Economic Order' and the Struggle over Aid, Trade, and Foreign Investment, 1962-1981." *Humanity* 5, no. 2 (2014): 211–34.

Ohlin, Jens David. *The Assault on International Law.* New York: Oxford University Press, 2015.

Onuf, Peter, and Nicholas Onuf. *Federal Union, Modern World: The Law of Nations in an Age of Revolutions, 1776-1814.* Madison, WI: Madison House, 1993.

Orakhelashvili, Alexander. "The Idea of European International Law." *European Journal of International Law* 17, no. 2 (2006): 315–47.

Ørvik, Nils. *The Decline of Neutrality 1914-1941, With special reference to the United States and the Northern Neutrals.* 2nd ed. London: Frank Cass, 1977. Originally published in 1971.

Osgood, Robert. "Woodrow Wilson, Collective Security, and the Lessons of History." In *The Philosophy and Policies of Woodrow Wilson,* edited by Earl Latham, 187–98. Chicago: University of Chicago, 1958.

O'Toole, Patricia. *When Trumpets Call: Theodore Roosevelt after the White House.* New York: Simon and Schuster, 2005.

Papachristou, Judith. "American Women and Foreign Policy, 1898-1905: Exploring Gender in Diplomatic History." *Diplomatic History* 14, no. 4 (1990): 493–509.

Paulus, Andreas L. "From Neglect to Defiance? The United States and International Adjudication." *European Journal of International Law* 15, no. 4 (2004): 783–812.

Park, James William. *Latin American Underdevelopment: A History of Perspectives in the United States, 1870-1965.* Baton Rouge: Louisiana State University Press, 1995.

Parker, Kunal. *Common Law, History, and Democracy in America, 1790-1900.* Cambridge: Cambridge University Press, 2013.

Parkman, Aubrey. *David Jayne Hill and the Problem of World Peace.* Lewisburg, PA: Bucknell University Press, 1974.

Patterson, David S. *Toward a Warless World: The Travail of the American Peace Movement, 1887-1914.* Bloomington: Indiana University Press, 1976.

———. "The United States and the Origins of the World Court." *Political Science Quarterly* 91, no. 2 (1976): 279–95.

Paul, Arnold M. *Conservative Crisis and the Rule of Law: Attitudes of Bar and Bench, 1887-1895.* Ithaca, NY: Cornell University Press, 1960.

Pearce, Russell G. "Lawyers as America's Governing Class: The Formation and Dissolution of the Original Understanding of the American Lawyer's Role." *University of Chicago Law School Roundtable* 8 (2001): 381–421.

Pérez, Louis A., Jr. *The War of 1898: The United States and Cuba in History and Historiography.* Chapel Hill: University of North Carolina Press, 1998.

Perkins, Bradford. *The Great Rapprochement: England and the United States, 1895-1914.* New York: Atheneum, 1968.

Perreau-Saussine, Amanda. "A Case Study on Jurisprudence as a Source of International Law: Oppenheim's Influence." In *Time, History and International Law*, edited by Matthew Craven, Malgosia Fitzmaurice, and Maria Vogiatzi, 91–117. Leiden: Martinus Nijhoff, 2007.

Peterson, Harold F. *Diplomat of the Americas: A Biography of William I. Buchanan (1852-1909).* Albany: State University of New York Press, 1977.

Phelps, Nicole M. *U.S.-Habsburg Relations from 1815 to the Paris Peace Conference: Sovereignty Transformed.* Cambridge: Cambridge University Press, 2013.

Pike, Frederick B. *Chile and the United States, 1880-1962.* Notre Dame, IN: University of Notre Dame Press, 1963.

——. *The United States and Latin America: Myths and Stereotypes of Civilization and Nature.* Austin: University of Texas Press, 1992.

Pires, Homero. *Anglo-American Political Influences on Rui Barbosa.* Translated by Sylvia Medrado Clinton. Río de Janeiro: Casa de Rui Barbosa, 1949.

Piscatori, James P. "Law, Peace, and War in American International Legal Thought." In *American Thinking about Peace and War: New Essays on American Thoughts and Attitudes*, edited by Ken Booth and Moorhead Wright, 135–57. New York: Barnes and Noble, 1978.

Pitts, Jennifer. *A Turn to Empire: The Rise of Imperial Liberalism in Britain and France.* Princeton, NJ: Princeton University Press, 2005.

Pletcher, David M. *The Awkward Years: American Foreign Relations under Garfield and Arthur.* Columbia: University of Missouri Press, 1962.

——. "Caribbean 'Empire,' Planned and Improvised." *Diplomatic History* 14, no. 3 (1990): 447–60.

Plischke, Elmer. *U.S. Department of State: a Reference History.* Westport, CT: Greenwood Press, 1999.

Posner, Eric A. *The Perils of Global Legalism.* Chicago: University of Chicago Press, 2009.

Pugach, Noel H. *Paul S. Reinsch: Open Door Diplomat in Action.* Millwood, NY: KTO Press, 1979.

Rabban, David M. *Law's History: American Legal Thought and the Transatlantic Turn to History.* Cambridge: Cambridge University Press, 2014.

Rajkovic, Nikolas M. "'Global Law' and Governmentality: Reconceptualizing the 'Rule of Law' as Rule 'through' Law." *European Journal of International Relations* 18, no. 1 (2012): 29–52.

Rauchway, Eric. *Blessed among Nations: How the World Made America.* New York: Hill and Wang, 2006.

Raustiala, Kal. *Does the Constitution Follow the Flag? The Evolution of Territoriality in American Law.* New York: Oxford University Press, 2009.

Reid, Cecilie. "American Internationalism: Peace Advocacy and International Relations 1895-1916." PhD diss., Boston College, 2005.

Renda, Mary. *Taking Haiti: Military Occupation and the Culture of U.S. Imperialism, 1915-1940.* Chapel Hill: University of North Carolina Press, 2001.

Reynolds, David. *From Munich to Pearl Harbor: Roosevelt's America and the Origins of the Second World War.* Chicago: Ivan R. Dee, 2001.

——. *The Long Shadow: The Legacies of the Great War in the Twentieth Century.* New York: W. W. Norton, 2014.

Ricard, Serge. "The Exceptionalist Syndrome in U.S. Continental and Overseas Expansionism." In *Reflections on American Exceptionalism*, edited by David K. Adams and Cornelius A. van Minnen, 73–82. Staffordshire, UK: Keele University Press, 1994.

Rippy, J. Fred. "Antecedents of the Roosevelt Corollary of the Monroe Doctrine." *Pacific Historical Review* 9, no. 3 (1940): 267–79.

Roberts, Priscilla. "Paul D. Cravath, the first World War, and the Anglophile Internationalist Tradition." *Australian Journal of Politics and History* 51, no. 2 (2005): 194–215.

Rodgers, Daniel. *Atlantic Crossings: Social Politics in a Progressive Age.* Cambridge, MA: Harvard University Press, 1998.

——. "Exceptionalism." In *Imagined Histories: American Historians Interpret the Past,* edited by Anthony Molho and Gordon S. Wood, 21–40. Princeton, NJ: Princeton University Press, 1998.

Rosenberg, Emily S. *Financial Missionaries to the World: The Politics and Culture of Dollar Diplomacy, 1900-1930.* Durham, NC: Duke University Press, 2003.

——. *Spreading the American Dream: American Economic and Cultural Expansion, 1890-1945.* New York: Hill and Wang, 1982.

——. "Transnational Currents in a Shrinking World." In *A World Connecting, 1870-1945,* edited by Emily S. Rosenberg, 815–996. Cambridge, MA: Harvard University Press, 2012.

Rosenthal, Michael. *Nicholas Miraculous: The Amazing Career of the Redoubtable Dr. Nicholas Murray Butler.* New York: Farrar, Straus and Giroux, 2006.

Ross, Dorothy. *The Origins of American Social Science.* New York: Cambridge University Press, 1991.

Rossi, Christopher. *Broken Chain of Being: James Brown Scott and the Origins of Modern International Law.* The Hague: Kluwer Law International, 1998.

Rossini, Daniela, ed. *From Theodore Roosevelt to FDR: Internationalism and Isolationsim in American Foreign Policy.* Staffordshire, UK: Ryburn Publishing, Keele University Press, 1995.

Rotundo, E. Anthony. *American Manhood: Transformations in Masculinity from the Revolution to the Modern Era.* New York: Basic Books, 1993.

Rouleau, Brian. *With Sails Whitening Every Sea: Mariners and the Making of an American Maritime Empire.* Ithaca, NY: Cornell University Press, 2014.

Rubery, Matthew. *The Novelty of Newspapers: Victorian Fiction after the Invention of the News.* Oxford: Oxford University Press, 2009.

Rubin, Alfred P. "The Concept of Neutrality in International Law." In *Neutrality: Changing Concepts and Practices,* edited by Alan T. Leonhard, 9-34. New York: University Press of America, 1988.

Ruskola, Teemu. "Canton Is Not Boston: The Invention of American Imperial Sovereignty." *American Quarterly* 57, no. 3 (2005): 859–84.

Sacriste, Gillaume, and Antoine Vauchez. "The Force of International Law: Lawyers' Diplomacy on the International Scene in the 1920s." *Law and Social Inquiry* 32, no. 1 (2007): 83–107.

Saito, Natsu Taylor. *Meeting the Enemy: American Exceptionalism and International Law.* New York: New York University Press, 2010.

Salvatore, Ricardo. "The Making of a Hemispheric Intellectual-Statesman: Leo S. Rowe in Argentina (1906–1919)." *Journal of Transnational American Studies* 2, no. 1 (2010): 1–36.

Sanders, Elizabeth. *Roots of Reform: Farmers, Workers, and the American State, 1877-1917.* Chicago: University of Chicago Press, 1999.

Sands, Philippe. *Lawless World: America and the Making and Breaking of Global Rules from FDR's Atlantic Charter to George W. Bush's Illegal War.* New York: Viking, 2005.

Scarfi, Juan Pablo. *El Imperio de la Ley: James Brown Scott y la Construcción de un Orden Jurídico Interamericano.* Buenos Aires: Fondo de Cultura Económica de Argentina, 2014.

——. "In the Name of the Americas: The Pan-American Redefinition of the Monroe Doctrine and the Emerging Language of American International Law in the Western Hemisphere, 1898-1933." *Diplomatic History,* 40, no. 2 (2016): 189–218.

Schachter, Oscar. "The Invisible College of International Lawyers." *Northwestern University Law Review* 72, no. 2 (1977): 217–26.

Scharf, Michael P. "International Law in Crisis: A Qualitative Empirical Contribution to the Compliance Debate." *Cardozo Law Review* 31, no. 1 (2009): 45–97.

Scharf, Michael P., and Paul R. Williams. *Shaping Foreign Policy in Times of Crisis: The Role of International Law and the State Department Legal Adviser*. Cambridge: Cambridge University Press, 2010.

Schmidt, Brian C. *The Political Discourse of Anarchy: A Disciplinary History of International Relations*. Albany: State University of New York Press, 1998.

Schmitt, Carl. *The Nomos of the Earth in the International Law of the Jus Publicum Europaeum*. Translated by G. L. Ulmen. New York: Telos Press, 2003. Originally published in 1950.

Schmoeckel, Mathias. "The Internationalist as a Scientist and Herald: Lassa Oppenheim." *European Journal of International Law* 11, no. 3 (2000): 699–712.

Scholes, Walter V., and Marie V. Scholes. *The Foreign Policies of the Taft Administration*. Columbia: University of Missouri Press, 1970.

Schoonover, Thomas D. "Morality and Political Purpose in Theodore Roosevelt's Actions in Panama in 1903." In *The United States in Central America, 1860-1911: Episodes of Social Imperialism and Imperial Rivalry in the World System*, 97–110. Durham, NC: Duke University Press, 1991.

Schoultz, Lars. *Beneath the United States: A History of U.S. Policy Toward Latin America*. Cambridge, MA: Harvard University Press, 1998.

Schwarzenberger, Georg. "The Standard of Civilisation in International Law," *Current Legal Problems* 8:1 (1955): 212–35.

Schulzinger, Robert D. *The Making of the Diplomatic Mind: The Training, Outlook, and Style of United States Foreign Service Officers, 1908-1931*. Middletown, CT: Wesleyan University Press, 1975.

——. *The Wise Men of Foreign Affairs: The History of the Council on Foreign Relations*. New York: Columbia University Press, 1984.

Scott-Smith, Giles. "Attempting to Secure an 'Orderly Evolution': American Foundations, The Hague Academy of International Law and the Third World." *Journal of American Studies* 41, no. 3 (2007): 509–32.

Scully, Eileen P. *Bargaining with the State from Afar: American Citizenship in Treaty Port China, 1844-1942*. New York: Columbia University Press, 2001.

Sexton, Jay. *The Monroe Doctrine: Empire and Nation in Nineteenth-Century America*. New York: Hill and Wang, 2011.

Shea, Donald R. *The Calvo Clause: A Problem of Inter-American and International Law and Diplomacy*. Minneapolis: University of Minnesota Press, 1955.

Shinohara, Hatsue. *US International Lawyers in the Interwar Years: A Forgotten Crusade*. Cambridge: Cambridge University Press, 2012.

Shklar, Judith. *Legalism: Law, Morals, and Political Trials*. Cambridge, MA: Harvard University Press, 1964.

Siegel, Stephen A. "Francis Wharton's Orthodoxy: God, Historical Jurisprudence, and Classical Legal Thought." *American Journal of Legal History* 46, no. 4 (2004): 422–46.

——. "Joel Bishop's Orthodoxy." *Law and History Review* 13, no. 2 (1995): 215–59.

——. "Lochner Era Jurisprudence and the American Constitutional Tradition." *North Carolina Law Review* 70 (1991): 1–111.

Silbey, David J. *A War of Frontier and Empire: The Philippine-American War, 1899-1902*. New York: Hill and Wang, 2007.

Simmons, Beth A., and Richard H. Steinberg, eds. *International Law and International Relations*. Cambridge: Cambridge University Press, 2006.

Simpson, Gerry. *Great Powers and Outlaw States: Unequal Sovereigns in the International Legal Order*. Cambridge: Cambridge University Press, 2004.

Siracusa, Joseph M. "Progressivism, Imperialism, and the Leuchtenberg Thesis, 1952-1974: An Historiographical Appraisal." *Australian Journal of Politics and History* 20 (December 1974): 312–25.

Skowronek, Stephen. *Building a New American State: The Expansion of National Administrative Capacities, 1877-1920*. New York: Cambridge University Press, 1982.

Slaughter Burley, Anne-Marie. "International Law and International Relations Theory: A Dual Agenda." *American Journal of International Law* 87, no. 2 (1993): 205–39.

Slotkin Richard. *Gunfighter Nation: The Myth of the Frontier in Twentieth-Century America.* Norman: University of Oklahoma Press, 1992.

Sluga, Glenda. *Internationalism in the Age of Nationalism.* Philadelphia: University of Pennsylvania Press, 2013.

Smith, Daniel Malloy. "National Interest and American Intervention, 1917: An Historiographical Appraisal." *Journal of American History* 52, no. 1 (1965): 5–24.

——. *Robert Lansing and American Neutrality, 1914-1917.* Berkeley: University of California Press, 1958.

Smith, Neil. *American Empire: Roosevelt's Geographer and the Prelude to Globalization.* Berkeley: University of California Press, 2003.

Solberg, Winton U. *The University of Illinois, 1894-1904: The Shaping of the University.* Urbana: University of Illinois Press, 2000.

Sparrow, Bartholomew. *The Insular Cases and the Emergence of American Empire.* Lawrence: Kansas University Press, 2006.

Spiermann, Ole. "'Who Attempts Too Much Does Nothing Well': The 1920 Advisory Committee of Jurists and the Statute of the Permanent Court of International Justice." *British Year Book of International Law 2002* 73 (2003): 187–260.

Spiro, Peter J. "The New Sovereigntists: American Exceptionalism and Its False Prophets." *Foreign Affairs* 79, no. 6 (2000): 9–15.

Sproat, John G. *"The Best Men": Liberal Reformers in the Gilded Age.* New York: Oxford University Press, 1968.

Stanley, Peter W. *A Nation in the Making: The Philippines and the United States, 1899-1921.* Cambridge, MA: Harvard University Press, 1974.

Steigerwald, David. The Reclamation of Woodrow Wilson?" *Diplomatic History* 23, no. 1 (1999): 79–99.

——. *Wilsonian Idealism in America.* Ithaca, NY: Cornell University Press, 1994.

Steinberg, Richard H., and Jonathan Zasloff. "Power and International Law." *AJIL* 100, no. 1 (2006): 64–87.

Stephanson, Anders. *Manifest Destiny.* New York: Hill and Wang, 1995.

Sterzel, Fredrik. *The Inter-Parliamentary Union.* Stockholm: P.A. Norstedt & Söner, 1968.

Stevens, Robert. *Law School: Legal Education in America from the 1850s to the 1980s.* Chapel Hill: University of North Carolina Press, 1983.

Strachan, Hew. *The First World War.* New York: Viking, 2004.

Strout, Cushing. *The American Image of the Old World.* New York: Harper and Row, 1963.

Stuart, Graham. *The Department of State: A History of Its Organization, Procedure, and Personnel.* New York: MacMillan, 1949.

Sullivan, William Maurice. "The Rise of Despotism in Venezuela: Cipriano Castro, 1899-1908." PhD diss., University of New Mexico, 1974.

Suganami, Hidemi. *The Domestic Analogy and World Order Proposals.* Cambridge: Cambridge University Press, 1989.

——. "A Note on the Origin of the Word 'International,'" *British Journal of International Studies* 4, no. 3 (1978): 226–32.

Suskind, Ron. "Faith, Certainty, and the Presidency of George W. Bush." *New York Times Magazine,* October 17, 2004.

Suzuki, Shogo. *Civilization and Empire: China and Japan's Encounter with European International Society.* New York: Routledge, 2009.

Sylvest, Casper. "Continuity and Change in British Liberal Internationalism, c. 1900-1930." *Review of International Studies* 31 (2005): 263–83.

——. "The Foundations of Victorian International Law." In *Victorian Visions of Global Order: Empire and International Relations in Nineteenth-Century Political Thought,* edited by Duncan Bell, 47–66. Cambridge: Cambridge University Press, 2007.

——. "International Law in Nineteenth-Century Britain." *British Year Book of International Law* 75 (2005): 9–70.

——. "'Our Passion for Legality': International Law and Imperialism in Late Nineteenth-Century Britain." *Review of International Studies* 34 (2008): 403–23.

Tamanaha, Brian Z. *Beyond the Formalist-Realist Divide: The Role of Politics in Judging.* Princeton, NJ: Princeton University Press, 2010.

——. "What Is Law?" Washington University in Saint Louis School of Law Legal Studies Research Paper Series no. 15-01-0. January 2015.

Tananbaum, Duane. *The Bricker Amendment Controversy: A Test of Eisenhower's Political Leadership.* Ithaca, NY: Cornell University Press, 1988.

Tansill, Charles Callan. *America Goes to War.* Boston: Little, Brown, 1938.

Thompson, John A. "Wilsonianism: The Dynamics of a Conflicted Concept." *International Affairs* 86, no. 1 (2010): 27–48.

——. "Woodrow Wilson and World War I: A Reappraisal." *Journal of American Studies* 19, no. 3 (1985): 325–48.

Thomson, Janice E. *Mercenaries, Pirates, and Sovereigns: State-Building and Extraterritorial Violence in Early Modern Europe.* Princeton, NJ: Princeton University Press, 1994.

Throntveit, Trygve. "'Common Counsel': Woodrow Wilson's Pragmatic Progressivism, 1885-1913." In *Reconsidering Woodrow Wilson: Progressivism, Internationalism, War, and Peace,* edited by John Milton Cooper, Jr., 25–56. Baltimore: Johns Hopkins University Press, 2008.

Tompkins, E. Berkeley. *Anti-Imperialism in the United States: The Great Debate, 1890-1920.* Philadelphia: University of Pennsylvania Press, 1970.

Tooze, Adam. *The Deluge: The Great War, America and the Remaking of the Global Order, 1916-1931.* New York: Viking, 2014.

Tucker, Robert. *Woodrow Wilson and the Great War: Reconsidering America's Neutrality 1914-1917.* Charlottesville: University of Virginia Press, 2007.

Tucker, Robert W., and David C. Hendrickson. *Empire of Liberty: The Statecraft of Thomas Jefferson.* New York: Oxford University Press, 1990.

Turner, Charles W. *Ruy Barbosa: Brazilian Crusader for the Essential Freedoms.* New York: Abingdon-Cokesbury Press, 1945.

Tuveson, Ernest Lee. *Redeemer Nation: The Idea of America's Millennial Role.* Chicago: University of Chicago Press, 1968.

Tyler, Tom R. *Why People Obey the Law.* Princeton, NJ: Princeton University Press, 2006. Originally published by Yale University Press in 1990.

Tyrrell, Ian. *Reforming the World: The Creation of America's Moral Empire.* Princeton, NJ: Princeton University Press, 2010.

Unterman, Katherine. "Boodle over the Border: Embezzlement and the Crisis of International Mobility, 1880-1890." *Journal of Gilded Age and Progressive Era* 11, no. 2 (2012): 151–89.

Vallenilla, Nikita Harwich. *Asfalto y Revolución: la New York & Bermudez Company.* Caracas: Monte Avila Editores, 1992.

van Alstyne, Richard. "The Policy of the United States Regarding the Declaration of London at the Outbreak of the Great War." *Journal of Modern History* 7 (1935): 434–47.

Vauchez, Antoine. "The Making of the International Professional: The Drafting of the first World Court and the Genesis of the International Way of Expertise." Unpublished manuscript in the author's possession.

Veenswijk, Virginia Kays. *Coudert Brothers: A Legacy in Law: The History of America's First International Law Firm, 1853-1993.* New York: Truman Talley Books, 1994.

Veeser, Cyrus. *A World Safe for Capitalism: Dollar Diplomacy and America's Rise to Global Power.* New York: Columbia University Press, 2002.

Vincent, Paul. *The Politics of Hunger: The Allied Blockade of Germany, 1915-1919.* Athens: Ohio University Press, 1985.

Vivian, James F. "The Taking of the Panama Canal Zone: Myth and Reality." *Diplomatic History* 4, no. 1 (1980): 95–100.

Vitalis, Robert. "Birth of a Discipline." In *Imperialism and Internationalism in the Discipline of International Relations,* edited by Brian C. Schmidt and David Long, 159–81. Albany: State University of New York Press, 2005.

Waldron, Jeremy. "The Concept and the Rule of Law." *Georgia Law Review* 43, no. 1 (2008): 1–61.

Walters, Ronald G. *American Reformers, 1815-1860.* Rev. ed. New York: Hill and Wang, 1997. Originally published in 1978.

Watts, Sarah. *Rough Rider in the White House: Theodore Roosevelt and the Politics of Desire.* Chicago: University of Chicago Press, 2003.

Weiler, J. H. H. "The Geology of International Law: Governance, Democracy and Legitimacy." *Zeitschrift für Auslaendisches Oeffenlisches Recht und Volkerrecht* 64 (2004): 547–62.

Weiner, Mark S. "Teutonic Constitutionalism: The Role of Ethno-Juridical Discourse in the Spanish-American War." In *Foreign in a Domestic Sense: Puerto Rico, American Expansion, and the Constitution,* edited by Christina Duffy Burnett and Burke Marshall, 48–81. Durham, NC: Duke University Press, 2001.

Weitz, Eric D. "From the Vienna to the Paris System: International Politics and the Entangled Histories of Human Rights, Forced Deportations, and Civilizing Missions." *American Historical Review* 113, no. 5 (2008): 1313–43.

Werking, Richard Hume. *The Master Architects: Building the United States Foreign Service, 1890-1913.* Lexington: University Press of Kentucy, 1977.

Wertheim, Stephen. "The League That Wasn't: American Designs for a Legalist-Sanctionist League of Nations and the Intellectual Origins of International Organization, 1914-1920." *Diplomatic History* 35, no. 5 (2011): 797–836.

West, Rachel. *The Department of State on the Eve of the First World War.* Athens: University of Georgia Press, 1978.

Wetter, J. Gillis. "Diplomatic Assistance to Private Investment: A Study of the Theory and Practice of the United States During the Twentieth Century." *University of Chicago Law Review* 29 (1961–62): 275–326.

Whitaker, Arthur P. *The Western Hemisphere Idea: Its Rise and Decline.* Ithaca, NY: Cornell University Press, 1954.

Whitman, James Q. *The Verdict of Battle: The Law of Victory and the Making of Modern War.* Cambridge, MA: Harvard University Press, 2012.

Wiebe, Robert H. *The Search for Order, 1877-1920.* New York: Hill and Wang, 1967.

Wiecek, William M. *The Lost World of Classical Legal Thoughts: Law and Ideology in America, 1886-1937.* New York: Oxford University Press, 1998.

Wight, Martin. "The Balance of Power and International Order." In *The Bases of International Order: Essays in Honour of C.A.W. Manning,* edited by Alan James, 85–115. London: Oxford University Press, 1973.

Williams, Walter L. "United States Indian Policy and the Debate over Philippine Annexation: Implications for the Origins of American Imperialism." *Journal of American History* 66, no. 4 (1980): 810–31.

Williams, William Appleman. *Empire as a Way of Life.* New York: Oxford University Press, 1982.

———. "The Legend of Isolationism in the 1920's." *Science and Society* 18, no. 1 (1954): 1–20.

———. *The Tragedy of American Diplomacy.* Rev. ed. New York: W. W. Norton, 1972. Originally published in 1959.

Willis, James F. *Prologue to Nuremberg: The Politics and Diplomacy of Punishing War Criminals of the First World War.* Westport, CT: Greenwood Press, 1982.

Witt, John Fabian. "Law and War in American History." *American Historical Review* 115, no. 3 (2010): 768–78.

———. *Patriots and Cosmopolitans: Hidden Histories of American Law.* Cambridge, MA: Harvard University Press, 2007.

———. *Lincoln's Code: The Laws of War in American History.* New York: Free Press, 2012.

Wood, Molly. "'Commanding Beauty' and 'Gentle Charm': American Women and Gender in the Early Twentieth-Century Foreign Service." *Diplomatic History* 31, no. 3 (2007): 505–30.

Wrange, Pål. "Impartial or Uninvolved? The Anatomy of 20th Century Doctrine on the Law of Neutrality." PhD diss., University of Stockholm, 2007.

Zakaria, Fareed. *From Wealth to Power: The Unusual Origins of America's World Role.* Princeton, NJ: Princeton University Press, 1998.

Zasloff, Jonathan. "Law and the Shaping of American Foreign Policy: From the Gilded Age to the New Era." *New York University Law Review* 78 (April 2003): 240–373.

——. "Law and the Shaping of American Foreign Policy: The Twenty Years' Crisis." *Southern California Law Review* 77 (March 2004): 583–682.

Zimmerman, Warren. *First Great Triumph: How Five Americans Made Their Country a World Power.* New York: Farrar, Straus and Giroux, 2002.

INDEX

Academy of International Law at The Hague, 98
ACJ. *See* Advisory Committee of Jurists
Adams, Brooks, 9
Adams, Henry, 41
Adams, John Quincy, 28
Adler, Felix, 43
Adolphus, Gustavus, 18
Advisory Committee of Jurists (ACJ), 170–71
AIIL. *See* American Institute of International Law
AJIL. See American Journal of International Law
Alabama claims, 30, 101, 217n99
Alsop claim, 124, 223n145
Álvarez, Alejandro, 161, 168
American exceptionalism, 83–84, 211n216
American Institute of International Law (AIIL)
    founding of, 67, 118, 161
    Moore's criticism of, 161–62
    "Recommendations of Havana," 162
American Journal of International Law (AJIL), 67,
    71, 81–82
American Peace Society, 28–29
American Society for Judicial Settlement of
        International Disputes (ASJSID)
    manly identity and, 74, 76*f*, 208n140
    Marburg and, 68, 206n80
    overview about, 68
American Society of International Law (ASIL), 1
    Carnegie Endowment for International Peace
        and, 98
    founding members of, 2, 67, 188n12
    founding of, 66–67
    LEP and, 157, 233n56
    permanent court and, 78
    Scott and, 80
    seal of, 74, 75*f*
    women and, 74, 75*f*
Ames, James Barr, 64
Ancient Society (Morgan), 21
Anderson, Chandler P., 137, 145, 227n17
Anderson, Luis, 119
Aquinas, Thomas, 16

arbitration. *See also* Permanent Court of Arbitration
    Alabama claims and, 30, 101, 217n99
    American public and, 104
    court procedure versus, 77, 93
    Dominican Republic and, 113
    "International Arbitration" address, 60, 203n7
    McKinley and, 31
    North Atlantic Fisheries, 217n100
    NY&B and, 115
    professionalization and, 75, 77
    Roosevelt, Theodore, and, 103–4
    Scott and, 60, 77, 99, 101, 203n7, 217n100
    Taft and, 102–4
    tolls exemption and, 99–101, 102
    treaties associated with, 30
    US as champion of, 30–31
    US-Mexican Mixed Claims Commission
        and, 30–31
    US submitting to, 101–2
Argentina, 122
arms export, 143, 229n71
ASIL. *See* American Society of International Law
ASJSID. *See* American Society for Judicial
        Settlement of International Disputes
Asser, Tobias, 19
Austin, John, 62, 69, 142

Bacon, Robert, 119, 188n12
Baldwin, Simeon, 46
Barbosa, Rui, 92–93
Bayard, Thomas, 34
belligerent rights, 139–40
Bello, Andrés, 120
Benton, Lauren, 8
Berlin West Africa Conference
    Congo and, 31–34
    US non-entanglement and, 15–16
    von Bismarck and, 15
Bikle, Henry W., 46
Bolívar, Simón, 119
Bolton, John, 177

Borah, William E., 165, 172–73
Borchard, Edwin, 80, 168, 175
Bourgeois, Léon, 20, 171
Brewer, David J., 51
Briand, Aristide, 174
Britain
    arms export and, 143
    Germany compared with, 146–47
    international law violations of, 143–45
    neutrality and, 143–44
    Order in Council and, 143, 144
    reacting to, 142–48
    Root and, 230n115
    Scott and, 146
Brown, Henry Billings, 47
Bryan, William Jennings, 188n12
    background about, 127
    Colombia and, 226n234
    cooling off peace treaties and, 127
    interventionist tendencies of, 134
    Mexico and, 129
    Moore and, 128
    Nicaragua and, 134
    Root and, 50
Buchanan, James, 130
Buchanan, William I., 119
Bunau-Varilla, Philippe, 53, 55, 201n78
Burritt, Elihu, 29
Bush, George W., 177
Bush administration, 177–78, 182
Butler, Nicholas Murray, 73

CACJ. *See* Central American Court of Justice
Calvo, Carlos, 120, 121
Carnegie, Andrew, 67, 88, 119
Carnegie Endowment for International Peace, 12,
        67, 205n74
    ASIL and, 98
    court campaign of, 95–98
    Institut de droit international and, 95, 97–98
    legal publications subsidized by, 98
    Oppenheim on, 74
    "Peace Through Victory" slogan of, 150
    Scott and, 67, 96–98
    tolls exemption and, 100
Carnegie Endowment's Division of International
        Law, 67, 80, 96, 98, 141, 159
Carranza, Venustiano, 132
case method
    Langdell and, 63–64
    Scott and, 65–66
Cases on International Law (Scott), 65–66
Cass, Lewis, 54
Castro, Cipriano, 111, 115, 123
Central American Court of Justice (CACJ)
    creation of, 119
    dissolution of, 127
Chamberlain, Joseph, 42, 80
Chile, 124, 223n145
Choate, Joseph, 79, 87
    at The Hague, 90–94

Christianity, peace movement and, 28
"Chronicle of International Events" (*AJIL*), 71
civilization
    Colombia and, 57
    empire and, 21–24, 43
    etymology of term, 193n29
    Latin America and, 120–21
    mission of, 23–24
    moral mandate from, 56–57
    nationalism and, 194n43
    overcivilization, 104
    race and, 22
    sociopolitical organization and, 21–22
    standard of, 21
    unidirectional, 172
Civil War
    neutrality and, 139
    peace movement and, 29–30
Clark, J. Reuben, 124, 223n150
classical legal thought
    business interests and, 69
    criticism of, 68–69
    customary law and, 70–71
    historical jurisprudence and, 69–70
    individual rights and, 70
    international law and, 68–74
    judicial supremacy and, 71
    nuanced perspective on, 69–70, 206n91
    objective truth and, 70
    peace and, 72–73
    science and, 72
    synonyms for, 206n84
    variety within, 69–70
    world government and, 71–72
coastwise, 99, 215n71
codification, 71, 95, 173
Colombia, 53–55, 57, 226n234
Columbia University, 35, 60
Comité Consultatif de la Fondation Carnegie,
        97, 215n67
Congo
    innocents abroad in, 31–34
    Institut de droit international and, 32
    International Association
        of the Congo, 32–33
Conrad, Joseph, 33
Constitution of the United States, 25
    made safe for empire, 45–49
contraband, 140–41
Coolidge, Calvin, 174
cooling off peace treaties, 127
Corollary to Monroe Doctrine, 112
Coudert, Frederic, 157
Creel, Enrique C., 119
Cromwell, William Nelson, 53
Cuba, 40–41, 118. *See also* Platt Amendment.
customary law, 70–71

Davis, George B., 111
Declaration of Independence, 24–25
Declaration of London, 140

Declaration of Rights and Duties of States, 236n139
Declaration of the Rights and Duties of Nations, 161
Declaration of the Rights of Man, 168
decolonization, 180–81
De Jure Belli ac Pacis (Grotius), 16, 17, 18
Dennis, William Cullen, 57
de Tocqueville, Alexis, 29
Dewey, John, 174
Díaz, Porfirio, 128
Dickman, John, 41
A Digest of International Law (Moore), 36, 57–58, 136
diplomatic precedent, 219n50
Dodge, David Low, 28
dollar diplomacy, 124–25, 134
Dominican Republic, 134
    arbitration and, 113
    Corollary to Monroe Doctrine and, 112
    Grant and, 2
    Moore and, 112–15
    Roosevelt, Theodore, and, 113–14
    SDIC and, 112–15
Dorr v. United States, 48
Downes v. Bidwell, 47
Drago, Luis María, 120, 121–22
Drago Doctrine, 120, 121–22, 222n129
Draper, Andrew, 59
Dred Scott v. Sanford, 45
Le droit international théorique et pratique (Calvo), 120
Dunne, Finley Peter, 47

education
    peace movement and, 73
    professionalization and, 78–79
Edwards, Jonathan, 37
Elements of International Law (Wheaton), 21, 29
Eliot, Charles, 63, 64
empire
    anti-imperialism and, 41
    civilization and, 21–24, 43
    Constitution made safe for, 45–49
    embracing of, 177–78
    era of, 42
    imperialist proponents and, 42–43
    international, 11, 191n45
    international law against, 34–38
    international law and, 5–9, 34–38
    justification of, 12
    legitimizing of, 6
    Moore and, 36
    of nation-states, 8, 110, 191n45
    in Philippines, 49–52
    US as legalist, 2–3
entrepreneurs. *See* transnational norm entrepreneurs
An Essay on a Congress of Nations (Ladd), 28
Europe. *See also specific country*
    civilization and empire and, 21–24

international law origins in, 16–18
exceptionalism. *See* American exceptionalism

Fauchille, Paul, 80, 210n190
LaFeber, Walter, 56
Fenwick, Charles, 175
Fiske, John, 9
Fleming v. Page, 45
folk international law, 7
foreign policy
    American tradition of, 24–26
    commerce over politics in, 25
    establishment of, 2–3, 188n13
    Latin America and, 116–19
    legalist expertise and, 116–19
    Manifest Destiny and, 25–26
    Monroe Doctrine and, 25
    US values of, 25–26
Foster, John W., 87
Franco-Prussian War, 19
Franklin, Benjamin, 24
Frelinghuysen, Frederick, 31–32
Fuller, Melville W., 48

Galván, Manuel de Jesus, 113
Garrison, William Lloyd, 28
gender roles, 208n140
General Orders No. 100, 50
Germany
    arms export and, 143
    atrocities and, 146, 230n106
    Britain compared with, 146–47
    Lansing and, 145, 147–48
    nationalism of, 147
    Oppenheim and, 146
    Order in Council and, 143, 144
    reacting to, 142–48
    Root and, 147
    stance against, 145–46
    submarine blockade and, 145–46, 149, 231n142
Gompers, Samuel, 41
Gonzales, Alberto, 177
Grant, Ulysses S., 2
Gray, George, 113
Great War. *See* World War I
Grotius, Hugo, 16, 17, 18, 86
The Hague
    Academy of International Law at, 98
    Barbosa at, 92
    Choate at, 90–94
    judicialists promote international court at, 88–95
    Peace Conference of 1899, 86-87
    Peace Conference of 1907, 87-88
    Porter Convention adoption at, 122
    presence at, 88
    Roosevelt, Theodore, and, 89–90
    Scott at, 90–94
    selection of judges and, 91–92
    sovereignty and, 94

Haiti, 134, 225n211
Hall, W. E., 114
Harding, Warren G., 172
Harlan, John Marshall, 48
Harris, Susan, 199n20
Harrison, Benjamin, 31
Harvard method of legal instruction, 63–65
Hay, John, 115
Hay-Bunau-Varilla treaty, 57
Hay-Pauncefote Treaty, 99
Heart of Darkness (Conrad), 33
Henkin, Louis, 6
Hershey, Amos, 147
Hershey, Omer, 78
Herzberg, Henry, 99
Heureaux, Ulises, 112
Hilfrich, Fabian, 199n20
Hill, David Jayne, 166
historical jurisprudence, 69–70
history
    civilization and empire and, 21–24
    of international law, 7–8
    international law's origins in, 16–18
    Latin America and, 119–20
    neutrality and, 138–39
    overview, 12
    of professionalization, 18–21
*History and Digest of the International Arbitrations
    to Which the United States Has Been a Party*
    (Moore), 36
Holland, T E., 22
Hollweg, Theobald von Bethmann, 147
Holman, Frank, 181
Holmes, Oliver Wendell, Jr., 59
    Langdell and, 68–69
Holt, Hamilton, 155
Hornbeck, Stanley, 159
Hudson, Manley, 169, 234n91
Huerta, Victoriano, 129, 131, 132,
    224n195
Hughes, Charles Evans, 170
Hugo, Victor, 29
Hunt, Michael, 2

impartiality, 139, 227n32
individual rights, 70
The Inquiry, 163, 234n91
In re Ross, 45
insignias, 74, 75f, 76f, 208n140
Institut de droit international
    Carnegie Endowment for International Peace
        and, 95, 97–98
    Congo and, 32
    Declaration of Rights and Duties of States and,
        236n139
    Declaration of the Rights of Man endorsed
        by, 168
    establishment of, 19
    positivism and, 20

postwar challenges of, 167
Root and, 167
Scott and, 167–68
Scott's Washington invitation to, 167
Institutes of the Law of Nations (Lorimer), 21
"International Arbitration" (Scott), 60, 203n7
International Association of the Congo, 32–33
international empire, 191n45
    American principles spread via, 11
internationalist constitutionalism, 118
international law. *See also* professionalization, of
        international law
    American foreign policy tradition and, 24–26
    appeal of, 9–12
    Austin and, 62
    authority for, 17–18
    Britain violating, 143–45
    civilizing mission of, 10
    classical legal thought and, 68–74
    conclusions about, 177–83
    as coordinating mechanism, 6, 189n32
    debated in US, 99–106
    against empire, 34–38
    of empire, 5–9
    empire of nation-states and, 8, 191n45
    erosion of popularity in, 180–82
    folk, 7
    global politics and, 6
    Grotius and, 16, 17, 18
    as hegemonic technique, 122–23
    historical analysis of, 7–8
    history leading to, 16–18
    Koskenniemi and, 207n108
    from law of nations to, 16–18
    modern, 168–70
    natural law and, 17–18, 192n12
    positive law and, 17–18, 192n12
    positivism era in, 19–20
    state compliance to, 6–7
    transnational norm entrepreneurs and, 7
    US and, 26–31, 99–106, 180–82
    US as champion of, 26–31
    Vitoria and, 17
    Wilson, Woodrow, as skeptic of, 125–28, 131–32
    Wilson, Woodrow, on, 61
International Prize Court, 214n55. *See also* Prize
        Court Convention
isolationism
    critiques of, 192n2
    non-entanglement versus, 15

Jackson, Robert H., 239n17
Jay Treaty, 30
Jefferson, Thomas, 25
Jessup, Philip C., 181
Jèze, Gaston, 23
judge myth, 74
judicialism, 188n16
judicialists

The Hague and, 88–95
international court promoted by, 88–95
sensibility, 3, 68
jus gentium (law of peoples), 16

Kasson, John, 32
Kellogg, Frank, 174
Kellogg-Briand Pact, 173–75
Kent, James, 29
Ker v. Illinois, 45
Kinley, David, 59
Kirchwey, George, 66
Klüber, Johann, 20
Knox, Philander C., 116
dollar diplomacy and, 124–25
Latin America and, 123–24
on nationalism and internationalism, 171–72
Outlawry of War movement and, 174
Taft and, 123
Kohler, Joseph, 147
Koskenniemi, Martti, 122–23, 207n108
Kramer, Paul, 191n45
Kuehl, Warren, 216n97

Ladd, William, 28
Lake Mohonk Conference, 66, 158
Langdell, C. C., 46
case method and, 63–64
on constitution and empire, 46
Holmes and, 68–69
legal science and, 63–64
on women in law, 65
Lansing, Robert, 144
background about, 141–42
Germany and, 145, 147–48
Paris Peace Conference and, 153
as realist, 141
sovereignty and, 142
State Department and, 133
Latin America. *See also specific country*
AIIL and, 161
Alsop claim and, 124, 223n145
civilization and, 120–21
continuities and departures in US policy
toward, 132–35
Corollary to Monroe Doctrine and, 112
Declaration of the Rights and Duties of Nations
and, 161
dollar diplomacy and, 124–25, 134
foreign policy state and, 116–19
globalization and intervention and, 111–15
instability in, 107
international institutions of law and, 118–19
internationalism history in, 119–20
Knox and, 123–24
legalist expertise and, 116–19
overview, 13
Root and, 107, 121–22
sovereignty and, 120

state submission and, 121–22
Wilson, Woodrow, as international law skeptic
and, 125–28
law of peoples. *See jus gentium*
Lawrence, T. J., 20, 96–97
League of Nations, 4
anti-legalist, 162–67
covenant of, 163
Hill and, 166
PCIJ and, 171, 173
Root and, 165–66, 235n111
US rejection of, 164
Wilson, Woodrow, vision of, 162–63, 234n89
League of Universal Brotherhood, 29
League to Enforce Peace (LEP)
articles of, 154
ASIL and, 157, 233n56
cartoon commemorating first meeting of, 159, 160f
dissenting legalist and, 156–58
enforced law and, 154–56
founding of, 154
intellectual and institutional struggles, 158–62
legalist-sanctionist view of, 162
Lowell and, 154–55
lynch mob analogy for, 158
membership, 154, 155–56, 157, 232n15, 233n56
Moore and, 157–58
popularity increasing for, 158–59
Root and, 164
Scott and, 157, 158–60
second public meeting of, 155–56
Taft and, 154
legalism
conclusions about, 177–83
defined, 3, 188n16
domestic jurisprudence shaping, 68–74
eclipse of, 167–70
future for, 182–83
mirages of interwar, 170–76
popularity of, 4
public opinion and, 73, 208n128
Roosevelt, Theodore, and, 4
science and, 9, 72
split in ranks of, 13–14
strategic, 50
US elites embracing, 12–13
US government embracing, 4, 12–13, 86–90
violent expansion and, 4–5
Wilson, Woodrow, and, 4, 126–27
world government and, 71–72
legalists
dissenting, 156–58
foreign policy and, 116–19
future for, 182–83
League of Nations and, 162–67
legalist-sanctionist view, 162
LEP and, 156–58, 162
Paris Peace Conference and, 152–53
US as empire of, 2–3

legal realism. *See* classical legal thought
Leopold II, 32–33
LEP. *See* League to Enforce Peace
Levinson, Salmon, 173–74
Lieber, Francis, 19, 22, 29, 30–31, 50
Lieber Code, 29–30
Lochner v. New York, 69
Lodge, Henry Cabot, 42
Loomis, Francis B., 53, 115, 201n69
Lorimer, James, 21
Lowell, Abbot Lawrence, 48, 154–55, 159
Lusitania, 149
lynch mob analogy, 158

Madero, Francisco, 128–29, 224n195
Maguire, Peter, 50
Mahan, Alfred Thayer, 45, 58, 139
Mandelstam, Andre, 168
Manifest Destiny, 25–26
manly identity, 74, 76*f*, 104, 208n140
Mann, Michael, 222n134
Marburg, Theodore, 68, 83, 161, 206n80
Mare Liberum (Grotius), 16
Marti, José, 31
McCarthy, Joseph, 181
McKinley, William
    arbitration and, 31
    Hague Peace Conference and, 87
    Root and, 39
merchantmen, 148–50
Merignhac, Alexandre, 23
Mexico
    Bryan and, 129
    Moore and, 129–31
    nonrecognition and intervention in, 128–32
    possible war with, 131–32, 225n219,
        225n223
    recognition and, 130–31, 225n217
    revolution in, 128–29
    Wilson, Woodrow, and, 128–32, 225n206,
        225n217, 225n219, 225n223
Mill, John Stuart
    on savage humanity, 22–23
    on savage life, 21–22
Miller, David Hunter, 153
mirages of interwar legalism, 170–76
Monroe, James, 25
Monroe Doctrine
    challenges to, 43–44
    Corollary to, 112
    foreign policy and, 25
Montague, Andrew J., 97
Moore, John Bassett, 2, 61, 97, 137
    AIIL, criticism of, 161–62
    background of, 34
    Bryan and, 128
    cartoon of, 133*f*
    at Columbia University, 35
    conservatism of, 48–49
    A Digest of International Law and, 36, 57–58, 136

diplomatic precedent and, 219n50
Dominican Republic and, 112–15
duties of, 35
empire and, 36
Lawrence and, 96–97
LEP and, 157–58
memorandum to Roosevelt, Theodore, by, 53–
    55, 201n69, 201n78
Mexico and, 129–31
moral mandate from civilization and, 56–57
Panama Canal and, 53
Panama policy and, 55–56, 202n93
Paris Peace Conference and, 153
PCIJ and, 237n183
positivism and, 35
Prize Court Convention and, 140
as realist, 35–36
recognition of Mexico and, 130–31
resignation of, 132, 133*f*
State Department and, 34–35, 117
State Department confidants of, 219n31
treaty rights and, 56
Venezuela and, 114–15
Wharton and, 197n102
Wilson, Woodrow, and, 35, 128, 131–32
works of, 35, 36
Morgan, Lewis Henry, 21
Moynier, Gustave, 19

nationalism
    civilization and, 194n43
    of Germany, 147
natural law, positive law and, 17–18, 192n12
Nazis, 180, 239n17
neoliberal institutionalism, 189n32
neutrality
    armed merchantmen and, 148–50
    belligerent rights and, 139–40
    Britain and, 143–44
    changing conceptions of, 138–42
    Civil War and, 139
    connotations of, 139
    contraband and, 140–41
    history surrounding, 138–39
    impartiality and, 139, 227n32
    Mahan and, 139
    The Neutrality Laws of the United States, 141
    Scott and, 141
    self-interest versus, 27
    submarines and, 148–50
    trusteeship and, 142–43
    US as champion of, 27–28
    Wilson, Woodrow, and, 137–38, 227n20
    World War I and, 137–42, 227n20
Neutrality Act (1935), 175
The Neutrality Laws of the United States (Carnegie
    Endowment's Division of International
    Law), 141
"New Aspects of International Law" (Politis), 168–69
New Sovereigntists, 177

New York & Bermudez Company (NY&B)
    arbitration and, 115
    Loomis and, 115
    precedents of law and, 115
    Venezuela and, 111, 114–15, 123
New York Peace Society, 28
Nicaragua, 134
Nicholas II, 86, 212n9
non-entanglement
    Berlin West Africa Conference and, 15–16
    Washington and, 2, 15
Norris, George, 173
North Atlantic Fisheries arbitration, 217n100
NY&B. *See* New York & Bermudez Company
Nys, Ernest, 20, 23

objective truth, 70
O'Gorman, James, 105
Olivart, Marquis de, 98
Olney, Richard, 8, 44, 55, 57
Olney-Pauncefote Treaty, 30
Oppenheim, Lassa, 96
    on Carnegie Endowment, 74
    Germany and, 146
    positivism and, 197n100
    science and, 72
    on World War I, 136
Order in Council, British, 143, 144
O'Sullivan, John, 26, 29
Outlawry of War movement, 173–74
overcivilization, 104

Panama
    legalizing, 57–58
    Moore defending policy in, 55–56, 202n93
    moral mandate from civilization and, 56–57
    taking, 52–57
    treaty rights and, 56
    Woolsey, Theodore Salisbury, and, 55
Panama Canal
    coastwise and, 99, 215n71
    Moore and, 53
    Panama Canal Act, 99, 215n72
    tolls exemption and, 99–100, 104–5, 216n76
Paris Peace Conference
    Lansing and, 153
    legalists absent at, 152–53
    Moore and, 153
    Wilson, Woodrow, and, 152
PCA. *See* Permanent Court of Arbitration
PCIJ. *See* Permanent Court of International
    Justice
peace. *See also* Carnegie Endowment for
        International Peace; Hague Peace
        Conference; League to Enforce Peace; Paris
        Peace Conference
    American Peace Society, 28–29
    classical legal thought and, 72–73
    cooling off peace treaties, 127
    New York Peace Society, 28

Women's International League for Peace and
        Freedom, 172, 174
peace movement
    Alabama claims and, 30
    Christianity and, 28
    Civil War and, 29–30
    education and, 73
    Lieber Code and, 29–30
    societies founded in, 28–29
    transatlantic scope of, 29
    US as champion of, 28–30
Peace of Westphalia, 17
"Peace Through Victory" slogan, 150
Penfield, Walter, 120
Permanent Court of Arbitration (PCA), 87
    intervention and, 111–12
    overview about, 77
Permanent Court of International Justice (PCIJ)
    critics of, 173
    features of, 170–71
    League of Nations and, 171, 173
    Moore and, 237n183
    Scott and, 171
    US congressional votes on, 238n186
Philippines
    anti-imperialists and, 41
    end of war in, 52
    expansion proponents and, 42
    imperialist arguments surrounding, 42–43
    law and empire in, 49–52
    Root and, 50–51
    Treaty of Paris and, 40
    Woolsey, Theodore Salisbury, and, 51–52
Platt Amendment, 56, 118, 123, 134
Politis, Nicolas, 168–69
Porter Convention, 122, 222n129
positive law, natural law and, 17–18, 192n12
positivism
    era of, 19–20
    Institut de droit international and, 20
    Moore and, 35
    Oppenheim and, 197n100
Pound, Roscoe, 69
Principios del Derecho de Jentes (Bello), 120
Prize Court Convention, 140
professionalization, of international law
    arbitration and, 75, 77
    Cases on International Law and, 65–66
    classical legal thought and, 68–74
    creation of, 66–68
    education and, 78–79
    elites and, 64–65
    Harvard method and, 63–65
    history of, 18–21
    insignias related to, 74, 75f, 76f, 208n140
    judge myth and, 74
    judicial identity affirmation and, 74–81
    law school gatekeepers and, 63–64
    legal science and, 63–64
    masculinity and, 62–63

professionalization (*Cont.*)
    need for, 61–66
    overview about, 12, 60–61
    permanent court and, 77–78
    Scott and, 79–80
    universities and, 61
    US power and, 81–85
public opinion, 73, 208n128

race, civilization and, 22
Ralston, Jackson, 72, 82–83
Randolph, Carman, 45
Recommendations of Havana (AIIL), 162
Reed, James, 173
regenerative militarism, 2
Reinsch, Paul, 81
*Revue de Droit International et de Legislation
        Comparée* (Institut de droit international), 19
Rolin, Albéric, 146
Rolin-Jaequemyns, Gustave, 19, 20
Roosevelt, Franklin D., 175
Roosevelt, Theodore, 88, 212n9
    arbitration and, 103–4
    Colombia and, 226n234
    Corollary to Monroe Doctrine and, 112
    Dominican Republic and, 113–14
    The Hague and, 89–90
    imperial paths not taken and, 107
    legalism and, 4
    Moore defending Panama policy for,
        55–56, 202n93
    Moore memorandum and, 53–55,
        201n69, 201n78
    Republic of Panama recognized by, 55
    Root and, 90, 213n27
    on unlimited adjudication, 159
    Venezuela and, 111
Root, Elihu, 2, 47, 67, 75
    ACJ and, 170
    Alsop claim and, 124, 223n145
    background about, 107–9, 108f
    Britain and, 230n115
    Bryan and, 50
    Cuba and, 118
    debt collection, armed, and, 121
    Drago and, 121–22
    empire of nation-states and, 110
    General Orders No.100 and, 50
    Germany and, 147
    Institut de droit international and, 167
    judicial recall and, 79
    justification for international court, 88–89
    Latin America and, 107, 121–22
    law enforcement and, 164
    on law-making power, 95
    League Covenant and, 163
    League of Nations and, 165–66, 235n111
    LEP and, 164

    persuasion and, 123
    Philippines and, 50–51
    Prize Court Convention and, 140
    public opinion and, 73
    Roosevelt, Theodore, and, 90, 213n27
    Scott and, 79–80
    secretary of war, 39
    on self-restraint, 71–72
    skills of, 109
    sovereignty and, 94
    State Department aims under, 110–11
    State Department and, 110–11, 116
    success of, 123
    tolls exemption and, 100, 104–5
    worldview of, 109
    World War I and, 143
Ross, John, 45
Rowe, Leo, 46

San Domingo Improvement Company (SDIC)
    Dominican Republic and, 112–15
    negotiations with, 112–13
    victory of, 113–14
Scheer, Reinhard, 149
Schurz, Carl, 83
science
    legal, 63–64
    legalism and, 9, 72
"The Science of International Law: Its Task and
        Method" (Oppenheim), 72
Scott, James Brown, 2, 87, 90
    admiration for, 80–81
    AIIL founding by, 161
    America's founding and, 156
    arbitration and, 77, 99, 101
    ASIL and, 80
    background about, 59
    Borchard and, 168
    Britain and, 146
    Carnegie Endowment for International Peace
        and, 67, 96–98
    case method and, 65–66
    Comité Consultatif de la Fondation Carnegie
        and, 97, 215n67
    cooling off peace treaties and, 127
    court of nations and, 84–85
    critics of, 80
    Fauchille and, 80, 210n190
    at The Hague, 90–94
    Institut de droit international and, 167–68
    "International Arbitration" address by,
        60, 203n7
    International Prize Court and, 214n55
    Lake Mohonk Conference and, 66
    LEP and, 157, 158–60
    neutrality and, 141
    North Atlantic Fisheries arbitration and,
        217n100

O'Gorman and, 105
pacifism and, 63
PCIJ and, 171
professionalization and, 79–80
Recommendations of Havana and, 162
on reformers, 75
Root and, 79–80
shipping and, 148–49
Snow and, 205n60
State Department and, 116–17, 124, 223n149
Taft and, 161
transatlantic links and, 96
University of Illinois and, 59–60
Venezuela and, 123
on world government, 156
World War I and, 136, 143, 144, 145–46
Scott-Smith, Giles, 215n67
SDIC. *See* San Domingo Improvement Company
self-determination, 129, 225n202
shipping, 148–50
Shipstead, Henrik, 173
Shotwell, James, 174
Sluga, Glenda, 67
Smith, Jacob H., 49, 50
Snow, Freeman, 205n60
sociological jurisprudence, 69
sovereignty
  Lansing and, 142
  Latin America and, 120
  New Sovereigntists, 177
  Root and, 94
Spanish-American War, 39–40
Stanley, Henry M., 31–32
State Department, US
  archives of, 220n70
  claims recording and, 116–17
  Clark and, 124, 223n150
  Cuba and, 118
  international lawyers influence at, 117
  Lansing and, 133
  legal capacity expansion within, 117–18
  Moore and, 34–35, 117, 219n31
  Office of the Legal Advisor, 170
  pecuniary claims and, 116
  reformation of, 116
  Root and, 110–11, 116
  salaries at, 117
  Scott and, 116–17, 124, 223n149
  staff expansion at, 117
  World War I growth of, 137, 227n17
Stimson, Henry, 170, 175
Stowell, Ellery C., 80
strategic legalism, 50
Straus, Oscar S., 1, 66
Strong, Josiah, 9
Strout, Cushing, 11
submarines, 145–46, 148–50, 231n142
Sumner, Charles, 29

Sumner, William Graham, 41

Taft, William Howard, 200n61
  arbitration treaties and, 102–4
  background about, 51
  colonization and, 2
  dollar diplomacy and, 124–25
  judicial recall and, 79
  Knox and, 123
  LEP and, 154
  Scott and, 161
Taney, Roger, 45
Thayer, James Bradler, 46
Tillman, Benjamin R., 41
tolls exemption, 99–100, 102, 104–5, 216n76,
  218n131
Torres Caicedo, José María, 120
transnational norm entrepreneurs, 7
A Treatise on Extradition and Interstate Rendition
  (Moore), 35
Treaty of Ghent, 30
Treaty of Guadelupe Hidalgo, 31
Treaty of Paris, 40
Treaty of Versailles, 164–65
Treaty of Vienna, 20
trusteeship, 142–43
Twain, Mark, 41, 50

United States (US). *See also* State Department, US
  AJIL and, 81–82
  arbitration and, 30–31, 101–2
  Bush administration and, 177–78
  as champion of international law, 26–31
  civilized ethic and, 83–84
  debating international law in, 99–106
  exceptionalism and, 83–84, 211n216
  foreign policy tradition of, 24–26
  foreign policy values of, 25–26
  global leadership rise of, 152
  interests and values and, 180
  international law and, 26–31, 99–106, 180–82
  League of Nations and, 164
  legalism embraced by, 4, 12–13
  as legalist empire, 2–3
  metaphorical world power clothing of,
    1–2, 10–11
  neutrality and, 27–28
  non-entanglement and, 2, 15
  PCIJ and Congress and, 238n186
  peace movement and, 28–30
  professionalization and power and, 81–85
  regenerative militarism in, 2
  violent expansion of, 4–5
  as weak and strong, 8
University of Illinois, 59–60
US. *See* United States
US Court of China, 116
US-Mexican Mixed Claims Commission, 30–31

Vásquez, Horacio, 113
Venezuela
  Moore and, 114–15
  NY&B and, 111, 114–15
  persuasion and, 123
  precedents of law and, 115
  Roosevelt, Theodore, and, 111
  Scott and, 123
Vesnitch, Milenko, 80, 210n190
Villa, Francisco "Pancho," 132
Vitoria, Francisco, 17
von Bismarck, Otto, 15
von Martens, Georg Friedrich, 20

Wambaugh, Eugene, 137, 144, 227n17
War Inconsistent with the Religion of Jesus Christ
    (Dodge), 28
Washington, George
  farewell address of, 25
  foreign entanglements and, 2, 15
Webster, Daniel, 28
Weld, Angelina Grimké, 29
Wellman, Walter, 44
Westlake, John, 19, 20, 22, 23
Wharton, Francis, 197n102
Wheaton, Henry, 21, 29
White, Andrew Dickson, 86, 87
White, Edward D., 47, 48
White, Harold F., 100
Williams, Talcott, 46, 158–59
Williston, Samuel, 80–81
Wilson, Henry Lane, 129, 224n195
Wilson, Woodrow
  distrust of lawyers by, 153
  dollar diplomacy and, 134
  on international law, 61
  interventionist tendencies of, 134
  Lansing and, 133
  League of Nations vision of, 162–63, 234n89
  legalism and, 4, 126–27
  liberal capitalist vision of, 126, 224n166
  Mexico and, 128–32, 225n206, 225n217,
      225n219, 225n223
  Moore and, 35, 128, 131–32
  neutrality and, 137–38, 227n20
  Paris Peace Conference and, 152

racism and, 225n206
recognition of Mexico and, 130–31, 225n217
self-determination and, 129, 225n202
shipping and, 149–50
as skeptic of international law, 125–28, 131–32
tolls exemption and, 105, 218n131
war with Mexico and, 131–32, 225n219,
    225n223
women
  ASIL seal and, 74, 75f
  Langdell on, 65
Women's International League for Peace and
    Freedom, 172, 174
Woolsey, Theodore Dwight, 37
Woolsey, Theodore Salisbury
  background of, 36–37
  courses taught by, 61
  expansion opposition of, 49
  Panama and, 55
  Philippines and, 51–52
  views of, 37–38
world government
  classical legal thought and, 71–72
  Scott on, 156
world power
  criterion for achieving, 2
  US emerging as, 1–2, 10–11
World War I
  armed merchantmen and, 148–50
  arms export and, 143, 229n71
  Britain, reacting to, during, 142–48
  despair over, 136
  Germany, reacting to, during, 142–48
  interest in law and, 136–37
  neutrality, changing conceptions of,
      and, 138–42
  neutrality and, 137–42, 227n20
  Oppenheim on, 136
  Order in Council and, 143, 144
  overview, 13
  Root and, 143
  Scott and, 136, 143, 144, 145–46
  special interests and, 229n82
  State Department growth during, 137, 227n17
  submarines and, 148–50
world safe for law and, 150–51